P9-DZN-579

HELPING THE ELDERLY

PERSPECTIVES ON MARRIAGE AND THE FAMILY
Bert N. Adams and Reuben Hill, Editors

HELPING THE ELDERLY
The Complementary Roles of Informal Networks and Formal Systems
Eugene Litwak

COMMUTER MARRIAGE
A Study of Work and Family
Naomi Gerstel and Harriet Gross

WIFE BATTERING
A Systems Theory Approach
Jean Giles-Sims

Helping the Elderly

The Complementary Roles of
Informal Networks and Formal Systems

EUGENE LITWAK
Columbia University

FOREWORD BY ROBERT N. BUTLER

THE GUILFORD PRESS
New York   London

To Eleanor

© 1985 The Guilford Press
A Division of Guilford Publications, Inc.
200 Park Avenue South, New York, N.Y. 10003

Library of Congress Cataloging in Publication Data

Litwak, Eugene, 1925-
  Helping the elderly.

  (Perspectives on marriage and the family)
  Bibliography: p.
  Includes index.
    1. Aged—Care and treatment.   2. Aged—Institutional
care.   3. Aged—Family relationships.   4. Social
structure.   5. Social groups.   6. Small groups.
I. Title.   II. Series.
HV1451.L59 1985   362.6′042   85-7985
ISBN 0-89862-077-5

Acknowledgments

This book would not have been possible without the help of a marvelous group of research associates. Their contributions cannot be measured by any specific items but are based on countless discussions. I want to thank them all—John Dono, Cecilia Falbe, Barbara Kail, Steve Kulis, Sam Marullo, Roger Sherman, and Dave Siegel. In addition, thanks are owed to Rose Dobrof, whose commitment and enthusiasm helped initiate this project. Doing this study required the cooperation of administrators of institutions for the aged at a time when they were under public scrutiny and had little to gain. I want to thank those who helped obtain this cooperation—Eleanor Kay, Barbara Blum, Margaret Jacks, Richard Sena, and Joe Spinelli—as well as the administrators who agreed to cooperate. To the respondents who participated because they were told this research would help improve the life of older people, I hope this book meets that promise.

Funds provided by the National Institute on Aging (Grant No. R01 AG00564) and the National Institute of Mental Health (Grant No. R01 MH30726) permitted the collection of the statistical data presented in this book. However, these agencies cannot be held responsible for any of the conclusions reached.

To those who work with statistical data, it is no secret that they are often meaningless unless one has an organizing framework. The last gift my parents, Isaac and Bessie, and my mother-in-law, Lena Smith, gave to me before they died, was an understanding of what it means to grow old in the United States. The organizing framework in this work owes much to them.

To the editors of this series, Bert Adams and Reuben Hill, I owe special thanks. Their enthusiastic support, close reading, and detailed comments were invaluable. Finally, I want to thank my wife, Eleanor Smith Litwak, for the initial editing (bringing to bear her considerable expertise in the field of gerontology and her practical experience as a helping daughter) as well as for those crucial intangibles of love and encouragement.

Foreword

Losses and grief are the frequent accompaniments of old age to which both formal and informal community and social arrangements have responded throughout the centuries. In this volume by Eugene Litwak we now have an increasingly empirical and refreshing theoretical understanding of such networks and systems. Litwak shows the important basis of sociology to social policy and policy making: the necessary practical translation of social theory to effect social policy directives and practice.

Perhaps most of all Litwak shows that irresponsible, frightened, or mistaken declarations that modern society's creation of large-scale formal organizations has led to decline of the family and the community are not accurate. Modern researchers are continually rediscovering the value of informal groups, primary groups. The effectiveness of large-scale organizations depends on a close alliance with informal organizations. The alliances of formal and informal groups is of special importance to the quality of life and, indeed, the survival of older people. One important task, of course, is to assure appropriate mechanisms to link the two types of organizations to minimize fatal conflict. Mobilization of all of our society's structures— acquaintances, friends, neighbors, "blocks"—and more formal, public structures must be accomplished to meet the challenge of the increasing absolute number and relative proportion of older persons. It is with special pleasure that I note that funding by important national agencies, the National Institutes on Aging and Mental Health, helped make this work possible—an example of the alliance of private creativity and public support.

This book not only documents the crucial services of formal organizations and informal networks, but contrasts relations between the two. For example, it is important to know when and how formal organizations can provide substitute services for family groups and when and how they cannot. Especially noteworthy is Litwak's clear description of the "modified extended family structure" where members legitimate geographic mobility while at the same time exchanges by kin are maintained over distances. It is certainly important to modern society that this modified extended family system provides more kinship as well as more organizational services.

If we are to deal prudently with the impact of the demographic or longevity revolution, we cannot constantly adopt short-term ad hoc policy decisions. We must have a broad vision and long-term strategies. This scope requires the general principles described here that follow from the data Litwak also provides. Short-term solutions are not necessarily prudent; for example, it would be unwise to revive old laws of filial responsibility. These may bring in money, and children are the best caretakers of the chronically ill old. However, legal reestablishment of family responsibilities are not realistic. They are not consistent with modern social or economic life or the contemporary character of the family.

The so-called impersonal mass society can actually enlarge responsibility through facilitation of affection rather than through harsh, lock-stepped, class-stratified discharge of responsibilities through obligation. Mass organizations provide relief and fluidity in the discharge of responsibility, supplementing, sustaining, and building upon the family and other informal networks. However, informal networks may be beset by life's vicissitudes— death, illness, poverty—and it is easier to express affection, duty, or respect when one is not living on the margin.

Formal structures do provide professional care, the technical expertise needed, as we better understand the problems of health, illness, and stress for people of all ages, including old age. It is a proper division of labor and the sharing of tasks. If we do not understand the underlying rationale and interdependence of formal and informal organizations, we may put at risk those people and communities who would be served by both. If we make members of informal groups, such as neighbors and family, feel guilty or overstressed, their capacity to do what they do and their bridge-building with formal organizations will be reduced. If they perceive that formal organizations are bureaucratic and insensitive, they will keep their distance. Political ideology must be supplanted by the kind of scholarship we find in this work.

Robert N. Butler, MD

Contents

HELPING THE ELDERLY

1

An Overview

This book asks the question, "Which groups are best suited to provide which services to older people?" In order to answer that question in an enduring way, it is necessary to have some understanding of the theoretical properties of various groups and services. Otherwise one is left with answers that are limited to a given time and place. Readers interested in older people may feel a certain impatience when confronted with a seemingly abstract discussion of theories of group structure and tasks; however, if they will be patient and follow the development of these abstract principles, the practical dividends will be substantial. What the book provides are guidelines as to which groups can perform which tasks in a wide variety of present and future situations. At the same time, I would ask those interested in the theoretical properties of group structure and in which structures are best suited for which tasks not to be turned off by the seemingly narrow empirical focus on aging. The fact of the matter is that the theories of matching group and task structures that are presented in this book grow out of developments in the literature on formal organizations and primary groups. They apply to all groups, not just the aged. As such, they should be of basic interest to organizational and primary-group theorists (such as family sociologists), as well as to gerontologists.

With these thoughts in mind, I should like to review very briefly what this book covers. In Chapter 2, I provide the theoretical rationale for the study. The basic thesis is that in a modern society one must have both large-scale formal organizations and small primary groups (i.e., family, neighbors, friends) to manage most tasks. This differs from the views of past writers, who have suggested that society is confronted with a draconian choice between formal organizations with their high states of technology and family-like groups with their humanitarian values. This dilemma is rejected because both the empirical data and the theory suggest that there is no possibility of such a choice. The large-scale organization cannot perform effectively without close cooperation from strong primary groups, and primary groups cannot function without formal organizations. However, those who speak about the conflict between the two structures are partly correct. The reason why formal organizations and primary groups manage different aspects of the same tasks is that they have very different and often contradictory structures. The primary group puts much greater stress on motivating people by affection and duty, while the formal organization emphasizes impersonal economic incentives. The primary group stresses everyday knowledge and diffused relations, while the formal organization stresses technical knowledge and specialized ties. Earlier writers have assumed that this conflict in structure would make it impossible for strong forms of primary groups and large formal organizations to exist side by side. This assumption does not take into account the fact that these two types of groups also need each other because they manage complementary aspects of the same goals. As a result, most prior writers have not dealt with the crucial problem of a modern society: That is, how do large-scale formal organizations and primary groups exist side by side, despite their conflicts?

At this point, those interested in older people might be getting a little impatient. What bearing can this abstract discussion have on who provides help to older people? The answer to that query lies in one of the solutions as to how organizations with contradictory structures live alongside each other. They can alter their structure so as to reduce the amount of conflict to a tolerable level. In the case of the primary groups, the need to deal with problems of differential geographic and occupational mobility that the formal organization requires has led to each primary group's developing a slightly different structure. The modern kinship system gives up the dimensions of continual face-to-face contact that traditional primary groups had; the modern neighborhood gives up the long-term commitment of the traditional primary group; the modern marital household reduces its size below that of the traditional primary group and moves toward a model of role substitutability in gender relations; and the modern friendship group gives up long-term commitment for intermediate time commitments, as well as stressing affection rather than duty. It is the fact that primary groups must differentiate themselves along these lines that is most relevant to gerontologists, because this structural differentiation means that these primary groups no longer provide the same set of services.

In Chapter 3, I take the theoretical analysis and generate from it the principle that groups can optimally manage those tasks that match them in structure. This principle in turn explains which services older persons will receive uniquely from neighbors, which from friends, which from spouses, and which from kin. This principle is empirically demonstrated with eight services from a survey on older people. It provides the basis for classifying any task in the present or future so that one can say which group will optimally manage it. Not only is the principle of practical interest to gerontologists, but it provides primary-group theorists with a theory of an integrated network of groups, which in turn explains a widespread set of prior findings—namely, that different primary groups seem to do different things and are not easily substitutable for one another.

In Chapter 4, the same basic principle for matching task structure with group structure is applied to nursing homes (i.e., one type of formal organization) to show which sorts of services nursing homes can take over from primary groups, which must be retained by primary groups such as the kin, and which will be lost. Again, the importance to gerontologists of this application is self-evident. However, it also provides organizational theorists with an understanding of the relationship between formal organizations and community primary groups.

In Chapter 5, the findings of the earlier chapters are brought together in a model of change that enables one to deal with a problem endemic to aging: Who provides services when the older person moves from a state of health to a state of chronic illness in the community to institutionalization? For the sociological theorist, the model suggests a theory of network change over one section of the life cycle. Again, the practical significance of this to gerontology is obvious. But equally important is the presentation of a theory of relations between a network of primary groups and formal organizations.

In Chapter 6, the simplifying assumption that all people in society adhere to the ideal form of kinship structure is dropped. The rationale for atypical structures based on ethnicity, class, illness, and gender is examined. It is shown how the principle of matching can be elaborated to show which services kin can deliver over which geographic distances, which require the same social class and generation, which can cross class and generational barriers, and which benefit from larger-sized groups.

In Chapter 7, the optimum form of husband–wife relations is discussed. It is pointed out that the small size of the marital household unit and the need to maintain a semiautonomous status puts a limit on the amount of household services a primary-group helper can provide. To some extent, the tension can be minimized when the helper is single. It is pointed out that "role substitutability" between husband and wife is also most likely to guarantee marital household services to older people. It is argued that the delivery of marital household services to older people who are sick is generally managed by women helpers in our society, but what prior investigators have not fully emphasized is that they in turn require help from their husbands, since they can deliver such services only when the older persons move close to them.

Chapter 8 shows that the same forces that produce the modified extended family structure and the marital household based on role substitutability also produce the mobile neighborhood. This is a neighborhood based on the fact that neighbors may have only short tenure, but still remain cohesive because they have rapid modes of integration. It is in such neighborhoods that neighbors are most likely to provide neighborhood services. Moreover, because older persons need different helping groups at different stages of aging, it is argued that older people who live the full life span have institutional pressure to make at least three major moves: (1) when feeling well, to move to age-homogeneous neighborhoods; (2) then, when ill, to move to age-heterogeneous ones; and finally (3) to move to institutions when they need 24-hour care. Older people who do not make these moves will suffer major losses of services from key helping primary groups at each stage. This analysis is of some interest to neighborhood theorists, because it further elaborates the mechanisms by which groups can maintain cohesion despite rapid membership turnover. It also provides an explanation of how to deal with a perennially puzzling problem—that is, setting the geographic boundaries of neighborhoods. For the gerontologist, it suggests which features of the neighborhood should be strengthened if older people are to receive optimal help; it also has important implications for housing and urban planning policy.

Chapter 9 points out that the same forces that produce the modified extended family and the mobile neighborhood also produce the concept of time-based friends—that is, short-term, intermediate-term, and long-term friends. It is argued that the rapidity of changing statuses, coupled with the differential rates of change among age peers, has made it very difficult to maintain lifelong friends who have common roles. This problem is especially severe with older people, for whom the relationship with age peers, illness, and death make it unlikely that they will have large numbers of viable long-term friends. As a result, it is argued that one has several types of friends—that is, very short-term friends, intermediate-term friends, and long-term friends—who in turn perform different services. However, it is suggested that the key group may be intermediate-term friends (i.e., those who have been friends for 3–20 years). These have been friends for a short enough time period so as to have matches on key role statuses, such as occupation, marital status, and social interests. At the same time, they have been friends for a long enough time to build up reciprocities based on affection, which are necessary for the delivery of many friendship services. It is shown that in fact where people do have mechanisms of quick integration that permit such friendships, they are most likely to utilize friends for delivery of services. It is also shown that where people do have matching on some key status (which in our sample tends to be age), they are more likely to use friends for friendship services. For the gerontologist, Chapter 9 provides some guidelines as to what forms of behavior are likely to enhance friendship ties and services among the aged. For the sociological theorist, it will expand prior views that there are different kinds of friends, as well as open up considerations of some of the mechanisms of integration that are necessary to maintain these different types of friends in a modern society.

Finally, in Chapter 10, I point out how these considerations of basic social theory provide potential guidelines for evaluating the various types of programs used to buttress failing marital household groups of older people. For instance, I suggest which groups will and will not be helped by some of the following programs designed to support older people who can no longer maintain a household on their own: (1) homemaker services provided by an agency; (2) direct payments to kin, friends, or neighbors to provide home-maker services; (3) foster parent programs, in which individuals are paid to take care of an older person in their homes; (4) group communal homes, in which older people live jointly in a large apartment or home, with one housekeeper to take care of things like shopping, cleaning, and cooking; (5) meals-on-wheels programs; and (6) low-cost meal programs.

In conclusion, in this book I have tried to show that a proper under-standing of sociological theory can be beneficial in providing practical guidelines to helping older people. At the same time, examining the practical problems of older people provides a substantial stimulus to sociological theory.

2

The Theoretical Bases for Primary-Group Networks and Formal Organizations in Modern Industrial Society

Despite the statements often made that ours is an impersonal mass society, it has become increasingly apparent to both social scientists and to practitioners that in order to get things done, it is essential to take into account family, friends, and neighbors, or what sociologists call the primary groups (Cooley, 1909). These are groups who exchange services not on the basis of economic rewards, but rather on that of affection, duty, or respect.

The discovery of the importance of such informal groups has emerged in all areas of modern life. Some have pointed out its major role in the heartland of the contractual impersonal arena, the world of business (W. F. Whyte, 1956; Shils, 1951; Pennings, 1975; LaRocco, House, & French, 1980). Others have pointed out that primary-group ties are essential for understanding the effectiveness of combat troops (Shils & Janowitz, 1948). Still others have pointed out that the mass media could not operate effectively without supporting primary groups (Katz & Lazarsfeld, 1955); the importance of primary groups in preserving health (Cobb, 1976; Berkman & Syme, 1979) and in education (Z. S. Blau, 1981) has also been emphasized. Some have even argued that the noninstrumental, affective ties of primary groups are possibly growing stronger in modern society (Fischer, Jackson, Stueve, Gerson, & Jones, with Baldassare, 1977; Anderson, 1977). In any case, the utility of primary groups for the management of problems of older people has become a dominant theme of contemporary researchers in aging (Shanas, Townsend, Nedderburn, Friis, Milhoj, & Stehouwer, 1968; Rosow, 1967; Dono, Falbe, Kail, Litwak, Sherman, & Siegel, 1979; Cantor, 1979; Dobrof & Litwak, 1977).

What is very important to understand is that these investigators have not just been saying that such informal groups exist; they have been saying that such informal groups are essential for the achievement of the goals of the very formal organizations that were once thought to have replaced them.

There is a seeming paradox in the idea that for a factory to make the most profits, it must use groups whose forms of compliance are noneconomic. The paradox seems even greater that the mass media, the personification of mass society, require these very small groups (with limited scope and idiosyncratic norms) to be effective.

In the past, social scientists and humanists have taught that a dilemma arises from the need to choose either the highest standards of living brought about by formal organizations and by science and technology, or the humanistic values of affection that are stressed by family and friendship groups. A choice appeared necessary because the organizations seemed to have opposing structures. The formal organization requires segmental ties, impersonal, objective evaluations, and economic motivations, while families necessitate permanent ties, affective, loving evaluations, and diffused relations. This is the basis for the draconian choice between high standards of living and a humane society. This book argues that such a choice is not possible. The nature of modern society requires primary groups if one is to have well-functioning formal organizations. The dilemma confronting us is how to maintain these types of groups alongside each other, despite their contradictory structures. It is not only that past writers have not seen the nature of the dilemma; they have, as a result, not focused on the key problem facing our society—that is, how society can maintain groups working side by side despite continual conflict. In this book, two solutions to this paradox are discussed: altering the structures of primary groups, and altering the structures of formal organizations. A third solution, the use of linkage mechanisms that continually adjust the social distance between formal organizations and primary groups, is also given. In each case, the point is made that conflict between these two groups can be reduced sufficiently to enable them to coordinate their efforts, despite the states of conflict still existing.

The Decline of Primary Groups and the Rise of the Mass Society: A Popular Delusion

In order to understand the principles guiding the operation of primary groups within the modern industrial society, it is necessary to understand why people thought that such groups would decline in a modern industrial society. Though many social scientists commented on the decline (Toennies, 1940; Wirth, 1938; Mills, 1956; Nisbet, 1969; Stein, 1960), the rationale for this decline was most clearly spelled out by Weber (1947).

Weber's rationale was very simple. In a modern industrial society, people with technical knowledge could solve problems better than people without such knowledge. The maximizing of technical knowledge required bureaucratic organizations that were contradictory in structure to primary groups.

Thus Weber argued that to maximize technical knowledge, it was necessary for people to be hired and fired on the basis of their technical knowledge. By contrast, in primary groups, people were assessed on the basis of their ability to handle everyday problems. Recruitment was based on such criteria as birth, love, and friendship, which require no technical knowledge.

Weber further argued that to increase technical knowledge, it is necessary to have a detailed division of labor, which would permit people to become experts by concentrating their full time in very small areas. This, in turn, meant that people would have only limited contact with others. It also meant large groups. This was the precise opposite of the primary groups' demands that people should have diffuse ties and that groups should be small.

Weber pointed out that where there are large groups with detailed specialization, and consequently with geographic dispersion as well, the only effective way to coordinate their behavior is through rules. For instance, if the group had 60 members, each would have 1 minute of discussion every hour; if it had 600, each would have 6 seconds. That is why it is necessary to use rules to coordinate people. For those rare circumstances where there are no rules, someone with authority should make the decisions, thus preventing the problems of large discussion meetings or the chaos of individuals each going their own way. The stress on rules and hierarchies for coordination contrasts with the primary groups' stress on face-to-face contacts, common life styles, and collegial peer ties.

As Weber also pointed out, to motivate people in a way that will insure that they evaluate one another only on the basis of technical expertise, it is necessary to stress impersonal relations rather than affectionate ties. If people are emotional, they will evaluate others on the basis of love or hate rather than merit. Weber argued that in a modern monied economy, money can be used to motivate people because it is a generalized means of achieving most goals. When people can pay one another, they have some sense that they have provided a proper incentive, and at the same time they do not have any emotional tie. This strongly contrasts with primary groups, which stress two internalized forms of compliance: (1) affection and (2) responsibility for the survival of the group as a major goal per se.

Without going into all the details, the central point of Weber's argument can be well understood: That is, to develop technical expertise properly, it is necessary to encompass it within a network of social ties that is the very antithesis of the informal primary group. Furthermore, technical experts are generally able to solve problems better than nonexperts. Even where the primary group can handle some goals better than the formal organization, it is still confronted with the problem of how to maintain its structure in a society dominated by organizations with conflicting structures.

Weber implied yet another basis (other than technical knowledge) for the formal organization's effectiveness. The formal organization can take complex tasks, can subdivide them into smaller units, and by so doing can make each subunit simpler to do. As a result, the total task can be done faster, more reliably, and with less expenditure of energy. This may be called "task simplification" by a division of labor. The classic illustration of task simplification is the assembly line: The individual job on the assembly line may require little technical knowledge. To develop such task simplification, one needs the same organizational prerequisites as are required for the development of technical knowledge (i.e., a large organization, with detailed division of labor, coordinated by rules and hierarchies, and motivated by economic incentives with stress on impersonal ties and *a priori* limits of rights and duties). As such, the use of task simplification also requires organizational structures that are the antitheses of the primary group.

The rationale behind task simplification is especially important for the aged, because many formal organizations, such as nursing homes, are fundamentally seeking to replace everyday family tasks by task simplification and not by technical knowledge.

The implication of Weber's formulations for the field of aging is clear: Society should concentrate on the development of formal organizations to handle problems of the aged. Such a position would applaud the proliferation of institutions for the aged and would decry the various efforts at deinstitutionalization, such as the movement from hospital to community mental health centers or the effort to expand community "natural support" groups.

The logic of Weber's work seems extremely plausible. As indicated earlier, it has many past and current supporters. Perhaps Ogburn (1953) presented the evidence most simply and cogently when he pointed out that in all major areas of life, such as food production, clothing manufacturing, health, and protection, there has been an enormous growth in formal organizations.

The only thing that prevents acceptance of Weber's view is that it is not consistent with most of the empirical evidence. As already indicated, much of the empirical evidence has suggested that large-scale formal organizations actually operate best when they work in close conjunction with primary groups.

The Mutual Need of Primary Groups and Formal Organizations for Each Other despite Their Conflicting Structure

There have been several attempts to present theories that deal with the paradox described above (Parsons, 1944; Katz & Lazarsfeld, 1955; Mayhew, 1970). The one pursued in this volume is referred to as the "theory of shared functions" (Litwak & Figueira, 1970; Sussman, 1977). According to this theory, most goals have one component that can be best handled by people with specialized training and another that requires everyday experience and continual contact to handle. Therefore most tasks require both primary groups and formal organizations for their accomplishment. This raises at least two intellectual paradoxes. First, what tasks can conceivably be managed better by nonexperts than by experts or through "task simplification"? Second, how can contradictory organizational structures exist side by side if they cannot be completely isolated from each other but must remain close so as to coordinate their efforts?

The idea that a task cannot be handled better by technical experts seems hard to believe. What kind of activity cannot be handled better by a person with trained skills? Part of the answer to this question is to understand what is meant by "nontechnical knowledge." What is meant is knowledge learned through everyday socialization in the primary groups (e.g., the first spoken language, getting dressed, preparing food, administering first aid, shopping, driving a car, etc.). By contrast, technical knowledge is learned in special schools or on-the-job training in a formal organization.

Granted that distinction, why should it be the case that a person with advanced technical training is not able to manage all activities better than the person who has only learned through his or her primary groups or minor forms of technical training? I submit that the following situations do not permit the effective use of technically trained people:

1. *Unpredictable events.* For extremely unpredictable events, detailed experts often cannot be used because (a) they cannot be trained in time to make a difference; or (b) they cannot be brought to the scene in time to make a difference; and (c) their work cannot be easily supervised, which makes it difficult to motivate them by money alone.

2. *Too many contingencies.*[1] When the number of contingencies is greater than the technologies' capacities to coordinate them, then technical knowledge generally cannot be used effectively because (a) the technical experts cannot be coordinated in time to make a difference; or (b) personnel are insufficient to permit the training of all the technical experts needed, so that large gaps in services occur; and (c) it is difficult to supervise their work, so they cannot be easily motivated by money alone.

3. *Tasks not easily subdivided.* Using technical knowledge for tasks that cannot benefit from a division of labor generally involves slower decision-making processes because (a) nothing is gained by use of the experts; and (b) the costs of coordination, such as costs of communication, selection, training, and evaluation, slow up decision making.

In short, the argument is made here that these three conditions (unpredictability, too many contingencies, and tasks not easily subdivided) are basic to everyday life and cannot be handled by technical knowledge. I refer to these three conditions and the tasks characterized by them as "nonuniform" situations, events, or tasks. It is argued that nonuniform tasks are most effectively managed by primary groups, that they are central parts of most tasks, and that they cannot be eliminated in the foreseeable future. To understand why primary groups handle these tasks better, it is necessary to show more specifically why each dimension of the formal organization will fail and why its counterpart in the primary group will succeed.

At this point, some readers may ask whether this is really necessary. Are there not an enormous number of studies showing that primary groups are important? The answer is that there are, but that there are no good explanations as to *why* primary groups are important. To develop principles as to which tasks primary groups can best manage, and which services different primary groups can best manage, such an explanation is essential. With that in mind, the reader should recall that to use and develop technical knowledge or task simplification, one needs an organizational structure characterized by a division of labor, appointment by merit, the use of rules and hierarchies for coordination, and a strong economic component for motivating workers. Now the question might be asked: How effective are such ties when one has unpredictable events?

To give this point some meaning, let us consider an unpredictable event that might confront an older person. For instance, an older man has a stroke and becomes paralyzed in the middle of the night. Who is to help him? There are a number of specialists who can do something for him, such as the internist, the surgeon, the anesthesiologist, the nurse, the ambulance driver, and the hospital intake clerk. But the likelihood of any such specialist's being present in this man's home at the time of the stroke is small. If this stroke victim is to survive, someone must be by his bedside, or within hearing distance, who can either take him to the hospital or call an ambulance. The very division of labor that permits the development of specialized knowledge requires that the experts only deal with people in segmental, specialized circumstances, and not have continual face-to-face contact with them. By contrast, primary groups (such as marital dyads, neighbors, friends, or relatives) have as one of their major objectives the continual face-to-face proximity of their members.

In the same way, police are not available for spotting a burlgar's attempt to break into a home. That requires someone who is within continual visual contact and knows household members sufficiently well to realize that someone climbing in through the window is a stranger and not a household member who has lost his or her key. Only a neighbor or a spouse would have a high probability of performing this task. In short, the detailed specialization that produces technical knowledge is not very useful when dealing with many unpredictable events. In such cases, primary-group members, with their diffuse generalist training and continual proximity, are far more effective.

Weber (1947) also pointed out that for technical experts to be used effectively, they must be coordinated by written rules for most of their activities and by hierarchies in the small percentage of cases where rules do not fit. However, it is impossible to write rules and use hierarchies where the majority of events are unpredictable or there is a time emergency. Thus, in the case of the stroke victim, there is no way to write a rule that will indicate that the ambulance driver, internist, hospital intake clerk, surgeon, or anesthesiologist should anticipate that individual X will have a stroke at a given date and time and should be prepared for it. Any attempt to write such rules would lead to many wasted trips. In short, spending time and energy writing rules and setting up hierarchies where there are many unpredictable events is likely to lead to slower, more costly, and less effectual decisions. For handling tasks that are typically unpredictable and do not require large numbers, the primary group's structural emphasis on small size and continual face-to-face contact is superior to the formal organization's stress on rules and hierarchy.

The formal organization also stresses economic motivation and impersonal social ties so as to minimize favoritism and to optimize the use of technical knowledge. However, in the course of unpredictable events, it is often very hard to assess objective merit. For instance, if a person had a stroke in the middle of the night and the spouse did not call the hospital until mid-morning, was it dereliction of duty, or did the healthy spouse just think that the ill mate was sleeping late? If a burglar breaks into a home and it is not reported by the neighbors, is it because of dereliction of duty, or is it because the neighbor happened to be doing some household chore and did not spot the burglar? What is characteristic of many unpredictable events is the difficulty of evaluating the performance of those people who are supposed to help. Because of this fact, motivation that emphasizes instrumental economic rewards is generally not useful. If outcomes cannot be evaluated, then the person motivated by money can do what is easiest for him or her. In this regard, the primary group's stress on affectionate relations rather than impersonal ones and its stress on survival of the group as a good in itself are both noninstrumental, internalized motivations that stress the value of helping as a goal in itself. Therefore, the primary group as a structure generally provides a better motivation base than the formal organization for handling nonuniform events.

This particular point is very important in the field of aging, because the older person who becomes ill is often in the position of paying people who cannot be closely supervised to provide everyday household services, which in turn are characterized by unpredictability and many contingencies. Night nurses are hired to turn bedridden patients so they will not develop bedsores or clogged lungs. What characterizes the night nurse's situation is that no one is in a position to evaluate how well she is performing her services. Clogged lungs can occur even when people are turned. In such situations, the use of primary-group members, with their stress on internalized motivations, is often better than using people from formal organizations with their economic incentive.

Without going into all of the details (Litwak & Figueira, 1970), what has been argued is that all of the attributes of the formal organization that are designed to increase the use of technical knowledge become dysfunctional when one is dealing with unpredictable events. By contrast, all the attributes of the primary group become very functional for dealing with such nonpredictable events.

So far, I have only spoken about one aspect of nonuniform tasks (i.e., unpredictability), and only one basis for the advantage of formal organization (i.e., development of technical knowledge). However, for the study of aging, the central issues revolve around the other basis for formal organization (i.e., task simplification through a detailed division of labor) and the other basis for nonuniformity (i.e., tasks that have too many contingencies for current technology and cannot be simplified by a division of labor). The reason is obvious. The major services of formal organizations for the aged are designed to replace activities that are normally handled by primary groups. This is basically what programs for homemakers, or delivery of hot meals, or nursing homes are doing.

What characterizes these tasks performed by primary groups is that they do not involve technical knowledge, but, as noted, are unpredictable, have many contingencies, and are already so simple that they do not benefit from further division of labor. To handle the problems of many contingencies and unpredictability, the formal organizations must reduce them to routine tasks and then gain efficiency more through a division of labor and task simplification than through technical knowledge.

The problems can be illustrated with everyday activities of getting dressed. What characterizes getting dressed is that it is a simple event where the use of detailed division of labor is not likely to develop economies through task simplification or greater technical knowledge. For instance, if society decided to develop job specialization so that one person puts on the underpants, one the undershirt, one the stockings, one the shirt, one the pants, and one the belt, it would not increase specialized knowledge or job simplification to the point where the dressers could do the job faster or more effectively than the normal individuals dressing themselves. However, it would lead to enormous problems in coordination. To do the job properly, these specialists would have to meet and spend much time deciding which combination of clothes to put on. Two problems arise: First, the problem of coordination has no compensating expertise or task simplification. This leads to slower services. Second, if coordination is not possible because some specialists are ill or cannot be trained because of the shortage of personnel, people could end up missing crucial items of clothing. The idea of gaps in service takes on a literal as well as a figurative meaning.

The central point of this discussion is that the very structure of the formal organization, which produces technical experts and task simplification, is ineffective when dealing with tasks that are unpredictable, have many contingencies for the given state of technology, and cannot be easily sub-

divided—that is, nonuniform tasks. By contrast, the primary-group structures, which are ineffectual for developing technical knowledge, are very
effective for such nonuniform tasks.

Some readers might at this point scream "foul." Have I not compared
the primary group to an extreme type of formal organization? Are there no
formal organizations, such as the "human relations" model, that could
manage these nonuniform tasks? The answer is mixed. Modern organizational theorists do argue that there are many different types. What is
proposed here and developed below (Litwak, 1978b) is that there is a
continuum of organizational structures as well as one of tasks. Primary
groups can handle the most extreme nonuniform tasks, human relations
structures can manage moderately nonuniform tasks, and rationalistic structures can manage nonuniform tasks least of all.

What the reader now has is a rationale for the use of primary groups in
modern society that does fit the data from the empirical world, which show
that primary groups are active in all areas of life, since nonuniform tasks can
occur in all areas of life.

However, before this formulation can be accepted, several puzzling
questions must still be answered. Are not nonuniform tasks the very things
that science and technology reduce? If so, will it not be the case that in the
long run, all nonuniform tasks and therefore primary groups will disappear?
Furthermore, if primary groups and formal organizations have such contradictory structures, and if they must work cooperatively together over a
broad spectrum of activities, how can they exist side by side in the same
society? More specifically, how does one explain the empirical data that
suggest that there are times when formal organizations and primary groups
actually perform more effectively when they are closer together? The un-
raveling of these seeming paradoxes must be undertaken if a plausible
argument is to be made that primary groups are vital in a modern society.

The Role of Science and Technology in
Maintaining Primary-Group Tasks

Will not science reduce unpredictability, develop means to keep track of
many contingencies, and find ways to apply technical knowledge to simple
everyday tasks? We (Litwak & Figueira, 1970) and others (Foote & Cottrell,
1955) have suggested that such an analysis is a half-truth. Science and
technology do indeed reduce uncertainty and provide technology (e.g., computers) to handle many contingencies. They have also taken simple family
tasks and, through technology and science, have applied expertise and large-
scale organizations to handle them more effectively (e.g., manufacturing of
clothing, provision of protection by police and insurance, mechanization of
farming, etc.) (Ogburn, 1953). Because it is a half-truth, there is a compelling

quality to the argument that sciences and technology will reduce nonuniform events.

However, an equally compelling case can be made for the view that science and technology, through their innovation, have increased uncertainty in contemporary society. To some, it is a simple function of the rapidly accelerating speed of innovation (Emery & Trist, 1965; Bennis, 1966; Terryberry, 1968). In addition, science and technology can create knowledge and machinery that are simple enough to be used by individuals with minimal training and can be purchased with the primary group's resources (cars, home appliances, typewriters, hand calculators, home computers, home urine tests, etc.). Insofar as that is the case, it is always more efficient to let primary groups handle such knowledge and such machinery, because the primary groups will be able to handle the more idiosyncratic elements of a task as well as the technical ones.

Finally, it must be understood that science and technology are as likely to open up new frontiers as they are to close down old ones. Thus each new discovery has generally been accompanied by the opening up of a new set of unknowns of which there was no prior knowledge. The introduction of the automobile had varied and unanticipated consequences, including new courtship behaviors, new industries, new forms of death, new types of police enforcement, new urban settlement patterns, and new forms of illness (from smog). If one considers the accumulations of one invention on top of another, it is no wonder that some argue that ours is a society faced with constant uncertainty (Emery & Trist, 1965; Bennis, 1966; Terryberry, 1968). The argument is also a half-truth.

For these reasons, we (Litwak & Figueira, 1970) have argued that science and technology have an equal probability of producing nonuniform and uniform events. Therefore, we have suggested that nonuniform events will continue to exist for the foreseeable future. As such, there will be a need for primary groups in the foreseeable future.

The Importance of Primary-Group Tasks
in a Modern Society

The question must still be answered as to how important these nonuniform events are. The answer is that they are as important as the uniform ones, the reason being that most tasks consist of both types of events, and failure in one type would lead to failure in the other. Medical care requires doctors to handle technical problems, while primary groups provide emergency first aid, initial diagnoses, and preventive care. How else can one explain the Berkman and Syme (1979) findings that people with informal networks live longer?

The importance of nonuniform tasks is especially obvious in dealing with older people who can no longer handle those nonuniform tasks that the average person manages (e.g., shopping, housecleaning, cooking, dressing, bathing, etc.). Some of these are life-and-death matters. In short, I would argue that nonuniform events are significantly related to all major goals and, as such, are of major importance.

One Solution for Dealing with Conflict between the Structure of Formal Organizations and Primary Groups: The Differentiation of Primary-Group Structures

Thus far, I have dealt only with one aspect of the dilemma raised—that is, that primary groups and formal organizations have complementary goals, which means in most cases that they will have to coordinate their efforts. How does one deal with the problem of their contradictory structures? There are basically two ways. The first is the use of linkage procedures that adjust the amount of contact to minimize friction. For some theorists (Weber, 1947; Parsons, 1944), the principle governing such linkages is to minimize contact. The shared-function formulation suggests a more complex principle called the "balance theory of coordination" (Litwak & Meyer, 1966, 1974). According to the balance theory, there must be some middle point of distance between types of groups, close enough to enable them to coordinate goals, but not so close as to lead to destructive conflict between group structures.

The second procedure for minimizing conflicts was suggested by Parsons (1944), who argued that groups might accommodate to contradictory pressures by altering their structures so as to minimize conflict. Parsons saw this alteration as consisting of the shrinking of primary groups in size to the two-adult marital household (with young children). Only one member of this household would have a major career in the labor force. Parsons never considered the possibility of altering the structures of formal organizations or alternative ways of modifying primary groups.

To understand the variety of ways in which primary groups can be modified to reduce friction, it is necessary to be more specific about the sources of friction. Parsons (1944) pointed out that the chief factors producing conflict were the formal organizations' need to allocate labor all over the country and the need to promote people on the basis of their merit. Such requirements of large-scale formal organizations led to a high probability that members of the same primary group in the labor force might be forced to move to different locations, as well as ending up in different social classes. Differential geographic and social mobility was thought to be incompatible with primary groups' demand for continual face-to-face contact, affectivity, common life style, and the primacy of the family tie. How could primary-group members retain their affection and noninstrumental orientation if they did not have continual face-to-face contact (i.e., live in the same place) or if one member was in a higher social class than another?

Kinship Primary Groups

Specifically, the question must be asked as to how large kinship networks (relations between parents and adult children, siblings, etc.) keep together if their job demands require members to move to different geographic locations. Many social scientists would argue that continual contact is a basic condition for common identity (Homans, 1950) and primary-group ties (Wirth, 1938). Yet, despite the logic of this argument, there is empirical evidence that kinship systems retain significant forms of identification and exchange over geographic distance (Adams, 1971; Litwak, 1960c; Sussman, 1965; Lansing & Mueller, 1967; Fischer et al., 1977). The answer to the seeming paradox is that in a modern industrial society there are techniques of quick communication over geographical distance—that is, the telephone, the automobile, and the airplane; these mean that even when people do not live within immediate walking distance of one another, they can still retain contact. Furthermore, most if not all of the modern industrial nations are monied economies, which means that money is a generalized means to most goals. It is also easily transportable over great distances, so that one primary-group member can provide important services to another by sending money, even though they may be many hundreds of miles apart. On these bases, it has been argued that a modern kinship system with many members who live at some distances from one another can still retain significant contacts—that is, sufficient to maintain many of the properties of the classic primary groups, such as noninstrumental ties, affectional ties, and long-term commitments. What must be emphasized is that though such groups are viable, they do not have face-to-face contact, which means that they cannot handle the full range of tasks managed by traditional primary groups. They cannot handle tasks requiring immediate proximity, such as providing emergency first aid or transportation to the hospital. However, there are many tasks they can handle that do not require immediate proximity, such as flying in to help in home nursing and care of a relative laid up for a week or two, or providing emotional support over the phone for a relative suffering from the death of a spouse. Furthermore, other primary groups, such as the neighbors, may handle problems of immediate emergencies.

A second contradiction between kinship systems and formal organization arises because formal organizations demand that all those in the labor force be promoted on merit. Since there is no reason to assume that all people from a given primary group such as a kinship system will be equally good at their jobs, or that all industries provide the same opportunities for mobility, it is quite possible that class differences will arise between members of the same primary groups. Those class differences can lead to different standards of living and cultural values (Hyman, 1953; Kohn, 1969), specialized languages (Labov, 1972; Bernstein, 1964/1970), different life styles, and different social statuses. Two questions are raised by the possibility of differential mobility. First, how can people from two different cultures retain their noninstrumental, affective, face-to-face ties? Second, how does one prevent family norms of love and affection from leading to nepotism in the formal organization? For example, what is to prevent the sibling who has been successful from using his or her position to help a less able sibling to get a job ahead of better-qualified people?

With regard to the first point, the argument is made that in modern societies there are class differences, but there are class similarities as well. Thus, the various mass media and other mass production organizations tend to give the society many areas of common culture, despite class differences. Communalities in religion, ethnicity, region, nationalism, sports, and the like, may overlap with class differences (Dahl, 1966).

In addition, it should be pointed out that families who end up in different classes have the same class origin. This is especially the case where the kinship unit consists of parents and their married children. If one child becomes a doctor and the other a skilled laborer, and the father was an unskilled laborer, they all shared in common the status of unskilled labor when they were growing up. People do not necessarily forget the language and culture of their origin. This is obviously the case with children of immigrants, who may become completely Americanized and yet may retain sufficient language skills to understand their parents, who still speak a foreign tongue. In other words, families that are separated by virtue of differential success in the labor market may, through the phenomena of multiple languages, multiple cultures, and a common class history, find the process of communication sufficiently open to make significant exchanges.

Furthermore, empirical evidence suggests that people who rise to the top are often helped by their families (Sussman & Burchinal, 1962), and that they may well reciprocate with help when family members such as their parents need help. The bulk of the empirical findings, with few exceptions (Stuckert, 1963), suggest that those who are upwardly mobile do not abandon their families (Litwak, 1960a; Adams, 1967; Streib, 1958).

To point out that kinship units can cross class lines does not mean that such help will be the same as that of a traditional kinship system, where everyone is in the same social class. That is, where kin or primary-group members are from different classes, there will be areas of life that they do not share, and therefore they might not be able to provide exchanges. It would be my prediction that this particular vacuum will be filled by friends, who can be freely chosen to match common generation, stage in the family life cycle, and occupational and class milieux. The central point is that essential elements of kinship systems can exist despite class and geographical distances.

However, these modified extended kinship systems do differ from traditional ones.

The problem still remains with these modern kinship systems as to how to prevent the intrusion of kin norms into the work situation, or, alternatively, how to prevent work norms from being introduced into kin relationships. There are several barriers to such intrusions in a modern society. First, the major socialization agencies and consequently social norms lead primary-group members to restrict themselves to nonuniform tasks, and so many of their actions can be isolated from work by time and place (Goode, 1960; Merton, 1957). Second, with the development of formal organizations, there is an increasing separation of work production from the specific tasks of hiring and evaluation. As a result, the bulk of the workers are not in a position to hire or promote their kin directly. Third, with the restriction of jobs to uniform tasks, the criteria for job performance have become more public and objective, so intrusion of family or primary-group norms can be more easily spotted and rejected. Finally, the larger kin unit is not the key consumption unit; rather, it is the smaller marital household. There is therefore less incentive for kin to engage in nepotism in the work setting. This is not to say that discrimination and non-merit-based advancement do not exist, but only that they are less likely in the more industrialized societies.[2]

In any case, the major point is that mechanisms exist to prevent family norms from undermining norms of merit in the formal organization. This does not as yet deal with the problem of work norms undermining family norms. For instance, Parsons (1944) pointed out that having two or more members of a family in the labor force can lead to invidious status competition—a norm that is acceptable in the world of work, but destructive within primary groups based on affection. We (Litwak & Figueira, 1968) have pointed out in rebuttal that marital household units are common consumption units. This means that each member can gain in social status from the income of the other, which can reduce status competition between husband and wife. We have further suggested that the invidious status competition that exists between husbands and wives today may be related to prejudice based on traditional gender-linked roles, rather than being intrinsic to the occupational order. With the increased stress on merit-based advancement in formal organizations, and the merging of sex roles, this form of prejudice may be declining.

Neighborhood Primary Groups

The modifications in kinship structure described above are consistent with primary groups such as the family, where the underlying assumption is that biological–legal and cultural norms make it difficult if not impossible to waive the condition of long-term commitments. But can a primary group such as a neighborhood manage in modern society, which requires some members of the group to move to one area while others move to another? After all, the minimal criterion for a neighborhood is that members live in close proximity to one another.

For groups to retain the criterion of immediate proximity while at the same time remaining subject to demands for differential geographic mobility, there would have to be some way by which people who have only short-term commitments to each other could retain some form of identity, noninstrumental ties, affection, and contact. That such groups can exist seems to be demonstrated empirically (Festinger, Schachter, & Back, 1963; W. H. Whyte, 1956; Litwak, 1960b, 1961a; Wilensky, 1961; Fellin & Litwak, 1963; Jackson, 1977). The key to the seeming dilemma is the speed with which groups incorporate new members and release old ones. The theoretical and empirical argument has been made (Litwak, 1960b, 1961a; Fellin & Litwak, 1963) that where groups have systematic mechanisms for speeding up the incorporation of new members and releasing old ones, they can make up for many of the problems of short tenure.

One mechanism of integration is a group norm that strangers are good and change is ordered. It would be my argument that such a mechanism of rapid integration is systematically encouraged by large organizations, which must shift staff members around while at the same time encouraging them to work as a team (Fellin & Litwak, 1963; Kohn, 1971; Wilensky, 1961). Another mechanism of quick integration is the adoption of nationally based life styles, which means that strangers have much in common when they meet, so that the processes of integration can be speeded up. This is systematically encouraged by the development of nationally based mass media and nationally based organizations. Yet another mechanism of coordination is the locally based voluntary organization that is specifically set up to help integrate newcomers. The evolution of Welcome Wagons; the assignment of local PTA members to greet newcomers; the aggressive outreach recruitment of newcomers by priests, ministers, and rabbis, the church socials for newcomers—all these are instances of the use of voluntary organizations to speed up the integration of strangers into the community. These local voluntary organizations also promote quick integration of individuals (Litwak, 1960b, 1961a) by virtue of their public access, which permits newcomers to identify them quickly (through the telephone directory if nothing else); by virtue of a membership consisting of local neighborhood people, so that new people can meet their neighbors quickly; and by virtue of discussing local issues, so that the newcomer becomes quickly exposed not only to neighbors but to the local norms. I have not attempted to develop the idea of mechanisms of quick integration completely here, but I hope that the reader can get a sense from what has been provided that such mechanisms can exist and that there is much reason for their systematic development in a modern industrial society. However, neighborhoods that utilize quick mechanisms of integration are not like traditional neighborhoods. They cannot handle problems that require long-term commitments. Thus neighbors may not be willing to provide home care on a long-term basis to a chronically ill person. However, they can manage many other tasks that require proximity but not long-term commitment: providing first aid, spotting break-in attempts and calling the police, or providing loans of such small household items as salt or Band-Aids. These new types of neighborhoods are called "mobile" neighborhoods, as distinguished from traditional ones. The same force that has produced the modified extended family has produced the mobile neighborhood.

Friendship Primary Groups

Aside from problems of differential mobility, there are two other stresses that formal organizations put on traditional primary groups. First, the incredibly detailed division of labor means that there are nonuniform events associated with work and problems of work that affect families and that can only be understood by those in precisely the same occupation, career point, and point in the family life cycle. Second, the speed with which innovation is introduced into the system means that people with small differences in age are subject to very different socializing experiences. Primary groups such as family and neighbors are unlikely to contain within their structure people who are at the same point in the family life cycle, in the same precise occupation, and at the same point in their careers in that occupation. Therefore, they cannot manage those nonuniform events that demand precise matching if people are really to be able to exchange services.

To have precise matching under conditions of change requires a primary group whose members have easy entrance and egress. Friendship groups have this structural characteristic, because membership is based predominantly on mutual affection and interest. Kinship and marital ties also stress affection, but, in addition, they include the notion of long-term commitment. As a result, they cannot so easily change their membership to reflect occupational and family life cycle changes. The comparative intractability of kinship and marital ties is reflected in laws that complicate or prevent their dissolution, while friendship ties can be broken by either partner's whim. The neighborhood that has short-term commitments is still inflexible, because it is basically controlled by geographic proximity; it is difficult to guarantee that one's immediate neighbor will have precise matching, and to change neighbors requires a major household move.

To get some idea of the impact of the modern division of labor and the consequent need for friendship groups, consider two siblings who both become engineers. There may be 20 different types of engineers, and the siblings may in addition differ according to their particular industries, the success of their particular firms within the industries, and their different personal abilities. If one sibling is an aeronautical engineer and the other is a civil engineeer, one sibling's family may be confronted with unemployment while the other is flourishing. One may require several geographical moves while the other is stable. One firm may stress international customers while the other is domestically based, so that one sibling might encourage positive feelings toward foreign countries while the other discourages them. In short, the two siblings and their families may have many areas where they cannot provide services to each other, because they lack the same everyday experiences necessary for such services.

The same point can be made about the family life cycle. Two sisters born 4 years apart will reach retirement at different ages. They may be widowed at different ages. They may have children of different ages and sexes and as a result may have different ties to their children's families. All of these factors may affect how they must deal with the world. To get practical, everyday advice on how to handle such problems, they may have to have friends who have gone through precisely the same situations at the same times.

Only the friendship structure permits the necessary flexibility in choice of members so as to provide precise matching in terms of job and stage in the family life cycle. But to provide such matching in contemporary society (with its many changes in roles), friendships may require a shorter time frame than traditional friendships. Therefore, they may not be able to manage all of the activities of the traditional friendship groups.

Marital Household Primary Groups

Many activities require both long-term commitments and close, continual proximity. Typical of such tasks are daily activities, such as preparing food three times a day, dressing oneself, straightening up the house, shopping, and handling everyday problems of home maintenance. Handling such tasks in a primary group becomes a major problem when the formal organizations demand differential geographic and social mobility for those in the labor force. The two structural solutions offered so far by the larger kinship system and the neighborhood will not work for this type of task. The first solution requires waiving face-to-face proximity, while the second involves waiving long-term commitments. To deal with tasks that require both long-term commitment and continual proximity, it is necessary to have a primary group with the fewest possible number of people in the labor force. A group with only one member in the labor force does not have to worry about differential mobility. That is, of course, the solution that Parsons (1944) offered when he spoke about the isolated nuclear family with a permanent gender-linked division of labor. While rejecting Parsons's view that the marital unit must be completely isolated or that there must be a permanent gender-linked division of labor, one can still accept his view that the smaller the primary group, the fewer problems there are with handling tasks that require both long-term commitment and continuous proximity. Thus it is argued that the marital dyad must be autonomous in residency and occupation from the larger kinship system. Other key features, such as role substitutability, have been mentioned (Litwak & Figueira, 1970). To say that the contemporary marital unit is viable because of its small size and role substitutability is not to say that it can do the same things it did when it was a subunit in the traditional family structure.

What has been stated thus far is that one way of managing the conflict between formal organizations and primary groups is for the traditional primary group to become differentiated into several groups, each with its own structure and each as a consequence able to handle some of the tasks of the traditional primary group but not all of them. However, as a total system they can precisely replace the traditional primary group.[3] From a theoretical point of view, what is being offered is a statement as to why a stable network of groups is likely to arise in a modern society. It provides a rational explanation for finding that different groups manage different tasks and are not easily substitutable for one another (Rosow, 1967; Babchuk, 1965; Litwak & Szelenyi, 1969; Gordon, 1977; Lopata, 1979; LaRocco et al., 1980; Fischer, 1982).

A Second Solution for Dealing with the Conflict:
The Differentiation of Formal Organizational Structures

It is also possible that formal organizations can be modified to minimize the friction between formal organizations and primary groups. In order to understand how organizations can vary their structure, it is necessary to expand the concept of "organizations" in two ways. First, one should not see organizations as involving a dichotomy between bureaucracies and primary groups. The fact of the matter is that organizations can be arranged on a continuum: At one extreme are the highly monocratic structures (i.e., impersonal, hierarchical, rules-oriented, etc.) that Weber (1947) spoke about; between the extremes are human relations structures (i.e., more personal and collegial in nature), with emphasis on committees (W. F. Whyte, 1956; Pennings, 1975); and at the other extreme are primary groups (Litwak, 1978b). Second, it is necessary to understand that one organization may have multiple tasks that require different administrative styles. The idea of having a single organization with multiple administrative styles is a well-understood development in modern organization theory (Litwak, 1961b, 1978b; Perrow, 1967; Thompson, 1967; Etzioni, 1969; Galbraith, 1973; Mintzberg, 1979). Let us explore each of these ideas in greater detail.

The Organizational Continuum

If one considers Weber's (1947) dimensions of monocratic bureaucracy, such as appointment and evaluation by merit, detailed specialization, rules and hierarchies, impersonal and economic forms of motivation, and separation of policy and administration, it can be argued that each of these can be viewed as a continuum (Litwak, 1978b). That is, an organization can be characterized as having 90-100% of its activities evaluated by merit, 90-100% covered by detailed specialists, 90-100% coordinated through rules, 90-100% motivated by impersonal economic factors, and 90-100% capable of being separated into administrative and policy sectors. Other organizations might have 80-89% of their activities handled in that way, while still others may have 70-79% of their activities so classified, and still others may have 60-69% of their activities so classified. At this point, organizations are often referred to as "human relations structures." At the other end of the continuum, organizations may have only 0-10% of their activities so classified, and they are then referred to as primary groups.

Examples of groups at different points on the continuum are as follows: The Social Security administrative unit that deals with establishing eligibility on retirement for pension payments has a task that involves few contingencies; this unit comes close to the ideal monocratic bureaucracy described by Weber. The welfare departments that establish eligibility for welfare clients in most cities and states have a task that involves more contingencies, and their structures tend to be less monocratic. A social work agency that delivers social services may have a task with still more contingencies and an organizational structure that has even fewer monocratic dimensions. A senior citizen center may have activities that have even more contingencies than those of the social work agency; these are often handled by older people themselves, so such a center is run on an even less monocratic basis. At the far end of the continuum, one comes to the nuclear family unit and the individual, whose activities are highly idiosyncratic and whose organizational structure is that of the primary group.

What is important to understand is that there is a range of formal organizational structures even before one reaches the voluntary associations and the primary groups at the high-contingency, low-monocracy end of this continuum. Once it is understood that there is a range of organizational styles and not just a dichotomy between formal organizations and primary groups, or even a limited choice between two types of formal organizations (that is, the monocratic and human relations structures), then it is possible to conceive of balancing contradictions between formal organizations and primary groups by adjustments of administrative styles. This leads to a proposition: The greater the extent to which administrators can move the organizational structure toward the primary-group end of the continuum, the smaller the conflict between primary groups and formal organizations will be. As such, the friction between formal organizations and primary groups can be far less than that anticipated by Weber (1947) and Parsons (1944). However, as indicated above, this solution is constrained by the fact that the further one moves formal organizations toward a primary-group structure, the less likely one is to have technical expertise and economies of task simplification.

Multiple Administrative Styles and
Multiple Task Organizations

A second factor, which makes the first even more important, is that organizations can sometimes segregate uniform and nonuniform tasks by staff, place, and time, and can have two or more different administrative styles within the same organizational structure. Thus modern organizational theorists have pointed out that one section of an organization might be organized strictly on a Weberian monocratic model, such as the payroll departments in a modern university or hospital, while another section might be organized on a human relations structure, such as the academic departments at the university or the collegial relationships among doctors in the hospital. These organizations are sometimes referred to as "matrix organizations" (Galbraith, 1973), while others refer to them as "compartmentalized organizations" (Litwak, 1978b); still others give no particular name, but discuss these types of organizations (Thompson, 1967; Perrow, 1967). When an organization can be compartmentalized so that the staff members who must relate to the community primary groups are organized in a more "human relations" way, it will minimize conflict.

The central theoretical point that I wish to make at this juncture is that formal organizations and primary groups can live side by side in a strong form in a modern industrial society, because each type of group can modify its structure to minimize the conflicts between them.

Before closing this discussion, there is one final option I should like to discuss. Though modifications in structure of formal organizations and primary groups can minimize and in some cases can eliminate friction, it is still the case that the structure of the majority of formal organizations and the majority of primary groups contain elements that are contradictory. Thus members of the modified extended family still stress noninstrumental orientations of affection and family survival as their central motivational devices, while the majority of the formal organizations must have a strong emphasis on economic motivation and only a minor emphasis on affection and the value of membership ties. If these two groups become too closely intertwined, there would be dangers of introducing nepotism into the organization or instrumentalism into the kinship relationship.

This leads to a final procedure for moderating conflict between the two types of organizations—that is, linkage mechanisms that keep primary groups and formal organizations at some distance from each other to avoid such conflict, but not so far apart as to disturb coordination of shared function.

A Third Solution for Dealing with the Conflict:
A Balance Principle of Coordination under Conditions of Conflict

Parsons (1944), in his formulations, suggested that one major way to deal with problems of conflict between formal organizations and primary groups is to keep them at a great distance. However, the present analysis of non-uniform tasks, which suggests that they occur in all areas of life and often in close conjunction with uniform ones, would suggest that dangers might arise from keeping the two groups at maximum distance. For instance, if a doctor did not communicate to a patient new forms of symptoms that indicate the onset of a given disease, the patient might not spot the disease in time to make a difference. If the patient neglects to tell the doctor about his or her symptomatology, then the doctor will be less successful in treating the patient. As already indicated, this is the message that has come from studies on armies' fighting capacities (Shils & Janowitz, 1948), on mass media diffusion (Katz & Lazarsfeld, 1955), on medical care (Berkman & Syme, 1979), and on diffusion of scientific information (Coleman, Katz, & Menzel, 1957).

To point out that Parsons's ideal of complete isolation is not suitable is not to disagree with his proposition that the primary groups and the formal organizations have contradictory structures and therefore should avoid too much contact. The fact of the matter is that both propositions are right. For coordinating efforts with formal organizations, primary groups should have frequent contact with them. However, because their structures are also contradictory, they should avoid frequent contact. Given that both propositions are right, what should be the ideal distance between the two types of organizations? It has been argued (Litwak & Meyer, 1966, 1974; Litwak, Meyer, & Hollister, 1977) that organizations and primary groups must maintain some midpoint of social distance, where they are close enough to provide moderately good coordination but not so close as to have their structures lead to major conflict. Thus, at any point in time, a formal organization and a primary group may be too close, too distant, or at a balance point. Therefore, at any given time, organizations and primary groups must seek linkages to open a gap, to close it, or to maintain the status quo in social distance if they are to optimize their goals. The two central theoretical problems of linkages involve their capacities for opening and closing distance, and a typology of situations most likely to produce blockages in coordination.

The idea of linkages that moderate the distance between the formal organizations and primary groups is one that has rarely been discussed or researched by organizational or family theorists (Litwak *et al.*, 1977; Sussman, 1977). However, it is something that practitioners are in fact concerned about and do research on, though the concept is often called something other than "linkages" and is so task- and situation-specific that the general principles governing linkages are hard to see. Thus many of the problems of closing social distances were examined in research on mass media in areas such as advertising, where the basic problem was to get closer to the client but where only minor variations in a given linkage (i.e., the mass media) were considered. By contrast, social work practitioners interested in community organizations have spoken about a wide range of linkages to close distance, such as storefront services (Cloward & Elman, 1967), indigenous workers (Katan, 1974), local information centers (Kahn, Grossman, Bandler, Clark, Galkin, & Greeawait, 1966), or other types of outreach services, such as having youth counselors work with delinquent gangs. Neither type of research, however, discussed the problem of groups' moving too close or formulated the linkage problem generally enough to deal with the whole range of problems.

We (Litwak & Meyer, 1966) sought to remedy these deficiencies by combining a typology of barriers developed by Hyman and Sheatsley (1947) with the underlying dimension of linkages necessary to overcome these barriers. The importance of our formulation is that it specifies the types of linkages that can be used to push community primary groups away and the types that will draw them closer. It further suggests that where organizations and primary groups have severe barriers, they should use linkages that increase the frequency of face-to-face contact, while those that are already too close might do better by using linkages that will cut down on the number of face-to-face contacts (Litwak *et al.*, 1977; Dobrof, 1976; Dobrof & Litwak, 1977). In this book, I do not deal with the use of linkages to manage the conflict between formal organizations and primary groups.[4] Rather, I examine changes in primary groups and formal organizations.

The Principle of Matching Task and Group Structures
as the Best Predictor of Which Groups
Can Optimally Provide Which Services

Though in this book the emphasis is on the primary groups, a consideration of the historical development of primary groups and formal organizations is enlightening, in that it highlights one of the basic theoretical principles that is advanced in this book: *A group can optimally manage those tasks that match it in structure.* Behind this proposition is the assumption that both groups and tasks can be classified in terms of common categories.

To understand what is new about this formulation, one must first recognize that the early sociologists assumed, and even today many sociologists still assume, that there is one ideal type of primary group or formal organization that is optimal for all tasks. Thus, Cooley (1909) spoke about one primary-group structure for friends, families, and neighbors. In more contemporary times, one finds people like Cobb (1976), who speaks of all support groups as having the same basic dimensions; Cobb's support groups, in turn, overlap with Cooley's primary group. Researchers such as Berkman and Syme (1979) speak about the importance of informal groups and tend to treat them conceptually as though all are cut from the same cloth. The idea that primary groups vary in structure is a relatively new development (Litwak & Szelenyi, 1969; Gordon, 1977; Cantor, 1979), and one that is far from accepted by many researchers in this field. What is even rarer is the understanding that there is a need to have a conceptual scheme for classifying services. This is especially paradoxical, in that the bulk of the empirical research by the modern primary-group theorists has invariably suggested that different groups manage different tasks (Rosow, 1967; Lopata, 1979; LaRocco et al., 1980; Fischer, 1982).

The theoretical vacuum in the primary-group area is highlighted if it is contrasted with the history of organizational theory. The early organizational theorists, such as Weber (1947), like the early primary-group theorists, assumed that there was one organizational structure (monocratic bureaucracy) that was ideal for all tasks. The second-generation organizational theorists disputed those of the first in terms of the ideal model. They argued that the human relations structure is ideal (W. F. Whyte, 1956; P. Blau, 1955; Penning, 1975). However, they also still argued that there was one ideal type that was optimal for all tasks. However, the third generation of organizational theorists has very clearly argued that there is not one ideal model, but different ones, depending on the tasks (Litwak, 1961b; Woodward, 1965; Perrow, 1967; Thompson, 1967; Etzioni, 1969; Galbraith, 1973; Mintzberg, 1979). What they have done, in addition, is to develop a conceptual scheme for classifying tasks, as well as to argue that it is necessary to match the structure of the organization with the structure of the task to know which group can optimally handle a given task. In that regard, they are ahead of the primary-group theorists, who had no scheme for classifying tasks. The organizational theorists have used a variety of terms for describing the theoretical dimension of tasks, but in general have referred to the same underlying dimensions (such as predictability, contingencies, and the degree to which tasks can be subdivided) that have been used here and elsewhere to define uniform and nonuniform tasks (Litwak, 1978b).

In this work, I hope to expand on this classification scheme of the organizational theorists by showing that tasks and groups can be classified by precisely the same dimensions. Thus Cooley's (1909) characterization of primary groups as having continual face-to-face contact can be used to classify services as well. For instance, to have a good chance to spot an attempted break-in at a residence, a person must live within visual contact of that residence. By contrast, providing emotional succor over the telephone can be managed at some distance. Once it is recognized that tasks and groups can be classified by the same dimensions, and that both groups and tasks may systematically vary in structure, then the principle that groups can best manage tasks that match their structure has both theoretical power and great practical consequence. It is this proposition that I seek to develop and to demonstrate empirically for the reader during the course of this book. If this analysis is correct, it should be shown that the initial classification of tasks as uniform and nonuniform is a special case of this more general proposition.

Summary and Conclusion

In this chapter, the underlying rationale as to why formal organizations and primary groups are interdependent as well as in states of conflict has been presented. It has been pointed out that conflict can be reduced by altering the structure of primary groups and formal organizations. This in turn suggests the specific way in which the traditional primary groups have been changed to produce the modified extended family, the mobile neighborhood, the mobile friendship, and the marital unit with flexible gender roles. Understanding these differences is the first stage in making the second point: Each of these groups provides unique services. One cannot fully substitute for another.

In what follows, I elaborate this point so that the reader can see how these theoretical considerations permit the specification of which groups will provide which services to older people.

Notes

1. Some researchers have equated number of contingencies with number of variables. On this basis, it would seem that sending a rocket to the moon would have many more component parts than a chess game; the rocket may have several thousand components, while a chess game has only 32 pieces. Yet the chess game has many more contingencies than putting the rocket up, the reason being that the several thousand parts of the rocket have one or a small number of relations to one another, which are invariant over time. Thus 2000–3000 elements may have no more than 20,000 possibilities. By contrast, each figure in the chess game may have from 3 to 22 moves. Furthermore, the relationships are not invariant over time, so after each move a complete new set of moves is possible. The possible combination of moves is so great that the largest computers we have cannot store them. It is therefore not just the number of factors, but the number of ways they can relate to one another and how these change with time that become

crucial in defining the number of contingencies. This is also why child-rearing may have far more contingencies than sending a rocket to the moon.

2. For instance, there is considerable evidence that members of primary groups, such as friends, play a key role in locating jobs (Granovetter, 1974). However, a close look at Granovetter's analyses suggests that such help from friends may not involve immediate violation of rules of merit. What Granovetter points out is that where there are many applicants, all of whom meet the merit criteria, then the primary groups play a great role. Primary-group criteria are generally used as secondary criteria, and only after the merit requirements have been satisfied.

This is not to argue that the use of primary-group criteria as a secondary basis for job judgment cannot lead to distortions of merit in the long run (Litwak & Dono, 1977). But in the short run the effects are not fatal, and even in the long run they can be used to correct for past inequities as well as to increase inequities (Litwak & Dono, 1977; Granovetter, 1974).

3. In this initial explanation, no attempt is made to illustrate all the possible types of primary-group forms. In later chapters, the larger networks discussed by Granovetter (1974) and Horwitz (1977), as well as volunteers, are discussed. In addition, noninstrumental aspects of transactions by ethnic groups, as suggested by Zola (1966), Papajohn and Speigel (1975), and others, are analyzed. In all of these analyses, the major point is that aspects of modern society have led to tasks that require primary groups to differentiate their structure if tasks are to be successfully managed and conflicts with formal organizations muted.

4. For some application of this balance theory to the problem of aging, see Dobrof and Litwak (1977) and Dobrof (1976). For applications in health and education, see Litwak *et al.* (1977) and Litwak and Meyer (1974). For applications in social services, see Litwak (1970, 1978a).

3

Differential Structures and Tasks of Primary Groups: The Principle of Matching Task and Group Structures

In this chapter, I should like to develop in some detail the basic thesis that services can be classified by the same dimensions as primary groups. This leads to a central principle that a *primary group can best provide those services that match it in structure*. Because the idea that group structure and task structure must match has not been stated before, I should like to elaborate this point further and then use new empirical data from a study of older people in New York and Florida to show how this principle works.

Dimensions for Classifying Primary-Group Structures

There are various schemes that can be used to classify primary-group structures (Parsons, 1960; Fischer *et al.*, 1977; Cooley, 1909). It is felt that they all overlap (Litwak & Kulis, 1982). The one I use here is derived from Cooley (1909).

As indicated in Chapter 1, primary groups are characterized by the recruitment of members on the basis of everyday socialization, such as love, birth, or friendship, rather than technical skills or "merit." They emphasize diffused ties and small groups because they do not require technical knowledge or task simplification. They are coordinated by continual face-to-face contact, peer ties, and common life styles. The members are motivated by internalized, altruistic feelings and a sense of duty to group survival, which manifest themselves in the requirement of long-term commitments. These motivations contrast with the instrumental, impersonal economic incentives of the formal organizations.

Dimensions for Classifying Tasks

What previous investigators have not sufficiently appreciated is that these same dimensions describe not only the structure of the group, but the

31

services or exchanges provided by groups. I develop this idea here through a series of illustrations that I hope will have a face validity in their own right.

Tasks Requiring Continual Proximity or Distance

Let us start with the dimension of continual face-to-face contact. It would be my argument that some tasks require continual physical proximity, while for other tasks proximity is not relevant one way or the other, and for still other tasks, only people who live at a distance can exchange services effectively. Two underlying dimensions can be used to classify the proximity requirements of services: (1) the frequency with which the service must be delivered, and (2) the degree to which it requires face-to-face contact. Generally tasks that require both face-to-face contact and frequent contact can be classified as requiring continual proximity. For instance, emergency first aid in a household accident, supplying daily meals, making beds, reporting an attempted break-in, or emergency borrowing of small items all fit this category.

If a task does not require a physical presence and is infrequent, it generally can be performed at a distance. For instance, a widow may require a weekly or monthly call for emotional support. In the United States, people living at some distance can make such a call. It is also the case that where services require face-to-face contact but must be delivered infrequently, the helper can live at some distance. For instance, a person's breaking a leg and requiring household help for 2 or 3 weeks is a very infrequent event that requires face-to-face contact. A helper can fly in from across the country, perform this service, and fly back. This kind of help requires only ad hoc proximity. What characterizes the last two illustrations is that they can be performed by people living far away or close by.

There are some services that can best be provided when people are at great distances from each other. For instance, a retired older person contemplating a move to a retirement community might want to get information on everyday living. Such information is best provided by a primary-group member who lives in that community.

The crucial things for the reader to understand are that all activities can be classified as (1) requiring close continual physical proximity, or (2) performable under conditions of either close proximity or distance, or (3) requiring great distance in order to be handled effectively. This point, as obvious as it may seem, has not been taken into account by most theorists, policy makers, or researchers who study primary-group exchanges. At most, they have assumed that all services will suffer equally to the degree that the helper is distant from the older person. The formulation given above suggests that some services will suffer enormously from minor geographic distance, others will suffer little, and still others will benefit from major distances.

Tasks Requiring Long-Term or Short-Term Commitment

Exchanges between group members can also be classified in terms of whether they require members to have long-term or short-term commitments to each other. I think that there are several reasons why some exchanges require long-term commitments. First, nonuniform exchanges that place the future of one person in the hands of the other are best handled by primary-group members with long-term commitments. For instance, exchanges that require one primary-group member to manage the finances of another generally require long-term commitments. If the helper mismanages money, its consequences may affect not only the present state of the individual, but his or her future as well.

It is also the case that some activities require much greater expenditures of time and energy on the part of the helper. The helper who does regular household shopping for someone for the indefinite future will be investing more time and energy than the one who does it on an ad hoc basis in an emergency. The helper who comes in for 2 weeks to help out in home nursing care is putting in more time than the one who brings over food for a person laid up overnight.

Where activities do require much time and energy, then they are more likely to be performed by individuals who have long-term commitments, the reason being that primary-group exchanges are not rewarded by money, but involve exchanges in kind or in services. The greater the expenditures of time and energy, the more difficult it is for reciprocity to take place in the short run.

Some exchanges require long-term commitments because they can only be experienced in terms of historical shared experiences. Thus, seeing a current movie might remind one of a time in one's past. To truly enjoy these feelings, a person often requires someone who has shared these experiences and who can talk with him or her about them.

In contrast to the cases described above, there are many exchanges for which the length of the time commitment is not relevant; they can be handled by people who have long-term or short-term commitments. For instance, all activities that require very little in the way of large-scale resources, such as making ad hoc loans of salt or sugar or reporting attempted break-ins in a neighbor's home, can be handled by people with long-term or short-term commitments.

There may be tasks that can only be handled by people with short-term commitments. Simmel (1903/1950) spoke about the fact that for some exchanges, strangers are the best. For older people, there are very critical cases when long-term commitments may be harmful. For instance, residents in a nursing home may not want to make long-term commitments to other residents, since the empirical reality is that they will die within a year or so.

In summary, it would be the hypothesis that all tasks can be classified as (1) requiring long-term commitments, (2) being irrelevant for time commitments, or (3) requiring short-term commitments.

Tasks Requiring Large or Small Groups

Following a similar logic, it can be argued that some tasks require primary groups larger than the marital dyad and/or the individual. Others are not affected by size at all. Still others may require the smallest possible size—that is, the marital dyad or the individual.

The theoretical role of size has been developed in Chapter 2 and is only alluded to at this point. The addition of other people to the groups will make the task speedier and more flexible where the task can be broken into simpler components and where a larger number provides specialization, which increases the knowledge of the individuals doing the task. However, tasks such as personal grooming cannot be broken into simpler components that increase speed and efficiency, nor can they be used to develop special expertise. As a result, the larger group adds nothing to the efficiency with which the task is handled, but does have an added burden of coordination.

On the other hand, there are clearly some tasks that require more than the two-person group. For instance, people seeking emotional support when they are fighting with their spouses require someone other than their spouses with whom to discuss the matter. Individuals seeking to borrow small household items like sugar and salt in an emergency need someone other than their spouses (since the spouses share the same household goods).

There are some tasks for which size is less relevant. For instance, checking daily by telephone to see whether someone is all right may be done almost as effectively by one person as by 10.

Tasks Requiring Common or Different Life Styles

The idea that some tasks might require ties with people who have different life styles while other tasks require people who occupy a common one can be illustrated by using age and retirement status. It is argued that retirement, disability, and age are major determinants for life styles among older people (Z. S. Blau, 1961; Palmore, 1981; Riley, Johnson, & Foner, 1972). For instance, a newly widowed elderly woman who is seeking information on how to adjust to eating alone, how to arrange an escort for late-evening events, or how to go about establishing new friends may find that only another elderly widow can provide this information.

By contrast, there are other activities that do not require age and gender matching, but can be handled by people of either gender or at any age group.

For instance, spotting a break-in at a neighbor's house and reporting it to the police may be done by people at all age levels; providing someone with emergency loans of small items like salt and sugar are activities that do not require people from the same generation.

There are still other activities that do require people from younger generations. Activities that require great expenditures of physical strength and energy, such as taking care of a sick person for several weeks or carrying groceries for elderly persons who are physically frail, do require younger persons.

In short, there may be some tasks for which common generation plays a role, some tasks for which generation is not relevant, and yet other tasks for which cross-generational ties are important.

Tasks Requiring Internalized Forms of Motivation versus Those Requiring Instrumental Ones

All tasks can be classified in terms of the need to have some internalized form of motivation or some external, instrumental ones. As indicated earlier, the two internalized and altruistic forms of motivation that characterize the primary group are affection and the ideal that group survival is the major goal in its own right. This contrasts with the instrumental, bureaucratic forms of motivation, in which one works for economic rewards or prestige. The argument is that instrumental forms of motivation such as economic rewards are not very effective where it is hard for an outside observer to observe the outcomes or the conduct of the worker (D. I. Warren, 1968; Etzioni, 1969). The reason is that where neither work behavior nor outcome can be assessed, people will get rewards whether they use maximal or minimal effort. In such cases, those motivated primarily by money would opt for minimal effort. The only forms of compliance that will encourage maximal effort are those that operate through altruistic internalized goals.

With this thought in mind, the more specific question is that of what tasks are difficult to observe and what outcomes are difficult to check. Personal services, such as grooming and housekeeping, often cannot be supervised by older people because of memory failures or physical disabilities. For instance, if things are missing from the household, is it because the helper has stolen them or the older person has misplaced them? One would be reassured if there was a sense that the helper had a genuine affection for the older person or had a strong built-in sense that the relationship with the older person was important in its own right and must survive. Professionals may have a professional code of ethics that provides the same type of internalized motivation. However, professionals are generally not available for dealing with such nonuniform tasks.

In contrast to such situations, other situations involve tasks that can be observed or where internalization is disadvantageous. Thus all personal grooming tasks or household tasks that are being done for a housewife who is in good health and at home can be monitored continually and require far less internalized motivation on the part of the worker. It is also the case, as suggested earlier, that older people in nursing homes do not want to make deep internalized commitments to others because of the high mortality rate. They are afraid of paying the emotional costs of having someone they love die. To summarize, tasks can be classified in terms of whether (1) they require internalized modes of compliance, (2) they do not require internalized modes of compliance, or (3) internalization does not matter. Following the same logic, other dimensions of primary groups could also be used to classify tasks (e.g., need for everyday socialization rather than technical training).

The Matching of Primary-Group Structures with Tasks

What has been described so far is that exchanges between people can be classified in terms of the same dimensions as the primary groups that encompass them. Once that point becomes clear, the key principle stated earlier cannot be emphasized too much: *Groups will most effectively handle those tasks that are consistent with their structure.* What does that mean in practical terms? Our prior discussion suggests that groups consist of a set of dimensions, so tasks must be simultaneously classified by all dimensions. Thus a neighborhood has as its chief characteristics proximity, short-term commitments, and large size (see Table 3-1). It can handle tasks that have as their chief characteristics proximity, short-term commitment, and large size. As common-sensical as this observation may seem, it has seldom been articulated by researchers or policy makers. Thus it is more than common sense to say that reporting break-ins in a house, emergency borrowing of small household items, accepting deliveries for neighbors who are not at home, administering emergency first aid, providing information on local services, and visually checking people daily to see if they are all right all share in common the need for close proximity, do not require long-term commitments or common life styles, and do benefit from a group of larger size than the marital dyad. Having this theoretical framework allows one to classify all of these seemingly diverse services as sharing the same underlying dimensions and thereby as being consistent with neighborhood structures. Furthermore, it allows one to consider an infinite number of future services and to anticipate or predict whether neighbors will be able to handle them or not.

What characterizes most kinship systems in our society (see Table 3-1) is that they have long-term commitments, do not have close proximity, have large size, and permit different life styles (i.e., age heterogeneity rather than

Table 3-1. Forms of Differentiation in Primary-Group Structure That Have Evolved in Modern Industrial Society

Dimensions of Group and Task Structure	Some Typical Types of Primary Groups				
	Marital Dyad	Modified Extended Family	Friends	Neighbors	Formal Organizations
Face-to-face continual contact of group	Highest	Low	Low	High	Low
Long-term commitments	High	Highest	Moderate	Low	Lowest
Small size	Smallest	Large	Large	Large	Very large
Affection	High	High	High	Moderate	Lowest
Duty to group survival	High	Highest	Moderate	Low	Lowest
Common life style (age homogeneity)	High	Low	High	Moderate	Lowest
Peer ties	High	High	Highest	High	Low
Membership eligibility —everyday socialization	High	High	High	High	Low
Division of labor	Low	Low	Low	Low	High

Illustrations of Services That Match Dimensions of Groups in Columns Above

	Daily cooking, shopping, house-cleaning, laundry	Care for bedridden for 2 to 3 weeks; emotional support in death of spouse	Compan-ions for free-time activities; advice on daily living for widows	Reporting "break-ins" while out on daily chores; emergency loans of small house-hold items	Major surgery; 24-hour perma-nent care of older person; selling food; arresting criminals

age homogeneity). As a result, kin should be able to handle the following "diverse" tasks: (1) taking care of people who need home nursing for 2 or 3 weeks; (2) managing financial matters that do not involve daily expenditures but do involve monthly bills and checks; (3) providing emotional support for marital quarrels or illnesses that can be managed over the telephone or on weekly or monthly visits; and (4) providing temporary supplemental loans or acting as guarantors of larger loans, which in turn may be used for a variety of things. These seemingly diverse tasks all share the same underlying "kinship" dimensions.

What characterizes friendships in our society is that they have a large size and emphasize common life styles or roles, which for older people tend to be defined by age and stage in the family life cycle (Z. S. Blau, 1961; Lazarsfeld & Merton, 1954; Jackson, 1977; Lopata, 1979). In our society, there may be several types of time-based friends—that is, long-term, inter-mediate-term, and short-term—or, as Jackson (1977) refers to them, "com-mitted and utilitarian friends" (Wolf, 1966). One would expect shorter-term friends to be able to handle tasks that have shorter-term commitments, are age-homogeneous, and do not involve close proximity, but do require rela-tions larger than the two-person dyad. Thus a shorter-term task might be serving as an ad hoc companion for free-time activities, such as a pick-up game of cards at a senior citizen's center. Intermediate-term friends would have the same stress on age homogeneity but would exchange services that reflect changes in major role but a common life style, as in the case of a recent widow or a recent retiree seeking information on the everyday prob-lems of living. Long-term friends stress services centered around slow-changing roles, such as ethnicity, religion, or advice on how to handle the behavior or one or another member of a long-standing social group (e.g., marital disputes).

Factors characterizing the marital household unit are that it has con-tinual proximity (by virtue of sharing a common household), long-term commitments, very small size, and common life styles (i.e., age peers). Such groups can handle all tasks that require small size, continual contact, and long-term commitment. Activities illustrative of these dimensions are per-sonal grooming, daily household financial matters, daily housekeeping activities, laundry, and daily food preparation.

Five dimensions of the primary groups have been reviewed here: size; length of commitments; degree of proximity; degree of noninstrumental, internalized commitment; and degree of common life style/age homogeneity. It has been suggested that both tasks and groups can be classified into unique combinations of these dimensions, and that, using these combina-tions, one should be able to predict which primary groups will perform which tasks most efficiently.

There are several things to keep quite clear in this formulation. First, it is argued that various primary groups (e.g., neighbors, kin, friends) in American society *tend* to have different combinations of dimensions. Second, it is argued that the dimensions of the group must match the dimensions of the task if one is to know which group will handle which task. The two points are independent. The second point, on matching, will hold even if the primary groups do not have the predicted dimensions. For instance, if older parents live with their married children in one household, or friends live in the neighborhood, the first point will say that this is an atypical group. The second—that is, the theory of matching groups with tasks—will tell what kinds of tasks these atypical groups can handle. More generally, this means that groups with very strange combinations of dimensions, such as urban communes, or groups that do not exist as yet but that "futurists" speculate about, can also be evaluated in terms of the types of tasks they can and cannot handle.

Empirical Evidence from the 1978 Survey of Older Persons

Nature of Sample

At this point, I should like to begin to introduce some data based on a survey in 1978 of 1818 people who were 65 or older. Half the people lived in the New York metropolitan area (i.e., New York City, Long Island, and West-chester and Rockland Counties), and half lived in Dade and Broward Counties in Florida (i.e., the Miami–Fort Lauderdale area). The sample consisted of 399 people who lived in some institutional setting and 1419 who lived in the community. The community sample was stratified by economic area and old-age homogeneity of neighborhood into four equal groups: low-income/old-age-homogeneous, low-income/old-age-heterogeneous, high-income / old-age-homogeneous, and high-income / old-age-heterogeneous groups. The present results represent this stratification process and have not been reweighted to give estimations of the population. The homes in the institutional sample were selected at random from a list of licensed homes provided by state agencies, but the people within the homes were mostly selected by staff members as those being physically able to be interviewed. (For a complete description of the sample, see Appendix A.)

Typical and Atypical Primary-Group Structures

Potential exchange partners were classified into six basic groups: close friends, neighbors, kin (i.e., both children and other relatives), spouses, the individual respondent, and formal organizations (which included all people who were paid for their help). The theoretical formulation suggests that these common-sense designations should roughly correlate with groups that have different primary-group dimensions. Some empirical indicators suggested that this was so in the 1978 survey. For instance, as one indicator of continual face-to-face contact, people were asked where the members of each of these groups lived. According to the theoretical expectation, it should be the case that spouses should have the closest continual proximity, neighbors next, followed by friends, and lastly kin. It was the case that 98% of those married shared households with their spouses, 88% said that their best-known neighbor lived on their block, 49% had close friends who lived on the same block, and 23% had kin who lived in the same house or block. Basically the same pattern emerged if the amount of daily contact (i.e., either talking to each other on the phone or seeing each other) was used as a measure of proximity: 98% of the respondents had daily contact with spouses, 76% with neighbors, 59% with friends, and 49% with kin.

Another key dimension of primary groups is the extent to which exchange partners make long-term commitments. According to the theoretical expectations, kin and spouses should have the longest commitment, friends next, and neighbors least. A rough indicator of length of commitment is the length of time people have known each other. In the survey, neighbors who had just about the closest proximity to respondents had the least longevity, with 47% of the respondents knowing their neighbors for more than 10 years. Kin helpers who had the least proximity had the most longevity, with 98% knowing the respondent for 10 or more years. Marital households who had the closest proximity also had the next to the longest commitment, with 92% knowing their current spouses for more than 10 years. Friends who had an intermediate proximity also had an intermediate commitment, with 69% of the respondents saying that they had known their close friends for more than 10 years.

Yet another dimension of primary groups is the degree to which members share a common life style. Among this population of older people, the empirical indicator was being in the same generation or living in the same household. Respondents were most likely to be of the same generation as friends (51%) and least likely to share a common age with kin helpers (29%) or neighbors (35%). With regard to daily style of life, only 14% shared a household with someone other than a spouse or "companion" (i.e., a common-law spouse).

To conclude, the point is being made that in the 1978 sample, key family helpers, neighbors, and friends typically followed the structural characteristics in regard to length of commitment, proximity, age homogeneity, size, and noneconomic incentives that have been suggested by the prior theoretical formulation (Litwak & Szelenyi, 1969). However, it is also true that there were substantial exceptions. I begin here with the simplifying assumption that each group did indeed represent a unique bundle of dimensions, and then show how the theory of matching groups and tasks materially increased predictions when these atypical cases were taken into account.

Nature of Services

With the structures of groups in mind, the next step is to see whether different types of primary groups are best able to handle different services, as suggested by the principle that groups can best manage tasks that match their structure.

There were two services measured in this survey that highlight the need for neighborhood primary groups by virtue of stressing proximity and large numbers, and permitting short-term commitments. They were measured by the following items:

> Suppose you had to go out of the house for an hour, to go to the store or to the doctors, and while you were out someone tried to break into your place. Tell me which of these people (CARD A), if any, would be likely to see what is going on and call the police or tell you about it. (CHECK AS MANY AS APPLY.) Neighbors, close friends, children, relatives, spouse or companion, someone else (SPECIFY), or no one.

> Suppose you were in a situation where you had to borrow something small in a big hurry—like salt or sugar—as you were sitting down to eat, or a Band-Aid for a cut finger. Tell me from which of these people (CARD A), if any, would you be able to borrow such things in a hurry? (CHECK AS MANY AS APPLY.) Neighbors, close friends, children, relatives, spouse or companion, someone else (SPECIFY), or no one.

Respondents were able to choose as many different groups as they wanted for each question. I initially report only on the people living in the community. As indicated in Table 3-2, 73% of the respondents said that neighbors would watch their houses and 69% said that they would borrow small household items from neighbors when in a hurry. No other type of primary group was chosen by more than 14% of the respondents. The only other primary group that stresses proximity besides neighbors is the conjugal unit. However, the majority of respondents in this sample (61%) did not have spouses. Therefore, they could not take advantage of the proximity feature. Where they did have spouses, then a substantial percentage chose them for watching the house (33%).

SERVICES REQUIRING COMMON LIFE STYLE, LARGE SIZE,
INTERMEDIATE TIME COMMITMENT, AND AD HOC PROXIMITY:
FRIENDSHIP SERVICES

It has been argued that friendship ties stress the need for age-homogeneous ties. Given the retirement of most older people and the resulting unique daytime patterns, items on leisure are likely to emphasize generational uniqueness. The following item was used to measure this type of service:

If you wanted someone to join you in your favorite free-time activities, tell me which of these people (CARD A), if any, would join you? (CHECK AS MANY AS APPLY.) Neighbors, close friends, children, relatives, spouse or companion, someone else (SPECIFY), or no one.

As Table 3-2 shows, the largest percentage of respondents chose friends (42%). Neighbors, relatives, and spouses were chosen by 29%, 31%, and 27%, respectively. What should be stressed is the dramatic shift in choice of helping primary group by virtue of changing the task. Whereas only 11% chose friends to watch their houses, 42% chose them as companions; whereas 73% chose neighbors to watch their houses, only 29% chose them as companions.

SERVICES REQUIRING LONG-TERM COMMITMENTS,
DIFFERENT LIFE STYLES, LARGE SIZE, AND AD HOC PROXIMITY:
KINSHIP SERVICES

The question now arises as to what kinds of tasks match kinship structure—that is, demand long-term commitments, large size, and ad hoc proximity, but not common generation. Three services measured in the survey fit this description. First, respondents were asked:

Now, I'd like you to think about people who might help you if you got ill and had to stay in bed for 2 or 3 weeks. Who, if anyone, would be helpful in feeding you your daily meals, helping you in and out of bed, bringing you water when you needed it, and many things like that? Tell me which of these people (CARD A), if any, would be able to do this kind of job for 2 or 3 weeks, either at your place or theirs. (CHECK AS MANY AS APPLY.) Neighbors, close friends, children, relatives, spouse or companion, someone else (SPECIFY), or no one.

This question was used to measure long-term commitment because being bedridden for several weeks is a major drain on helpers, and there is no guarantee that a helper will have a similar catastrophe within the immediate future to warrant that magnitude of time, money, and energy. However, if people have spent 20 to 40 years together, then there is a good chance that during that period one or more of them has needed some help of this magnitude (Sussman, 1965; Hill, 1970). It also measures ad hoc proximity, since people living far away can fly in, provide help, and fly back. This is possible because it is an infrequent event. Finally, given the age of this population, such physically vigorous activity is likely to require help from younger individuals. A second set of items asked:

Tell me which of these people (CARD A), if any, have done these things for you in the last 6 months:

    a. Talked to you when you were feeling upset or low and made you feel better?

    b. Checked on you daily to see if you were all right?

(CHECK AS MANY AS APPLY.) Neighbors, close friends, children, relatives, spouse or companion, someone else (SPECIFY), or no one.

The problems that cause older people to feel depressed might involve increasing physical frailties, death of someone close to them, or lack of income, all of which may make carrying out everyday tasks difficult. Younger people are the ones who have the physical and economic resources to provide such services and therefore can provide the optimal reassurance. In addition, age peers, because of their physical frailty, may be too vulnerable even to discuss such issues. Finally, both of these services can be delivered over considerable physical distance by a combination of telephoning and ad hoc visits.

    Table 3-2 indicates that in each of these cases, the group most likely to be chosen was the kinship unit: 55% of the respondents said that kin had talked to them when they were feeling low and had made them feel better. The groups chosen after kin were friends and spouses; 27% of the respondents chose each of these groups. Similarly, most chose kin as the group that had checked up on them daily to see if they were all right (52%). The group chosen next most often was neighbors; 32% chose them. For home nursing, kin were chosen by the highest percentage (44%), and spouses were chosen by the next highest percentage, 32%.

    What is again stressed is the remarkable shift in the percentage choosing a given group, depending on the task dimensionality. Of the respondents, 55% chose kin as the persons to whom they talked when feeling low, and 31% chose them as potential free-time companions, but only 9.6% chose them as people who might watch their houses.

SERVICES REQUIRING SMALL SIZE, CONTINUAL PROXIMITY,
COMMON LIFE STYLES, AND LONG-TERM COMMITMENTS:
MARITAL HOUSEHOLD SERVICES

As indicated above, the marital household unit tends to share in common all the features of the other groups: proximity, long-term commitment, common life styles, and peer group ties. What clearly differentiates the marital unit is its small size (i.e., never more than two adults) and the capacity to handle activities requiring both long-term commitments and continual proximity.

    With this thought in mind, we asked individuals:

Tell me which of these people (CARD A), if any, have done these things for you in the last 6 months:
    a. Helped with money matters, like keeping track of bills, medical payments, Social Security, bank accounts, and things like that.
    b. Stored things for you, like seasonal clothes or valuables, or took care of laundry or cleaning.

Table 3-2. Percentage of Older Persons Saying They Received Services, by Relation to Helper and Type of Service

| | Percentage Respondents Choosing Each Group[d] | | | | | | | |
| | Neighborhood Services | | Friendship Services | | Kinship Services | | Individual or Marital Household Services | |
Helper's Relation to Respondent[a]	Watch House while Shopping[b]	Borrow Small Things in Hurry[b]	Join as Companion for Free Time[b]	Check Daily	Provide Home Nursing Care[b]	Provide Emotional Succor when Upset	Store Clothes and Do Laundry	Manage Money, Bills, Bank Account, Social Security
Neighbors	73.0	69	29	32	18	25.7	1.0	1.0
Friends	11.0	14	42	26	19	27.0	1.9	1.9
Relatives (and children)	9.6	11	31	52	44	55.0	22.0	22.5
Spouse or respondent	10.1	4	27	24	32	27.3	20.0[c]	19.5[c]
Formal organization	8.1	1	0	2	8	3.7	1.8	2.4
No one	13.0	18	14	17	12	14.2	59.0[c]	58.0[c]
n	(1396)	(1406)	(1402)	(1419)	(1411)	(1414)	(1403)	(1371)

Note. To test the hypothesis advanced in the text, it is necessary to show that items for each type of service had a higher rank-order correlation in the percentage using each primary group than items between services had. In this regard, the rank-order correlation for the neighborhood items was .94, for the kin services .81, and for the marital household services .94. They were all significant at the .01 level. By contrast, the correlation of items between services was on the average −.01, which was not statistically significant. Where more than two items were compared, the rank orders were derived from Kendall's coefficient of concordance. For two items, Spearman's rank-order correlation was used.

[a]The respondent could choose as many groups as he or she wanted. Therefore, each cell in the table has the same population base, and totals for each task (column) can be more than 100%.

[b]Four items—watching house, borrowing small items, providing home nursing, joining for free time—measured hypothetical exchanges. The other four consisted of the respondent's estimate of who actually provided these services in the last 6 months.

[c]For all tasks, except marital household services, a response of "no one" would mean that the task could not be done because it required some person other than the respondent. For the two items listed as marital household services, it is very likely that a "no one" response meant the task was handled by the respondent. As such, these numbers should be combined as indicators of the individual or marital dyad. This remains true throughout this book.

[d]Only noninstitutionalized respondents are considered.

(CHECK AS MANY AS APPLY.) Neighbors, close friends, children, relatives, spouse or companion, someone else (SPECIFY), or no one.

According to Table 3-2, the majority indicated that no one did these things for them: 59% of the respondents said that no one helped with laundry, and 58% said this about money management. In this case, "no one" is interpreted to mean that these tasks were handled by individuals themselves. This is what Rix and Romashko (1980) found when they asked a similar question but included the category of the respondent as well. This interpretation contrasts with those about questions where a task could not be done without two or more individuals (e.g., watching the house while one is out, loaning small items in a hurry, or doing home nursing when one is bedridden).[1]

Therefore, for these two items, the combination of "no one" and spouse represented the percentage of help coming from the household unit. This means that for such services as managing money and doing laundry, 78% and 79% of the respondents, respectively, used the household marital dyad. This contrasts with the use of spouses or the individuals themselves for home nursing, which was 32%; or with the use of spouses as free-time companions (27%) or for watching the house (10%).[2]

To summarize the results to this point, this set of items was handled by very different primary groups in a way that is consistent with the principle that groups can best handle tasks that have matching structures.[3] This analysis, as well as the larger theory, should give considerable pause to those studying network exchanges. What it very strongly suggests is that, depending from which part of the task universe an investigator draws items, he or she could come out with very different conclusions as to which groups are most important, as well as what it is primary groups can do (Dono *et al.*, 1979; Litwak & Szelenyi, 1969).

Effects of Primary-Group Structure
and Functional Substitutability

The analysis above raises two problems. First, though the figures go in the right direction, there are clearly "deviant cases." For instance, while 42% of the people chose friends as free-time companions, 29% also chose neighbors and 31% relatives. How can one explain these "deviations"? It may be that the deviance comes from the fact that the survey did not use direct measures of group structure, but rough correlates (i.e., friends are more likely to be of the same generation than neighbors and kin). However, if relatives are cousins or siblings from the same generation, or if older parents live with their children, or if neighbors have long-term ties, they may handle activities requiring a common life style.

The poor measurement may in part arise because the theoretical statement speaks about typical shapes of primary groups.[4] It is quite possible for atypical cases to exist as long as they remain a minority (Litwak, 1965). If it is either the case that the survey did not define the primary groups well or that there were atypical cases, the general situation should still be summarizable by the principle that groups can manage tasks that match their structure. If that principle is correct, one of two consequences should follow. First, the so-called "deviant cases" should be atypical primary groups, which match the structure of the typical ones that ordinarily handle the tasks in question. Second, for those who do not have such atypical primary groups, the loss of a given group should generally mean a loss of services.

NEIGHBORHOOD EXCHANGES AND FUNCTIONAL SUBSTITUTABILITY

The analysis to this point indicates that most people will overwhelmingly choose their neighbors for watching their houses and for borrowing small household items in an emergency. The question then arises as to what people do who have little contact with their neighbors. Do they choose friends, kin, or spouses, or do these become lost services? We measured availability of neighbors by asking respondents how much contact they had with their neighbors. The respondents were classified into those who had daily contact, those who had weekly contact, and those who had monthly or less frequent contact. We found that the percentage of the people (1058)[5] using neighbors for watching the house went from 78% for those with daily contact, to 66% for those (187) with weekly contact, to 44% for those (147) with monthly or less frequent contact. There was a drop of 34% between those having daily and monthly contact. The question then arises as to whether those without active neighbors would lose these services or whether an atypical group (structured like neighbors) would pick up the service. The number of people who said "no one watches" increased from 19% to 33% when they had infrequent neighborhood contact. This is certainly what would be predicted if one argues that group structure and task structure must match.

Nevertheless, some respondents did choose other groups. The theory would suggest that these groups should share the neighborhood dimensions of proximity and large size. This indeed turned out to be the explanation. For those (205) with a close friend living within a 10-block radius, 15% said that a friend would watch their house. This dropped to 4% for those (64) whose close friends all lived more than 10 blocks away. Where the respondents had spouses living in the same household, 33% said that their spouses would watch the house. It dropped to 2% where the spouses did not live with them. Where the older person lived in the same house or within 5 blocks of a kin helper, 25% said that their relatives would watch. This shrank to 4% when the helpers lived more than 1 hour away.

In other words, where other groups had one of the key structural features of the neighborhood (i.e., proximity), there was some functional substitutability. In this regard, it must also be noted that typically neither friends nor family members lived on the same block as the respondents. As such, these findings conform to the theory that groups can only handle tasks that match them in structure, as well as to the theory of primary-group differentiation.

FRIENDSHIP EXCHANGES AND FUNCTIONAL SUBSTITUTABILITY

Let us continue to examine this principle, but now shift to friendship activities, where the stress is on common age statuses. What happens to people seeking companions for their favorite free-time activities when they have no friends? In the survey, there was an increase in the percentage of respondents who said that no one was available to join them when they reported having no friends. Of those who reported having four or more friends (551), 7% said they had no one with whom to share free-time leisure activity. Of those who had one to three friends (582), 11% said this. By contrast, 44% of the respondents with no friends said that there was no one who could join them in their favorite free-time activities.

But, clearly, some still chose leisure companions from primary groups other than friends. According to the theory, people will choose from such groups when they match the friendship group's key structural characteristics (i.e., share the same style of life). In our study, there were two objective measures of common life style: (1) same generation, and (2) belonging to same household (i.e., same consumption unit).[6]

It was found that where individuals had spouses, 65% chose them as companions for their favorite free-time activities. The fact that they were not chosen more often in the overall population is a function of the small size of the conjugal dyad, which meant that in 61% of the cases older people had no spouse.

The other findings were that where respondents lived in neighborhoods where a majority of the neighbors were 65 or older, 38% were likely to choose neighbors as companions in their free-time activity. By contrast, when neighbors were likely to be under 65, then 21% chose their neighbors as companions. Perhaps the situation where age homogeneity is complete and where life styles are most likely to match is that of the nursing home. Fellow residents are almost 100% in the same age group and have the same daily time schedules, the same leisure-time programs, the same problems of dealing with the same staff members, and so on. In the survey, 55% of nursing home residents selected fellow residents in that situation. There was also a close match in style of living when relatives, like spouses, lived in the same households as the respondents. In such cases, 54% of the respondents said that relatives would provide them with companions for favorite free-time activity.

The basic point is that where friendship primary groups do not exist, then other primary groups do not generally provide functional substitutes.

However, in the atypical cases where the other primary groups share the same style of life and size as the friendship group, then they can substitute.

KINSHIP EXCHANGES AND FUNCTIONAL SUBSTITUTABILITY

The same point can be made with regard to the "deviant" cases that are associated with kinship exchanges. When the item that asked who would provide the respondent with home care if he or she were bedridden for 2 or 3 weeks is examined, it can be seen which groups substituted when the kin were not available. To measure the presence or absence of the most significant kin, all respondents were classified by the number of children they had. When there were no children, 28% chose relatives for home care. By contrast, when there were three or more children, 62% chose relatives for home care, as predicted by the principle of matching. Among those without children, 19% said that no one helped in home care, while only 7% said that no one helped when there were one or more children. The question must be asked as to what extent other groups provided these kin services because they overlapped with children in having long-term commitments and resources. Length of time for which people had known the respondents was used as a measure of length of commitment, and proximity was used as a measure of resource. Proximity was viewed as a resource for older people because the service in question requires face-to-face contact, and taking a bus, car, or plane to provide care is difficult for the very advanced aged. Of those who had known their neighbors the longest (10 years or more), 19% said they would choose neighbors for several weeks of home nursing care. By contrast, this was true of 11% who had known their neighbors for less than a year.

The role of proximity becomes relevant to understanding the relationship between friendship and home care for the bedridden. Long-term friends do not provide more services to bedridden friends. At first glance, this may seem to negate the principle of matching the structure of groups with that of tasks. However, what it reveals is the necessity to match on several dimensions simultaneously. Long-term friends suffer in comparison to long-term neighbors in that they lack proximity, while they suffer in comparison to children in that they may be physically more frail and have less money.

There is some confirming evidence for this line of reasoning. Of those respondents with very short-term friends, 65% lived on the same block as their friends, while 55% of those who had intermediate-length friends and 26% of those with long-term friends had them living on the same block. Furthermore, when friends lived closer, they were chosen more often as those who would provide home nursing services (i.e., 15% vs. 4%).[7]

Where people lived with their spouses, 78% said that they would choose them for home care. Of the people married in this sample, 92% had been married for longer than 10 years. The chief problem with the marital dyad is its very small size, which means that it has a very good possibility of being disrupted by illness or death (e.g., 61% of the respondents in our study were single).

In short, where neighbors stressed structural dimensions close to those of kin (long-term ties) and had resources (i.e., close proximity), or where conjugal units had long ties and shared a common household, these groups tended to be chosen for help with home nursing.

CONJUGAL FUNCTIONS AND SUBSTITUTABILITY

The question is now asked as to which groups can substitute for the marital household unit. The marital household services examined in this study were managing money and doing laundry and storage of clothing. When those situations where the conjugal unit was complete are contrasted with those in which it was not, it can be seen that kinship units acted as functional substitutes for the marital household. The use of kin for money management went from 10% when spouses lived at home (512) to 23% when the individuals lived alone (629). Virtually none of the respondents used friends, neighbors, or formal organizations when spouses were absent; they managed money themselves. Thus the percentage of respondents who chose no one (or themselves) went from 45% of those with spouses to 68% of those without spouses. The fact that kin were chosen is understandable, since kin have long-term commitments. The fact that kin were not chosen as much as spouses is also understandable, since most kin do not have the continual face-to-face contact that spouses have.

This point becomes clearer if the group of 165 respondents who shared the same households with children is isolated. In this group, there was very close structural matching between the marital household and the kin group; that is, they both had long-term commitment and close continual proximity. In these cases, 60% chose kin for money management.[8]

In summary, the data show that different groups handled different problems, and that when individuals did not have the full range of groups, they were likely to miss some services unless they could locate groups with the same dimensions as the missing groups. These were generally atypical groups. The data provide powerful documentation for the principle that groups can only provide those services that match them in structure.

Resources Other than Group Structure

In the discussion thus far, attention has only been paid to the structure of the group. Yet it is clear that there are other, equally important resources that could affect the extent to which services are delivered. Three of the more obvious ones are mentioned here to show that the principle of matching primary-group structures and services prevails under most resource conditions. In the survey, the more disabled, the poor, Latin Americans, and East Europeans were more likely to get help from kin but less likely to get it from friends and neighbors. However, it was still true that the disabled, the two ethnic groups, and the low-income group would use neighbors more for neighbor tasks, such as reporting a break-in; kin for kin tasks; and so forth. Put statistically, all disability groups,[9] income groups,[10] and ethnic groups[11] followed the same overall pattern (special use of neighbors, friends, kin, and spouses) exhibited in Table 3-2, even though they varied in the percentage using each group. In the following chapters, I expand upon and discuss the important effects of income, disability, and ethnicity on the delivery of services. At this juncture, what is being stressed is that these larger social factors do not alter the basic proposition that primary groups can best handle those tasks that match them in structure.

Summary and Conclusion

In this chapter, an attempt has been made to document the principle that groups can optimally provide those services that match them in structure. In this analysis, two ideas have been emphasized. First, services delivered by primary groups can bc classified by the same dimensions that are used to classify primary groups. Second, primary groups can most effectively deliver those services that match them in structure.

This seems such a simple and self-evident principle that the reader might well ask whether it is not a truism. Astonishing as it may seem, very few, if any, primary-group researchers have ever sought to classify services provided by groups to their members. In almost all cases where one wanted to know which group provided which service, the services were selected in a haphazard manner or in terms of some immediate pragmatic need, or a measure was used that was assumed to correlate with all services (e.g., the number of contacts between a group and an older person).

This simple proposition, that groups can only manage those services that match them in structure, permits researchers to answer on a theoretical level a basic research question addressed by many researchers—that is, to what extent are primary groups substitutable for each other (Rosow, 1967; Babchuk, 1965; Cantor, 1979)? Or, to put the question another way, what is it that each group uniquely contributes to goal achievement (Litwak & Szelenyi, 1969; Gordon, 1977; Cantor, 1979; Dono et al., 1979)? It is unlikely that primary groups can completely substitute for one another, given the fact that modern industrial society seems to demand that kin, neighbors, friends, and marital households have different structures. Yet some substitution seems to be called for in order to provide services to the chronically disabled aged.

These questions have relevance, in that some writers propose that older people might be helped if their children would take them into their households (Sussman, 1980), while others propose a return to laws of filial responsibility that have not worked in the past, as Schorr (1960) has shown. In the following chapter, the principles of matching groups and task dimension are used to show which groups can substitute for which tasks with minimal disruption to the larger society. Some significant policy implications are developed in Chapter 10.

The same proposition (i.e., that groups can best provide those services which match them in structure) goes a long way toward explaining discrepant research findings on the relative importance of kin, friends, and neighbors. As pointed out elsewhere (Dono et al., 1979; Litwak & Szelenyi, 1969), investigators who have a well-defined universe of services can immediately see that researchers who select all of their services from that part of the universe that stresses continual proximity, long-term commitment, and small size must end up with a finding that the marital dyad is the only unit of importance. This, indeed, explains the conclusion of Rix and Romashko (1980) that all primary groups except the marital dyad are mostly irrelevant for older people. The services they used to measure relevance were cooking, shopping, housecleaning, and money management among the aged. By contrast, if one selects items that require long-term commitment and large group size, but not continual proximity, then one would find, as Sussman did (1965) and as Cantor did (1979), that kinship plays a significant role. If investigators selected their services from a range of areas, they would find that different groups handle different tasks, as has been found by many writers (Litwak & Szelenyi, 1969; Gordon, 1977; Rosow, 1967; Lopata, 1979; Muir & Weinstein, 1962; Babchuk, 1965; Adams, 1971). In short, instead of a series of ad hoc and sometimes discrepant findings, there is now a well-understood pattern.

In the next chapter, I should like to show how the principle of matching group structures and primary groups can be extended to formal organizations. This in turn sets the stage for showing which groups in the network will provide which services as older people move from a healthy state to illness and then to institutionalization.

Notes

1. Furthermore, hypothetical tasks were defined in terms of the respondent's needing help (e.g., "Who would help you if you were bedridden for 2 to 3 weeks and needed someone to help you in and out of bed, bring food, etc.?"). To answer "no one" to such a question suggests that the service would not be performed. However, the item on money and laundry was not hypothetical. It asked "Which of any of the following people helped you keep track of bills, etc., during the last 6 months?" A respondent who said "no one" could say this because he or she did not need help. However, it is the case that for the severely ill, those who said "no one" may indeed

have had no one. I examine this in the course of the analysis below. The combination of severely ill and those saying "no one" is a small percentage of the survey population; only 1.6% of the people were severely ill, and 4% of them were moderately ill. So the use of "no one" to indicate that the respondent managed the service only leads to slight overestimation.

2. These low percentages occurred because most of the population had no spouse. They are presented this way because the lack of a spouse is a consequence of a key dimension of the marital household, its small size.

3. From a statistical point of view, what one would like to establish is that within a task area (e.g., a neighborhood), people using the various services measured by different items will use primary groups in the same rank order of preference, and that this ranking will be different from the one these people use when they are using services from a different task area (e.g., kin). A rank-order correlation for the 1978 survey was derived from Kendall's coefficient of concordance. It was found that the rankings between task areas were not related to each other. The average rank-order correlation was −.01. By contrast, the rank-order correlations of items within the same task area (e.g., neighborhood items with each other or family items with each other) were much higher and were statistically significant. Thus the two neighborhood items had a rank-order correlation of .94, the three family items had a rank-order correlation of .81, and the two marital household items had a rank-order correlation of .94. All were significantly associated at the .01 level. Since the friendship area had only one item, no rank-order correlations were possible within it.

4. The deviant cases may also have arisen because of ambiguity in the questions. For instance, the question on who checked on the respondent in the last 6 months to see if he or she was all right did not specify whether the checking was done visually or by telephone. If visual checking was measured, then a neighbor would be in a much better position to do it, while if it had been done by telephone, then a relative might be in a better position. The fact that so many respondents chose neighbors on this question might mean that they had felt that "checking" referred to visual checking. Those choosing family members may have had in mind telephone checking. Rather than two groups' overlapping in services, it could be that the responses represent two different kinds of services. For instance, a neighbor who is close by can respond with emergency help that families living at some distance cannot provide.

5. Throughout this book, when percentages are given without an accompanying table, the population upon which the percentages are based is given in parentheses.

6. The only real objection to this formulation might be spouses, whose gender difference does produce differences in some aspects of style of living (Neugarten, 1964). However, others have argued that the gender difference also produces complementary needs (Ktsanes & Ktsanes, 1962; Winch, 1958). For older people who are retired and infirm, there may also be far less incentives to maintain traditional sex roles, since each may have to handle both roles (Cameron, 1968).

7. In our qualitative interviews, we did find a type of older person who had no children who tried to use friends in place of kin. Malowsky (1976) points out that these "friends" are often service people who come in contact with them (e.g., occupational therapist, postman, grocery clerk, etc.). The empirical phenomenon is one in which the older person views such a person as a close friend, and for a brief period the friendship flourishes; then it burns out, whereupon the older person goes to a new "friend." It is hypothesized that the instability of the friendship is based on the fact that such an older person is asking for major time commitments from someone with whom he or she has no past reciprocity or future potential reciprocity. Once the younger person feels the full burden of the request, he or she drops out. In this regard, it is important to note that though people with short-term friends are most likely to choose friends to provide housekeeping services, they are also most likely to have the largest number of people who say that no one helps. I touch on this matter again in Chapter 9.

8. If one looks at the cases where "live-in" helpers were relatives who were not children, it can be seen that 27% (25) of the people chose relatives. This is not as high as the percentage of those who chose relatives when children lived with the older persons. This may be a function of

the fact that relatives who are not children may not have the necessary physical resources or long-term commitment. Only children combine both attributes.

9. For the effects of disability, this matter can be put statistically using rank-order correlations derived from Kendall's coefficient of concordance. If task and group structure are important, then the rank order in which different primary groups are used to deliver services should be the same for individuals at different stages of disability, as long as the services are in the same task area. By contrast, the rank order should be different for individuals at the same stage of disability when groups are supplying services in different task areas. If disability plays the major role, then all the ranks from those in the same disability category should be the same, regardless of task area, while all the ranks between disability categories in the same task areas should differ. First, it can be pointed out that within a task, those survey respondents with different states of disability used primary groups in the same rank order. The average rank-order correlation derived from the Kendall coefficient of concordance was .89 for the neighborhood tasks, .60 for the friendship task, .79 for the kinship tasks, and .85 for the marital household tasks. The overall average was .78. By contrast, the average rank-order correlation between task areas for groups at the same level of disability was .27, with the rank-order correlations being .03 for those with no disabilities, .04 for those with a disability score of 1–3, .35 for those with a score of 4–7, .09 for those with a score of 8–15, and .56 for those with a score of 16 or more. The two highest were significant at the .05 level.

In short, all statistical evidence points to the centrality of task structure and a second but lesser effect for disability.

10. If one considers the effect of income, the average rank-order correlations of primary groups on the two services within the neighbor task area across each income level was .50; for the friendship tasks, it was .78; for the kinship tasks, it was .74, and for the marital household tasks, it was .78. All were statistically significant. The overall average of these correlations was .70. By contrast, the rank-order correlation of services by the lowest-income group for the four task areas was .28; for the middle-income group, it was .09; and for the high-income group, it was .18. The average correlation for rankings between tasks was .18. Only the low-income group was statistically significant. In short, task structure played the major role and income a secondary one.

11. All people born in a foreign country, with two exceptions, were given the nationality of that country. Those born in this country were asked which, if any, nationality, religious, or racial groups they were part of. Those who gave a response other than "American" were classified by that response. There were two exceptions, the blacks and the Jewish people. People were asked what their religion was, and all who identified themselves as Jewish on this question or who identified Jewish people as the group they felt closest to in the prior question were classified as Jewish, no matter where they were born. Blacks and Orientals were identified by an interviewer rating. The average rank-order correlations between ethnic groups for the neighborhood area was .99; for the friendship tasks, it was .80; for the kin tasks, it was .85; and for the marital household tasks, it was .88. These were significant at the .01 level.

The correlations between task areas for each ethnic group were much smaller and, with the exception of the Latin Americans, not significant. For the assimilated Americans, the rank-order correlations in the way primary groups were used in different task areas was .28; for the West Europeans, it was .20; for the Jewish people, it was .12; for the blacks, it was .29; for the East Europeans, it was .21; and for the Latin Americans, it was .46.

4

Formal Organizations: A Further Application to Nursing Home Settings of the Principle of Matching Task and Group Structures

Formal Organizations and Primary Groups: Opposite Ends of the Same Dimensions

Thus far in this analysis, I have discussed how differences in primary-group structure permit one to anticipate which types of nonuniform tasks primary groups can perform. However, in Chapter 2, I have pointed out that differences in structure between formal organizations and primary groups also permit one to anticipate what it is that formal organizations can do, as distinct from primary groups. In this chapter, I should like to join these two streams of thought, so it can be seen that one principle holds for both primary groups and formal organizations. The principle of matching group structure with task structure can enable one to predict which services formal organizations, such as nursing homes, can take over from primary groups; which must remain with the primary groups even when older people go into nursing homes; and which ones will be lost.

Nursing homes are particularly good groups to study if one wants to examine the principle of matching. The reason is that the major job of the nursing homes is to take over services that are generally provided by primary groups, such as marital households. According to the principle of matching, the only way the nursing home can do this is by changing the structure of the services or by changing its own structure to be more like a primary group. To understand why the same principle can be used for both formal organization and primary groups, it must be recalled, from Chapter 2, that the structure of the formal organization involves precisely the same dimensions as the primary group, except that each of its characteristics is at the opposite extreme of each dimension. Theorists in each field have frequently used different names to define the dimensions, so it is not always apparent that they have been referring to opposite ends of the same dimensions.

I briefly review this discussion here so that it is fresh in the mind of the reader. Weber (1947), in his description of the monocratic bureaucracy, said that people are recruited for such an organization by merit—that is, evaluated by their training in formal organizations, job experience in formal organizations, or written examinations that reflect any combination of the two. By contrast, primary-group theorists have said that members of such groups are recruited by birth, love, friendship, arranged marriages, and the like. What characterizes all these latter elements is that they require no experience or training in formal organizations, but are a product of everyday socialization in primary groups. They are at the opposite end of the continuum from what has been labeled by organizational theorists as "merit." In a similar fashion, organizational theorists have spoken about coordination through written rules, hierarchy, and separation of private life style from work, while primary-group theorists have spoken about the opposite of each of these qualities— that is, coordination through face-to-face meetings, peers, and stress on common life styles. Organizational theorists have spoken about motivating people by impersonal instrumental incentives such as economic rewards, which would prevent favoritism; primary-group theorists have spoken about motivating people by personal, internalized, and altruistic modes, such as affection or duty to group survival as an end in itself. Organizational theorists have spoken about the need to make all commitments contingent on performance and changes in technology, while primary-group theorists have spoken about lifelong commitments based on common values, such as duty to survival of ties. These commitments stress permanence rather than change and values rather than technology.

In short, theorists from these two groups have been dealing with the opposite ends of the same dimensions. It would seem to follow logically that the same analysis that holds for primary groups should also hold for formal organizations. Furthermore, the analysis in Chapter 2 should be understandable in terms of the principle of matching group structures and services. In that analysis, I have pointed out that because of their differences in structure, primary groups can best manage nonuniform services and formal organizations can best handle uniform ones. In other words, the terms "uniform" and "nonuniform" have been used to classify services in that case, while in Chapter 3 services have been classified by the same dimensions as tasks—that is, as involving continual face-to-face contact, common life style, and so on. The question now arises of how to reconcile these two ways of proceeding.

The idea that services can all be classified in terms of their degree of nonuniformity is directly inherited from theories of formal organizations (Litwak, 1961b). Though different theorists use different terms, such as "degree of analyzability" and "number of exceptions" (Perrow, 1967), or "pooled, sequential, and reciprocal interdependence" (Thompson, 1967), or "number of contingencies" (Pennings, 1975), I would argue that these are basically different words for describing the same things—that is, the number of contingencies, the degree of predictability, and the extent to which the task can be broken into simpler components (Litwak, 1978b). What all of these theorists have explicitly or implicitly argued was that all dimensions of organizations are related to task contingencies in the same way. Thus, degree of specialization, written rules, hierarchical authority, and economic motivations are all negated by tasks that have many contingencies or are unpredictable.

Theoretical Short Cut for Applying Principles of Matching to Formal Organizations: Routinization and Medicaid Legitimation

What the organizational theorists have discovered is a theoretical "short cut" in the principle of matching. Instead of analyzing each dimension of formal organization separately (e.g., division of labor, rules, hierarchy, economic motivation, etc.), it is only necessary to determine whether the task is uniform or not, because this particular aspect of the task is related to all dimensions of group structure in the same way. Since formal organizations are at the opposite ends of the same set of dimensions as primary groups, and since each of these dimensions relates to uniformity of tasks in the same way, knowing the degree of uniformity of the tasks should permit a precise matching with the structures of these two groups, as well as between formal organizations at two different places on the continuum—that is, rationalistic and human relations.

These questions now arise: How can it be said that primary groups are the opposite on all dimensions after it has been shown that primary groups differ from one another, and why has the same simplification not been used in the analysis of primary groups? The answer to the first question is that although primary groups vary in dimensions among themselves, they are generally closer to one another in structure than to formal organizations. Thus the modified extended family is larger than the marital unit, but generally is closer to it in size than to formal organizations. Therefore, under any gross comparison between primary groups and formal organizations, all primary groups can be treated as one group. To use an analogy, if people are compared to apes, all people are alike. However, if one wants to differentiate among people, it is possible to do so by sex, size, education, and other characteristics.

The answer to the second question is that such a simplification is not possible, because a detailed examination of primary groups shows that their various dimensions do not change together. Thus the kinship system has less continual face-to-face contact, neighbors have less long-term commitment, and so forth. As a result, it is no longer possible to find one dimension of tasks, such as nonuniformity, that will correlate with all dimensions of the group. Rather, the task has to be broken up into its component dimensions, as it has been in Chapter 3.

Why would not a detailed examination show the same problem for formal organizations? The answer is that a detailed analysis would show that the same problem arises in formal organizations (Litwak, 1978b; Litwak & Meyer, 1974), but that organizational theorists, for the most part, have not dealt with the issue. For instance, an authoritarian organization might have all of the features of a monocratic organization, but might not recognize the *a priori* character of written rules. This means that the persons on top can fire people who have followed the rules by declaring the rules null and void whenever it pleases them. Religious organizations, like the Roman Catholic Church, may have detailed written rules, hierarchy, and a well-worked-out division of labor, but they may motivate their personnel far more by internalized altruistic incentives than by economic ones. Similarly, organizations characterized by charismatic leaders often have hierarchy, but lack written rules or economic incentives, stressing altruistic and internalized ones instead. If one looks at the situation when each of these forms of organization is viewed positively, then one will find it necessary to introduce separate dimensions of task structure rather than to speak about the degree of uniformity.

For the most part, these "deviant" organizational types have been swept under the conceptual rug by organizational theorists and lumped together with one of the major classifications of human relations structures or rationalistic organizations. However, if one is interested in more precise predictions, it is necessary to take these differences in dimensions of tasks and dimensions of structure more seriously, as is to be done in this chapter for nursing homes. This is not to deny the importance of the uniform and nonuniform distinction developed by organizational theorists. It is still a very quick and easy way to deal with differences between most of the services that differentiate formal organizations from primary groups. However, when it comes to nursing homes, one element that must be considered, in addition, is that of economic motivation.

As noted in Chapter 3, the 1978 survey of older persons included a number of nursing home residents. Because of the nature of nursing homes in 1978, neither the individuals receiving the services nor the individuals providing the service had the final say on which services would be economically rewarded. The fact of the matter was that treatment for close to 92% of the people in nursing homes in New York was funded by Medicaid, while this was true of 54% of those in Florida. The people who determined which activities could be funded and which could not be funded in nursing homes were legislators who were in turn responding to politically powerful individuals and organizations in the larger public. These members of the larger public often had no primary-group members in nursing homes, nor were they necessarily positively oriented toward providing the maximum number of services to residents of nursing homes. Their wishes, and therefore the economic incentives, could vary separately from the fact that the task could benefit from a division of labor, rules, or hierarchies, or that the staff could be motivated by economic incentives. Therefore, to differentiate between formal organizations and primary groups, it was necessary to make two distinctions: the degree to which a task was routinizable, and the degree to which it was legitimated by Medicaid. The routinizability of the task was a "quick and dirty" way of matching the dimensions of the task with the formal organizational dimensions of merit, division of labor, hierarchy, written rules, and impersonal instrumental economic incentive, while the use of Medicaid rules on eligibility allowed one to capture an element of economic incentive that varied independently. Therefore, if the tasks I have previously examined could be classified in terms of their routinizability and the degree to which they are legitimated by Medicaid, then one should be able to predict which one of them will be picked up by the nursing home, which will be left to primary groups, and which will be lost when an older person enters a nursing home. What the reader must keep in mind is that though I am classifying the task in terms of routinizability, that is only a shorthand way of taking into account each of the dimensions of group structure.

To make it perfectly clear that classifying tasks by their uniformity or routinizability permits one to match up all dimensions of group structure, let us illustrate in what ways nursing homes must routinize primary-group tasks in order to take advantage of their division of labor, rules, hierarchies, and economic incentives of the staff and then illustrate why economic legitimation by Medicaid must be treated separately from routinization.

First, let us examine the provision of daily meals. What do nursing home staff members have to do to take over this primary-group activity? If one considers the number of main dishes and side dishes and how they are each cooked, as well as the time of eating and who eats with whom, then it is the case that with 100 families in a community, one is very likely to have close to 100 different situations. In order to benefit from a division of labor in which one person cooks for 100 nursing home residents, the nursing home staff must reduce the number of contingencies by serving one main dish as well as one set of side dishes to all 100. Furthermore, residents must sit in the same place with the same companions at each meal, and this must be designated through a written and fixed schedule. Any conflict is decided by administration. Furthermore, the staff is discouraged from displaying primary-group affection, which may lead to favoritism as well as to rapid "burnout" occasioned by the high mortality rate among the residents.

By eliminating all the individual contingencies surrounding meals, it is possible to see how a detailed division of labor, with *a priori* written rules and hierarchical authority, can be very efficient. In a similar fashion, one nurse's aide can make 10 beds and get 10 residents dressed very quickly, if the residents are awakened at approximately the same time, if they are next to each other, if clothing can be selected and put on without much concern for the residents' personal taste, and if aspects of personal grooming such as hair styling can be simplified and standardized (e.g., by cutting hair short or by drawing it straight back and tying it with a string).

Particularly instructive is the way in which nursing homes increase predictability in going to the bathroom for those with various degrees of incontinence. They put diapers on such older persons and change these diapers on a routine basis. Thus an unpredictable event becomes routinized. The degree of routinization for any given specialist, such as a cook, is further accelerated by the need for each specialist to coordinate efforts with others. Thus the fact that the nurse's aide has to awaken the residents at 6:30 in the morning is in part a consequence of the residents' having to be washed and dressed in time to be fed by the cook, who in turn has to coordinate his or her schedule with the occupational, vocational, and recreational specialists.

The need to routinize is highlighted by what happens when nursing homes must manage tasks that cannot be routinized. Nonroutinizable tasks must be handled by the staff of the nursing home, because they have 24-hour custody. What happens in such cases is that nonroutinizable tasks are lost unless an external primary group provides the service. For instance, residents who are so ill that they can no longer manage such aspects of personal grooming as putting on makeup or brushing their teeth may simply end up with no makeup put on and with their teeth unbrushed. This is not done out of staff maliciousness. If the staff members did decide to provide such individualized services, it would mean neglecting their present standardized tasks, neglecting most residents in favor of a few, and/or working well beyond the limits of the normal work day. Since these options are generally rejected by the staff, these nonstandardized services are lost. What is extremely important for the reader to understand is that this loss is a consequence of formal organizations' having to routinize services that are normally performed by primary groups in a nonroutine way. The loss can only be prevented by changing the structure of the formal organization to be more like a primary group or by asking outside primary groups to provide such services.

Routinization in the analysis given above is related to a division of labor, written rules, and hierarchical structure. It can also be related to the fact that formal organizations such as nursing homes stress economic incentives for the staff (Spilerman & Litwak, 1982). But it must be kept in mind that such a relationship does not fully exhaust the contribution of economic incentives, since they are also related to the rules of the funding source.

To make this distinction clear, let us first look at the relationship of economic incentives to routinization. One of the basic characteristics of an instrumental motivation such as an economic incentive is that it requires an observable outcome or work procedure in order to be used effectively (D. I.

Warren, 1968; Etzioni, 1969; Merton, 1957). Nonuniform tasks, because they are defined in terms of excessive contingencies or unpredictability, are difficult to observe. As a result, economic incentives are generally not effective. For instance, nursing homes seek to guard the possessions of residents against theft. They can standardize the problem in part by asking residents to store their valuables in a central office or in a safe. They can also insure that doors are locked at night. Such standardization is generally a good safeguard for property that is not required for everyday use. However, such standardized procedures cannot guard against the theft of possessions in everyday use, such as sweaters, underwear, stockings, cigarettes, shoes, cosmetics, or hair brushes. This is the case because (1) many residents are so incapacitated that they do not notice when such items are missing; (2) there is easy and necessary access to the residents' rooms by the staff; (3) these articles can be easily concealed; and (4) staff members cannot continually watch other residents, who also have easy access to one another's rooms. In other words, there are too many contingencies to permit nursing homes to routinize the guarding of everyday possessions. If the staff's motivation was mostly economic, there would actually be an incentive to steal, since there is some economic gain and little risk. In any case, there is little economic incentive to put time and effort into preventing such thievery, since such efforts cannot be assessed, and staff members are paid whether they do it or not.

Perhaps even more dramatic is the relationship between economic incentives and routinization of medical care. Typical in this regard is the need to turn bedridden patients periodically. Older people have poor circulation; therefore, bedsores can lead to gangrene and amputation, as well as to lung infections, which in turn lead to high death rates. Not turning a patient has serious consequences. However, there is no real way to be sure that the staff has turned a bedridden resident unless there is a continual one-to-one supervision. A staff member who is motivated mainly by economic concerns would find it advantageous to do that which takes the least effort—that is, to turn a resident as little as possible and as routinely as possible.

Thus far I have discussed the relationship between economic incentives and routinization. However, as suggested above, there are also aspects of economic motivation that are not directly related to routinization. It is possible to have services that can be routinized but for which there are no economic incentives. For instance, in 1978, Medicaid gave low priority to such routinizable activities as developing storage space for seasonal clothing or providing cleaning facilities for residents' clothes, and had somewhat mixed policies in regard to doing residents' laundry. Since nursing home staff members are mostly motivated by economic incentives, the lack of such incentives generally means that the services in question will not be provided.[1] In other words, when the 1978 study was being done, the Medicaid rules were pretty good indicators of what services nursing home staff members would provide as part of their regular job.

With that in mind, it is possible to argue that nursing homes will generally perform those services that can be routinized and for which there is economic legitimation by Medicaid. The concept of "routinization" in this case stands for the correlated cluster of task dimensions, such as detailed division of labor, coordination by rules, hierarchical authority, and economic incentives that are related to observability of performance.[2] Medicaid rules stand for one dimension—in this case, economic incentive—that is not correlated, so that the task must be assessed separately on this dimension. As such, the logic of matching group dimensions and service dimensions is precisely the same as that used for primary groups. The only differences are that an entire cluster of dimensions can be dealt with under the heading of "routinization," and that the discussion is dealing with the opposite ends of the same dimensions used to describe primary groups.

The principle of matching should therefore permit an assessment of (1) which primary-group services will be taken over by the nursing home, (2) which services will be continued to be managed by primary groups, and (3) which will be lost. The ones that will be taken over will be those that can be routinized and economically legitimated by Medicaid. The ones that will continue to be managed by the kin will be those that cannot be routinized or cannot be legitimated by Medicaid and that do not require continual proximity or common life style, or at least require only the most modest time commitments. Those services that will be lost will be nonroutinized services that require continual face-to-face contact and resources.

To document these assertions empirically, I now examine people who live in institutions rather than in the community.[3]

Empirical Illustration of Tasks That Match
Nursing Home Structures:
Routinizable and Legitimated

Let us first classify the services that can be routinized and that can be legitimated for economic payment by Medicaid. As a first step in classification, it is important to know that questions designed to measure services could take on different meanings, depending on the social context of the respondents. The question in a community context could have been viewed as involving nonuniform events, while in the institutional context, it could have suggested uniform tasks. For instance, let us look at the wording for the survey item on who would provide nursing care for 2 or 3 weeks:

> Now I'd like you to think about people who might help you[4] if you got ill and had to stay in bed for 2 or 3 weeks. Who, if anyone, would be helpful feeding you your daily meals, helping you in and out of bed, bringing you water when you needed it, and the many things like that? Tell me which of these people (HAND RESPONDENT CARD A),[5] if any, would be able to do this kind of job for 2 or 3 weeks either here or at their place. (CHECK AS MANY AS APPLY.)

Respondents answering this in the context of their own homes, where paid staff members were not available, answered in terms of a primary-group member. Only 8% suggested someone other than a primary-group member. A person answering such a question in a nursing home context, however, assumed the presence of paid staff members and the routinized care of nurse's aides—that is, that the aides would come routinely to change sheets, bring water, and so forth. Such services are also reimbursable under Medicaid rules. The important point is that the question, as worded, permitted respondents in the community to interpret the exchange in a nonuniform way, while those in a nursing home interpreted it in a uniform way. Another service that can be defined as economically legitimated as well as involving a routine activity for the nurses' aides was measured by this item:

> Tell me which of these people (CARD A), if any, checked up on you daily to see if you were all right. (CHECK AS MANY AS APPLY.)

Two other items, not previously discussed because only information on helpers was available, are now introduced. The first has to do with handling small household repairs; it was measured by this item:

> Tell me which of the following things (INSERT HELPER'S NAME) has done for you in the last 6 months. . . . Helped fix things around your place, like putting up curtain rods, unjamming stuck windows, screwing fixtures into the wall, fixing broken furniture. . . .

Such maintenance roles are legitimate for payment by Medicaid. Also, because of the way the question was asked, it could be interpreted by the respondent as a routinizable activity provided by the maintenance staff of the nursing home.

Respondents were also asked:

> Tell me which of the following things (INSERT HELPER'S NAME) has done for you in the last 6 months. . . . Helped in light housekeeping tasks like making the bed or straightening up rooms. . . .

Again, these are mandated services under Medicaid rules and can be viewed as the regular routinized tasks of nurse's aides for respondents in a nursing home context.

Empirical Illustration of Tasks That Must Be Managed by
Kin of Nursing Home Residents: Nonroutinizable

Let us now examine services that are nonroutinizable events in both the nursing home context and the community context. Respondents were asked:

> If you wanted someone to join you in your favorite free-time activities, tell me which of these people (CARD A), if any, would join you. (CHECK AS MANY AS APPLY.)

Though some leisure activities of the nursing home residents were routinized, this question specifically addressed the nonroutinized part, the free time of the residents. Staff members of nursing homes typically do not have sufficient similarities to residents in terms of their age, their physical state, their status of being staff members rather than residents, or their matching periods of "free time" to fit the more idiosyncratic aspects of the residents' free-time needs. Therefore the task was classified as not routinizable. The group that had precisely the same time schedule and style of life was that of other residents. However, most residents in nursing homes, because of great physical and psychological disabilities, can only provide services to each other that require the most minimal efforts. Therefore, it is very important to note another dimension of this item, the amount of commitment. The wording of the question indicated nothing about the time and effort involved; it was rather left up to the residents to define these aspects in terms of their own capacities. In the nursing home context, this could mean that the service supplied required very little of other residents, such as sitting together to watch television.

Yet another service that cannot be routinized by the staff was measured by the following question:

> Who, if anyone, helped with money matters like keeping track of bills, medical payments, Social Security, bank accounts, and things like that?

In our society, because money is a generalized means to most goals, it is easy for helpers to use older persons' money for their own goals. They have enormous incentives to do so if their major work motivation is economic and if the theft of money cannot be easily observed. To the extent that household expenses (such as payment of rent) are standardized, they can be observed— that is, easily supervised. However, to the extent that household expenditures reflect idiosyncratic and unpredictable desires for certain soaps, magazines, small snacks, or small articles of clothing, it is almost impossible to keep track of these expenditures for a large population, such as residents in a home for the aged. Putting staff members in charge of handling them would mean that they could not be easily supervised.[6]

There are two other services that can also be classified as not standardizable and not legitimated for Medicaid payment. Respondents were asked if their chief helpers had helped them in the last 6 months with the following:

a. Helped you enjoy your meals by bringing you special food treats, or having you to dinner, or taking you out to dinner, or cooking for you.
b. Gave you things for your place which made it more homey, like pillows, bedspread, pictures, plants, radio, or TV.

These items explicitly referred to aspects of tasks that are not routinizable in the nursing home context. Nursing homes provide standardized daily meals. What they explicitly do not provide is special food treats, bedspreads, or room furniture to meet the idiosyncratic taste of individuals.

Further Empirical Illustration of Tasks
That Must Be Managed by Kin of Nursing Home Residents:
Not Legitimated by Medicaid but Routinizable

With the classification above in mind, one can now clearly isolate services
that are capable of being standardized but that would not be reimbursed by
Medicaid. Typical in this regard is the service measured by the following
question:

> Tell me which of these people (CARD A), if any, have done these things for you
> in the last 6 months (CHECK AS MANY AS APPLY.). . . . Stored things for
> you (like seasonal clothes or valuables), or took care of laundry or cleaning. . . .

As already noted, with the possible exception of laundry, these are activities
for which nursing home staffs will generally not be reimbursed by Medicaid,
even though they could easily be routinized. As a result, they are generally
not provided by staff, with the possible exception of laundry.

Another service that falls into this category is one measured by the
following item:

> Tell me which of these people (CARD A), if any, have done these things for you
> in the last 6 months (CHECK AS MANY AS APPLY.). . . . Talked to you
> when you were feeling upset or low and made you feel better. . . .

Providing some kind of emotional support can possibly be thought of as a
routinizable service; there are professionals, such as social workers, who
could deliver this service, and Medicaid does legitimate the hiring of such
professionals. However, it does not legitimate their delivering this kind of
support, the reason being that the ratio of residents to staff members is so
high and the number of demands on the social worker is so high that such a
person is lucky if he or she can spend 10 minutes a week with each resident
for any kind of direct contact. It is for this reason that the provision of
emotional support is classified as a task for which Medicaid does not
legitimate payment.

Services That Are Lost Because No Matches Can Be Made with
Kin of Residents or Staff of Bureaucracy:
Nonroutinizable Tasks Requiring Long-Term Commitment
and Continual Proximity

There are two services measured in the 1978 survey that are nonstandardizable
and also require close continual proximity and more commitment than
nursing home residents can give. As such, the theory would suggest that
these are lost functions, as discussed above. The respondents were asked:

> Suppose you had to go out of your room for an hour or two and while you were out someone tried to steal something from it. Tell me which of these people (CARD A), if any, would be likely to report it or tell anyone about it. (CHECK AS MANY AS APPLY.)

In this wording, the question was most likely to be focused on everyday possessions and therefore on nonstandardizable events. The reader may ask why fellow residents or roommates could not be relied on (just like neighbors in the community who would perform this service for community respondents). The comparison with neighbors is not apt. Roommates and even other residents have much more ready access to nursing home residents' rooms than neighbors do to people's homes, but far less physical capacity to observe and often less altruistic motivation. People often become roommates in nursing homes because of the availability of a bed, not because of friendship.

The physical frailties of residents often lead to a loss of services. This point is illustrated in yet another service, which was measured in the survey by the following item:

> Suppose you were in a situation where you had to borrow something small in a big hurry, like you were taking a bath or shower and needed bath powder or cologne. Tell me from which of these people (CARD A), if any, would you be able to borrow such a thing in a hurry. (CHECK AS MANY AS APPLY.)[7]

For such a service, what must be taken into account is that staff members do not live at the nursing home, so they are unlikely to have such articles around. For residents to replace such items often requires a major effort if they are physically or mentally frail. Therefore, neither fellow residents nor staff members might be a good source for borrowing such items because they do not have them readily available; even if the fellow residents do have them, they might be reluctant to loan them, since it takes some effort on their part to replace these items.

Systematic Empirical Evidence from the 1978 Survey

With these classifications of services in place, this question can now be raised: To what extent does the principle of matching task dimensions with group dimensions permit one to explain (1) which services are taken over by nursing home staff, (2) which services are retained by primary groups, and (3) which services are lost in a nursing home context? Table 4-1 has been set up to show for each service what percentage of the residents in the institutions used staff help, what percentage used the chief primary groups,[8] what the differences were between the percentage using primary groups in the community and those using them in nursing homes, and what percentage in the institutions received no services at all. There is complete information on

Table 4-1. Percentages of Institutionalized Respondents Choosing Staff (Paid Help) or Chief Primary Group,[a] According to Degree to Which Task Can Be Routinized

| | Percentage of Respondents Choosing Each Group | | | | |
Services Delivered by the Staff or Primary-Group Members	Staff or Paid Help	Chief Primary Group	Community minus Institutional Primary Group	No One Provided Services	Institutional Population (n)
Highly routinized and economically legitimated					
Provide housekeeping care for bedridden for 2 or 3 weeks	83	11	−33	4	(381)
Check daily to see if older persons are all right	54	27	−24	16	(393)
Do light housekeeping	——[b]	6	−14	——	(393)
Do home repairs	——	8	−22	——	(396)
Nonroutinizable but no matching primary group					
Spot break-in when older people out on daily chores	40	32	−42	31	(381)
Provide emergency loans of small household items	30	33	−36	25	(396)
Nonroutinizable but matching primary group					
Store seasonal clothes or valuables, do laundry or cleaning	25	41	+19	——[c]	(395)
Help keep relatives in touch	——	53	+6	——	(393)
Talk to respondents when feeling low and cheer them up	24	74	+2	14	(399)
Provide special food treats	——	49	−3	——	(393)
Serve as companion for favorite free-time activities	10	55	+13	18	(387)
Give small household gifts	——	45	+1	——	(393)
Keep track of household bills, Social Security check, bank accounts	10	43	+19	——[c]	(399)

[a]Since people could choose as many groups as they wanted, the chief primary group was the one chosen by the highest percentage of the population. This percentage is, of course, lower than the percentage of respondents who chose all primary groups. For five items, the chief primary group consisted of children or relatives. For three items—that is, for spotting break-ins, providing emergency loans of small household items, and serving as a companion in favorite free-time activities—the chief primary group consisted of fellow residents. Because multiple groups could be chosen, the row totals can add up to more than 100%.

[b]Tasks with blanks only had information on helpers; there was no information on staff or on other primary groups, and no statement that no service was delivered.

[c]For these two items, respondents' saying "no one" probably meant that they handled the problem themselves, not that the activity was not provided. See Chapter 3 for detailed explanation.

eight services; for the other five services, only the differences between those who used primary groups in the community and primary groups in the institutions are available.

The first thing to note is that as one goes from tasks classified as routinizable and economically legitimated to tasks classified as not routinizable and/or not economically legitimated, one finds a decline in the percentage of respondents using staff members, as would be anticipated by the principle of matching. Thus, of respondents answering items measuring the most routinizable tasks, 83% said they would use staff for care when bedridden and 54% used them for daily checking. For those services that have been classified as nonroutinizable but for which there was no available primary group (such as reporting thefts), between 30% and 40% of the respondents used staff, while for those services rated as nonroutinizable and/or not economically legitimated, from 10% to 25% used staff. The reader should keep in mind that the respondents could have chosen both staff and primary groups or said that "no one" helped, so that the use of staff and the use of primary groups must be examined separately. It is the case that the percentage of those using primary-group members as their helpers declined from tasks that are routinizable and legitimated to those that are not. Thus, for routinized tasks, the percentage using primary groups ranged from 11% to 27%. For those tasks for which there was no suitable group, the range was 32–33%, while for nonroutinizable or not economically legitimated services, the range was from 41% to 74%.[9]

What must be especially noted is the idea that older people in a nursing home might experience increased services from kin rather than a decline in services. The popular stereotype is to assume that once older people enter nursing homes, they are abandoned by their relatives. Table 4-1 shows why this stereotype might arise, since it is a fact that nursing homes take over many activities of families. However, the explanation for this take over should not center on abandonment, because in many areas, the kin services actually increased.[10] This point can be seen in the column of Table 4-1 that shows the differences in the percentages using primary groups in institutions and in the community.[11] Residents in nursing homes suffered a drop in routinizable services, which ranged from 14% for light housekeeping services to 33% for home care when bedridden. For the services that had no suitable primary group in the nursing home context, those living in institutions also had a loss in the use of primary groups as contrasted to respondents in the community, with the differences in percentages ranging from 36% to 42%. By contrast, if one looks at services that have been labeled nonroutinizable but for which there was a matching primary group, respondents living in nursing homes have either equal or greater services from primary groups than those living in the community. The percentage increase, with one exception, ranged from 1% for bringing small gifts to make their place more homey to 19% for storing seasonal clothes or doing laundry or cleaning.

The question now arises as to what extent the data suggest that lost services are characterized by tasks requiring continual proximity and at least a moderate commitment. Empirically, the percentage of respondents who said that "no one" provided a given service supplies a measure of this (see Table 4-1). For this purpose, two items must be ignored—that is, doing the laundry and cleaning, and keeping track of bills, Social Security checks, and bank accounts. For these items, it is not possible to distinguish between respondents who did it themselves and those who had no service. If the other items are examined, it can be seen that two very different types of services were least likely to suffer from loss of function. First, respondents were least likely to say that "no one" helped for services classified as routinizable and legitimated by Medicaid. The percentage saying that "no one" would help with housekeeping when they were bedridden was 4%, and that "no one" checked daily was 16%. The second group of services for which respondents were least likely to say that "no one" helped were those services classified as nonroutinizable and/or not legitimated by Medicaid, but for which there was a matching primary group. In this group of services, 14% said that no one helped to cheer them up when they were low, while 18% said they had no companion for free-time activities.

It was among the services classified as nonroutinizable, and for which there was no matching primary group, that the highest percentage of respondents said that "no one" helped. That is, 31% said that no one helped watch their rooms, and 25% said that there was no one from whom to borrow small items in an emergency. These findings are in the right direction, but it is also clear that among the services studied, there was really no case of extreme loss of function.[12] However, the overall pattern represented in Table 4-1 is very clear.

The understanding that formal organizations such as nursing homes can only handle routinized tasks has now completed a crucial phase of the present analysis. Now I am in a position to state the general principle guiding changes in primary-group networks as the older persons move from health to disability and to institutionalization. This is precisely what is done in the next chapter.

But before proceeding with that analysis, I explore some further points on the nature of organizational structure.

The Organizational Dilemma of Nursing Homes,
Possible Variations in Administrative Styles,
and the Populations for Which They Are Suited

The analysis above suggests a basic dilemma of nursing homes: They are asked to take over primary-group services for which they are structurally incompatible. This means that, in order to take over the services, the formal organization must (1) routinize them, which generally means they will be viewed as humiliating; (2) be responsible for nonuniform services, which will be ignored or which give staff members an opportunity for exploitation because they cannot be easily supervised; or (3) alter their structure to become more like a primary group—that is, become a "human relations" organization. However, human relations organizations are labor-intensive and must have staff members who operate on an internalized altruistic incentive. Running an institution on such a basis would require a considerable increase in cost. Given the limits of social resources, the dilemma of nursing homes can be clearly stated: Should they move in the direction of primary-group structures and provide nonhumiliating services to a few, or should they move in the direction of the more rationalistic formal organizations and provide basic, life-sustaining, but humiliating services to many?

The principle of matching group structures and tasks, when carried over to organizational theory, suggests a range of administrative alternatives that can be used to moderate the dilemma. These alternatives have been explored elsewhere (Litwak & Spilerman, 1982; Spilerman & Litwak, 1982; Dobrof & Litwak, 1977) and so are only sketched out here. One solution to the dilemma is to separate tasks that differ in their uniformity and to have different groups whose structures match the different tasks provide the services. This is what has been more or less suggested in the present analysis of nursing homes and community primary groups.[13] As surveyed in 1978, nursing home staff managed the routinizable services (such as daily meals), and community groups managed the nonroutinizable ones (such as special food treats).

However, it is not always possible to divide standardized and nonstandardized services clearly enough so that they can be assigned to different groups. The staff of the nursing home must often manage both types of tasks. Where that is the case, it is sometimes possible to divide the services according to staff and place. Where this can be done, one can assign the uniform tasks to one group of staff members (e.g., providing daily meals), while other groups can get the less uniform tasks (e.g., providing recreational services). In such cases, these groups of specialists can be governed by different administrative styles; those handling the uniform tasks can have a rationalistic structure (Weber, 1947), while those handling the less uniform tasks can have a structure that more closely resembles the "human relations" style (W. F. Whyte, 1956). Modern organizational theorists suggest that it is possible to have an organization with subunits governed by different administrative structures (Litwak, 1961b; Perrow, 1967; Thompson, 1967).

But yet another situation must be considered—that is, where different staff members cannot handle different services, but the same persons must manage both the routinizable tasks and the nonroutinizable ones. For instance, the nurse's aides are responsible for getting the residents dressed and out to breakfast on a routinized basis. At the same time, they must also deal with the respondents' idiosyncratic feelings, which may cause them to resist dressing or going to breakfast. To manage such feelings, the nurse's aides have to learn to tailor their reassurances to each respondent's temperament. This calls for internal role segregation on the part of the aides. Where the routinized and nonroutinized tasks cannot be separated by roles, the only way to moderate the dilemma is by emphasizing the goal that is weakest. That can only be done by altering the whole administrative style. Thus, one can increase the number of nurse's aides so they have more time to develop individual rapport with each resident (in a human relations style of administration), or one can decrease the number of aides so they have less time for individual treatment of patients (the rationalistic bureaucracy). It depends on which value is more under attack—humane services, or basic life-sustaining services to many.

It should also be clear that any formal organization that serves people by taking over primary-group activities will suffer from the same dilemma as nursing homes. Thus, agencies that deliver meals or housekeeping services share with the nursing homes the fact that they are seeking to handle activities that customarily are handled by primary groups. In the case of organizations delivering meals, the problems are very much like those of the nursing homes. They have to provide standardized meals and routinized delivery times for a large population, and cannot possibly match the clients' idiosyncratic food tastes, arrive at the idiosyncratic times at which clients want to eat, or provide table companions with whom they would like to eat.

The delivery of housekeeping services stresses another problem of formal organizations in handling nonuniform primary-group tasks. It is the problem of motivating paid people to handle tasks that cannot be easily supervised because of many contingencies or uncertainties. Housekeeping involves many contingencies, and if older persons are disabled, senile, or depressed, they are not in a position to provide close supervision. It is then virtually impossible to determine whether the housekeeper is doing an adequate job or not.[14] Under such circumstances, a helper motivated basically by money is likely to work as little as possible and to do things that will increase his or her economic well-being, such as steal things from the older person. As a result, programs providing homemaker services suffer from complaints of abuse of older people by the homemakers.

In short, contemporary organizational theory, which uses a principle of matching group structures with tasks, suggests a variety of solutions to the dilemma of formal organizations' providing primary-group services. Different solutions are necessary for different problems.

Summary and Conclusion

This chapter has sought to point out how the principles of matching group structures can be applied to formal organizations and to the classification of tasks as uniform and nonuniform. The nursing homes are theoretically interesting, because they are formal organizations that seek to substitute for disabled primary groups. The principle of matching tells us that the only ways in which formal organizations can manage nonuniform (that is, primary-group) services are by reducing contingencies and making them into uniform services; permitting primary groups to retain management of some of the services; ignoring many services; altering their formal structure to become more like a primary group; or any combination of these solutions. Some empirical data have been used to show that the principle of matching group structures to tasks allows one to anticipate which service will follow each of these paths in a nursing home context.

One of the more spectacular predictions generated from this formulation is that families are likely to increase some services to the aged in nursing homes. This is a far cry from the popular stereotype that institutionalization means abandonment. This prediction is consistent with what others have found in nursing homes (Gottesman, 1972; Dobrof, 1976). Another derivation from this theory is that some of the major humiliations to residents in nursing homes derive from the fact that a nursing home is a formal institution seeking to take over primary-group tasks. Such humiliations will occur even with the best-trained staff members, since the problem is in the inherent mismatch between the structure of nursing homes and the primary-group services they seek to take over. This is not to argue that one should seek a primary-group alternative to nursing homes, since for the most part those solutions are even worse for people needing 24-hour care. What the principle of matching suggests is a series of administrative solutions that will lessen the humiliation (Litwak & Spilerman, 1982; Spilerman & Litwak, 1982).

The central point of this chapter is that one can utilize the principle of matching to show which tasks the formal organizations can take over from the primary group and which it cannot. With this analysis in place, the stage is now set for a complete theoretical statement of how older people use their network of supporting groups as they move from states of health to states of illness to institutionalization. It is to this task that the next chapter is directed.

Notes

1. Staff members will clearly do many small things without extra pay, but these cannot be major aspects of services, since the bulk of their time is taken up with services for which they are paid. Volunteers can provide some services, but in terms of principles of matching, I argue here that they generally can only provide services that do not require individual continuity. This is explored in the discussion of friendships in Chapter 9.

2. Here the labels of organizational theorists are being used. The concepts of the primary-group theorists could have equally well have been used (e.g., diffused ties, face-to-face contact, etc.).

3. These institutions were selected at random from a list of licensed nursing homes and congregate living facilities supplied to us by New York State and Florida. Over 80% of the

homes approached agreed to permit the interview. However, the residents in the nursing homes were not selected at random, but consisted of residents who were judged by staff members as well enough to talk and who volunteered. In many nursing homes, those well enough to talk were a small minority. The primary-group ties of the incapacitated group have not really been studied and require a separate effort. In addition, in this chapter and what follows, I am using the term "nursing home," despite the fact that there were some non-health-related facilities in the 1978 study. I have used the term "nursing home" because I feel that what I have to say applies basically to nursing homes. In the following chapters, I more clearly isolate those institutionalized aged who were very ill, and it will be seen that the findings on these persons are more distinctive.

4. For those in nursing homes who were bedridden, the wording was changed to "who does help you."

5. For a respondent in a nursing home, Card A in the question included the chief helper, residents, close friends, children, relatives (other than children), husband or wife, nurse's aides, someone else (the respondent indicated who), or no one. The same list was used for all eight questions that gave the respondent a choice of possible helpers. For those in the community the same list was used, except that "neighbors" was substituted for "residents," and "nurse's aides" was dropped as a category.

6. In addition, Medicaid rules expressly forbid staff to interfere with a small fund that is meant to provide the residents with the equivalent of household money. This Medicaid provision reflects very strong social norms; these norms are further reflected by laws in some states that forbid staff to control bank accounts of residents who are not under Medicaid funding.

7. This was the wording for female respondents. Male respondents were asked, "Suppose you were shaving and needed to borrow shaving cream."

8. For all services except three, the chief helpers were children or other relatives. For emergency borrowing of small items and for watching one's room, the chief helpers were neighbors or fellow residents. For free-time companions, they were friends or fellow residents.

9. Although the data go in the direction anticipated, there is considerable variation. The question arises as to why this variation should exist. There are several possible explanations. First, the difference between routinized and nonroutinized tasks is not a dichotomy, but indeed a continuum, since classification depends on such factors as the number of contingencies and the degree of predictability, which are also continuums. The second possibility is that these were badly worded questions. The third possibility has to do with variation in socialization, which leads some staff to violate the norms of merit and rules of standardization and to treat some residents as though they were members of their own primary group. Differential socialization might also be a consequence of membership in different ethnic, racial, and class groups. In the chapters that follow, these issues are explored more thoroughly.

10. In this research, no pretense is made that the crucial areas of community primary-group participation have been fully examined. In that regard, a more systematic statement has been made elsewhere (Dobrof, 1976; Dobrof & Litwak, 1977). It must be recalled that the respondents in the 1978 study were limited to nursing home residents who could talk and were well enough to be interviewed. In many homes, this constituted a small minority. Yet it is very likely that for residents who are mentally incompetent or so ill they cannot be interviewed, their community primary groups may have to deliver very different services. For instance, they would have to be far more concerned with guarding against staff abuse or neglect.

11. Such comparisons must be given as only tentative assessments. For a real test of the proposition, the same people would have to be studied before and after they entered the institutions. The process of selective recruitment as to who comes to nursing homes could operate so that people with kin who provide services are most likely to come. This is a highly unlikely hypothesis, but it could be very valid for severely ill people.

12. To get at such a clear empirical case, the survey questions would have had to be worded more precisely. For instance, with regard to watching one's room, the mention of specified

articles (e.g., cosmetics, underwear, and cigarettes) might have produced a higher percentage of those saying that no one could guard such items. In addition, if one or more items had touched on personal grooming (e.g., applying makeup), I would argue that there would be a higher percentage saying "no one."

13. Key issues regarding the optimal forms of linkage by which formal organizations and primary groups best coordinate are developed in Dobrof (1976), Dobrof and Litwak (1977), Litwak *et al.* (1977), and Litwak and Meyer (1966).

14. If housecleaning agencies send in a team of workers to clean a house, it might be sufficiently routinized housecleaning to permit adequate supervision. In this case, however, it is likely to suffer from the complaints of routinization—the workers come at the wrong time and do not clean to suit the clients' idiosyncratic tastes.

5

Dynamics of Network Change
from Community to Institutionalization

Up to this point, an attempt has been made to show which groups can best handle which tasks at a given point in time. The theoretical concepts are now in place for the discussion of a more dynamic problem: which primary group best provides which services with each change in the health status of the older person.[1] In this chapter, it is shown that by using the principles of matching dimensions of groups with those of tasks, it is possible to solve this problem for older people.

The Basic Sequences of Primary Groups and Nursing Homes in Managing Marital Household Tasks

To begin this analysis, the reader should be again reminded of the unique structural features of modern primary groups. To deal with the problems of differential mobility and rapidity of change required by modern formal organizations, the kinship system (i.e., parents, adult children, siblings, etc.) had to give up continual proximity and common life style in order to retain its intrinsic quality—that is, long-term commitments. The neighborhood, under the same organizational pressure, had to give up long-term commitment and common life style in order to stress its unique character—that is, continual proximity. The friendship group, in order to maintain its basic feature (i.e., common life style), had to give up long-term commitments and, to some extent, continual proximity. Facing the same problem, the marital unit had to shrink its household to a very small size (i.e., two adults), while retaining all of the other features of the traditional primary group—that is, long-term commitment, continual proximity, and common life style.

   In Chapter 3, it has been shown that tasks can be classified by the same dimensions as groups, and that groups can optimally manage those tasks that match them in structure. What has been stressed up to now is the difficulty that one type of group has in substituting for another, since they have unique structures and so each is best equipped to manage unique tasks.

However, the empirical fact is that when older people get ill and spouses die, other primary groups often must provide substitute services, imperfect though the provision may be. The principle of matching can be used to indicate which of these primary-group alternatives can optimally substitute for the collapsed marital unit.

To see how this principle can be used, it is necessary to clarify one prior statement about the classification of tasks. There are basically three ways in which a task can be classified. The task can stress one pole of a given dimension (e.g., continual proximity), or it can stress the opposite pole (ad hoc proximity), or it can be indifferent to proximity (e.g., it can be managed by people who live close by or far away). It is the characteristic of indifference that now becomes central. For instance, providing emotional support to an individual who has suffered an unpleasant experience with a Social Security official can be provided by a spouse who lives close by in a face-to-face contact, or it can be supplied by a child who lives at some distance by telephone.

The central idea is that the marital household, which is characterized as having a very small-sized structure, long-term commitments, continual proximity, and common life style, can manage tasks that have these precise dimensions, *or tasks that have some of them but are indifferent to others.*[2] With this qualification in mind, it means that a marital household does not manage just one type of task (characterized by small size, long-term commitment, continual proximity, and common life style), but several different types, depending on which of these four dimensions is not required for the task.

Kin as a Matching Primary Group

For instance, a spouse can manage tasks that require small group size and long-term commitment but do not require continual proximity or a common life style. Typical marital household tasks that match this combination of dimensions would be filling out health insurance forms for the family, taking care of weekly or monthly household bills, providing small household repairs, or taking clothes to the cleaners. What characterizes all of these tasks is that they do not require that a person share the same household or live next door, because they are weekly or monthly tasks and can be managed by phone, mail, or ad hoc visits. A helper can live close by or at a moderate distance and still manage such tasks. They can also be managed by people of different or the same life style, but they all require long-term commitments, because they either involve the future well-being of the respondent or require sufficient effort so that no one will provide them on an unpaid basis unless there is long-term reciprocity.

In general, these tasks are typically managed by one spouse for the other, because they benefit from the speed and flexibility of very small numbers. But when the marital unit is no longer viable, the principles of matching suggest that the kinship system is the optimal substitute, even though it is not the equal of the marital unit. The neighborhood unit stresses short-term commitment and continual proximity, while the friendship unit stresses common life style and is indifferent to length of commitment.

Neighborhood as a Matching Primary Group

Another combination of task dimensions that the marital household best manages would be one that stresses small size and continual proximity, but not necessarily long-term commitment or common life style. Typical tasks that spouses provide for each other that fit this combination would be provision of emergency first aid for household accidents, calling the doctor or ambulance for illness, calling the fire department for a house fire, and accepting packages for a spouse who is not home. What characterizes all of these tasks is that the individual must live very near by, usually within voice or visual distance. They are tasks that have an ad hoc character about them and require little effort, and so do not demand long-term commitment. Finally, they can be managed by people with either different or the same life styles. However, such tasks do benefit from the combination of small size and very immediate proximity that only the marital household can provide. If the marital household is dissolved through death and illness, the neighborhood primary group is the one that comes closest to matching the dimensions of this task. It is the only one that stresses continual proximity. The kinship system stresses ad hoc proximity, while the friendship system at best is indifferent to proximity.

Friendship as a Matching Primary Group

Yet another combination of dimensions that the marital unit might generally manage is one that puts stress on small size and common life style, but not necessarily on continual contact and long-term commitment. For instance, a spouse can serve as a social escort to parties, movies, or church affairs, as well as a confidant on problems of everyday living in retirement. These are all tasks that benefit a great deal from a common life style and the small size of the unit. However, these tasks are relatively indifferent to proximity. If necessary, they can be managed by people who do not share the same house but live a moderate distance away. These tasks do not necessarily require long-term commitment, either. Where the marital unit dissolves because of death of a spouse, the friendship unit has the structure that most closely matches these services.

Classification Scheme for Marital Household Tasks

At this point, it should be clear to the reader in what sense it can be argued that the marital unit can manage a variety of tasks, even under the principles of matching task dimensions with those of group structure. Furthermore, the reader can understand why it is that when the marital unit breaks up, the principles of matching can tell one which group can optimally take over given tasks. A reasonable question that might occur to the thoughtful reader is this: Is there some way to classify all combinations of task dimensions systematically, so that researchers and policy makers can have an overall framework for locating all activities the marital unit can manage, either now or in the future? All that is required for such a framework is to put the various dimensions together in all possible logical sequences.

A first, and somewhat simplified, scheme is presented to the reader in Table 5-1. Three dimensions consistent with the marital unit are considered. Each is a dichotomy, with one pole saying that the dimension is required while the other pole indicates that it is not relevant. Thus each task will require continual proximity or be indifferent to proximity, require long-term commitment or be indifferent to length of commitment, or require common life style or be indifferent to life style. What are left out of this scheme are all tasks requiring the opposite dimensions.[3] To insure that all combinations of these variables are unique to the marital unit, the condition is set that all tasks must benefit from small size.[4] If these conditions are accepted, there are eight logical combinations of dimensions, as indicated in the first four columns of Table 5-1. Thus row 1 of Table 5-1 represents a task that requires small size and long-term commitment but is indifferent to life style and proximity (e.g., filling out health insurance forms for reimbursement). As already indicated, this pattern most closely matches the kin structure once the marital unit dissolves.

Row 2 in Table 5-1 highlights services that require small size, a common life style, and long-term commitment, but no continual proximity (e.g., serving as a partner in a long-running bridge group). As indicated above, this matches the pattern of a long-term friendship once the spouse has died.

Row 3 in Table 5-1 suggests a logical combination of dimensions that includes small size and continual proximity but is indifferent to long-term commitment and common life style (e.g., calling an ambulance for a household accident). As pointed out above, when the marital unit dissolves, the neighborhood structure most closely matches the dimensions of this task.

What this systematic presentation suggests is that one can separate services requiring long- and short-term friends (e.g., companion for an ad hoc game of cards vs. a member of a long-term card game), as well as those requiring neighbors with the same or different life styles (e.g., a buddy system for neighbors to check on each other daily to see if they are all right

Table 5-1. The Underlying Dimensions of Tasks Normally Managed Only by Spouses and the Primary Groups That Most Closely Match Them, at Two Stages of Health

	Dimensions of Household Services Normally Provided Only by Spouses[a]				Helping Primary Groups at Two Stages of Health	
Row	Tasks Require Small Size?	Tasks Require Same Life Style?	Tasks Require Continual Proximity?	Tasks Require Long-Term Commitment?	Marital Household Healthy and Intact	Primary Group Most Closely Matching Dead or Disabled Spouse's Function
1	Yes	No	No	Yes	Marital dyad	Kin[b]
2	Yes	Yes	No	Yes	Marital dyad	Long-term friend[c]
3	Yes	No	Yes	No	Marital dyad	Neighbors; age difference possible[d]
4	Yes	Yes	Yes	No	Marital dyad	Neighbors; age similarity necessary[e]
5	Yes	Yes	No	No	Marital dyad	Short-term friends[f]
6	Yes	Yes	Yes	Yes	Marital dyad	Lost function or atypical joint household with friends or siblings[g]
7	Yes	No	Yes	Yes	Marital dyad	Lost function or atypical joint household with children[g]
8	Yes	No	No	No	Marital dyad	Tasks that may be managed by all groups but emphasized by none

[a] All tasks that spouses provide for each other must require small size, a common life style, continual proximity, and long-term commitment, or they must be indifferent to these dimensions. However, they cannot require the opposite—that is, large size, different life styles, ad hoc proximity, and short-term commitment. As a result, all tasks provided in the marital household can consist of any combination of these four dimensions, with the understanding that when it is said that the task does not have a given dimension, it means that the task is indifferent to the dimension, not that it requires the opposite of that dimension.

[b] Row 1 represents tasks that are normally provided by one spouse for another, but in fact emphasize only two of the four dimensions that typically characterize marital households—that is, small size and long-term commitment. These services can be provided where the helper and recipient do not share the same generation or live in the same household, even though they would benefit from both. Typical tasks that fit this particular combination are household maintenance (e.g., putting up curtain rods) and managing weekly or monthly bills. The primary group external to the marital unit that most closely matches these task dimensions is the kin group composed of adult children. For the detailed rationale, see text.

[c] Row 2 represents tasks that spouses normally perform for each other that stress three of the four dimensions of the marital household—that is, small size, common life style or age, and long-term commitment, but not continual proximity (i.e., living in the same household). One service that typifies this category of tasks would be the provision of a steady companion for various social events (parties, shows, vacations, etc.). It is argued that the primary group external to the marital dyad that most closely matches these dimensions is that of friends.

vs. calling an ambulance for a household accident). It also suggests a pattern, row 8, in which all helping groups would provide an equally good match— that is, the case in which small size is required, but the service is indifferent to all other dimensions. Since none of the helping primary groups stresses any given dimension, it would be hypothesized that a service characterized in this way would not be especially favored and is likely to be lost.

More explicitly, this systematic presentation suggests at least two patterns where there are not typical helping primary groups. Rows 6 and 7 suggest a combination where both continual proximity and long-term commitment are required. The only typical primary group that has such a pattern is the marital household. Any other group having such a pattern is atypical in a modern society. Thus, where children or other relatives live with the individual, then it would be atypical but would meet the condition of continual proximity and long-term commitment. The same would be true of long-term friends who decided to live together. Row 6, which stresses common life style, is more likely to consist of a common household of friends or siblings, while row 7 is likely to consist of individuals who live with adult children. Since these are atypical groups, the likelihood is that for

---

[d]Row 3 represents tasks that stress two dimensions of the four that typically characterize marital households—that is, small size and continual proximity—but do not emphasize people having the same life style (i.e., same age) or long-term commitments. For instance, if one spouse falls down in the house or immediately outside it and breaks a leg, the other spouse will call for an ambulance. It is argued that, where a spouse is not available, a neighbor matches these dimensions most closely.

[e]Row 4 is like row 3, but, in addition, represents tasks that stress the need for age similarity or life style similarities. This in turn means that only neighbors who have the same life style or age can manage these tasks. For instance, in some buildings for the aged, "buddy" programs have been developed by neighbors, where each day one person is to check to see if the other is up and walking. Such activities are normally provided by spouses. But it is only aged neighbors with missing spouses who see it as a necessity.

[f]Row 5 represents tasks that stress small size and common generation, but not continual proximity or long-term commitment. For instance, if an individual had an unexpected free moment and wanted to fill it with some leisure-time activity, that person and his or her spouse might have an ad hoc game of cards, or discuss a movie they had seen, or watch a television program together. When one no longer has a spouse, such ad hoc and spontaneous leisure activities, with no future commitments, might be filled by more casual acquaintances, such as people one meets at a senior citizen center. I refer to these more casual friendships as "short-term" friends.

[g]Rows 6 and 7 stress both long-term commitments, continual proximity, and small size. In modern industrial society, only the marital household unit stresses both continual proximity (i.e., the same household) and long-term commitment. Tasks that generally require these three dimensions are daily food preparation, personal grooming, and daily housecleaning. When one spouse dies, there are generally no external primary groups, such as the kin, neighbors, or friends, that combine both continual proximity and long-term commitment. There are atypical groups, such as older parents who live with their children or friends. In such cases, children (row 7) and friends (row 6) can provide help in personal grooming, daily food preparation, and housecleaning. Otherwise, these services will be lost.

many people the service represented by this pattern is likely to be lost. Typical services that spouses provide for each other that require both continual proximity and sufficient physical effort for long-term commitment are preparing daily meals, personal grooming (e.g., dressing, brushing teeth, combing hair), and daily housekeeping activities (e.g., garbage disposal).

Though this classification is simplified, in that it does not include all the dimensions of the group or all the combinations of these dimensions, it is adequate for indicating how the theories of matching can be used to understand the dynamics of network change (which groups will pick up the tasks of the marital household unit) when it dissolves. With all of its limitations and complexities, the reader must recognize the enormous simplifications provided by the conceptual scheme represented in Table 5-1. Whereas prior researchers and policy makers were faced with a bewildering and undefined universe of marital household tasks, they now have in principle a comparatively simple way of classifying all existing and future services of the marital unit. This is not to say that the problem of actually classifying tasks will be easy; it must be acknowledged that there are still many complexities to consider. However, now researchers have a specific framework around which to focus their efforts, rather than a vague undefined classification called "marital household tasks" that is continually subject to change and relates to helping primary groups in unknown ways.

Changes at Each Stage of Health

There is yet one further step that must be taken if one is to use the principle of matching dimensions of groups with tasks to formulate a theory of network change for older persons. To make this analysis complete, one has to include a last stage in which people are so ill they can no longer manage to live in the community and must be institutionalized. In Chapter 4, it is pointed out that the principles of matching group structures to tasks can be applied to formal organizations such as nursing homes as well. If a task is routinizable and legitimated by Medicaid for reimbursement, it very likely matches the structure of the nursing home.

With this last piece of information in mind, it is now possible to utilize the principles of matching to say which group will pick up which task at each stage of health. For tasks that originate in the marital household unit, there are basically three patterns, as indicated in Table 5-2, rows 1, 2 and 5. One pattern consists of services that are initially managed by the marital household when spouses are healthy. They are taken over by another primary group when the marital unit is incapacitated, and finally they are managed by the staff of the institution when the individual becomes so ill that he or she must be institutionalized. This pattern has been labeled "partial primary-group expansions" and is displayed in row 2 of Table 5-2. This partial

Table 5-2. Overall Patterns of Primary-Group Help as Older Persons Move from Health to Institutionalization

| | Stages of Health | | | |
Row	First Stage: Married with Minor Ailments	Second Stage: Single with Major Ailments	Third Stage: Institutionalized, Single, Major Ailments	Name of Sequence
1	Task handled by individual or spouse	Task handled by helping primary group (e.g., kin, friends, neighbors)	Task continues to be handled by helping primary group and not by institution	Complete primary-group expansion
2	Task handled by individual or spouse	Task handled by helping primary group (e.g., kin, friends, neighbors)	Task handled by institution	Partial primary-group expansion
3	Task handled by helping primary group (e.g., kin, friends, neighbors)	Task continues to be handled by helping primary group	Task continues to be handled by helping primary group	Primary-group continuation
4	Task handled by helping primary group (e.g., kin, friends, neighbors)	Task continues to be handled by helping primary group	Task handled by institution	Primary-group decline
5	Task handled by individual or spouse	Task not handled by helping primary group or institutions	Task not handled by institution or helping primary group	Lost function or atypical primary group

Note. These are not all the possible patterns, but the ones that are hypothesized to be most prevalent. There is one possible major omission—that is, older people in the second stage who have no help, but who move into the third stage and receive institutional help.

primary-group expansion can refer to either a kinship, friendship, or neighborhood group, depending on which combination of dimensions characterizes the task (see Table 5-1).

Two services investigated in the 1978 study have the characteristics of this pattern of change: (1) providing light housekeeping services (e.g., dusting rooms), and (2) providing small household repairs (e.g., putting up curtain rods). The theory of matching suggests when the marital unit is intact, the combination of small size and long-term commitment that characterizes these two tasks makes that group the ideal match. However, when the marital unit dissolves, the kinship unit, with its stress on long-term commitment, is the best alternative match. Where a person becomes so ill that he or she must be institutionalized, then these two tasks can be routinized and are legitimated for Medicaid payment, so the staff of the nursing home provides the ideal match.

To highlight the theoretical issues, this and other patterns of change are empirically illustrated with three selected groups from the 1978 survey population: (1) respondents who were married and healthy; (2) respondents who were seriously disabled and single, but still in the community; and (3) respondents who were institutionalized as well as seriously disabled.[5] With this in mind, the "partial primary-group expansion" pattern is represented in a curvilinear relationship between kinship aid and the stages of disability. That is, only 14% and 19% of the respondents had kinship aid for light housekeeping and home repairs, respectively, when they were healthy and married; these respective figures went up to 34% and 46% when they were ill and living in the community, and down to 7% and 10% when they were ill and single and living in institutions.[6] To make this clear, the percentages of kinship aid for the two items have been averaged and are presented in Figure 5-1.

A second pattern of change suggested by the principle of matching is called "complete primary-group expansion" (Table 5-2, row 1). It involves services that are optimally managed by a healthy marital unit and that, once it fails, are taken over by another primary group. However, these services cannot be routinized or legitimated by Medicaid, and therefore the helping primary group must and can provide these services even when the individual is institutionalized. Again, the primary group can be either kin, neighbors, or friends. In the 1978 study, there were two tasks with dimensions that fit this pattern: keeping track of household bills and bank accounts, and storing seasonal clothes or sending clothes to the cleaners. These differ from home repairs and light housekeeping tasks in that they are not legitimated by Medicaid and so cannot be handled by institutions. Also, as noted earlier, everyday personal expenditures cannot be standardized. Since these tasks require only small size and long-term commitments, the kin group most closely matches them, once the marital unit fails.

If Figure 5-1 is examined again, it can be seen that the "complete primary-group expansion" pattern for kin has a shape that is distinctively different from the "partial primary-group expansion" pattern. The "complete" pattern has a monotonic relation to health, while the "partial" pattern has a curvilinear one. For the individual items, 7% of the respondents without disability had kin help in money matters, and 13% had help in storage, cleaning, and laundry. These figures rose to 46% and 35%, respectively, for those who were sick and single in the community. It continued to rise to 54% and 44%, respectively, for those who lived in institutions.[7]

A third pattern of change that can logically occur (Table 5-2, row 5) is one where the service is managed by the marital household unit in the first stage, but there are no typical helping primary groups that match the service, so it is lost in the second stage; or it cannot be standardized, so it is lost in the third stage; or both things happen, so it is lost in both stages. If it is lost in the second stage but not the third, it is called a "partial primary-group loss." If it is lost in the last stage but not the second, it is called a "partial

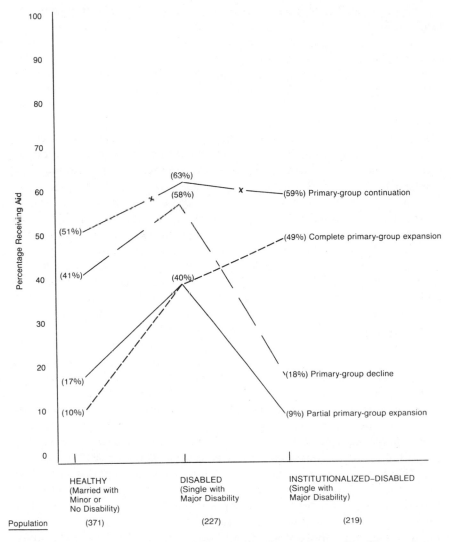

Fig. 5-1. Patterns of kinship aid with changes in states of health. *Primary-group continuation* included either inviting respondents to dinner or bringing food to them, providing small household gifts such as radios, helping respondents keep in touch with relatives, and cheering up respondents by talking with them. *Complete primary-group expansion* included helping respondents keep track of household bills, and doing laundry, cleaning clothes, or storing seasonal clothes or valuables. *Primary-group decline* included checking daily to see if respondents were all right and providing home care for those temporarily bedridden. *Partial primary-group expansion* included providing small household repairs and doing light housekeeping (e.g., making beds and dusting). The percentages in this figure are the average of the specific items in each pattern.

institutional loss." If it is lost in both stages, it is called a "completely lost function."

The pattern of "partial primary-group loss" is illustrated by such marital household services as daily preparation of food and daily housekeeping tasks (e.g., removing garbage). As already indicated, these services are generally lost once the marital unit fails, because no other typical primary group has both long-term commitment and continual proximity, which are both required to manage such tasks. Since these activities are legitimated by Medicaid and can be standardized, they are also picked up again when the older person is institutionalized. Prior to institutionalization, the lost function is manifested by respondents' suffering from poor nutrition and having filthy residences.

In the 1978 study, the light housekeeping services came closest to illustrating the "partial primary-group loss," even though these have been classified above as representing the "partial primary-group expansion." The reason for this is that the item used to measure light housekeeping referred to services that were weekly as well as daily. In the analysis given above, the weekly services have been stressed, but to illustrate the lost function, the daily character of these services is now emphasized. To highlight this difference, light housekeeping is compared with the service of providing "small household repairs," which has also been classified as "partial primary-group expansion" but which is unambiguously a less frequent event (i.e., a monthly or less frequent occurrence). Therefore, household repairs can be managed at a greater distance than can daily housekeeping. Both services require long-term commitment, in that they are both continual over time and demand much physical effort. To highlight the lost function, the 1978 population is split in Figure 5-2 into those who had typical households (i.e., lived more than five blocks from their helpers) and those who had atypical households (i.e., lived in the same residence as or next door to their helpers).

What can be seen in Figure 5-2 is that for those older persons who lived more than five blocks away, only 8% of the population received household help from their kin at the first stage of health. This figure went to 14% in the second stage and to 6% in the third stage. It is graphically represented as a relatively flat line. By contrast, small household repairs show a distinctive curvilinear pattern: 13% of the respondents had help from kin at the first stage, 30% at the second stage, and 11% at the third stage. If a marital household function is lost to the primary group at the second stage and picked up by institutions at the third stage, then the percentage of kin who helped should be extremely low at each stage, or a straight line.[8] It has been argued that only those living in atypical households, such as with adult children, can receive such services. As can be seen in Figure 5-2, where respondents lived in the same household as their helpers, there were virtually no differences in the percentage of respondents using kin for light housekeeping and household repairs; both percentages were very high.

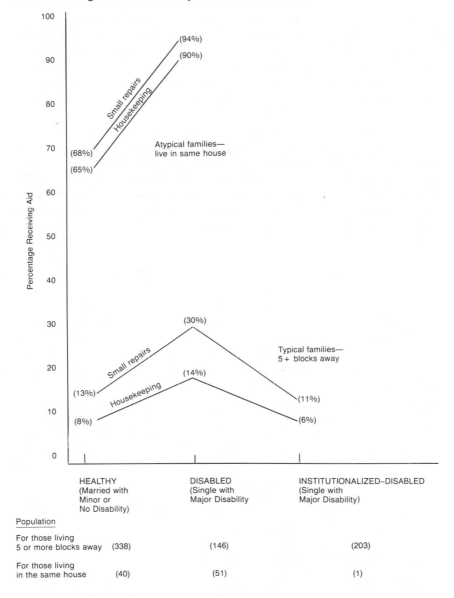

Fig. 5-2. Partial kinship exchanges by distance from helper.

In this study, there was no service that illustrated the completely lost function. However, the theoretical formulation indicates what they should look like, and qualitative observations have suggested several. Theoretically, these services require close continual proximity and long-term commitment, and cannot be standardized or are not mandated by Medicaid in a nursing home context. Putting on makeup for a woman, combing a respondent's hair, and brushing his or her teeth would be illustrative of such services. If the individual can no longer manage these activities, they will be lost unless the helper lives in the same household or very near by. Furthermore, they require very individualized attention, so they are generally not provided by the staff in nursing homes. The only concession interviewers saw in the 1978 study to hair grooming for women was to cut it short and leave it uncombed or to pull it straight back and tie it with a string. Generally, teeth were not brushed, and cosmetics were not applied.[9]

The Basic Sequences of Primary Groups and Nursing Homes in Managing "Normal" Helping Services

What I have examined so far is the use of larger primary-group support systems that substitute for the marital household unit when it is disabled. Now I should like to consider services that are normally provided by primary groups other than the marital household even when the marital dyad is complete and well. What happens to these tasks when the marital household unit becomes permanently disabled? Generally, where the task is handled in conjunction with the marital unit (e.g., help in home care when a spouse is bedridden for 2 or 3 weeks), then the larger primary-group network will have to increase its services a little to compensate for the loss of the spouse. Where the service is provided independently of the marital unit (e.g., loaning small household items in an emergency), then the larger support system may continue without being affected by the marital unit's disability. It is also possible, but rarer, for the helping primary group to discontinue all services once the marital unit dissolves.[10]

The same set of dimensions, with one exception, can be used to characterize services normally provided to the marital unit by other primary groups (see Table 5-3). The one exception is that all services require a large-sized group.[11] What differentiates these patterns empirically from those in Table 5-1 is that in each case the healthy intact marital unit starts out with a high percentage of help from other primary groups. If the services are not routinizable or not legitimated by Medicaid, the primary group will have to continue them (Table 5-2, row 3) or they will be lost (Table 5-2, row 5). If they can be routinized, the nursing home staff will take them over (Table 5-2, row 4). The continuation of nonroutinizable services has been labeled "pri-

Table 5-3. Dimensions of Tasks Normally Managed by Spouse in Cooperation with Other Primary Groups or Solely by Other Groups, and the Primary Groups That Most Closely Match Them at Two Stages of Health

Row	Dimensions of Services Normally Provided by Spouse and Other Primary Groups				Helping Primary Groups at Two Stages of Health	
	Large Size Required?	Same Life Style (Age) Required?	Continual Proximity Required?	Long-Term Commitment Required?	Marital Household Healthy and Intact	Marital Household Broken by Death or Disability
1	Yes	No	No	Yes	Kin	Kin[a]
2	Yes	Yes	No	Yes	Long-term friends	Long-term friends[b]
3	Yes	No	Yes	No	Neighbors, age-heterogeneous	Neighbors, age-heterogeneous[c]
4	Yes	Yes	Yes	No	Neighbors, age-homogeneous	Neighbors, age-homogeneous
5	Yes	Yes	No	No	Short-term friends	Short-term friends[d]
6	Yes	Yes	Yes	Yes	Atypical joint household (friends)	Atypical joint household (friends)
7	Yes	No	Yes	Yes	Atypical joint household (children)	Atypical joint household (children)
8	Yes	No	No	No	Can be managed by all but not emphasized by any	Can be managed by all but not emphasized by any

[a] Sample task: Provision of emotional support when spouse is seriously ill.
[b] Sample task: Companionship for "free-time" activities.
[c] Sample task: Emergency loan of small household items, such as salt or sugar.
[d] Sample task: "Pick-up" game of cards.

mary-group continuation," and the continuation of routinizable services has been labeled "primary-group decline."

To provide empirical documentation for this framework, two services from the 1978 survey that fit the kinship version of the "primary-group decline" sequence (Table 5-2, row 4) are examined here. Respondents were asked whether anyone had checked on them daily to see if they were all right during the previous 6 months; they were also asked to state who would help them if they were sick in bed for 2 or 3 weeks (by bringing food, helping them in and out of bed, etc.). What characterizes both of these helping patterns is that they often require a primary group larger than the marital household unit even when the marital unit is intact and basically well. Both are activities that can be managed through ad hoc contact (i.e., by a visit for a few weeks in the case of invalid assistance, or by a telephone call in the case of checking) rather than requiring close continual proximity (e.g., a common household). Both require sufficient expenditures of time and energy that only a person with long-term commitments would undertake these activities on an unpaid basis. In short, both have in common dimensions that fit the structural demands of the kinship system (Table 5-3, row 1). In addition, once a person is institutionalized, both of these activities (as measured by the survey questions) are economically reimbursable and routinizable.

The 1978 data show that among married couples in the first stage of health (i.e., good health), 35% said that they would use kin for home nursing, and 47% said that kin had checked on them daily over the last 6 months. In the second stage of disability, these figures rose to 53% and 63%. But in the third stage, where the institutions took over, these figures dropped to 11% and 25%. These patterns follow the decline pattern, with the exception that in the second stage, there is some increase before the decline takes place. It is hypothesized that this exception occurs because at the first stage the spouse helps kin, and therefore when the spouse dies, the kin must increase aid. This point is elaborated below. However, what should be emphasized at this time is that the pattern is very different in one major respect from the "partial primary-group expansion," which also has a curvilinear shape. Where they should differ (as indicated in Figure 5-1) is at the first stage of health. That is, people at the first stage of partial kin expansion had 17% receiving services, while in the first stage of kin decline 41% received services. In both cases, the third stage led to a low percentage saying that kin did or would help.[12]

Let us now turn our attention to the sequence of network supports that has been called "primary-group continuation"; that is, the individual uses the primary group (here, kinship) in all three stages of disability (Table 5-2, row 3, and Table 5-3, row 1). This resembles "primary-group decline" in all respects but one—that is, the institutions do not see the tasks as central or routinizable. In the 1978 survey, four tasks fit this pattern. Respondents were asked whether in the last 6 months anyone had talked to them when they were feeling low and made them feel better. They were also asked whether in the last 6 months anyone had helped them keep in touch with their relatives, had taken them out for dinner or brought them special food, or had bought them small items to make their place more homey (e.g., pillows, bedspreads, or a television set). Because of the way in which the questions were worded, two of these items clearly represent nonroutine tasks that institutions cannot manage—that is, providing residents with their own special food preferences and room furnishings. The other two services— talking to people when they are feeling low and helping people keep in touch with relatives—are low-priority services for staff members, given the limited resources of nursing homes.

These four seemingly diverse helping patterns share in common the fact that most of them can be carried out over the telephone or by ad hoc contact, do not require a common household, and take enough time and energy to require long-term commitment by an unpaid primary-group member. The 1978 data show that this pattern of "primary-group continuation" starts like the pattern of "primary-group decline," with physically robust marital households having a high percentage of their populations using these kin services: The range went from 42% providing household gifts to 72% using kin to talk to when they were feeling low. In the second stage of disability, where the respondents were single and ill, the figures ranged from 51% using kin for household gifts to 84% who used them to talk to when they were feeling low. In the third stage, the range sank slightly, starting at 46% for household gifts and going to 75% for talking to kin. However, there were more people in the third stage using kin than in the first stage. Therefore, these figures do indeed illustrate the pattern of "primary-group continuation."[13] The average of these services for this pattern is also presented in Figure 5-1.

The theory as set forth in Table 5-3 indicates that other supporting primary groups have different structures and therefore supply different services, but the same principles of matching structures that have been illustrated here for kinship hold. Two items from the 1978 survey characterize neighbors' services. The first question asked who, if anyone, might spot a burglary attempt in the respondents' homes while they were out and report it to the police. The second question asked from whom the respondents could borrow a small household item (e.g., a Band-Aid, shampoo, salt) in an emergency. These seemingly diverse tasks can be classified as having the following theoretical dimensions in common: (1) They require close, continual proximity; (2) they require a larger group than the one- or two-person household; (3) they can be handled by persons of either the same or different generations; and (4) they do not require long-term commitments (Table 5-3, row 3). What further characterizes these activities, as indicated in Chapter 4, is that they are only partially accepted by institutions for the aged as central and routinizable, but neither are they manageable by the primary group, so a substantial percentage of individuals lose these services in the third stage.

Given these dimensions, one could expect a neighborhood version of the sequence I have called "primary-group decline" (Table 5-2, row 4). It resembles the kinship version of primary-group decline (see Figure 5-1) in two respects. In the first stage (i.e., the robust marital household), there is a heavy use of a supporting large primary group (i.e., neighbors), and in the last stage there is a very substantial decline in the use of the supporting primary group. The 1978 data show that at the first stage (i.e., robust marital household units), 81% said that neighbors would spot and report a break-in, and 75% said that neighbors would loan small household items in an emergency. These figures dropped to 68% and 61% for the respective tasks when the members of the household units were disabled, and then there was a substantial drop to 31% and 32%, respectively, when older persons were institutionalized.[14]

To illustrate the dynamics of network exchanges further, data on acquaintances or short-term friends are also considered here. Unlike the services provided by neighbors, services provided by short-term friends require matching life styles. In this context, a consideration of primary groups established within institutions among residents is cogent. Though nursing home residents have the basic neighborhood features of proximity and short-term commitment, they also have a shared life style that is more typical of friends or spouses (e.g., same food, same recreational program, same staff to relate to, same generation, similar major disabilities, etc.). If they are friends, it is likely that they are short-term friends with very limited resources, or possibly that they resemble what Granovetter (1973) has called persons with "weak ties." If this description of fellow residents is acceptable to the reader, it provides the basis for discussing the friendship version of "primary-group continuation." To measure exchanges among friends, we asked all our respondents the following question:

> If you wanted someone to join you in your favorite free-time activity, tell me which of these people (CARD A), if any, would join you. (CARD A read as follows: Neighbors, close friends, children, relatives, husband/wife/companion, someone else [WHO?], no one.) (For those in nursing homes, the category of "aide" was added, and "residents" was substituted for "neighbors.")

This question may be classified theoretically as requiring a common generation, given the retired status of most of the population, but being indifferent to length of commitment[15] (Table 5-3, row 2 or 5).

It has been argued in Chapter 4 that the staff in nursing homes cannot provide such free-time companionship. As a result, this behavior falls under the pattern called "primary-group continuation" in Table 5-2, row 3. The assumption is that in the robust healthy stage, a significant percentage of individuals will choose friends for free-time companions, and that they will continue to do so even when institutionalized. The 1978 data show that 41% of those respondents who were married and healthy chose friends. This figure went down slightly to 35% in the second stage of disabled household units, but went up to 62% choosing residents in the institutional stage. If this friendship version of the "primary-group continuation" sequence is compared with the kinship version, it can be seen that they have in common two features. In the first stage (i.e., the robust household), a substantial part of the population chose a member of a group other than their household units. In the third stage, a very substantial number still chose such a person.

Though there are similarities between these patterns, there are also differences.

The Same Sequences with Assumptions of Continuous
Rather than Dichotomous Dimensions of Tasks

The fact that the empirical data from the 1978 survey are related to the theoretical expectations in general, while having some unanticipated bulges and squiggles in particular, suggests that some complexities are not being considered in the deliberately simplified theoretical statement that has been presented here. Some of the simplifying assumptions are now dropped in order to explain these "deviant cases." One simplifying assumption has been that tasks require groups of small size (Table 5-1) or large size (Table 5-3). Tasks that are indifferent to size (i.e., that can be managed by either large or small groups) have been ignored. What cannot be entertained in such a simplified scheme are tasks that can be simultaneously managed by the marital household and a helping primary group. However, some of the kinship services have precisely this character. For instance, providing home nursing care to an individual who is bedridden for 2 or 3 weeks is likely to be managed by the spouse in conjunction with a relative who has specifically come to help out. By contrast, there are other services that require large size (i.e., where only the helping primary group can provide the service) and the spouse cannot help out. For instance, a respondent who wants to borrow a small household item (e.g., sugar or a Band-Aid) in an emergency is unlikely to get it from a spouse, since the spouses share the same household. They generally can only get such emergency help from neighbors.

Introducing this complexity permits one to explain the differences in shape between the kinship and the neighborhood versions of the "primary-group decline" pattern. It will be recalled that the kinship version shows an increase in the percentage of helpers called upon during the second stage of illness and then a decrease, while the neighborhood version shows a modest and then a sharp decrease. This is the case because in the first stage of health, both spouse and kin provide kinship services; therefore the kin must increase their services in the second stage, when the spouse has died, to compensate for the loss of the spouse. However, for the neighborhood services, kin do not participate in the first stage, so the neighbors do not have to increase their services when the spouse has died to maintain the same level of services.[16] These speculations can in part be empirically verified. For two of the kin services and two of the neighborhood ones, respondents were asked which groups did provide the services, allowing the respondent to choose as many as they wanted. Let us examine, for these four items, how many of the respondents chose their spouses at the first stage.

For the kinship items, 58% said that their spouses had checked on them daily in the last 6 months, and 77% said that their spouses would help if they were homebound for 2 to 3 weeks. By sharp contrast, for the neighborhood items, 22% said that their spouses would be able to watch their homes when they were out on daily chores, and 9% said that their spouses would loan them small household items. In other words, it is the two items on kin that are most likely to be affected by a loss of the spouse and therefore to require increased kin support in the second stage. The same rationale explains the increased use of kin during the second stage in the kinship version of "primary-group continuation." The 1978 data provide a measure of the use of spouse for only one of the four items in this pattern (i.e., whom the respondents had talked to when feeling low who made them feel better). In the first stage of aging, 63% used their spouses. The loss of the spouse in the second stage should be significant and should call for an increase, not just a continuation, of kin aid, if the same level of help is to be delivered.

Can the same reasoning be applied to the third stage, where there are again substantial variations in the predictions of decline? There may indeed be services that are indifferent to routinization. In this case, the variations may arise because of variations in staff help. The reader will recall from Chapter 4 that there are measures of staff members' providing services for some of these items.

First, let us contrast the items where primary groups declined in the third stage with items where they remained active in the third stage.[17] According to the theory, the first set of items should show more use of staff or paid help in the third stage than the second set of items. For eight of these items, there were measures of staff help.

It is the case that in the third stage of health, staff members were more likely to handle services that were classified as primary-group decline or partial primary-group expansion. There were four items, and on these items, from 30% to 83% of the respondents received help from staff. By contrast, exchanges classified as primary-group continuation or complete primary-group expansion were in fact handled by paid staff less (i.e., from 8% to 24%). Though these findings go in the right direction, it is also clear that they do not constitute a dichotomy, but a continuum.

If that is the case, then it perhaps explains the dip that occurs in the third stage for those items that are included in the kinship version of primary-group continuation. There is one item (i.e., someone to talk to when feeling low) from the kinship version of the continuation pattern for which there are measures of who helped. It can be seen that 24% of the institutional population said that they used staff or paid help as people they talked to when feeling low. The view that this item measures a noninstitutional task is correct, in that this 24% is much lower than the 71% who used kin. Nevertheless, for some significant part of the population (24%), there was a use of staff. I believe that this is in part the reason that there was a dip in the use of kin in the third stage (i.e., from 79% in the second stage to 71% in the third).[18] It is also important to note that other items that measured the kinship version of continuation exhibited no decline in help in the third stage; these were managing money and serving as a free-time companion. In those cases, the use of paid staff in the third stage was the lowest (10% and 8%, respectively).[19]

What is central is that some of the major discrepancies in the original "predictions" can be understood, once the simplifying assumptions are dropped and classifications that permit continuous dimensions[20] and the possibility of two or more primary groups helping simultaneously are used. In this book, the simpler scheme has been emphasized, since it works well enough for most purposes; as an introductory statement, it is sufficiently complex in its own right to make it difficult for the uninitiated to follow.

There is one more "deviant" case that should be commented upon because of its theoretical importance. It is always true that kin managing tasks that are normal to them (as in the kinship versions of primary-group continuation and decline) constitute a higher percentage of those who provide services than do those kin who substitute in tasks normally managed by the marital dyad (as in the kinship versions of partial and complete primary-group expansion). In Figure 5-1 it can be seen, at the second state of health, that the kinship versions of partial and complete primary-group expansion had smaller percentages than the kinship versions of decline and continuation, while at the third stage, complete primary-group expansion had a smaller percentage than continuation. Furthermore, a smaller percentage of respondents reported the partial primary-group expansion pattern for kin than the primary-group decline pattern in the second and third stages of health. These differences are not true deviant cases from the predictions based on principles of matching group structures with task dimensions. These principles state that the kinship group is the best substitute but not the best primary group for managing these marital household services. The marital dyad is the optimal structure. However, the kinship group is the best group for managing normal kin exchanges, and that is why there were higher percentages managing the kin exchanges than the marital exchanges in the patterns mentioned above.

The Effects of Economic and Cultural Factors on Dynamics of Network Change

I have thus far proceeded with the analysis as though all individuals have equal economic resources and more or less the same cultural values as, and equal access (i.e., proximity) to, their helpers. If these factors are considered, they add to the complexity of the analysis, but do not basically alter the major sequences of primary-group aid that accompany each stage of health and disability. As before, instead of trying to elaborate the full implications of such factors as family income, ethnic–racial differences, and distance from helpers, I view them narrowly to show that they do not basically alter the relations between stages of health and services, even though they do very much affect the delivery of services.

In order to highlight this point, the stages of health in the 1978 survey are examined, with income, ethnicity, and the distance at which helpers lived from respondents held constant. This is a way of asking how the relationship between stages of health and the provision of services would look if the respondents all had the same mixture of ethnic–racial statuses, the same mixture of incomes, and the same mixture of distances from their helpers. The question can be answered by the use of regression equations, which can be found in the bottom rows for each service in Appendix C, Table C-2. From these equations, it is possible to compute what the percentages of those receiving help would be like if individuals at each health stage had the same income, the same racial–ethnic composition, and the same range of distances from their helpers. These standardized percentages are located in Figure 5-3; it will be noted that they form the same patterns as the percentages in Figure 5-1. The average difference between the standardized and non-standardized percentages is 4.6%, with only two differences being higher than 7%—that is, 8% and 10%.

To point out that services are related to stages of health when these three variables are controlled for does not mean that ethnicity, income, and distance do not play very important roles in the delivery of services. From a statistical point of view, including these variables permits one to account, on the average, for four times the amount of variance as would be accounted for by the use of stages of health alone. In the following chapters, I explore how each of these elements affects the helping networks. But central throughout this explanation is the principle that matching the structure of groups with the dimensions of services permits one to anticipate which services each group provides as older persons move through the stages of health.

Summary and Conclusion

At this point, the major themes of this book come together. In Chapter 3, the point is made that primary groups vary in structure. It is also argued there that all exchanges between group members can be classified by the same dimensions as primary groups themselves. This in turn leads to the principle that primary groups can best handle those tasks that match them in structure. In Chapter 4, the further point is advanced that the dimensions of the primary group constitute one end of a continuum and that the dimensions of formal organizations constitute the other end. From this analysis, it is argued that matching organizational structure with task structure means

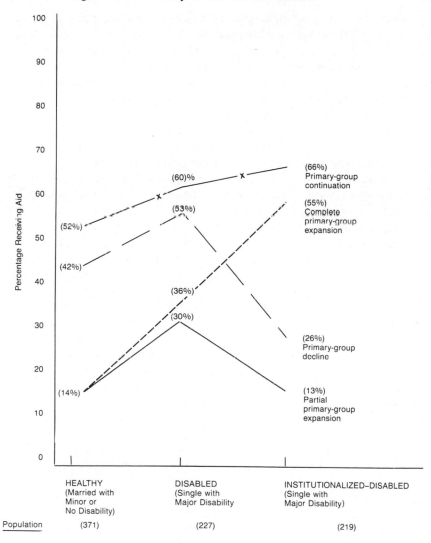

Fig. 5-3. Patterns of kinship aid with changes in states of health; percentages standardized for income, ethnicity, and distance respondents lived from helpers. For tasks representative of each pattern of aid, see Figure 5-1.

that formal organizations can best handle tasks that can be routinized. In this chapter, the effort has been made to employ all of these points and principles to deal with change produced by disability. The question of dynamics of change has then been "boiled down" to two specific questions: First, what are the range of activities carried on within the marital household units? Second, which of these activities come closest to the structure of other primary groups or nursing homes?

The answer to the first question can be found by looking at all possible combinations of four key primary-group dimensions that characterize the typical marital household unit (i.e., continual proximity, long-term commitment, common life style, and small size of the group).[21] To understand which group will typically take over those activities when the marital household unit breaks down, it is only necessary to see which groups come closest to matching each of the possible combinations. A conceptual table providing the theoretical solution has been presented to the reader (see Table 5-1).

What has emerged from this analysis is a theoretical statement on the dynamics of primary-group help over the life cycle of older people that is empirically testable and that provides both researchers and policy makers with relatively few variables for handling an otherwise impossibly complex problem. Instead of having to look at an infinite set of services in combination with a large set of groups, which may be affected by disabilities in many unknown ways, one has a small number of dimensions to characterize both tasks and groups, with a principle of matching that indicates which group can substitute for which others for which tasks. Through the principle of matching, there is a systematic way of indicating the effects of disability on the processes described above.

To say that the theoretical problem has been simplified does not argue either that it is simple, that the empirical task of classifying services is easy, or that all of the theoretical issues have been clearly solved. Quite the contrary: This formulation raises some formidable questions. The major difference from the past state of affairs is that the present construct offers a coherent scheme on the differential role of primary groups that can be verified, altered, or rejected,[22] as contrasted with the currently stated ambiguity (R. Kahn & Antonucci, 1980).

Notes

1. The discussion of this chapter focuses on change. However, it must be kept in mind that the data are based on a cross-sectional survey. As such, they can only be viewed as consistent with the theory of change, rather than as definitive tests (Palmore, 1981). The empirical material presented should be viewed more narrowly as showing that groups with different degrees of disability receive different forms of help, which is interesting in its own right.

However, the dynamics of change provide a more comprehensive way of looking at these issues, and as such are well worth developing where longitudinal data are not available.

Presenting the problem in this way has the virtue of motivating researchers and policy people to collect longitudinal material. It also has the virtue of suggesting interesting research and policy problems, as long as the respective groups are aware that without both time-series and cross-sectional data, some serious misinterpretations are possible (Palmore, 1981).

2. This leads to a very important qualification of the prior formulation that different types of primary groups cannot substitute for one another. The proposition should state that primary groups cannot substitute for one another, except where the tasks have structures that overlap two or more groups. For instance, a task that is indifferent to the dimensions of size, proximity, and common life style but requires long-term commitment would overlap both the marital dyad and the kinship system, and so could be managed by either or both simultaneously. To illustrate, a mother seeking some financial aid to take care of the future of a retarded child may seek support from a spouse or a parent, both of whom may have long-term commitment. Since negotiations for such help can take place through telephone or mail as well as through personal contact, it is a task that is indifferent to distance; since providing such help can be managed by people who share the same or different life styles, it is also indifferent to life style. Finally, since it can be managed by either a small or a large group, it is indifferent to size.

3. All tasks that require ad hoc contact, short-term commitment, large size, or different life styles are ruled out of this classification because they are inconsistent with the marital dyad.

4. If size is treated as a dichotomous variable like the others, then the scheme would include some tasks that could be managed by either the marital household or some other group, as indicated in footnote 2. For simplicity's sake, this combination is not considered now, but is discussed later. Its inclusion would make for a more complex statement, but would not alter the fundamental assertion.

5. Groups omitted are those married individuals with serious disabilities and those single individuals with minor disabilities. Also omitted are those who were institutionalized but with minor disabilities (e.g., living in congregate living facilities rather than nursing homes). The figures for the complete population are in Appendix C, Table C-1. The inclusion of these groups does not alter our findings; it only makes the pattern harder to visualize.

6. For later comparative purposes and statistical tests, I have put these figures in the form of a regression equation, with disability treated as a dummy variable. I am using unstandardized regression coefficients. The constant stands for the percentage of healthy married couples who have kin help; b_1 is the percentage difference between the healthy married couples and the single seriously disabled people living in the community; and b_2 is the difference between the institutionalized seriously disabled and the healthy married couples living in the community. All asterisked coefficients are significant at .05 or beyond. The partial primary-group expansion is captured by a regression equation that has a low constant, a large positive b_1, and a small positive or negative b_2. I am more interested in the pattern of constants and coefficients than in the R^2. The regressions for this and following services are in Appendix C, Table C-2. It can be seen in Table C-2 in the top row for each service that the predicted pattern is there. It would have been perfect if the b_2 for kin repairs ($-.08$) had not been significant. However, it is significantly lower than the constant, while the b_1 is significantly higher, so that the predicted curvilinear relation is significant.

7. If this kinship version of the primary-group expansion pattern is put into a regression form, one would expect the constant to be low and b_1 and b_2 to be both high and positive. Table C-2 in Appendix C shows b_1 and b_2 to be statistically different and positive. It contrasts with the kinship version of primary-group decline, where b_2 is negative.

8. It is also possible that meals-on-wheels programs or homemaking services may be used in the second stage to provide services. In this sample, very few respondents used these services.

9. Partially lost institutional functions—that is, those lost only in the third phase of health—tend to be activities that are managed by friends or neighbors in the community. The reason for this is that friends and neighbors external to the nursing homes generally do not have the commitment or physical resources to help individuals once they are institutionalized. The major exceptions to this assertion are services that require virtually no personal resources or

services for people who reside in non-health-related institutions. Fellow residents of such institutions do play a very significant role. In our study, two services, reporting attempted break-ins and borrowing small household items—both neighborhood services—had elements of this pattern. This point has been developed in Chapter 4.

10. This pattern is not developed here. However, in the qualitative part of the 1978 study, it was noted that neighbors' services were often contingent on the respondents' kin being present. Where kin were not present, the respondents often sought to use neighbors for kin services, and the neighbors, having no long-term commitment, found these demands excessive and stayed away. It was also the case that loss of neighborhood services occurred because the respondents were too ill to maintain the ties or to establish new ones when old neighbors left and others came in.

11. Those services that are indifferent to size are discussed below.

12. The distinctiveness of the primary-group decline model can be seen if we examine the regression coefficient for this model. What is expected is a much higher constant, a negligible b_1, and a large negative b_2. Table C-2 in Appendix C, which compares the regressions, indicates this pattern of differences. What is important is to note that the b_1 is still smaller than those from the prior two patterns, as anticipated, and that all other comparisons among the three patterns are as anticipated.

13. The regression equation for primary-group continuation should show a high constant and small b_1 and b_2. Table C-2 in Appendix C indicates that this is indeed the pattern; thus the constants range in size from .41 to .73, making them like those for primary-group decline (.48 and .35), which they should resemble, and higher than those for the partial and complete primary-group expansion, which range from .08 to .20. It has a b_1 that should be small (i.e., range from +.07 to +.19) and similar to that for primary-group decline (i.e., +.16 and +.18), but smaller than that for complete primary-group expansion (+.23 and +.39) and partial primary-group expansion (.20 and .29). Its b_2 (i.e., .06 to .17) should be as small as that for partial primary-group expansion (.08) but smaller than that for complete primary-group expansion (+.32 to +.49) and larger than that for primary-group decline (−.23 and −.25). As Table C-2 suggests, the inequalities follow the predicted direction, but there are some substantial differences within each inequality, suggesting that other factors seem to be playing a role as well. I discuss these below.

14. In terms of the pattern of inequalities of the regression coefficients, the neighborhood version of primary-group decline follows the same pattern as the kinship version. (See Table C-2 in Appendix C.) There is one difference, in that the neighborhood version exhibits decline at each stage of health, while the kinship version exhibits decline only at the last stage. This is discussed below.

15. The question did not say anything about whether these are short- or long-term commitments. It gave the respondents discretion to take account of their physical frailties as well as their living conditions. Thus, those who had only short-term companions (i.e., lived in institutions for the aged) may have viewed the exchange as short-term.

16. The reason for the moderate decline is explained in footnote 10.

17. These would involve the kinship versions of partial primary-group expansion and primary-group decline and the neighborhood version of decline, as contrasted with the kinship versions of complete expansion and continuation and the friendship version of continuation.

18. It should be noted in the second stage only 1% used any form of paid help or non-primary-group members, so that such help played no significant role outside of the third stage.

19. The only real exception to this analysis involves the functions of storing clothes or laundry. Here there was no decline in kinship aid, even when staff aid was as high as that for emotional support.

20. There are three reasons for a continuum. First, the dimensions of group structure are not dichotomous. This is apparent for dimensions such as "continual face-to-face contact," where one can differentiate among hourly, daily, weekly, monthly, and yearly contact. The other two reasons for a continuum have to do with measurement error. First, socialization is

never perfect; people do not always conform to roles. Therefore, for example, there are always some staff and residents who develop primary-group ties. The second type of error has to do with item ambiguity (Dono *et al.*, 1979). Thus the question that asked "Who has checked on you daily?" without specifying whether the check was visual or by telephone would receive an answer of "neighbor" or "kin," depending on which meaning respondents gave to the question. Measurement errors of these two types often account for two or more groups' overlapping in exchanges.

21. For purposes of this analysis, all primary groups are assumed to have internalized noninstrumental motivations of affection or duty.

22. At present, there are several alternative schemes for classifying tasks and structure (Fischer *et al.*, 1977; Granovetter, 1973; Weber, 1947; Parsons, 1960). The principles of matching developed here could work with any one of these systems.

6

Ideal and Nonideal Forms of Kinship Structure and Exchange: An Elaboration of the Principle of Matching

Up to this point, the major focus of the inquiry has been on the theoretical principles of matching group structure with task structure. The empirical data have been supportive of the theory, while at the same time it has been clear that much has not been explained. To account more fully for the empirical data, it is necessary to drop the initial simplifying assumptions. The assumption up to this point has been that individuals are all in similar and ideal states of the primary-group structures. The only exception is the marital household unit, which has been treated in states of both complete and broken structure.

In this chapter, key simplifying assumptions about the modified extended family structure are dropped. The principle of matching group and service dimensions is examined in the following more complex situations:

1. *Variations of extended family norms and residence structures.* To what extent do people adhere to the residential requirements and the norms of the modified extended family, the traditional family, or the isolated nuclear family, and which services are affected?

2. *Face-to-face contact: Dichotomy versus continuum.* The assumption has been made that services are divided into two groups: marital household services requiring continual face-to-face proximity and normal kin services that can be managed over distance. This assumption is now dropped, and this question is asked: To what extent do different tasks require different distances, and, insofar as that is the case, is there a scheme for ordering the relationship between the very large number of tasks and distance points?

3. *Mixed life styles.* It has been assumed so far that a modern kin structure must be able to transcend differences in class and generation among its members. What, specifically, are the tasks that can be managed across these cultural barriers, and which ones cannot?

4. *Long-term commitments.* It has been assumed that a kinship system has long-term commitments. But individuals in fact may vary in terms of such commitments. The question thus arises: Which services are affected by length of commitments and which are not?

5. *Moderate size*. The assumption has been made that kin systems are larger than marital dyads and smaller than formal organizations. But within this moderate size, there may be significant variations in the number of key relatives available. Specifically, what difference does it make to the delivery of services if one has few or many children?

6. *Affectional ties*. The assumption has been made that relatives in a modern society do maintain affective ties, despite geographic and occupational distances. To what extent is this true, and what consequences, if any, do variations in affection have on the delivery of services?

7. *Shared function with formal organization*. It has been assumed that all kin systems would be equally helped by formal organizations. However, this is clearly not the case for the poor and those with less education. This question then arises: How does this affect services, and which services?

This chapter shows that the theory of matching, with its corollary of the modified extended family, can incorporate the variations listed above, and as a result can explain over four times as many data as under the simpler set of assumptions provided thus far.

Alternative Models of Kinship Structure
Proposed by Sociologists

Let us begin by reviewing the four basic kinship models that have been proposed by theorists. One of the most popular sociological models up until very recently was the view of the typical family in modern societies as a household made up of husband, wife, and young children, who have either very weak ties or no ties to other kinds of units (Parsons, 1944; Goode, 1963; Burgess, Wallin, & Schultz, 1953). This conjugal unit was said to provide the following services: procreation, early socialization, and adult tension management or companionship. This type has been variously referred to as the "isolated nuclear family" or "isolated conjugal family."

A second view that was presented by sociologists up until the late 1940s and early 1950s and is still among the most popular among psychotherapists and sociologists is that there are no meaningful primary groups, just individuals. This view was implicit in the works of people who referred to "mass society," such as Toennies (1940), Redfield (1947), Stein (1960), Nisbet (1969), and Mills (1956). More recently, psychotherapists, some women activists (Firestone, 1971), and many family sociologists have stressed the overriding importance of the individual by suggesting that an individual's need for self-expression and happiness should be the major criterion for judging marriages (Polsky & Duberman, 1979).

A third model of kinship relationships, which argues for a "modified extended" family, has evolved. It has been described in Chapter 2 as a kinship system consisting of a series of nuclear household units that are semi-independent of each other. That is, they deal only with the nonuniform aspects of exchange and leave the uniform aspects to the formal organizations. Furthermore, among themselves, they have a specific division of labor; some tasks are handled only by the nuclear household units, while others are exchanged between the nuclear subunits. My colleagues and I have developed this point of view (Litwak, 1960a, 1960c, 1965; Litwak & Szelenyi, 1969), as has Sussman (1965, 1977). It has received indirect support from evidence that many primary groups such as kin systems remain viable in modern industrial society (Fischer *et al.*, 1977; Fischer, 1982; Shils, 1951; Katz & Lazarsfeld, 1955; Adams, 1971; Streib, 1958; Shanas *et al.*, 1968; Lopata, 1979).

There is a fourth group of writers who have contended that primary groups such as kinship groups have survived and, if anything, have grown stronger in modern societies. However, these writers do not differentiate between modified and traditional extended family structures; therefore, their empirical findings have often been used to argue that traditional kinship ties are most effective in a modern society. The work of Young and Willmott (1957) has often been cited in this regard, and the work of Anderson (1977), Gans (1962), Talmon-Garber (1970), and Marris (1970) could be easily so interpreted.

What should be clear to the reader is that there is an entire range of kinship and marital household models from which to choose. Of this range, I have argued in Chapter 2 that there is only one model, the modified extended family approach, that is consistent with the empirical evidence and also provides a theoretical explanation as to how large organizations and primary groups can operate side by side, despite their contradictory structures. What must be understood is that the principle of matching dimensions of the group with dimensions of services can be applied to any of these alternative models, and that a prediction can be made as to which type of service the group can best manage. However, the assertion has been made that in a modern industrial society, only one model of the family is typical. This leads to two empirical questions: (1) What are the major sources of deviation from the model, and are the deviations truly atypical? (2) Granted that they are atypical, do they still manage different services as predicted by the principle of matching dimensions of groups and tasks?

Empirical Measures of Alternative Norms on Kinship Structure:
Their Source and Consequences for Exchange

An examination of these alternative models makes it clear that one area in which they disagree concerns the norms of autonomy that govern relationships between kin members. In the 1978 survey of older people, these norms were measured by two questions. First, the respondents were asked to evaluate kinship ties vis-à-vis occupational demands:

> If a married child has a chance to get a much better job out of town and it means moving away from his parents, should he turn down the job to stay near his parents or should he take it?

This question seems to force the individual to choose between kinship needs and occupational ones. This is precisely the choice that Parsons (1944) argued that most individuals in our society must confront; because of it, Parsons said, kinship ties cannot be viable.

Of respondents living in the community (1347), 91% said that the married child should take a job out of town even if it means leaving the parents. This seems to provide strong support for Parsons's position, as well as for those saying that primary groups are not viable in a modern society.

The second question was worded as follows:

> How important is it for parents and their married children to keep in touch? Would you say it is very important, important, not too important, very unimportant?

Of the respondents to this question (1047), 79% agreed that it is very important for people to keep in touch with their married children. This would seem to indicate overwhelming support for a norm that is consistent with the extended family model and completely opposed to the Parsons position. In short, these are two empirical findings that seem to be completely contradictory.

This seeming contradiction disappears if one adopts a modified extended family position. In such a position, it is perfectly consistent for people to make occupational choices independently of kinship ties, while at the same time reaffirming the importance of kinship ties. This is possible if kin can make meaningful exchanges across geographic and social distance. In fact, 71% of the community respondents (1347) adopted a modified extended family orientation; that is, they simultaneously said that it would be important for a married child to take a better job out of town away from the parents and that it is very important for married children to keep in touch with parents. Another 20% of this population adopted a position that might be consistent with the isolated nuclear family approach; that is, they said it would be very important for a married child to take a better job out of town, while also saying that it is not important for married children and their parents to keep in contact. Only 8% adopted a position consistent with the traditional family approach; these said that the married child should not take a job out of town and that it is important that parents and married children keep in touch.[1]

It could be argued that the stress on kinship occurs because the population interviewed was elderly—65 and older. Since it is possible that a younger group may hold less firmly to extended family norms, the 1978 survey also included interviews with the helpers of the aged,[2] who in 75% of the cases were their children. The average age of this helper group was

49 years. If one looks at the way in which this group answered the same questions, one sees, if anything, an increase in the percentage of traditional family responses. Thus 64% of the helpers (733) had a modified extended family orientation as contrasted with 71% of the older respondents (1347). Another 14% of the helpers had an isolated nuclear family approach as contrasted with 20% of the older group, and 19% of the helpers had a traditional kinship orientation as contrasted with 8% of the older group. Consequently, these findings suggest that the society is becoming more, not less, oriented toward extended family norms (Anderson, 1977).[3]

It is important to stress that the overwhelming majority of our population, both younger and older, adhered to norms that were close to the model of the modified extended family, while a minority adhered to isolated nuclear family norms and traditional family norms.

An examination of the relationship of these kinship norms to primary-group exchanges as well as to formal organizations is instructive. Older people who adhered to a traditional family norm had, on the average, a slightly higher percentage[4] receiving services [50% (99)] than those adhering to norms of the modified extended family [43% (943)], and both groups had substantially higher percentages than the group adhering to norms of the isolated nuclear family [29% (252)]. This is theoretically precisely what would be expected, since I am in part describing nonuniform services that require proximity when I speak of kinship exchanges. The modified extended family cannot manage all the nonuniform tasks that the traditional extended family can, because the modified extended family lacks the dimension of continual face-to-face contact.[5] The central argument of those advocating the modified extended family structure is not that the modified extended family delivers the same number of services as the traditional family, but that it delivers enough to maintain important services and forms of identification. The data are certainly consistent with such a formulation.

Furthermore, the reason why the modified extended family structure is thought to be ideal, despite the fact it cannot deliver the same number of kinship services as the traditional kin structure, is that it is better able to deal with formal organizations and with tasks that are closely intertwined between primary groups and formal organizations. For instance, a traditional kinship structure, which blocks the differential mobility of its members, ultimately decreases the economic opportunity of its members; it also encourages nepotism in the work place (Young & Willmott, 1957; Gans, 1962). If the traditional family structure were expanded so that it would constitute a majority in society, it would lead to a class-crystallized society as well as to a breakdown in formal organizations.

The 1978 study provides some supportive evidence for these theoretical assertions. Those older persons with a modified extended family orientation were more likely than those with a traditional family orientation to have held higher-prestige jobs[6] (59 % vs. 35%), while those with the isolated nuclear norm were in between (53%). Furthermore, if the helpers can be used as a rough indicator of children in general, it is the case that older people with a modified extended family orientation have children who have achieved more educationally than those with a traditional family orientation. It was the case that those respondents with a modified extended family orientation had helpers of whom 56% were college-educated, while those with traditional family norms had helpers of whom 31% were college-educated. Those with an isolated nuclear norm were in between, having 41% of helpers who were college-educated. Such findings would be consistent with other studies on the effects of parents' orientation on children's education achievement (Z. S. Blau, 1981).

Not only are such norms associated with occupational and educational achievement, but they are also associated with "atypical" kin structures in the way anticipated by the theory. People with a traditional family orientation were more likely to live in the same household with their adult children [23% (99)] than those with the modified extended family view [13% (943)] or those with the isolated nuclear norm [8% (252)]. If one considers a more liberal view of proximity—that is, living within a five-block area—then 41% of those with a traditional family orientation lived within a five-block area of their children, as contrasted with 27% of those with a modified extended view and 25% of those with an isolated nuclear family position.

In addition to this material on achievement and proximity, the 1978 study provides data on tasks directly related to formal organizations; these also show that those with a modified extended family norm did better than those with a traditional family one. There were two outcome variables that reflected the capacity to deal with formal organizations. The first asked all respondents the number of organizations for senior citizens, such as senior centers or Y's, to which they belonged. The other asked respondents in nursing homes how often they were not given attention by nurse's aides. There was a small but consistent advantage in each case for those having a modified extended family orientation. Those with a modified extended family orientation were more likely to belong to clubs [27% (943)] than those with a traditional family norm [20% (99)]. It was also the case that those with a modified extended family orientation were more likely to say that they were never neglected by the staff in nursing homes [64 % (943)], as contrasted with 36% (99) for those holding a traditional family orientation. In both cases, those with an isolated nuclear family orientation were in between, with 23% (252) belonging to voluntary organizations and 58% (252) saying that they were never neglected by nurse's aides.[7]

The advantages that accrue to the modified extended family because it can utilize both formal organizations and primary groups can also be seen by looking at outcomes of the 1978 study that were likely to reflect both formal organizations and primary groups. Respondents were asked how satisfied they were with their free time and whether they were happy most of the time.

I would argue that these states of mind can be helped by either formal organizations or primary groups, and are likely to be maximized when individuals have both. It was the case that 40% of those with modified extended family norms were very satisfied with their free time, as contrasted with 32% for those with a traditional kinship norm and 26% for those with the isolated nuclear norm. For happiness, these figures were 88%, 79%, and 85%, respectively.

In short, most of the 1978 sample had a modified extended family norm. In addition, the principle of matching dimensions of groups with services permits one to predict for which services the traditional kin structure is best and for which the modified extended family and the nuclear family structures are better.

Yet it is the case that in a modern society there are people who seem either to adhere to traditional kinship norms, or to reside in the same household as their adult children in what appears to be a traditional kinship structure. Though they are atypical, the question must still be asked: Can they be prototypes for the future, or can they be shown to be a systematic consequence of the reconciliation of formal organizations and primary groups, which means they will always be restricted to special groups? To answer this question, it must be recalled that the theory of matching argues that a modified extended family orientation is necessary, because the occupational system requires differential geographic and occupational mobility among kin so as to allocate labor rationally. If that is the case, the question can be further refined: Under what conditions would the theory of matching group structures with task structures predict that groups would be least subject to pressures for differential occupational mobility?

One fairly obvious condition would be found among those who are recent migrants from a less industrialized society. The very theory that argues that modified extended norms should evolve in a modern society would also argue that the traditional family ones should be more likely in preindustrialized society.[8]

To get some insight into this source of traditional values, all individuals in the 1978 survey were classified into six groups, based on the recency of migration and the degree to which they came from industrialized countries (Steinberg, 1981; Lieberson, 1980). The groups were given the following labels: "assimilated Americans," "West Europeans," "East Europeans," "Latin Americans," "American blacks," and "Jewish." However, the groups under these labels were more diversified than the labels suggest.[9]

The respondents were also classified in terms of the number of generations their families had lived in the United States, with those who were born in foreign countries listed as "first-generation," those born in the United States but with one or both parents born in a foreign country listed as "second-generation," and those born in the United States with both parents born there listed as "third-generation or longer." The first point to note is that the Latin American group (85) was composed exclusively of immigrants

—that is, 99% were first-generation. The East Europeans (141) had the next highest percentage of first-generation, 78%, followed by the West Europeans (207), 52%, and the Jews (347), 44%. The American blacks (65) should have had 0%, but it turns out that there were 8%, suggesting an interviewer error in classification. The assimilated Americans (429), by definition, had no first-generation members. If these ethnic groups are now examined in terms of family orientation, it turns out that the Latin American groups had the highest percentage with a traditional family orientation, 27%; the East Europeans had the next highest percentage, 14%; the Jewish and black groups each had 8%; and the West Europeans and assimilated Americans each had 4%. In short, the groups most likely to have the deviant values were those with members who had most recently come from a preindustrialized society. This is precisely one of the sources that would be predicted by the theory of matching group and task structures. As such, it is not at all inconsistent with that theory.[10]

Not only did the two ethnic groups with the most first-generation members have more traditional family orientations, but their members were also more likely to live in the same household with their adult children.[11] The Latin Americans had 25% who live in the same household; the East Europeans had 20%; the blacks had 16%; the West Europeans had 11%; the assimilated Americans had 9%; and the Jewish group had 5%. This structural deviation among the East Europeans and Latin Americans would also be consistent with the theory of matching group structures with task structures. What is important to note is that on the average the Latin Americans had 13% more helpers who provided household services normally provided by spouses and 17% more who delivered normal kin services[12] than did the assimilated Americans. The East Europeans had, respectively, 17% and 16% more who did so. Only the American blacks came close to this mark, with 11% more providing household services and 6% more delivering normal kin services. The West Europeans and the Jewish groups had approximately the same as the assimilated Americans.[13] In short, the finding that groups manage tasks that match their structure, as evidence by the way kinship groups picked up marital household tasks, can now be further elaborated in a way that is consistent with that theory: That is, groups that are recent migrants from less industrialized societies are more likely to adhere to traditional family norms and to live closer to each other, and as a result to deliver more household services, than would normally be expected.

However, recency of migration is only one source of "atypical" family norm and residence structure. It does not seem to account for the American blacks, who also delivered more family services than most other groups. Nor does it account for the behavior of the poor, of whom the blacks are a special case.[14] It is also true that the poor and the blacks have a higher probability of living in the traditional family mode (same household as their adult children), even though, in the case of the blacks, they do not adhere to traditional family norms. For instance, respondents whose helpers were in the lowest income quartile ($0 to $9,999) had 25% who lived in the same household as their helpers, those with incomes between $10,000 and $19,999 had 20% in such common residence; those with helpers whose income was between $20,000 and $30,000 had 12% sharing a common residence; and those with the highest income (over $30,000) had 5% who shared a common residence.

How can the theoretical framework proposed here account for this traditional family mode of residence, insofar as it can be isolated from the effects of first-generation migrants? Again, what must be kept in mind is that the requirement that adult children and their older parents have separate residences comes from the fact that there are multiple people in the labor force, and the need exists to allocate labor rationally. However, such pressures for differential mobility are far less for poor people who have unskilled occupations than for wealthier ones. Those in unskilled jobs can easily substitute for one another in any given job. Any place that has opportunities for one group of kin who are unskilled will provide equal opportunities for all. By contrast, if a kinship system is made up of people with specialized work experience, such as a chemist, an engineer, and a professor of English, there is absolutely no guarantee that if there is a job opening for one in a given city, there will also be a job opening for the others.[15]

The question thus arises as to why poor people should move closer together even if they are not pressured to move apart. The answer lies in their lack of money, which means that they generally have less access to the resources of formal organizations. As a result, any time they are in need, they must, like the traditional families of old, turn to kin for help. For instance, a wealthy older person who is feeling too tired to walk several blocks to the grocery store, or too ill to take public transportation to his or her doctor, or in need of recreational diversion, can pay respectively to have the groceries delivered or eat at a restaurant, to take a cab to the doctor, or to go to a movie. Poor older persons cannot afford such luxuries and have to ask their kin or friends to shop for them, borrow money for a cab or obtain help for public transportation, and see friends or kin for recreational diversion. It is because they lack access to formal organizations that the poor are under pressure to live close to kin.

The same theory that suggests that most people will be under pressure to move differentially from kin also suggests that very poor people will be under less pressure to live apart from their kin. The behavior of the blacks, as one of the poorest groups in our society, would be explained, in part, by this analysis.[16]

There is yet another form of deviant residential behavior suggested by the earlier data on illness—that is, single people who are chronically ill and cannot provide their own marital household services. As has already been indicated, these household services especially require continual proximity. If the modified extended family is to provide such services, the older person must move closer.

The question might well be raised as to whether this is not inconsistent with the requirement for differential mobility among kinship members. The answer is that the chronically ill have special needs, and that, being ill and retired, they are out of the labor force and not as subject to the demands of differential mobility. This is not to argue that there are not still pressures, since moves of older people closer to their helpers would put some limitation on the helpers' options to move. However, the stress is far less than would be the case if both the helpers and the older persons were active in the labor force.

What all of this means is that the modified extended family structure has a unique relationship to people who are ill, which differentiates it from the other three models. That is, the modified extended family model would suggest that as people move from states of health to illness, the kin services will shift from normal kin services to a mix of normal kin and marital household services. By contrast, those advocating an isolated nuclear unit would argue that there will be no shift, since there should be no normal kin service or marital services when people are healthy or ill. Those advocating the traditional family structure would also support no shift, because both normal and marital household services are provided by kin when people are both healthy and ill. Therefore, the modified extended family position can be illustrated with data from the 1978 survey by first grouping people into the three stages of health and looking at what combination of services they received.

The first thing to note is that, between people who were healthy and married and those who were ill and single, there was the precise shift in the mix of kinship services that the modified extended family concept suggests. For the people who were healthy and married, the single largest group consisted of those who received only normal kin services (55%) (see Table 6-1). However, among those who were sick and single, the single largest group, 63%, consisted of those who received a mixture of normal kin services and marital household ones. The individuals who received no services at both time periods (the position of the isolated nuclear family group) comprised 15% of those who were healthy and married and 9% of those who were single and ill. These percentage should have been high and constant if the isolated nuclear family model was dominant. The people who received both services in both periods of time (the position of the traditional family norm) comprised 29% of the healthy and married and 63% of the sick and single. To be consistent with the traditional family orientation, these percentages should have been high and constant. In short, the majority of those receiving services followed a pattern that is most consistent with the modified extended family model.

Also behind the modified extended family construct is the assumption that people who are ill might move closer to their helpers without necessarily adhering to a traditional kinship orientation. The data show that people who

Table 6-1. Percentages of Older Persons in the Community Receiving Each Combination of Services, According to Stage of Disability

		Percentage Receiving Services		
		Stage of Disability		
Marital Household Services[a]	Normal Kinship Services[a]	Healthy and Married ($n = 439$)	Healthy and Single or Ill and Married ($n = 657$)	Ill and Single ($n = 248$)
No	Yes	55	45	27
No	No	15	11	9
Yes	No	1	0	1
Yes	Yes	29	44	63

[a] "Yes" means at least one such service, while "No" means no services. "Marital household services" include doing light housekeeping, doing laundry, keeping track of household bills, and making small household repairs. "Normal kinship services" include checking daily to see if respondents were all right, inviting over for dinner, providing small household gifts, helping respondents to keep in touch with kin, and providing emotional support when respondents were low.

were married and healthy had a 10% chance of living with their helpers; people who were married and ill or single and healthy had a 13% chance of living with their helpers; and those who were sick and single had a 22% chance. In short, being ill seems to be a factor, like being a first-generation immigrant and being poor, that causes people to move closer together in expected ways.

If the assumptions of the modified extended family construct are correct, it should be the case that the normal kinship services should be less affected by shifts in states of health and proximity than the marital household services. This was indeed so in the 1978 survey: The standardized rate of increase[17] for marital household services with increased illness was 33%, while the same rate of increase for normal kin services was 7%. It was also the case that marital household services were more affected by shifts in distance than normal kin services. Those living in the same household had an average increase in the delivery of marital household services of over 121% over those living six or more blocks away. This contrasted with the increase of 31% for those receiving normal kin services. By these measures, household tasks were on the average almost 5 times as affected (4.7) by states of health as normal kin activities, and almost 4 times as affected (3.9) by shifts in distance.

To conclude, the argument is being made that the modified extended family construct would suggest that people must move closer if they are to provide household services to the chronically ill. This is not necessarily a measure of traditional family orientation, but reflects a phase in the family life cycle. With these thoughts in mind, three sources of seemingly deviant cases (i.e., ethnicity, income, and illness) are in fact very consistent with the modified extended family model. In addition, the typical and atypical groups conform to the principle that the dimensions of group structures and tasks must match if services are to be provided.

If such factors as ethnicity, income, illness, and proximity are brought into the explanatory model, they enable the model to explain a great deal more empirical data. To give some idea of this point, I have put all of these factors into a regression equation (see Appendix C, Table C-2) and compared them with the regressions based only on illness developed in Chapter 5. What happens is that the amount of variance explained for the household services goes from an average of 12% to 33%. The average amount of variance explained for the normal kin tasks goes from 5% to 16%. In short, relaxing the initial simplifying assumptions has added considerably to the ability to explain the data without requiring the violation of the basic theoretical propositions.

These equations also suggest that such factors as ethnicity, proximity, illness, and (to a more limited extent) income all seem to play a role in the delivery of services. However, the precise role that these variables play cannot be fully understood until we can provide a causal model that permits one to look at indirect as well as direct effects. Such a model is presented at the end of this chapter.

There are yet two further implications that can be drawn from these equations. The factors that have been discussed so far explain far more about marital household tasks than about the normal kin tasks,[18] and there seems to be a continuum of the way in which services are related to proximity, rather than the sharp dichotomy I have thus far proposed between marital household tasks and normal kinship tasks.[19] In part, the first assertion is expected. If normal kin tasks are indeed what every family has, then there should be little variation in a modern industrial society and therefore little explanatory power possible as long as one is dealing with a modern society. However, the idea that services may fall on a continuum in relationship to proximity opens up some very intriguing questions, which are now examined.

Variation in Proximity between Kin Members and
the Consequences for Exchange

So far in the analysis, the simplifying assumption has been made that the primary-group dimension of face-to-face contact or proximity can be treated as a dichotomy between those who share the same household and those who do not. This simplifying assumption is now dropped. Also dropped is the simplifying assumption that only two categories of services must be considered—those that require immediate, continual proximity and those that do not. Rather, it is now assumed that services can vary over distances that are significant for their delivery.

Dropping these simplifications seems to open up a theoretical Pandora's box, since there are a large number of services and infinite points of distance. To solve the seeming dilemma, one must first think back to the basic reasons why services are thought to be related to proximity. As suggested in earlier chapters, there seem to be at least two major elements. The first one is the frequency with which a service must be provided if it is to be meaningful (e.g., providing daily food vs. providing emotional support at the death of a spouse). The second feature that affects proximity is the extent to which the service requires the physical presence of the helper or not. Thus providing food requires a physical presence, while providing emotional support by talking does not. As will be recalled, both of these attributes considered together give some idea of proximity requirements. Where a service requires both frequent delivery and a personal presence, then it also requires immediate proximity (e.g., daily meals). When a service requires infrequent delivery and can be managed over the phone, then it can be provided by those living at a great distance.

Let us demonstrate this point with empirical data. All respondents in the 1978 survey were asked:

> Where does (INSERT NAME OF HELPER) live? Would you say in the same household, on the same block/apartment, within 5 blocks, within 10 blocks, or farther than 10 blocks?[20]

The percentages of older persons receiving each service were plotted according to the distances they lived from their helpers (see Table 6-2). For the sake of this discussion, the percentage of those who received services at each geographical point will be treated as the best estimate of the probability of that service's being delivered at that point. There are two services that best represent the prior simplifying assumption. The item that asked respondents who, if anyone, provided them with light housekeeping services (e.g., dusting the room and making the bed) represents a service that requires sharing the same household, in that it requires the physical presence of the helper and can be interpreted to be a weekly or even daily task. By contrast, the item that asked respondents whom they could talk to when feeling low represents a service that can be managed over the telephone and has no statement about frequency. If it can be assumed that the task can be handled in a monthly call, it should not be very much affected by distance at all. Empirically, that is what is suggested in Table 6-2. The first item was sharply affected by distance, in that people who lived over 30 minutes from their helpers had a very sharp drop in services from those who lived in the same house (i.e., from 82% to 6%, or a 76% drop). By contrast, the delivery of emotional support by talking went from 92% for those in the same house to 70% for those over

Table 6-2. Percentages of Older Persons Receiving Services from Helpers, According to Distance Older Persons Lived from Helpers and Type of Services

	Percentage Receiving Services				
	Distance from Helpers				
Type of Services	Same House ($n = 179$)	1 to 5 Blocks ($n = 202$)	6 Blocks to 30 Minutes ($n = 335$)	Over 30 Minutes ($n = 598$)	Rate of Decline
Marital Household Services					
Doing light housekeeping	82 (77)	26 (26)	12 (10)	6 (8)	57 (49)
Doing storage, laundry, cleaning	74 (75)	23 (28)	14 (16)	9 (15)	48 (37)
Managing household money, bills, Social Security	58 (49)	25 (25)	20 (20)	12 (16)	40 (30)
Doing small repairs on house	81 (85)	39 (48)	30 (35)	14 (21)	43 (37)
Average for all marital household services	74 (72)	28 (32)	19 (20)	10 (15)	47 (39)
Normal Kinship Services					
Checking daily	99 (95)	83 (86)	64 (61)	20 (23)	36 (34)
Taking older persons out for dinner or bringing in dinner or cooking	82 (78)	67 (68)	59 (57)	36 (40)	23 (20)
Providing small household gifts	79 (72)	49 (48)	47 (44)	35 (38)	22 (18)
Helping respondents keep in touch with kin	75 (69)	44 (45)	42 (40)	42 (45)	15 (11)
Talking to respondents when low and cheering up	92 (87)	83 (83)	79 (78)	70 (73)	9 (7)
Average for all normal kinship services	85 (80)	66 (66)	58 (56)	41 (44)	21 (18)

Note. The figures in the parentheses are the percentages computed with the following elements controlled: sex of helpers, income of older persons, illness–marital status of older persons, number of children of older persons, whether helpers were children, ethnic status, and traditional kin values of the older persons. These percentages have been recomputed from the regression coefficients in Table C-3 of Appendix C.

30 minutes away, or a 22% drop. Put in terms of standardized rates of decline,[21] light housekeeping services were over six times as affected by distance as providing emotional support by talking.

If that were all there was to it, the earlier simplification would be more than adequate. However, what Table 6-2 shows is that most of the services fall on a continuum. If the average rate of geographic decline is used to characterize each service, this becomes very obvious. As indicated, at one extreme is light housekeeping services, which were most affected by distance, with an average decline of 57%. Other household tasks ranged from a decline of 48% to one of 40%. Normal kin services went from a decline of 36% to one of 9%. Thus it is the case that marital household tasks require more proximity than the normal kin tasks, while it is also true that they are parts of a continuum. If these tasks are considered in terms of the frequency with which they must be performed and the degree of face-to-face contacts required, these assertions make sense. For instance, light housekeeping services as defined in the survey question require face-to-face contact and could refer to daily or weekly events. The item on laundry, cleaning, and storage of clothes also requires face-to-face contact and refers to events that are most likely to be weekly but could, in the case of storage, be monthly. Managing household bills can fluctuate between monthly to weekly, but often does not require close proximity, because the task can be handled by a combination of mail and telephone. Small household repairs such as putting up curtain rods can range from monthly to every 4 to 5 months. It can be further noted that when most factors, such as gender of helpers, income of older persons, disability of older persons, number of older persons' children, and so forth, are held constant, the effects of proximity remain very much the same. The standardized percentages are included in parentheses in Table 6-2 and would lead to the same conclusion.[22]

The dropping of the simplification of proximity is not just of theoretical interest but of great practical importance. Central to the study of older people is their growing disability and therefore the shifts in the frequency with which they need services. Shifts in frequency, in turn, imply shifts in proximity. These shifts may be on a continuum. Some insight into this issue can be gained if one can assume that the number of household services needed is roughly correlated with the degree of disability of older people. What the 1978 data show is that virtually all respondents living in the same house with their helpers received at least one household service [95% (79)]. Furthermore, a substantial percentage [43% (335)] received such services even when they lived up to 30 minutes away. Even for those living at the greatest distance (over 30 minutes), a little over a quarter of the population [27% (598)] still received at least one household service. However, in the case of respondents who needed four or more household services, even those living in the same house had only a 45% chance of receiving services. Those living within a five-block area had a 15% chance of receiving such services, while those living over 30 minutes away had only a 1% chance of receiving these services. The increasing constraints of proximity are indicated by the rate of geographic decline, which rose from 32% to 71% with the increase in number of household services. In short, it is again emphasized that different stages of health may require different frequencies of household services, which in turn require different distances.

Given the infinite number of geographic distances and frequencies, is there a reasonable way to allocate tasks to given distances? A discussion of technology may provide an answer, since all services are provided through technology.

Technologies can be classified, like services, by the degree to which they provide face-to-face contact (e.g., cars, airplanes, and trains vs. telephones, radio, and mail), as well as the speed with which they can cover distances (e.g., the telephone vs. the airplane vs. the car). In addition, technologies can be classified by the economic and technological resources necessary to use them (e.g., telephones and cars vs. trains and planes). If one considers walking as a natural technology, then it is the one that requires the least economic resources and technical knowledge. In an advanced industrial society, the telephone is next, and then cars, and then trains and airplanes. This order could, of course, change with transformations in technology. However, at the time this study was done, by using telephone contacts versus various face-to-face contacts, a pretty good estimate could be obtained of the general relationship of proximity to the two basic elements essential to defining proximity—that is, the frequency with which a service must be managed and the degree to which it requires face-to-face contact. This was done without examining any specific services, but just by asking the respondents how much of each type of contact they had. The major assumption in this procedure was that all services would have to be funneled through these two basic technologies, so anything known about their properties would be true of services as well. Once the basic relationships could be established, then a small theoretical subset of these could be used to classify all services.

In the 1978 study, two items were used to measure the two "technologies." First, respondents were asked:

How often will you talk with (NAME OF HELPER) on the phone? Would you say daily, weekly, monthly, yearly, seldom, or never?

Next they were asked:

How often will you see him/her either at your home or their home or some other place? Would you say daily, weekly, monthly, seldom, or never?

Answers to these questions were plotted by the distance at which the helpers lived from the older persons (see Table 6-3). The percentage of people having contact at each point and each frequency will be treated as the best estimate of the probability of that contact's being made at that point and frequency. These percentages can be plotted on a graph, and, by extrapolation, all intervening geographic points and frequencies can be estimated. Thus I have plotted in Figure 6-1 the set of telephone curves associated with daily, weekly, monthly, and yearly frequencies. In Figure 6-2 I have plotted the same set of curves for those in face-to-face contact. The proposition is made that all services can be located on one of these curves, depending on the frequency of contact they require and whether or not they demand a physical presence. In short, what is being suggested is that even though the numbers of services is infinitely large, the theoretical number of patterns they can follow is small and can be estimated from the set of curves in Figures 6-1 and

Table 6-3. Percentages of Older Persons in Contact with Chief Helpers, According to Distance Older Persons and Helpers Lived from Each Other and Type of Contact

| | Percentage in Contact with Helpers | | | | | | | | | |
| | Distance from Each Other | | | | | | | | | |
Frequency of Contacts	Same House (n = 172)	Same Block (n = 128)	2 to 5 Blocks (n = 71)	6 to 10 Blocks (n = 76)	11 Blocks to 30 Minutes (n = 259)	31 Minutes to 1 Hour (n = 187)	More than 1 Hour to 2 Hours (n = 91)	More than 2 Hours to 4 Hours (n = 190)	More than 4 Hours (n = 129)	Rate of Decline
	Telephone Contacts									
Daily	76 (72)	77 (76)	79 (82)	61 (62)	59 (55)	36 (37)	20 (19)	4 (2)	1 (4)	44 (34)
Weekly or more	78 (74)	85 (84)	96 (93)	91 (90)	95 (90)	88 (81)	78 (71)	52 (48)	45 (45)	4 (5)
Monthly or more	79 (78)	86 (86)	99 (99)	96 (94)	97 (96)	97 (98)	93 (91)	90 (88)	78 (78)	0 (−1)
Yearly or more	79 (78)	86 (86)	99 (100)	96 (95)	98 (97)	97 (99)	96 (94)	92 (91)	83 (84)	−1 (−2)
	Face-to-Face Contacts									
Daily	97 (94)	85 (85)	44 (44)	25 (26)	14 (8)	2 (2)	0 (1)	1 (1)	00 (03)	73 (63)
Weekly or more	97 (95)	99 (99)	99 (98)	88 (88)	81 (79)	55 (56)	23 (22)	3 (3)	03 (05)	37 (39)
Monthly or more	99 (97)	99 (100)	99 (99)	100 (99)	95 (95)	91 (92)	65 (67)	13 (12)	12 (14)	17 (17)
Yearly or more	99 (99)	99 (99)	99 (99)	100 (99)	97 (96)	97 (98)	96 (94)	88 (82)	76 (75)	5 (5)

Note. The numbers in parentheses are the percentages computed with the following elements controlled: sex of helpers, income of older persons, illness-marital status of older persons, ethnic status, and traditional kin values. These percentages have been recomputed from the regression coefficients in Table C-4 of Appendix C.

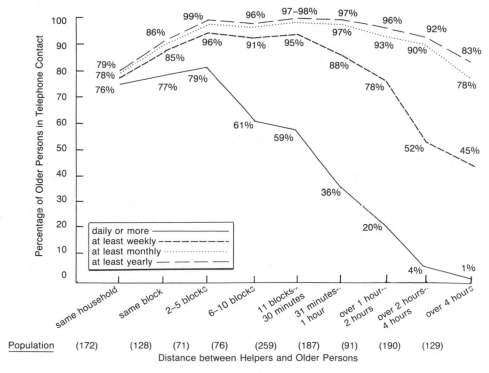

Fig. 6-1. Percentages of older persons in telephone contact, according to frequency of contact and distance from helpers.

6-2. They have also been standardized (the percentages in parentheses in Table 6-3) for factors known to affect proximity, such as economic status, disability, gender of helpers, marital status of older persons and helpers, number of children of the older persons, ethnicity–race, family norms, and age of the older persons. (The standardized percentages have been derived from the regression coefficients in Table C-4 of Appendix C.) However, these particular curves can only be viewed as a prototype, because of the nature of the sample and the fact that specific measures of each technology may be required. Even with these limitations, they provide a marvelous prototype to demonstrate that a theoretical lid can be put on the Pandora's box, as well as indicating the new kinds of questions that can be addressed and answered.[23]

For instance, where people have an opportunity to deliver a service either by the telephone or face-to-face, this question might arise: At what distances does using the telephone provide a higher probability of delivering the service? Specifically, if a helper has an opportunity to provide *daily* comfort to a parent (whose spouse is ill in a nursing home) by telephone or face-to-face contact, at what distances will the telephone provide a higher

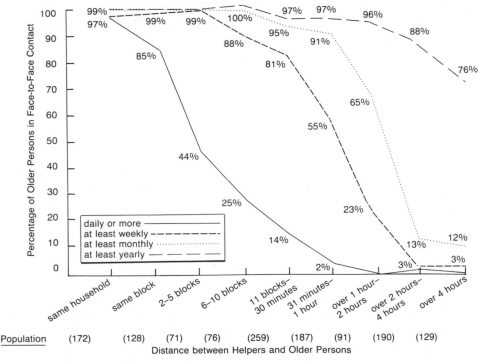

Fig. 6-2. Percentages of older persons in face-to-face contact, according to frequency of contact and distance from helpers.

probability of delivering the service? On a common-sense basis, one might argue that the telephone, by virtue of its capacity to cross great distances quickly, would always provide a higher probability than face-to-face contact. However, the probabilities in Table 6-3 suggest that for the 1978 sample, the advantage of daily telephoning over daily visiting only began for people who lived on a different block and only lasted for those who lived up to 2 hours away. Thus for those living two to five blocks away, those who used the telephone had a 79% probability of receiving the service, while those who depended on face-to-face contacts had a 44% probability. This gave those relying on telephones a 35% greater probability of making contact. For those living 1 to 2 hours away, using the telephone still provided a 20% greater probability. But after that point, there was no greater probability; people in daily telephone contact and those in daily face-to-face contact both had close to a zero probability of making contact. For those living in the same house or on the same block, then, relying on face-to-face contact should provide a greater probability of making contact than those relying on a telephone contact. There is no common-sense observation that could pinpoint the precise geographic distances at which one form of contact provides a greater probability of making contact than the other.

It should be noted that Table 6-3 also indicates how the advantages of telephoning for crossing geographic distance alter as an increasing frequency of services is required. For instance, in the 1978 survey, there was virtually no difference between telephoning and face-to-face contact for services that could be managed by each method and required contact of only once a year or less. The advantage of the telphone over face-to-face contact for services that could be delivered once a month only occurred when people lived more than 1 hour away. For services requiring weekly contact, the telephone's advantages began when people lived outside the 10-block area. For services requiring daily contact, telephoning had no virtues (in fact, it could have been a barrier) when people lived in the same house or on the same block. However, after that point (i.e., two blocks away), the advantages were very substantial.

Yet a different type of question can now be systematically addressed: How does the variation in frequency of a service affect the probability that it will be delivered? Again, common sense would suggest that the less frequent the service, the greater the chance it can be delivered, and that this should be true for all geographic points. For instance, suppose a helper who is providing laundry service has the option of providing fewer clothes and washing every day or providing more clothes and washing weekly. Both options require face-to-face contact. What Table 6-3 suggests, for the 1978 sample, is that the weekly face-to-face contact led to a higher probability of delivering services between two blocks and 2 hours away. Within two blocks and over 2 hours away, daily contact and weekly contact had the same probability of delivering services: Both had a high probability of providing services within 2 blocks and a very low one at over 2 hours' distance.

Still another issue that can confront the helper is whether he or she should deliver a service less frequently in person or more frequently by telephoning. Thus a person providing advice to an older widow on how to manage household tasks that were previously managed by the husband might do so by talking to her daily on the telephone or by coming down weekly and explaining such tasks in person. What Table 6-3 suggests, for the 1978 sample, is that the weekly face-to-face contact had a greater probability of delivering services than the daily telephone contact for those living up to 1 hour away. After that point, both methods were equal and quickly led to a zero probability.

What the 1978 study suggests is the inadequacy of the original notion that primary groups must be in continual face-to-face contact, as well as that of the modified extended family concept that tasks can be divided into those requiring proximity and those not requiring it. From the point of view of family theory, what is being proposed is a more powerful concept of a modified extended family structure, which has a variety of geographic limits and services. As a practical matter, it is the case that older people vary in their disabilities, and it would be very convenient if the sociologist could provide a set of rules that could be used to determine the ideal distances required for various combinations of services. This theoretical elaboration of the modified extended family structure moves in that direction.

Thus far in the analysis, only two attributes of technology have been discussed—that is, the degree to which different technologies permit face-to-face contact and the speed with which they can cover geographic distance. However, what has been assumed is that all technologies are equally accessible. Accessibility, in turn, is often indicated by the cost of the technologies and the knowledge required to use them. In the United States, telephones are sufficiently inexpensive and require a simple enough knowledge base that they are available to a substantial majority. By contrast, travel by airplanes, trains, or buses is beyond the financial capabilities of many families. However, the cost of a technology also depends on the frequency of use and the distance it must cover. Thus almost everyone in the United States could afford an airplane trip of 1000 miles if it were an event that happened only once or twice in a lifetime. This is significant, since many major crises, such as death of a spouse, are both important and infrequent.

In short, to evaluate the availability of technology properly, one must have some assessment of its cost over different distances and with different frequencies. As an initial attempt to make such an evaluation of telephone and face-to-face technologies, Table 6-4 is presented. It classifies respondents in the 1978 survey by the income of their helpers, the distances at which they lived from their helpers, and the frequency of contacts. Table 6-4 indicates that being rich did not seem to increase the probability of making daily or weekly face-to-face contacts. For our respondents, the percentage of people in the lowest-income group making such daily contacts (standardized for distance) was 31%, while the percentage of the highest-income group was 33%. For weekly face-to-face personal contacts, the standardized average for the lowest-income group was 69%, while for the highest-income group it was 68%.

There did seem to be some effect of income on telephoning. Helpers who were in the lowest-income group had an average of 44% who made daily telephone calls, once distance was standardized, while the highest-income group had 51%. For weekly telephone calls, these figures were 74% for the lowest-income group and 87% for the highest-income group. A closer inspection of this table indicates that the lowest-income group cut down on its contacts when members lived more than 10 blocks apart and had to make daily calls, or more than 30 minutes apart and had to make weekly calls.

For this sample, the basic assumption of the modified extended family construct seems to be supported: Technology is available to the bulk of the population and can deliver services over a variety of distances and with a

Table 6-4. Percentages of Noninstitutionalized Older Persons in Contact, According to Frequency and Type of Contact, Distance Older Persons Lived from Helpers, and Income of Helpers

| | Percentage in Contact | | | | | |
| | Distance from Helpers | | | | | |
Helpers' Income	Same House	Within 10 Blocks	11 Blocks to 30 Minutes	31 Minutes to 1 Hour	More than 1 Hour Away	Standardized Average[a]
Daily Telephone Calls						
$0–9999	69	82	47	20	4	44
$10,000–19,999	74	86	64	38	5	53
$20,000–29,999	84	77	56	48	5	53
$30,000 or more	71	71	64	37	11	51
Daily plus Weekly Telephone Contact						
$0–9999	69	92	94	80	33	74
$10,000–19,999	74	98	98	94	65	86
$20,000–29,999	84	88	97	91	58	84
$30,000 or more	86	90	100	93	64	87
Daily Face-to-Face Visits						
$0–9999	100	73	12	0	0	31
$10,000–19,999	95	74	14	0	0	37
$20,000–29,999	95	58	18	4	2	35
$30,000 or more	100	52	14	0	0	33
Daily plus Weekly Face-to-Face Visits						
$0–9999	100	97	82	60	8	69
$10,000–19,999	95	96	86	59	13	70
$20,000–29,999	95	100	88	48	7	68
$30,000 or more	100	100	75	53	11	68
Population Base for Each Cell						
$0–9999	(29)	(38)	(17)	(10)	(24)	
$10,000–19,999	(39)	(40)	(42)	(32)	(40)	
$20,000–29,999	(19)	(26)	(34)	(23)	(57)	
$30,000 or more	(07)	(21)	(28)	(30)	(56)	

[a] Average for each income group with distance held constant.

variety of frequencies. At most, a small segment of the lowest-income group, 8% of the 1978 sample, was affected when making daily face-to-face contacts over moderate to long distance, and 6% were affected when making weekly contacts over very long distances. These figures must be treated with caution, because they obscure two dynamic processes. First, poor people may move closer to their helpers because poverty prevents the use of technology. On the other hand, rich people may use modern technology to move their ill parents closer to them, and these figures might therefore underestimate the role of wealth in the use of technology for them. Even with these qualifications, the evidence still seems to provide overwhelming support for the proposition that technology is available to the large majority of older persons and their helpers.[24]

Similar and Dissimilar Social Status
and the Consequences for Exchange

This now brings us to a third major feature of the modified extended kinship system: its capacity to cross cultural barriers. The simplifying assumption has been made that kin services can cross class barriers and that social class raises the major cultural barriers. Both these simplifying assumptions are now explicitly examined. For older people, age differences may be a cultural barrier equal to if not greater than social class (Riley *et al.*, 1972). A review of the rationale as to how cultural barriers arise and how they block kin ties is in order. First, let us review why social class is a barrier. The occupational system demands that people be appointed on the basis of ability, and there is no insurance that members of the kin system have equal ability or that they will enter equally successful industries. There is a good probability that kin members may end up in different social classes. Therefore, kinship systems must be able to cross class boundaries if they are to exist (Litwak, 1960a, 1965).

Generally, there are two reasons as to why differential class position will disrupt kin systems. First, social classes have different life styles, different values, and different languages (Labov, 1972; Bernstein, 1970; Kohn, 1969). A second reason for loss of identity is that status differences are invidious in our society. People in higher status will not want to associate with those in lower status (Warner & Lunt, 1941). Because of this, those belonging to a strong kinship system will seek to reject occupational criteria of merit, either by discouraging its members from taking occupational promotions or by asking those who move up to give particularistic help to kin so they too can move up (Young & Willmott, 1957).

The same two factors of cultural differences and invidious status comparison can be applied to differences between retired older persons and younger working ones. As pointed out in Chapter 2, ours is a society subject to great technological changes and, consequently, to great social changes. People who are older might, as a result, end up with very different tastes in music, arts, and drama from those of younger people. They might end up with a different vocabulary, different norms on sex, different norms on dress, different norms on civility, and so forth (Kelly, 1955; Riegel, Riegel, & Meyer, 1967). These differences may lead to breaks in exchanges because of the inability of each group to communicate fluently with the other.

Even when parents and children share the same culture, they may not exchange because of "ageism" (a prejudice directed toward the old), which is like sexism and racism (Butler, 1974; Palmore, 1977, 1978). People in our society do not like to be identified as being old. In short, there are invidious status attributes attached to being old. If this were the only criterion, younger children and relatives might not want to associate with older, retired parents.

As indicated in Chapter 2, there are three elements in the answer to this line of reasoning, and they would apply to aging as well. First, there are two types of status gratification that people can achieve (Litwak, 1960a)—that is, association and deference. The first requires groups of the same status or higher, and the second requires groups of lower status. Links with kin of a different class and with friends of the same class typically permit individuals to achieve both forms of status gratification in an industrial society.

How can generational differences in language and values be overcome even if invidious status is not an issue? It has also been pointed out that modern society permits kin to reach across cultural differences because kin are multicultural with reference to key members. Parents and children shared the same language and values when the children were young. Both groups can still retain them while learning new ones as they grow older. As such, they have multiple group cultures and a common basis in communicating. Finally, whatever the differences in generations, there are clearly values and styles of life that are common to the larger society and embrace all age groups.

Given these views, it would be argued that there are some services that people can easily exchange across groups (e.g., services related to areas of common culture), while others will be lost (e.g., services related to the unique culture of each group). With these thoughts in mind, an empirical look at the ability to cross class and other cultural boundaries is now undertaken.

Social Class Differences

Educational groupings will be used here as the major indicator of social class.[25] The basic hypothesis I am advancing is that kin can provide non-uniform aid across social class lines because these tasks are often not related to social class or because kin use mechanisms of multiculture to reduce class differences.

The problem of studying this hypothesis in a kinship context among the aged is that educational or class differences are associated with family resources and geographic proximity, which also affect the delivery of service. First, let us consider resources. As indicated earlier, people with low incomes will provide more kin services because they have the greatest needs and the least ability to use formal organizational resources. The 1978 survey data do show that when education of both respondents and helpers was below the high-school level (32), the respondents received the most services. The average percentage receiving the nine services was 64%. By contrast, where both had education beyond high school (139), the average delivery of the nine services was 38%. There was a rank-order correlation of .82 between the groups' educational levels and the average percentages receiving the nine services.[26]

It was also the case that in a kinship context those who had the highest education were the ones to live furthest away from their helpers. For instance, where the helpers had less than a high-school education, they lived an average of 18 minutes away,[27] whereas when they had more than a college education they lived an average of 2½ hours away. The same pattern held true if one examined the older persons' education.[28]

The fact of the matter is that most exchanges in this study were affected to some degree by distance. The effects of proximity partially overlap with the notion that cultural similarity will lead to more exchanges. Where parents and children have little education, children will provide more services by virtue of living closer as well as by virtue of cultural similarity. By contrast, geographic distance will reduce the effects of cultural homogeneity among the highly educated.

With these thoughts in mind, let us see whether the effects of cultural differences can be unraveled from those of economic resources and geographical distance. As a first estimate, let us look at a question that did not touch on the delivery of services directly, but addressed perceived differences in style of life. "Style of life" involves services that are most likely to be related to class and generation. At the same time, since no delivery of services was involved, this question would be less likely to reflect geographic constraints or limited economic resources. The respondents were asked the following question about their helpers:

> If you consider your style of life, such as the kind of food you like, the kind of clothing you like, the kinds of TV programs you like, the kind of social activities you like, would you say that you and (INSERT NAME OF DESIGNATED HELPER) like: all the same things, most of the same things, about half the same things, some of the same things, none of the same things.

There was a perfect rank-order correlation between the respondents' estimate of a common life style and the degree to which they and their helpers had the same educational level. Of those respondents who had the same educational level,[29] 59% said that they had the same style of life as their helper. Those respondents who had a one-category educational difference with their helpers had 50% who said they had the same style of life, while those separated by two educational levels had 48% who said their life style was the same, and those separated by three educational levels had 40% who gave this response. An examination of the contingency tables suggested that level of education played little role in this response; those older people who had the same high educational level as their helpers had approximately the same percentage saying they shared their helpers' life style as those who had the same low level of education as their helpers.[30]

Accordingly, the respondents' subjective judgment of style of living generally does suggest that there are services that could be affected by educational differences. However, this does not as yet tell us which, if any, services reported in this study were affected by these cultural differences. In this regard, it is important to keep in mind that in providing kin services for older people, physical resources and commitment may be more important than style of life. To get a first estimate of this issue, averages for the nine kin services were examined in relation to the education of the helpers and the older persons. First, as already indicated and in contrast to the question on style of life, there was a resource effect, with a rank-order correlation of .82 between level of education and the delivery of services. The least educated received the most services.

In order to isolate the cultural effects, the education differences were further standardized by the distance that older people lived from their helpers. When this was done, it turned out that cultural differences played a minor role for marital household services but not for the normal kinship ones. For instance, for marital household tasks, those with matching levels of education had 38% who delivered marital household services; those who were one category apart in education had 32%; those who were two categories apart had 35%; and those who were three categories apart had 30%. For the normal kin services, these same figures were 63%, 67%, 61%, and 64%, respectively. What seems to be clear is that social class differences, as indicated by education, do not seem to constitute much of a barrier to the delivery of normal kin services or even marital household services. The chief elements related to the provision of services in the 1978 study seemed to be resources and family commitments.

The question arises as to why class differences seem to affect one set of services ("style of life" services) but not another (normal kin and marital household services). Part of the answer lies in the view that people in modern societies such as the United States have multiple noncorrelated group affiliations (Dahl, 1966). Some of these affiliations are defined by class, and some are defined by other criteria, such as religion, ethnicity, family, and the like. The ethnic group may contain people of different classes, and the class group may contain people of different ethnicities. "Style of life" activities may be related to the first, while marital household activities may be related to the second.

Another part of the answer lies in the view that even when kin have to manage tasks that include class differences, the fact that kin (i.e., parents, children, and siblings) shared a common class position at one time (e.g., through the children's early adulthood) provides a common cultural bridge. This operates through mechanisms of multiculture; that is, people retain the common bases even when learning new ones. I would further speculate that normal kinship and marital household services are related to familistic norms such as long-term reciprocity, and, for this older population, to physical and economic resources of the helpers.

Age Differences

To document these speculations, age differences between helpers and older persons are now examined. For older people, differences between those who are older and retired and those who are younger and working can be crucial. However, for this sample, age homogeneity between older people and their helpers is atypical, since those with children had to choose one of them. Therefore, when one speaks about age homogeneity, one is generally talking about people who had no children but relied on other relatives or friends.

To highlight the effect of age grouping, the older people were classified into two age brackets: those aged 65–74 and those aged 75 and older. Helpers, in addition, were grouped into those under 39, 40–49, 50–64, as well as 65–74, and 75 and over. First, the item that asked respondents how closely their style of life matched their helpers' is examined in relation to age. There was a perfect rank-order correlation between the age matching of older people and their helpers and the degree to which older people said they had the same life style. Those who were in the same age group as their helpers had 63% who agreed that they shared the same life style; those one age category apart had 55%; those two categories apart had 52%; those three categories apart had 49%; and those four categories apart had 36%.

However, as has already been suggested, the kind of exchanges that are being studied are not strongly imbued with generational differences in life style, but reflect, in the case of marital household tasks, the need for physical and economic resources as well as long-term commitment. In order to get some insight into this problem, the exchanges were classified into three groups so as to isolate those most likely and least likely to reflect the need for resources. The first group considered was made up of those exchanges that are most likely to stress cross-generational kin ties because they require long-term commitments as well as physical and economic resources. It was felt that the four marital household tasks (i.e., doing light housekeeping, doing small household repairs, managing money, and doing laundry and storage) would come closest to fitting this category. The second group of services consisted of those that are next most likely to call for cross-generational help, but do not depend as much on physical resources, because they touch on cultural norms associated with cross-generational family ties (i.e., helping older persons keep in touch with relatives) or because they deal with financial resources (i.e., providing small household gifts to make the place more homey). The third group of services consisted of those thought to be most likely to involve age-homogeneous helpers, because they make no physical demands and can be interpreted in terms of age-homogeneous problems as well as age-heterogeneous ones. These included inviting the older persons to dinner, talking to them when they were low, and checking on them to see if they were all right.

The helpers were classified by age and also by form of kin tie (i.e., as to whether they were children, relatives other than children, or nonrelatives). The assumption was that helpers who were children were more likely to have long-term commitments and were, by definition, age-heterogeneous; furthermore, the older they were, the more likely their parents were to require aid because of infirmities and advanced age. Thus age homogeneity can best be studied in this format by looking at ages of nonrelatives or relatives who were not children. For this group, all helpers over 65 were defined as age-homogeneous with the older person.

Exchanges requiring continual contact, much energy expenditure, or money control (i.e., the marital household activities) were more likely to be handled by younger relatives and nonrelatives. Thus, those respondents with helpers two categories younger (72) had 22% providing aid, those with helpers one category younger (79) had 18%, and those with helpers the same age (i.e., 65 or older) (154) had 15%. For tasks stressing economic resources of kinship ties (i.e., providing small household gifts, helping keep in touch with relatives), it was still the case that the younger generation helped more. Those with helpers who were two categories younger (72) had 51% providing aid, those with helpers one category younger (72) had 32%, and those with age-homogeneous helpers (154) had 28%. However, for tasks requiring minimal economic and physical resources (i.e., talking to older persons when low, inviting them to dinner, checking on them daily to see if they were all right), the younger helpers no longer provided more services. The percentages for the three groups were 59% (72), 60% (73), and 61% (154), respectively. In short, age homogeneity of helpers does seem to relate more to tasks that involve a common generational culture, but not to services requiring physical and economic resources or to family cultures. The earlier finding that age homogeneity is related to common life style would simply be a better illustration of the same point.

In conclusion, the data suggest that age and possibly social class can define meaningful cultural groups, and thus can act as barriers to some exchanges. What is crucial, however, is the understanding that such barriers do not block all services (e.g., those requiring long-term reciprocities), but only those specifically related to the culture of the group (e.g., "style of life" services). Dropping the simplifying assumption on "group–cultural barriers" enriches the understanding of networks by showing how one can enter class and age differences into the analysis.

Variation in Length of Commitment between Kin Members and the Consequences for Exchange

Up to this point, the simplifying assumption has been made that all kin, and especially parents and children, have long-term commitments. This assumption can now be examined; the question asked is this: What kinds of service suffer when one does not have long-term commitments?

As I have pointed out earlier, there are specific primary-group tasks that require long-term commitments. Let us review these. Generally, any form of unpaid exchange that involves much time, energy, or financial sacrifice requires long-term commitments to insure reciprocity. One must remember that primary-group help is given in terms of services. The longer the primary-group commitment, the higher the probability of a situation arising in which the helper will in turn need massive aid.

It is also the case that certain services can only be supplied by those who share a common history with the older person. Thus an individual seeing an episode in a movie that reminds him or her of a past experience might not be able to explore this fully unless someone else has shared this past experience. Similarly, it may be the case that certain events require some future time commitment in order to be undertaken. A person who manages an older person's finances can seriously affect the older person's future by creating debt.

Long-Term Reciprocity

The kinship system as it generally operates in modern urban societies, such as America, tends to establish long-term commitments through a combination of legal and biological definitions. Thus parents and children are tied together by a series of laws that make parents legally responsible for children.

Several unique issues arise in connection with long-term commitments of the aged. First, researchers (Sussman & Burchinal, 1962; Schnaiberg & Goldenberg, 1975; Hill, 1970) have pointed out that there is a regular pattern to aid between parents and children. These studies indicate that when parents have young children, aid goes from the parents to the young children, and the parents, in turn, receive help from their parents. When parents approach middle age, they are often in the position of moderating their aid to their children and giving more aid to their own parents. When parents become older, then their children tend to give them aid, and they do not have to give aid to their own parents because of their deaths. If the unsuspecting investigator were to cut into the family life cycle at one point in time, then he or she would get an erroneous picture of the exchange process. It would not look reciprocal. However, if the whole life cycle is taken into account, then it is reciprocal.

In the 1978 study, one question presented a list of nine exchanges and asked the respondents whether they had received any help in the previous 6 months on each of these types of services from their children (or, if they had no children, the persons they felt closest to). At the end of the nine items, the older persons were asked what, if anything, they had provided to the helpers. Though the wording of the two questions was not precisely similar, in that one included the specific list of nine and the second simply asked the respondents to think of any forms of exchanges they could, it is nevertheless instructive to look at the average number of exchanges the older persons said they received and those they said they gave. On the average, the older persons said they had received 3.7 exchanges in the previous 6 months, while they said they had given their children or other helpers 0.7 exchanges. This asymmetry in aid is perfectly consistent with the findings of prior investigators and reflects the unique problem of older persons in our society—that is, they tend to be receivers rather than givers at this point in their life cycle.

The point can be supported if one considers the following question:

> During your lifetime, have you given any money or gifts to your children (or persons raised like children), like giving them regular support payments; or helped with house mortgages or rent; or bought or loaned them money to buy major appliances, cars, or furniture? (IF NO CHILDREN, ASK ABOUT THEIR HELPER.) (The respondent could answer yes or no.)

Since "helpers" could be children, relatives (who could be further divided into siblings and nonsiblings), or friends, it is possible to see which groups might feel bound by long-term commitment. What we found was that among the cases (1020) where the helpers were children, 57% of the respondents said they had given major forms of aid to them. Where the helpers were siblings (120), only 17% had given such aid, and where the helpers were relatives other than children or siblings (88), 27% had given such major aid. In the cases where helpers were friends (120), 27% had given major aid. The helpers who were children were over twice as likely to have received aid from the respondents than any other type of helper. This indicates why children are so important for building up long-term reciprocities. It may be that no other group permits such continual long-term commitment for the aged.

It is also the case that long-term reciprocity is based on changes over time in who has resources. That is, when children are very young, they have few resources and parents have many, as do parents' siblings and friends. When parents are very old, they have few physical resources, as do their friends and siblings, while children have both economic and physical resources.

This is of course consistent with the just-concluded analysis that, where the older persons have age peers as helpers, the helpers are not as able to handle exchanges that require economic and physical resources. To emphasize the long-term commitment aspect, this issue is now examined again, but with the helpers now categorized into one of four groups (rather than only considering nonchildren): children, siblings, other relatives, and nonrelatives. The exchanges are classified into the same three groups considered previously: (1) those requiring either physical or economic resources but not necessarily common generational experiences; (2) those requiring common family identity but not necessarily resources; and (3) those requiring common generational identity but not necessarily economic and physical resources. There was a steady progression of choice in the 1978 results from closest ties to most distant ties for tasks that require physical and economic resources. Children were chosen most to handle household tasks such as light housekeeping [30% (1020)], then siblings [27% (93)], then other relatives [21% (88)], and finally nonrelatives [15% (120)]. For tasks that involve the family but do not require physical or economic resources (i.e., keeping in touch with relatives), then the basic division was between relatives and nonrelatives: 52% of the children, 44% of the siblings, and 47% of the relatives, but only 8% of the nonrelatives, were chosen. But on tasks that require fewer physical and economic resources and are not the exclusive domain of the family, nonrelative helpers provided services almost as much (59%) as children (60%), siblings (64%), or other relatives (60%). If this study had included services stressing common culture, the findings would have been more dramatic.

It is of some importance to note that there may be no functional substitutes for children in handling tasks that require long-term primary-group reciprocities. This point may be systematically overlooked by the larger public, because the central role of children may be apparent only to the advanced aged. That is, when people are young and their children are not yet married, parents may have friends and siblings with whom they have shared longer relationships than with their children. Friends at this age may be very vigorous, and major exchanges may be made between friends. It is only at the last stage of aging that the physical resources of children and the past reciprocities of parents to children so strongly outweigh those between parents and their friends.

I have tried to establish one point in this section: Where helpers vary in the length of their commitment, they will also vary in the type of services they provide.

Variation in Size of Kinship System and
the Consequences for Exchange

Let us now turn to another dimension of kinship structures—that is, their size. Up to now, the simplifying assumption has been made that kin systems are all the same size and are all larger than the marital household. Now the simplifying assumption is dropped, and key variations in kinship size are examined. Parents can have one adult child, two, three, or more. The question arises: How can such variations affect the type of services kin can deliver, and can the theory of matching group structures with task structures take variations into account? The reader will recall that in earlier chapters, it has been pointed out that some services benefit from large groups and some do not. For instance, it has been argued that most of the normal kinship services can benefit from large groups with virtually no costs of coordination. As such, the large groups would lead directly to more services being provided.

Several researchers have noted that when it comes to providing marital household services to older persons, generally one person assumes the role of prime caregiver. It is speculated that this is the case because such home services have very high costs of coordination and therefore cannot directly benefit from large groups. However, there may be indirect ways that large numbers of children help even when one person is the prime helper. A large number of children insures that there will be at least one who lives close by, who is willing to help, and who is physically and financially healthy enough to provide help.

With these thoughts in mind, let us examine the relationship in the 1978 survey between the delivery of services and the number of children an individual had. The general finding was that the more children one had, the greater the number of services that were delivered. For instance, in the category of exchanges normally handled by kin (e.g., checking daily, talking to someone when feeling low, etc.), 44% of those with one child (302) had had these services delivered. By contrast, of those with four or more children (149), 62% received such services.[31] In the category of exchanges in which the helpers provided marital household functions (housekeeping, laundry, money matters, etc.), 23% of those with one child (302) received aid, while 36% of those with four or more children (149) received aid.[32]

Since large families are associated with low income, it is possible that these findings really reflect income differences rather than size of the kinship unit. It is, of course, also possible that the findings on income might reflect size of kinship groups. In this regard, a consideration of the various models of family structure provides a clue as to how to unravel the effects of income and size of kin unit. Thus, the modified extended family model argues that household tasks should be performed by the marital unit. If the marital unit requires help and a formal organization can be used, the first priority should be to use money to supplement the marital dyad, rather than to move to a relative's home to provide marital household services. However, if individuals are poor and do not have money, or if they are sick and cannot supervise paid help, then they should turn to kin.

By contrast, the traditional family model does not recognize the distinction between marital household tasks and normal kin services. According to this model, all should be provided by the kinship unit, and family members should be utilized first and paid help second. Of course, for those who argue that kinship units are not viable (Parsons, 1944; Weber, 1947), the number of children is not relevant. One should get all resources from formal organizations.

Table 6-5 shows that having more children is very important for the lower-income groups if they are to receive more services. For the higher-income groups, having more children is not important. A rough measure of the effects of children can be estimated by comparing for each income group the amount of service provided to those respondents with one child and those with four or more. For instance, for the lowest-income group, those who had four or more children had a 27% advantage, on the average, in receiving marital household services. For the middle-income groups, those with four or more children had a 9% advantage. For the highest-income groups, such respondents had no advantage. In fact, there was a 1% decline in services for them.

In the provision of normal kinship services, the advantage of having four or more children over having one child was 18% for the lower-income groups and 15% for the middle-income groups. It was 7% for the higher-income groups. The pattern is the same, but the income effects are more muted. In short, the two resources of income and children are not additive, but follow an interactive pattern, which is more consistent with the modified extended family notion of semiautonomy and functional substitution. In addition, the path model presented at the conclusion of this chapter suggests that when all factors are considered, having many children leads to more services by insuring there will be one that lives nearby.

Variation in Affectional Ties of Kin Members and
the Consequences for Exchange

One of the most frequently mentioned characteristics of the primary group is that of affectional ties or positive sentiment. Up to now, the simplifying assumption has been made that kin members all have some internalized commitment, regardless of class and geographic distances. This assumption is now dropped.

This question was asked to measure the respondents' sense of affection:

Table 6-5. Percentage of Noninstitutionalized Older Persons Receiving Kinship Aid, According to Number of Children They Had and Older Persons' Income

| | Percentage Receiving Aid | | | | |
| | Number of Children | | | | Difference |
Older Persons' Income	One	Two	Three	Four or More	between Extremes
Marital Household Services[a]					
$0–3999	30	38	41	57	27
$4000–6999	20	19	21	30	9
$7000 or more	21	18	23	20	−1
Normal Kinship Services[b]					
$0–3999	51	55	66	69	18
$4000–6999	45	52	55	60	15
$7000 or more	44	50	48	51	7
Normal Neighborhood Services[c]					
$0–3999	8	6	11	22	14
$4000–6999	8	7	8	6	−2
$7000 or more	5	7	4	14	9
Population					
$0–3999	(90)	(91)	(58)	(50)	
$4000–6999	(93)	(111)	(44)	(40)	
$7000 or more	(88)	(113)	(51)	(33)	

[a]Doing light housekeeping, doing laundry and storage, doing small household repairs, and managing household finances.
[b]Inviting respondents for dinner, providing small household gifts, helping respondents keep in touch with relatives, checking daily, talking to respondents when feeling low.
[c]Watching house when occupant is out on daily chores, and borrowing small household items in an emergency.

How often do you have feelings of love and affection for the following people? Let me start with (NAME OF HELPER). Do you have feelings of love and affection toward (NAME OF HELPER) all the time, half of the time, some of the time, or never?

In the 1978 sample, the distance between older persons and their helpers had little negative effect on the respondents' sense of affection.[33] This finding is consistent with that of others (Adams, 1971; Fischer *et al.*, 1977). Of those who lived in the same household, 83% who said they felt affection "all of the time," while 86% of those who lived more than 1 day away made this statement. Some readers might object that such a question does not adequately measure the degree of affection, but rather taps a socially mandated effusiveness. Though there is no way that such a comment can be answered with the 1978 measures, it is reassuring to see that respondents did not have as high a percentage expressing such affection for others. For instance, 59% felt affection "all of the time" about relatives who were not helpers, while 48% expressed such affection for their close friends, and 34% felt this way about their best-known neighbors.

The second point regarding ties of affection is that they do not seem to be disrupted by class differences. Thus 93% of the respondents who were six or more income categories lower than their helpers said that they felt affection and love for them all the time. Among respondents who were at least two categories higher than their helpers, 94% felt love and affection all the time. Among the people whose income categories matched those of their helpers, 85% felt affection and love toward their helpers all the time. The difference between the percentage of those expressing affection who were in the same income group as their helpers and those who were in different ones is small and in the "wrong" direction. In short, neither geographic nor social distance seemed to mute bonds of affection for the survey respondents.

The issue that must still be addressed is that of the consequences of affection for delivering services. In the theory of matching groups and tasks, affection is viewed as an internalized and noninstrumental motivation. As a result, it is central for delivering services where outcomes cannot be easily observed. The 1978 data show that there was an association between affection and the delivery of services: 25% of those (1125) who felt affection for their helpers all the time received one of the four household services, on the average; 20% of those who said they were affectionate most of the time (170) received one of these services; and 7% of those having such feelings half the time or less (49) received one of the services. The problem with these findings is to establish causal direction, since affection and service were probably mutually interactive.[34]

Ideally, what one would like to have is some variation in the relation of affection to visibility of services so that one could demonstrate that affection was more highly related to tasks that had lower visibility. However, such differentiation could not be established with the services investigated in 1978.

In any case, what is suggested is that the data are consistent with the view that the typical older person does have some internalized commitment to kin, and the dropping of the simplifying assumption on affection permits one to explain more about service delivery.

The Web of Interrelations: A Causal Model of
Kinship Structure and Exchange

Thus far, this chapter has shown how some of the prior simplifying assumptions can be dropped and how a far richer, if somewhat more complex, analysis emerges. What is, of course, central in all of this is that the more complex assumptions are still accounted for by the principles that dimensions of groups and tasks must match. However, throughout this analysis one overall simplification has been made, and that is that each of the variables, such as physical distance, illness, ethnicity, number of children, kinship norms, and income, relates to the delivery of services in a direct way, with little or no relationship to the other variables.

Now I should like to drop that assumption and explore the web of relations that binds these factors to one another. Initially, this can be done by use of a simplified path model[35] (see Figure 6-3).

Let us start with the basic argument that in a modern industrial society there will be pressure from the occupational structure for a modified extended family system, with marital dyads managing household tasks, kin managing the "normal" kin exchanges, and the marital dyads living in separate households.

With that general framework in mind, it has been argued that several types of deviations from this typical structure can be expected. First, ethnic groups that are primarily composed of recent immigrants from less industrialized societies should have more traditional kinship norms. These in turn dictate that kin live close at hand and deliver marital household services as well as normal kin ones. The effects of ethnicity on services are indirect.

This set of speculations is presented in Figure 6-3 by an arrow from the first-generation groups (Latin American and East Europeans) to living in the same house (beta = .10), as well as an arrow from first-generation groups to views that parents who are too ill to live alone should live near their helpers (beta = .17). These views are in turn related to proximity (beta = .13). Proximity in turn relates to the actual services (betas ranging from .57 to .08).

Poor people comprise a second source of expected deviation from the modified extended family model. They are generally unskilled laborers, which means that their jobs are easily interchangeable, so they are therefore less affected by occupational pressures for differential mobility. At the same time, their level of income is so low that they are likely to need household help. There are many sources of poverty, including ethnic-racial discrimination (Lieberson, 1980; Bonacich, 1972). Thus one would expect the recent immigrants as well as the American blacks to be less well off. This is represented by the arrow from the first-generation groups (beta = −.30) to education, and by an arrow from blacks (beta = −.23) to education. Low education in turn relates to proximity (beta = −.12). It also leads to having more chil-

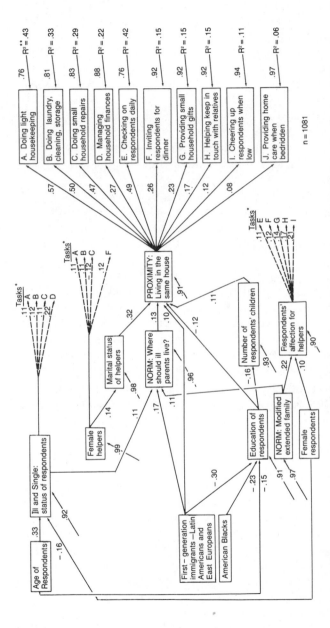

Fig. 6-3. Simplified path model for services. Only paths significant at the .01 level and with a standardized beta of .10 are shown. In the proximity variable, illness and marital status variable, and ethnicity variable, only the highest betas are shown, even though each of these variables consists of a series of dummy variables. In addition, only those direct paths to services are shown that have a pattern of relationships. For a complete definition of each variable as well as the first stage of the path model with unstandardized betas, see Appendix C, Table C-3. Where there may be a question of direction, the positive end of each variable is used in the labeling. *These tasks are the same as those indicated to the right with matching letters. They have been separated in this way and the paths drawn in dotted lines to highlight the role of proximity. **R^2 has been adjusted to take account of the number of variables.

dren (beta = .16), which likewise leads to proximity (beta = .11). Again, the interesting point is that education and number of children are related indirectly to the delivery of household services.

Yet another expected deviation from the modified extended family model occurs when people are so ill they can no longer perform household services within the marital household context. They therefore have great need and are out of the labor force, so are not as subject to pressures for differential mobility. In Figure 6-3, this group is represented by those who are sick and single. Being single and ill relates indirectly to services by causing people to develop norms that older people who are ill should move closer (beta = .11), which in turn leads to people actually moving closer (beta = .13). As indicated, living close leads to more services being provided. Thus being ill and single, like education and ethnicity, has an indirect relationship to providing services that depends on moving closer. However, it is the case that those who are ill and single will also be provided services directly. This is represented by the dotted arrows between being ill and single and marital household services A, B, C, and D, with betas ranging from .11 to .22. These values do not compare in magnitude with the betas for proximity and these marital household services, which range from .57 to .27.

Illness and marital status in the 1978 survey population were basically related to biological factors, as indicated by the arrow between age of the respondent and illness (beta = .33). Palmore (1981) and others point out that illness is also produced by poverty. But in this study education, the indicator of social class, had no such powerful relation.

Yet another expected source of deviation from the prediction is the gender of the helper. It is argued that in the recent past and still at the present, many women are more socialized to provide household help than males. If there is any deviation from the typical pattern of delivery of household services, it should be from those whose roles resemble the deviant behavior (Cloward & Piven, 1979). In Figure 6-3, this factor is reflected in dotted arrows between gender and marital household services A through C, and an arrow between gender and normal kin service F. The betas range between −.12 and +.12. The minus tells us that men helpers are more used for household repairs, while women helpers are more used for other household services. It is also the case that women helpers have indirect paths by which they deliver services. They are more likely to be single (beta = .14), which in turn leads to living in the same house as parents (beta = .32), which in turn leads to the delivery of services.

This touches on the issue of marital deviation, the final type of expected deviation that is discussed here. The modified extended family assumes the existence of a complete marital dyad. Where one has helpers who are single, there is far less need, under the modified extended family concept, to maintain distance between the households. This is reflected in the fact that the single most important source of proximity is the helper's being single (beta = .32). Of course, proximity is the major basis for delivering of household service. The role of gender and marital status is developed in the next chapter.

Finally, there is a positive relation between affection and delivery of normal kin services, but not marital household ones. This is represented in dotted arrows to services E through I, with betas ranging from .21 to .11. This reverses the pattern of proximity, gender, and illness, in that affection is more closely related to normal kin services. It is of some interest to note that the normative position of the modified extended family is the one most strongly related to affection (beta = .22).

There are two major points I wish to demonstrate with this path model. First, the nature of deviation from the modified extended family model can be accounted for in terms of the same theory that anticipates that the modified extended family will be the typical structure. Second, one cannot understand the process of exchange without taking into account the structure of the service. This is clearly seen in this path model, in that services that require proximity, such as the marital household ones, are best explained by factors that force the modified extended family to move closer. However, services that do not require proximity tend to emphasize elements, such as affection, that can be maintained over distance. This point can be made much clearer if one envisions some services that might benefit from distance. Thus the individual seeking to learn about the everyday living patterns in a retirement community in a different region of the country will benefit if he or she has a primary-group member who lives in that community. There are even some services that require a middle range of distance, neither very close nor very far. For instance, older persons who have some major medical problem but are still able to manage most household activities might want to move to the same community as their helpers in case help is needed. However, they might also want to be at a sufficient distance so they can still retain their own autonomy.[36] This is, of course, a condition that is familiar to many newlyweds, who want to be far enough from their parents for autonomy but close enough for exchanges.

With that limitation in mind, the more general features of this model can be discussed. First, as one moves from marital household services to normal kin services, there should be less variance explained, since, theoretically, it is expected that most people will have normal kin services. This turns out to be the case, with one exception. Thus, for the marital household services, the variance explained ranges from 42% to 22%. For those labeled normal kin services, with one exception, the variance ranges from 15% to 6%. The one exception is checking daily, for which 42% of the variance is explained; this service might possibly be better thought of as a mixture of normal and marital household services.[37]

The second point is that one expects proximity to play less of a role as one moves from marital household tasks to normal kin services. With the same exception, this pattern does indeed occur. The betas for marital household services and living in the same house range from .57 to .27, and those for normal kin services and living in the same house, with one exception, range from .26 to .08; the exception is "checking daily," which has a beta of 49.[38] In the most direct sense, the loss of variance explained is related to the diminished influence of proximity. But in the theoretical sense, the development of modern technology and the structure of normal kinship services mean that most people in the society can receive normal kin services regardless of distance, and that is the reason for the drop in both of these figures.

Waiving the initial simplifying assumptions permits one to explain more about the nature of service delivery. However, it also opens up complexities of relationships that are more difficult to follow. This path model is a first attempt to diagram these complexities in a form that readers can, with some effort, follow. It is presented as a conceptual device to show how atypical situations arise and can be related to typical ones, under the principle that the structure of groups and tasks must match.

Summary and Conclusion

In this chapter, the simplifying assumption that people typically have an extended kinship structure has been dropped, and variations in key dimensions have been examined within the framework of the theory that group structures and task structures must match. It has been shown that those with a modified family outlook are able to supply normal kin tasks almost as well as those with a traditional orientation, and at the same time are better able to deal with tasks associated with formal organizations and occupational mobility. Furthermore, it has been pointed out that kin's provision of "atypical" services (i.e., kin's provision of marital household services) arises from sources that would be predicted by the theory behind the modified extended family. These atypical exchanges take place among first-generation immigrant groups from preindustrial societies; groups outside the labor market who cannot manage household activities on their own, such as the chronically ill; and poor people who because of low occupational skills are never subject to intense pressures for differential mobility and have great needs for household services. It has been shown that these "atypical" groups have to have close proximity to deliver marital household services, which theoretically require such proximity. As such, they are consistent with the principles of matching.

The assumption that face-to-face proximity is a dichotomous variable has been dropped. It has been shown that there is no sharp dichotomy between services that can be managed at a distance and those that cannot, but rather a continuum, with different services requiring different degrees of proximity. It has also been shown how one can measure the central underlying dimensions that govern the relationship between services and proximity (i.e., frequency with which the service must be provided, plus the degree to which face-to-face presence is necessary) and derive a set of curves that permit one to estimate all possible services in terms of all possible frequencies at all geographic points.

The assumption that the kinship relationship can exist despite differences in social class and generation has also been explored. It has been pointed out that people are well aware that styles of life differ between class groups as well as between generations. Nevertheless, key services can be delivered across these culture barriers, because tasks vary in the extent to which they require common cultural, physical, and economic resources. For the old and chronically ill, style of life may be secondary to physical and economic resources, as well as to family norms of long-term reciprocity.

Yet another assumption dropped in this chapter is that kinship structures are all the same size; the consequences for the delivery of services of a family's having one, two, three, or more children have been examined. Evidence has been presented to show that services do benefit from large numbers, but that this is an indirect benefit—that is, it ensures the presence of a helper nearby.

Still another assumption made in earlier chapters has been that kin are able to maintain love and affection across geographic distance and occupational distance, even though the number of services provided over distance is less than those provided by the traditional family. This assumption has been empirically examined, and it has been shown that geographic and economic differences have little effect on the general expression of affection or love.

Finally, these different threads have all been brought together in a larger framework. I have tried to show that underlying the concept of the modified extended family is an intricate web of relationships, which in turn are all consistent with the principle that the structures of groups and services must match.

For policy makers and practitioners, there are very important implications in this formulation of the modified extended family. The fact of the matter is that many such individuals might not have a clear overview of the concept of the modified extended family, even though the bulk of service exchanges are governed by norms consistent with it. For instance, policy makers often do not recognize the difference between uniform and non-uniform forms of aid. As a result, they will seek legislation that will deduct any form of kinship aid from that supplied by the government. Alternatively, policy makers, troubled by the costs of aid, will turn to traditional family concepts and seek laws on filial responsibility to force kin to take over costs. The facts that these laws are inconsistent with norms of an open-class system and therefore cannot be easily enforced (Schorr, 1960), and that if they are enforced they tend to lead to a destruction of the kinship system (Anderson, 1977), cannot be seen by policy makers, because they lack the overall concept of the role of kin in a modern industrial society. They can only see short-term advantages.

These issues are explored more fully in Chapter 10. At this point, I turn to the issue of marital household units and the pressures put on helpers' households.

Notes

1. The remaining 1% of the population said that the married child should not take a job out of town and that married children should not keep in touch with their parents. This is a logically possible but theoretically meaningless response. It is thought to be a consequence of the way in which the items were dichotomized.

2. Interviewers were only able to establish such contacts with 55% of the sample, so the analysis only refers to a subgroup. There is some reason to believe that this group was one that was in closer contact with the older persons. They had, for instance, a slightly higher percentage who lived in the same household than those whose helpers were not contacted.

3. It could also reflect a biased sample of helpers; see footnote 2.

4. This is an average of nine services that helpers had provided to respondents in the previous 6 months: (1) doing light housekeeping, (2) storing seasonal clothing or doing cleaning or laundry, (3) keeping track of household bills, (4) doing small household repairs, (5) checking daily, (6) providing small household gifts, (7) taking respondents out for meals, (8) helping respondents keep in touch with relatives, and (9) cheering respondents up when feeling low.

5. The reader will recall from Chapter 4 that where older people had joint households with their adult helpers, the helpers were able to handle tasks that are normally difficult for kin to manage because of the need for proximity (e.g., light housekeeping and laundry).

6. "Higher-prestige" occupations for older people were all those occupations in the census classification of jobs that were above "craftsman." The same trends held for the helpers' occupations, with those holding a modified extended family orientation having 58% of their helpers in higher-prestige jobs, those having a nuclear family orientation having 55%, and those adhering to the traditional family orientation having 51%. Because of the radical differences in occupational structure between older people and their children, "higher-prestige" occupations for younger people consisted of those holding positions higher than clerical ones.

7. These findings may be confounded with those for occupation and education. However, such a confounding would not be spurious, but part of a causal path. I suggest such a path at the end of this chapter.

8. It should be clear that this statement does not challenge the various writers who have pointed out that the traditional family structure was not necessarily the norm in early industrial periods (Smelser, 1959; Furstenberg, 1966; Goode, 1963). What is being suggested is a milder statement—that is, that traditional family orientation would be more likely in the preindustrialized European and Latin American countries. In addition, these earlier writers often had to restrict themselves to measures of distance that involved those having common households versus those not having them. It would be expected that in a modern society distances between kinship group members must be much greater once one goes beyond the simple dichotomy of living in the same household or not. We (Litwak & Szelenyi, 1969) point out that people in a 1965 survey in a technologically more advanced society, the United States, were more likely to maintain family services over geographic distance than those in a technologically less advanced one (Hungary). The argument was made that this was the case because people in American society at that time (1965) were more likely to have automobiles and telephones.

9. The assimilated Americans consisted of all respondents who were born in the United

States and in answer to the following question said they did not identify with any group: "In addition to being an American, people sometimes think of themselves as a member of a nationality group, or cultural group, like Irish, Italian, Cuban, Puerto Rican, Jewish, black, and groups like that. Do you see yourself as part of any such group?" The West European group consisted of all people who lived in European countries west of those now included in the Communist sphere and not bordering on the Mediterranean. The only exception was France, which was included in the West European group. Also included in this group were England, Australia, New Zealand, and Canada. In the East European group were included all countries under the Communist sphere of influence, as well as all countries bordering on the Mediterranean. In the Latin American group were included all countries from South and Central America as well as the Caribbean. All other people were classified into a category called "others." This group was very small, given the fact that our sample came from people who were over 65 and lived in New York or Florida. There were two exceptions to the classification above. First, all people who on the question of ethnic identification or on a question of religion identified themselves as Jewish were classified as Jews, as were all people who said they were from Israel. Second, all people identified by interviewer observation as being black were classified as American black.

10. Lieberson (1980) makes a persuasive argument that American blacks should be classified by generation in terms of when they migrated to Northern urban areas. The 1978 survey does not provide the data to do this.

11. In this regard, it is important to note that for all groups the modified extended family was still the major family norm. This is a function of two factors. The people under discussion here were 65 and older, and though they were first-generation, they might well have been subject to powerful forms of socialization as a consequence of living in American society. Second, sociologists have pointed out that preindustrial societies in Europe had very substantial groups that did not adhere to the traditional family orientation (Smelser, 1959). As noted earlier, the present formulation simply speaks about a relative difference.

12. By "marital household services," I mean these four services: (1) light housekeeping, (2) doing laundry, cleaning, or storage of seasonal clothes, (3) keeping track of household bills, and (4) making small household repairs. By "normal kin services," I mean (1) talking to respondents when they were feeling low, (2) helping them keep in touch with relatives, (3) inviting respondents to dinner, (4) giving small household gifts to make a place more homey, and (5) checking on respondents daily to see if they were all right.

13. The assimilated Americans had 23% who delivered marital household services and 53% who delivered normal kin services. The West Europeans had the same for the first and 6% less for the second, while the Jewish group had the same for the first and 2% less for the second.

14. The average annual family income before taxes for each of the ethnic groups was as follows: Assimilated Americans, $6162; West Europeans, $6203; Jewish group, $5513; East European, $4707; Latin Americans, $4659; and American blacks, $3136.

15. This fact is well recognized for marital household units where both husbands and wives are in the labor force. It has been pointed out that one of the reasons that women may receive lower pay than men is because married women must give up their optimal career choices to follow those of their husbands (Marwell, Rosenfeld, & Spilerman, 1979). Think how much the problem is magnified if one is dealing with a kinship system that may have anywhere from 5 to 20 people in the labor force.

16. The poverty of blacks is in turn explained by racism (Lieberson, 1980; Steinberg, 1981), and there is good reason to believe that blacks, because of housing prejudice, are under much greater pressure to live close together (D. I. Warren, 1975).

17. The rate of increase is the difference in percentages between groups in the healthier state and those in immediately adjacent, less healthy states, divided by the percentage of those in the healthier state. The average rate is the average of these differences between two adjacent groups. The standardized rate is the average of these averages, giving each equal weight. The average rate for distance is compiled by subtracting the percentage of the most distant from the

percentage of the next closest and dividing by the most distant one. The rest is computed like that described for illness.

18. This is indicated by the amount of variance explained for each service. For the marital household services, it averages 33%, while for the normal kin services, it is 16%.

19. The betas for proximity fall on a continuum within the two groups.

20. Those responding "farther than 10 blocks" were asked how long it would take their helpers to come to their homes.

21. The rate of decline is the difference between the percentages on two adjacent points on a distance scale divided by the closest point. Once a percentage reaches 0% on the distance scale, the rate of decline is computed at 100%. This measure is intended to reflect two things. First, it provides a measure of the effect of distance independently of the frequency with which the service is provided under optimal circumstances (in this case, the same household). It is also intended to measure the speed at which a service reaches 0%, which means that there are no linear assumptions. No claim is made that these particular assumptions are universally necessary. For different purposes, different measures would be appropriate.

22. These standardized percentages have been derived from the regression coefficients in Table C-3 of Appendix C.

23. The problem is more complex than presented, since some services may be delivered by a mixture of technologies.

24. However, the empirical fact is that the 1978 survey really provides no hard and fast data on the use of various technologies and the extent to which specific groups were deprived. And in terms of social policy, a statement that 8% of this sample was deprived would be very important.

25. I have used education rather than income in this analysis for two reasons. First, for a substantial percentage of the sample, income figures could not be obtained for both the older persons and their helpers. Second, the same analysis was performed by income groups, with all the limitations, and it was found that the same patterns were better defined when education rather than income was used.

26. The educational levels of the helpers and the respondents were coded into four groups: 0–8 grades, 9–11 grades, 12 grades, and more than 12 grades. Their collective scores were added to give an overall education score. This rank-order correlation was significant at the .05 level for a one-tailed test of significance.

27. The estimate of time must be considered relative rather than absolute. For people living within 10 blocks, there was not a time measure, but a distance measure. The assumption was made that those who lived one block away would take 1 minute for travel, those who lived from one to five blocks away would take 5 minutes, and those who lived from 6 to 10 blocks away would take 10 minutes. Those who lived in the same house were assumed to be in instantaneous communication. Since the same assumptions were being made for well and poorly educated respondents and helpers, it is unlikely that a more precise measure would alter the direction of the findings. Following this same logic, those who had some high school lived 1 hour and 12 minutes away, while those who had graduated from high school lived on the average 1 hour and 24 minutes away.

28. What is especially interesting is that the educational effects of older people and their helpers were not additive. If either had a high-school education or if both had one, they tended to live the same distance apart.

29. These percentages were standardized to take account of the level of education, as well as whether the older persons were higher or lower than their helpers. The standardization was accomplished by giving equal weight to each cell in a contingency table that was composed of the helpers' and the respondents' education levels.

30. The rank-order correlation between agreements on style of life and level of education was a nonsignificant .39.

31. For those with two children (377), 49% received services, while of those (180) with three children, 53% received them.

32. The percentages for those with two and three children were 24% and 27%, respectively.

33. There was a .60 rank-order correlation between distance and affection—that is, the greater the distance, the more affectionate respondents were. This correlation was significant at the .05 level for a one-tailed test.

34. The data do not support the view that affection is simply a consequence of delivery of services. In the path model presented in the section below, it is shown that once proximity and other relevant variables are taken into account, affection relates to normal kin services but not to marital household ones. If affection were simply gratitude for services received, it would more likely relate to all services but especially to marital household ones, which require more effort and are given when the older person is in greatest need.

35. This path model has been simplified in several respects. First, only standardized betas significant at the .01 level and having a magnitude of .10 are presented. Second, categories have been collapsed and presented as though they were one (e.g., illness, marital state of respondents, proximity of the respondents, and ethnicity). The highest beta has been presented in such cases. Third, the direct effects of all variables, besides living in the same household, have been dropped except where there is evidence of systematic relationships. In those cases, the relationships have been drawn with dotted arrows. Fourth, no consideration has been given to most interactive effects or the assumption of two-way causality.

36. If one can assume that people who telephone weekly are basically delivering such services, while those seeing each other daily are delivering marital household services, and those telephoning monthly are delivering services that require distance, these alternative patterns of proximity can be illustrated. Thus, weekly telephone contacts are optimized when people live at a middle distance—that is, more than 10 blocks, but no more than 1 hour. The betas between this distance and weekly telephone calls range from .34 to .46. Those living closer have betas ranging between .24 and .27, while those living at a greater distance have betas ranging between .17 and .04.

By contrast, respondents who see their helpers daily follow the pattern indicated in our path model. The highest beta arises for those living in the same house, .72. It quickly drops to .21 for those living between one and five blocks away, and by the time one reaches the middle distance, the betas range from .12 to .02. At the farthest distance, the beta is .01. If making monthly telephone calls is examined, then it is the case that living very close is negatively related to contact, the beta being −.02. From this low point, the betas steadily increase with distance until the middle distance, where they range from .20 to .17. At the greatest distance, they drop off slightly but still remain higher than for those living very close (i.e., the betas range from .09 to .11).

37. This is partly a measurement problem. Of all the services, checking daily has the most linear relationship to distances. The marital household services tend to have a reverse "J" shape. As a result, the beta and the R^2 systematically underestimate the effects of proximity for those services. The measure of geographic decline is a better measure.

38. See footnote 37.

7

Ideal and Nonideal Forms of Marital Ties and Exchange: A Further Elaboration of the Principle of Matching

This chapter attempts to explore the structure of the marital dyad and its consequence for the kinship exchanges. The simplifying assumptions that helpers provide services without cost, that helpers have complete marital dyads, and that gender is not important in the delivery of services are now dropped. The principle of matching group and task structures is elaborated under these more complex circumstances. Three elements of the marital structure are stressed here: first, the fact that the marital dyad is an extremely small primary group with only two adults; second, the fact that as a structure it has a semiautonomous relationship to the rest of the kinship system (it is expected to exchange with other kinship units in some areas but to maintain its exclusivity in other areas); third, the fact that it is a bond based on cross-gender relations, with a tradition of a division of labor based on gender.

Among the advanced aged, these structural features lead to a major dilemma. Because of the first feature (i.e., small size), the advanced aged are very likely to have disabled marital household units, which means that they require help in household services. However, because of the second feature (i.e., semiautonomy), the other kin are not supposed to deliver household services; nor can they, without weakening their own marital units. The dilemma that confronts kinship systems is how to balance the needs of helpers' marital households against the needs of older persons' households in a situation where there is no ideal solution.

If kin systems did supply the marital household services, it would cause the helpers and their spouses to experience sharp conflicts between their occupational worlds and their kin. It would also mean a curtailment of the helpers' own household tasks, insofar as limited resources are withdrawn or attempts to incorporate older people into a joint household lead to diseconomies of large numbers.

The reader can get some insight into the problem by examining the literature on urban communes. These were "natural" experiments where people tried to create large primary groups to handle normal household functions. Two trends were generally reported (Houriet, 1971). First, people living in such urban communes could not engage in occupations that involved differential mobility among commune members. Members of such communes generally had to move to unskilled labor or home craft jobs. Alternatively, there were communes with high turnover rates, where it was difficult to get people to handle daily household services. What was perhaps more striking was the need to routinize everyday household tasks. Perhaps prototypical of the negative consequence of this routinization was the commune called "Harrad West" (Houriet, 1971). It was a commune that stressed the concept of group marriage. All men and women were supposed to love one another equally. To insure equality, the group of six was forced to make up a sleeping schedule, which was posted on the kitchen bulletin board. A group that had originally been created because it viewed the outer society as too regulated found itself scheduling personal behavior in a far more constrictive way because of its size.

Having pointed out the problems of trying to handle marital household activities within larger primary groups, it is nevertheless the case that many primary-group members might prefer this type of problem than the one that would ensue if an individual did not have a primary group at all. This is exactly the dilemma that confronts the older person who is sick and whose spouse is dead.

Of the various alternative theoretical models of kinship structure, it is only the modified extended family that systematically highlights the continual conflict engendered by the semiautonomous structure, such as the demand to balance the needs of a helper's household against those of an older person. For those who see the isolated conjugal unit as the "ideal" fit (Parsons, 1944) or advocate the centrality of the individual (Polsky & Duberman, 1979) there is in principle no conflict, since exchanges between marital units are not essential. For those who view the traditional kin structure as ideal, there is also no conflict in principle, because marital units in a kinship system share a common household and therefore there is no problem of household autonomy.

Costs to Helpers of Providing Services

The principle of matching group and task structures, as indicated in Chapter 5, suggests that to deal with the disabled marital household, one must ideally find a group that can duplicate it. However, the discussion in that chapter does not consider the conflict or cost to the helper or the structure of the helper's household. Let us begin this discussion with the cost to the helper of providing supplemental services. In order to get at the helper's sense of burden, helpers interviewed in the 1978 survey were asked:

> Does helping your parent put any great burden upon you and your family?
> Would you say it involves no sacrifice, minor sacrifice, some sacrifice, consider-
> able sacrifice, major sacrifice, or you can't do it at all?[1]

The first question to be asked is to what extent the sense of sacrifice increases
with the delivery of services. Is the answer not self-evident—that is, with
delivery comes sacrifice? The modified extended family theorist says, "No, it
is not self-evident." Delivery of normal kin services has few costs and leads
to many gains. It is only the delivery of marital household services to kin that
leads to major costs. And indeed this was what was found: The more the
helpers delivered marital household services, such as doing laundry and
light housekeeping, the greater the sense of sacrifice was.[2] Thus 22% of those
(485) who delivered one or more marital household services felt some
burden, compared to 12% of those (459) who delivered none. By contrast,
there was no greater feeling of burden when helpers delivered normal kin
services (e.g., cheering up older persons, providing small household gifts,
etc.); the percentages were 17% in each group.

A better understanding of the dynamics of exchange and sacrifice
requires the examination of the combination of the two types of exchanges.
This is the case because, as pointed out in Chapter 6, people almost always
supply the "emergency" household services within a context of providing
normal kin exchanges. The group of helpers with the highest percentage of
those feeling that help involves sacrifice were those who provided a combination of marital household services and normal kinship ones (22%). By
contrast, the helpers who provided only normal kinship exchanges had the
smallest percentage of those feeling that help involves sacrifice (11%). People
who provided neither type of service had a higher percentage feeling sacrifice
(17%). This does indeed suggest that the optimal state is achieved when one
delivers only normal kin services rather than none.[3] There were virtually no
people who provided only marital household services (only 4), so the consequences of this type of service delivery cannot be assessed. However, the
lack of such a combination is itself a confirmation of the modified extended
family construct.

A major reason why marital household services produce a sense of
burden is that, as indicated in Chapter 6, they require a common household
as well as much time and effort. To bring an older person into a helper's
household, or vice versa, will produce a great strain, given the autonomy
needs and the limited personal resources of the helper's marital unit. This
can be demonstrated by looking at the relationship between helpers' sense of
sacrifice and the proximity of the helpers to the older persons.

It is the case that the closer helpers lived to the older persons, the more
likely they were to have a sense of sacrifice when delivering services. Where
people lived in the same household, they had a greater sense of sacrifice [23%
(117)] than when they lived more than 30 minutes away [11% (304)]. The

discerning reader might well point out that the older persons living in the same household may have been sicker, and indeed it was this factor and not living in the same household that was crucial. When the same data are examined for older people who were matched on health status, it is still the case that where they shared a residence with their helpers, the helpers had a greater sense of burden. Thus, once health of the older person was held constant, 25% of the helpers who shared the same household said that providing service involves a sacrifice; 17% of the helpers who lived one to five blocks away said this; and 12% who lived more than six blocks away had this response. It is also true that where helpers were matched on how far away they lived, those providing service to older people who were sick and single always had a greater sense of sacrifice (24%) than those who provided service during intermediate stages of health (16%), as well as those who provided service to healthy and married older people (15%).

In other words, sharing a common household and illness of the older person contribute independently to the helper's sense of sacrifice. This is very clear if one looks at the two extreme groups. Among those helpers (34) who had older people who both lived in the same house and were single and ill, 41% said that providing services was a burden. In those cases (182) where the older person lived over five blocks away and was married and healthy, only 8% of the helpers felt this way.

Furthermore, if one also takes into account whether the helper delivered one or more marital household services, as well as the disability of the older person, it is still true that those helpers who lived in the same house as their older persons and delivered services had a greater sense of burden (26%) than those who delivered services and lived one to five blocks away (11%), or those who lived five or more blocks away (11%).[4] In short, there is some evidence that the sheer presence of an ill older person in the household leads to a sense of burden, even after one takes into account the amount of disability and whether services are provided. The data discussed above suggest a dynamic. When people become ill, they require more marital household services (i.e., 68% of the single and ill received such services, as opposed to 23% of the married and healthy). This in turn requires them to move closer to their helpers (i.e., 27% of those who were sick and single lived in the same household as their helpers, in contrast to 12% of the healthy and married). This in turn leads to the violation of the helpers' autonomy, which also increases their sense of burden.

Effects of Complete and Incomplete Marital Households
on the Helping Process

The analysis thus far has proceeded on the implicit assumption of a complete marital household of husband and wife. The question arises as to what might happen to the theoretical assertions if this assumption is dropped. What the modified extended family concept tells us is that the optimal family household structure is the marital dyad. However, it also provides the underlying dimensions of such a structure, and presumably any combination of people can be evaluated to see how closely they approximate the marital household unit. This in turn should permit one to make predictions about any combination of marital statuses resulting from interaction between helpers and older persons.

There are four possible combinations involving adult children and their parents: (1) The children and their parents can both be married, (2) the children can be married but the older persons single, (3) the older persons can be married but the children single, and (4) children and parents can both be single.

The question arises as to the structural properties of each of these combinations. Insofar as the combination consists of children and parents from the same unit of procreation, then all members will have long-term commitments based on past reciprocities. However, where a child helper is married, then there is introduced into the primary group one person who is less likely to have a sense of long-term reciprocity—that is, the spouse of the helper. The spouse has not received the 20 years or so of care that the parents have provided for the child. Where either the older person or the helper is a single person, there is an additional characteristic that has to be taken into account. The single-person household has limited human resources, and there is an incentive for it to join another to optimize the delivery of marital household tasks. This contrasts with the marital dyad, where the inclusion of others produces diseconomies of large size.

How do these two factors of commitment and optimum size affect the process of exchange? First, where there is an exchange between parent and child and both are single, there may be a strong incentive for them to form a joint household, because they both can benefit from the commitment and optimal size of a normal two-person household. From a structural point of view, such a dyad will be perfectly in tune with the larger society's needs for differential mobility and the short-term needs of exchanges. It is not possible as a regular long-term pattern for society, since it lacks the ability to deal with procreation, and because of age disparities the household is faced with asymmetry in its long-term commitment. The child would have no partner from his or her middle age through years of retirement.

It can be further stated that where there are two marital dyads in the same household, there will be the greatest probability of socially based friction. First, it would represent the largest number of people in a household, and thus would lead to loss of economies on a small scale. It would also be the greatest threat to differential mobility, because it represents the potential of four people in the labor force. Finally, it includes within its midst one person, the spouse of the child, who may have no long-term reciprocal relations with the helper's parents.[5] All of these factors prevent two marital dyads from forming a joint household, which in turn makes the delivery of household services to the older persons more difficult.

Given this analysis of the two extreme groups, what can be said about the mixed cases—that is, the situations where the older person is married and the helper is single, as contrasted with that where the helper is married and the older person is single? Of these two combinations, the first is more likely to lead to a joint household, because it consists of people who have all emerged from the same biological family and therefore share long-term commitments. It is the smallest household unit next to the two-person marital dyad. In addition, it suffers least from problems of differential mobility because both older people are likely to be retired, leaving only one person in the labor force. It is more likely to insure the delivery of marital household services than where the unit consists of the younger marital dyad and a single older person, because one member of this latter group is unlikely to have a sense of long-term reciprocity and may be in the labor force, doubling the chance of a move. It must be understood that this analysis defies the common-sense probabilities, because the largest pool of people consists of married younger persons and single older persons.

With these thoughts in mind, let us first examine the probabilities of each of these units forming a joint household. This is crucial, because it has been demonstrated that joint households (i.e., where parents and adult children share a common residence) are much more likely to be able to deliver marital household services. The probabilities of people in each combination forming a joint household, as assessed in the 1978 study, ranged from 29% for the cases (278) where both helpers and older persons were single, to 24% for the cases (133) where the helpers were single and the older persons were married, to 10% for the cases (508) where the helpers were married and the older persons were single, to 4% for the cases (372) where both helpers and older persons were married. The reader will recall that, in the path model of all the factors contributing to the establishment of a common household (see Figure 6-3), the marital status of the helper was the most powerful (beta = .32).

This formulation also predicts that single helpers should be more likely to deliver marital household tasks than married ones, because they live closer. The 1978 data show that among the single helpers, an average of 35% delivered marital household services, as contrasted with 23% of the married ones. However, the superiority of the single-person helper in delivering marital household services almost completely evaporated once the married and single were matched on distance between older persons and helpers. When they were matched on distance, the figures were 33% and 36%. This is illustrated in the path model with arrows going from marital status to proximity but not directly to service. It is important to recognize that none of the other models of kin structure can highlight the unique importance of the single helper.[6]

The question might well be asked whether the single person is not under greater strain than the married couple. In order to examine this issue, single and married helpers have been compared according to the stage of the older persons' marital disability and the number of marital household services received. What is found (see Table 7-1) is that the single and married persons had approximately the same sense of sacrifice, once the people they were helping were matched on disability and whether they were receiving services or not (16% for married and 12% for single). If anyone had a greater sense of burden, it was the married helpers. What Table 7-1 also tends to show are the autonomous effects of marital status in producing friction. Thus, among helpers who delivered no marital household services, the ones who felt the greatest tension were those helping older persons who were married and healthy (15%). The helpers of the sick and single manifested the least tension (4%). By sharp contrast, among those who delivered marital household services, it was not the marital state but the degree of illness that led to the

Table 7-1. Percentages of Helpers Saying Help Involves Sacrifice, According to Marital Status of the Helpers, Stage of Disability of the Older Persons, and Number of Marital Household Services Received

Older Persons' Stage of Disability	Percentage Saying Help Involves Sacrifice		
	Married	Single	Total
Helpers Provided No Marital Household Services			
Married and healthy	15 (131)	7 (36)	13 (167)
Married and ill or single and healthy	10 (117)	12 (41)	11 (158)
Single and ill	4 (28)	4 (12)	4 (40)
Helpers Provided One or More Services			
Married and healthy	16 (52)	16 (25)	16 (77)
Married and ill or single and healthy	21 (114)	8 (51)	17 (165)
Single and ill	27 (52)	22 (45)	25 (97)
Standardized for illness and service delivery by averaging the percentages in each column and giving equal weight to each one	16 (494)	12 (210)	

Note. The populations for the subgroups appear in parentheses.

greatest sense of burden. Thus 16% of the helpers delivering services to married couples who were married and healthy had a sense of burden, while 25% of those delivering services to those who were single and ill felt a burden.[7]

The role of marital status is further illuminated if the status of helpers is also considered. Thus the maximum tension was experienced by helpers who did not deliver services when both they and the older persons were married (15%). For those delivering services, the maximum tension arose when the helpers were married and the older persons were sick and single (27%).

From the viewpoint of resources, it is a paradox that the single helper can provide more services, but has the same or less of a sense of burden as the married helper. Why should not the married helper have less of a sense of burden, since presumably there are two people and therefore more resources? The answer I have suggested is that the helper who is married may see the provision of household services to kin as directly competitive with his or her marital needs. The single helper is much more likely than the married helper to form a household unit with the older person that matches the ideal marital household state. It is this functional substitute for the marital unit and not the fact of the helper's being single that is significant.

This same point can be demonstrated even more dramatically if attention is focused on the structure of the older person's household unit. The ability of the marital unit to prevent institutionalization is a measure of its power to deliver marital household services (Townsend, 1965; Palmore, 1976). To emphasize the importance of the two-person marital unit, an index was constructed of the respondents' disabilities. The index included the ability to perform everyday activities (e.g., shopping, managing stairs, and taking public transportation), as well as direct physical handicaps, such as the ability to see, hear, or speak, or missing limbs.[8] All respondents were also classified according to their marital status (i.e., widowed, divorced, separated, or never married). People in the community were compared with those in institutions for each combination of marital status and disability. This allowed for the probability of people from each combination in this sample being institutionalized.[9] The power of the marital dyad can be seen in the very low probability of members of a complete marital household being institutionalized until the very extreme of disability was reached. In Table 7-2, it can be seen that only 4% were institutionalized among the married older persons who were at or below the 27th percentile on the disability scale. By contrast, 10% of the single people in this score range were institutionalized. In the 28th–38th percentile range of the disability scale, 3% of the married were institutionalized, while 32% of the single group were so placed. In the 39th–59th percentile range, 6% of the married were institutionalized, while this was true of 30% of the single group. In the 59th–86th percentile range on the scale, 13% of the married and 47% of the single were institutionalized. Finally, among the most severely disabled people—that is, those above the

Table 7-2. Percentages of Older Persons Institutionalized, According to Disability Score and Marital Status

| | Percentage Institutionalized | | | | | |
| | Disability Score | | | | | |
Marital Status	0 (below 27th Percentile)	1–3 (28th–38th Percentile)	4–7 (39th–59th Percentile)	8–15 (59th–86th Percentile)	16+ (87th–100th Percentile)	Total
Married	4 (209)	3 (112)	6 (127)	13 (92)	22 (41)	6 (581)
Not married	10 (336)	32 (128)	30 (262)	47 (327)	40 (177)	30 (1230)

Note. The populations for the subgroups appear in parentheses.

87th percentile on the scale—22% of the married and 40% of the single were institutionalized.[10] To put it somewhat differently, just over three times as many single people as married in this sample were institutionalized, even when disability is standardized (10% vs. 32%). That is indeed a very impressive statement of the power and importance of the marital dyad for delivering household services.

One further point is highly revealing of the limits of marital household structure. If the rates of institutionalization of three groups of single people are compared, a very puzzling pattern emerges. Those who were widowed (937) had the lowest average rate of institutionalization (30%), while the divorced (144) had the next lowest rate (36%), and those never married (149) had the highest rate (40%). This remains the case even when the figures are standardized for disability (the respective standardized percentages being 24%, 29%, and 32%).

One of the speculations made by many investigators in the past is that those who were never married have learned how to live as single persons and therefore can handle the problems of being single better than widows can. Yet the 1978 data show the reverse pattern. The answer to this seeming paradox is that there are two elements other than medical disabilities that must be considered in estimating institutionalization. First is the older person's ability to live alone, and second is the question of primary-group resources available to the older person faced with illness. There is strong evidence that having primary-group resources is crucial in health (Berkman & Syme, 1979). In that regard, the process by which an older person becomes a single person is central. It can be argued that it is the widowed who have the highest probability of finding a helper among their kin. The widow has the following groups from which to choose: children, her own relatives, and her in-laws (Lopata, 1979). Those never married have the least probability of finding a helper. That is, they are least likely to have children, and they do not have in-laws. Friends, who are central when they are younger, may not

have the necessary resources when older unless they form a common household. Those who are divorced may not have any in-laws because of the
bitterness of the divorce, and may have a lesser probability than the widowed
of having children or children who are not alienated.

However, aid is a function not only of resources, but of need. All single
households have greater need than married ones. If both the need for kin aid
and the availability of kin are taken into account, we would expect the
widowed group to have the most household family help, the other singles to
have the next most, and the married group to have the least. It is of some
interest to see that the widows in the 1978 study (476) were the most likely to
receive marital household forms of support (34%); this figure was twice as
much as the 16% of the married persons (296), as well as higher than the 20%
of the divorced respondents (33), the 24% of the separated (21), and the 26% of
those who were never married (53).

The same line of reasoning would lead to different predictions for normal
kinship services, because characteristic of this type of service is the fact that
the marital dyad has normal need of them. Even though the widows still
received more normal kinship services than the married group (61% vs. 53%),
the advantage was smaller, and the married group received more than the
never married (46%) and separated (49%) and almost as much as the divorced
(59%).

What is important is not only that the concept of a modified extended
family structure and the principle of matching permit one to differentiate
between two-person and one-person households, but that one can differentiate which type of single-person household will receive aid, as well as the
nature of aid that most clearly distinguishes the single-person household
from the married one.

This principle of matching can be further demonstrated by contrasting
kin aid to married couples, to those living with nonspouses who were also
not helpers (e.g., a common-law spouse was defined as a spouse, not a
helper), to those living alone, and to those living with kin helpers such as
children. It can be shown that those living alone require more kin help than
those living with someone else. A second point is that the proximity of
helpers also affects the kind of services delivered. To highlight the need to
match the structure of the group with that of the tasks, all services have been
classified into four categories, based on their empirical relation to proximity
(see Table 7-3). Thus the household tasks have been split into two groups,
those requiring very close proximity (light housekeeping and laundry) and
those requiring less continual proximity (doing small household repairs,
keeping track of Social Security checks, etc.). The normal kin services have
also been divided into two groups: those that involve telephoning frequently
or face-to-face contact, and those that involve little proximity. It is assumed
that single older people need services requiring proximity most but that such
services can only be received from those who are very close, while for the

Table 7-3. Percentages of Noninstitutionalized Older Persons Receiving Services, According to Living Arrangements

Type of Services Received by Older Persons from Kin	Living with Spouse (n = 250)	Living with Someone— Not Spouse, Not Helper (n = 37)	Living Alone (n = 259)	Living with Helper (n = 111)
Percentage Receiving Services				
Household Services Requiring Very Close Proximity				
Doing light housekeeping	14	11	12	85
Doing seasonal storage, laundry, or cleaning	11	16	15	79
Average	13	14	14	82
Household Services Requiring Moderate Proximity				
Keeping track of household bills and Social Security checks	7	14	28	55
Doing small household repairs	17	20	34	84
Average	12	17	31	70
Normal Kin Exchanges Requiring Some Proximity				
Checking daily to see if all right	44	46	49	98
Inviting older persons out for meal or bringing over meal	48	62	59	81
Providing small household gifts	44	43	41	80
Helping keep in touch with relatives	51	49	46	77
Average	47	50	49	84
Normal Kin Exchange Requiring Little Proximity				
Talking to older persons when feeling low and cheering them up	77	81	81	93

tasks that do not require proximity the single people's needs are only modestly greater than those of married persons, and helpers who are close provide only modest advantages over helpers who are distant.

In Table 7-3, the effects of the interaction between the structure of the marital dyad and the nature of tasks can be seen. First, for tasks that require the most proximity (i.e., daily or weekly contact), it can be seen that the only group materially affected by kinship aid was that of respondents whose helpers lived in the same household (i.e., on the average, 82% received such help). The fact that older persons living alone need as much if not more help did not much matter if the helpers did not live in the immediate vicinity (i.e.,

14% of those living alone received such help). The fact that married persons living together did not receive this help is understandable, since as members of marital dyads they did not need it (i.e., 13% received such help). What is of course very interesting is that those who lived with friends also did not receive help (i.e., 14% received such help). According to the theory of substitutions, they did not receive help because they did not need it. However, it is hard to establish this fact with items that require high proximity.

To establish this point therefore necessitates some item that requires considerable proximity, but not so much that only people who live in the same household can manage it. The second category of household items— that is, those that have to be performed on a weekly or monthly basis—serves this purpose. An examination of this category shows, as would be expected, that those who lived in the same household as their helpers still received by far the most services (70%). However, now the group of those living alone is clearly differentiated from married couples or people who live with someone else, such as friends. Thus 31% of those living alone received such services, while 12% of the married couples and 17% of those living with others did. I take this as evidence for the fact that where some functional substitute can be found for a marital dyad (i.e., someone to live in the same household), the need for marital household help can be reduced.

But it must be recalled that this analysis assumes that the tasks being discussed require close proximity, long-term commitment, and small group sizes. A task that does not require close proximity and can be economically provided in a large group, but does require long-term commitment, is a service that both marital dyads and single-person households should receive in almost the same amounts. Living in the same household as the helper will have far less impact on the delivery of such tasks. Thus in Table 7-3 it can be seen that for such a task (talking to older persons when they felt low and cheering them up), those who were not married and living alone had almost the same percentage as those who were married and living together (i.e., 77% vs. 81%). Furthermore, the single persons who lived alone had the same rate as those who were single and living with friends (81%). What is most distinctive about this task is the fact that those living with their helpers had a much smaller advantage over other married or single household groups and that all groups received the service. If the services in Table 7-3 are ranked from those most demanding of proximity to those least demanding, the advantage of living with helpers over against the next highest group is 68%, 39%, 35%, and 12%. This is also indicated in the path analysis (see Figure 6-3).

In Table 7-3, I have tried to highlight several points about exchanges. First, the amount of kinship aid one receives depends, first, on the structure of the household, and, second, on the structure of the task. I have shown that where people do not have a marital dyad or its functional equivalent (friends or relatives sharing the same household), then they are unlikely to get kin to provide household services unless their kin helpers live in the same household. I have further argued that marital groups or their functional equivalent do not receive such aid because, under the modified extended family concept, such forms of aid are best handled within the household unit as long as the household unit is a marital dyad or its equivalent. Finally, I have argued that where the tasks have the structure of normal kinship exchanges, all older people will receive them, regardless of their household structures or their distance from their helpers.

If these findings were taken by themselves, there would be a great temptation to argue that children and their spouses should take in older parents who have become ill and widowed. But what must be remembered is the earlier set of findings showing that where a helper takes an older person into his or her household, it involves greater tension for the helper. More generally, a married couple taking someone into the household has two basic costs: first, the cost of trying to handle household tasks with larger numbers, and second, the cost of trying to deal with an occupational world that may require helpers of older persons to have differential occupational and geographic mobility. This translates for the helper into issues of having to move to places that are not beneficial to the older person, and of engaging in a style of life that the older person cannot really approve of or understand. The mechanism that kin ordinarily use to cross class and generational lines (i.e., keeping kin and friends separate) may be difficult to employ when kin are also part of one's household. Finally, from the point of view of social policy, there are severe stresses put on concepts of merit and open-class societies when parents must take it as a matter of course that they will eventually end up living with their children. With such expectations, parents will have far greater incentives than now to intervene in the occupational and social careers of their offspring so as to insure a proper home for themselves when they are older. Thus the initial view that the chronically ill can be cared for most effectively in the same household with their children or helpers must be treated with caution. Sussman's pioneering work (1980), which attempts to assess the immediate monetary costs of such care, must be interpreted in light of the fact that he made no attempt to measure the social and psychological costs of joint households.

The Division of Labor by Gender and
the Helping Process

So far in the analysis, the simplifying assumption has been made that both members of the marital dyad (in the case of married helpers) deliver help to the older person. However, the path model (see Figure 6-3) and the work of previous investigators have made clear that in a modern industrial society women are the ones who predominantly provide kinship services (Sweetser, 1966, 1968; Adams, 1971). If, indeed, husbands and wives have specialized roles in their marital household activities, then providing functional substitutes to older families who can no longer handle marital household tasks might also call for gender specialization among the providers. The burden of handling the resultant dilemma may belong solely to women. With this in mind, let us review the theoretical arguments for and against gender role differentiation.

One group has argued that with the shift from an agricultural society to a modern industrial one, there has been a separation of place of work from the family (Sweetser, 1966). In many agricultural societies of the past, if older people were to receive help, they had to be close to those family members who were the main breadwinners, since home and work were joined. Since males often inherited property, it was necessary for older people to live near or with male children, even though their wives might provide the actual services. A classic illustration of this point is Arensberg and Kimball's (1940) study of the Irish farmer. What Sweetser (1966, 1968) and others (Adams, 1971) have pointed out is that in a modern society, the formal institutions take care of many basic needs of the older person (basic income and basic medical support), and that therefore what older persons need is help in the traditional household activities. That is, they need someone to provide some help in shopping, some ad hoc nursing when they become sick, occasional help in housework, occasional chauffeuring to doctors or leisure activities, occasional psychological support when they are feeling low, and so forth. Women still provide these services, except that now because of separation of work and home, women are more likely to control the home. Therefore, in a modern society, one must be close to daughters if one requires kin support.

To this analysis of Sweetser must be added the analysis of Komarovsky (1953). Komarovsky starts from the fact that in American society of the 1930s and 1940s, the woman was the chief socializer of children through their adolescent years. As such, it meant that daughters had a more direct role model (i.e., that of housewife) than sons. Because of this direct role modeling, a special identification grew up between daughters and mothers.[11] Komarovsky implicitly accepts the argument that women manage household activities, and to it adds the idea that daughters will have special affinities to mothers in the kinship exchange processes. The empirical evidence supports the proposition that mothers and daughters do indeed tend to have more kinship exchanges than any other pairing (Adams, 1971).

One other body of literature must be added to this analysis. In the 1940s through the 1950s (perhaps culminating in the year 1960), a series of studies sought to show that men and women did different things in the home. At issue was not only the simple distinction between men being the main breadwinners and women being housewives, but, rather, the existence of specialized roles for men and women within the family activities (Blood & Wolfe, 1960; Adams, 1971). Thus women mended clothes and did the cooking and housecleaning, while men did small household repairs (e.g., fixing the faucets, putting up curtain rods, moving heavy furniture). The men also did household maintenance (e.g., cutting the lawn, taking care of the automobile, etc.). This analysis would suggest that in any family exchange, men would handle some problems and women others. Several studies have suggested that parents do indeed receive different forms of help from sons than from daughters (Lopata, 1979). Perhaps most persuasive in this line of inquiry are studies that were done on family decision-making power. These studies, which began with the question as to who exercised overall power in the family, concluded in the late 1960s that men and women each exercised power, but in different areas of life (Safilios-Rothschild, 1971). It would be my hypothesis that this finding reflected the fact that there was a role division within family activities. By doing a cross-cultural comparison as Strodtbeck (1951) did, it was possible to highlight the modern American pattern of role division, as opposed to cultures that stress patriarchal authority and matriarchal authority.

There are two competing theoretical formulations that can incorporate these speculations and empirical findings. The first is that of Parsons (1944), who pointed out that intrinsic to a modern society must be a permanently gender-linked division of labor. Such a division would permit the isolation of the primary group from the formal institutions of work. Parsons contended that such isolation was necessary in order to prevent nepotistic family norms from being introduced into the work situation (e.g., husband and wife helping each other). He also argued that such an arrangement made it possible for the family to be moved geographically and socially, based on the rational needs of formal organizations for allocating labor, since there were no conflicting career demands. Furthermore, it prevented occupational norms (such as invidious status competition) from being introduced into the family.[12]

An opposing position called "role substitutability" was suggested later (Litwak & Figueira, 1970). Role substitutability entails the notion that men and women should have the same range of roles. At any given moment in time, they may have some division of labor. What is central is that these divisions are never permanent or viewed invidiously; furthermore, they may be reversed at any point in time. It was argued that Parsons's (1944) formulation does not recognize that advanced states of science and technology work against any permanent gender-linked division of labor, because some activities are continually being removed from the family while others are being put back (Litwak & Figueira, 1970; Foote & Cottrell, 1955). This has been discussed in Chapter 2. As a result, technology is continually shifting family activities, and thus a permanent role division based on gender is antithetical to modern society. Studies that document this proposition show that norms on traditional gender roles are changing (Giele, 1978) toward greater overlap in roles. Furthermore, several studies suggest that marriages most likely to survive major shifts in roles are those in which spouses have greatest role flexibility (Litwak, Count, & Hayden, 1960; Komarovsky, 1940; Angell, 1936/1965).

To the problems of change introduced by science and technology must be added the special problems of change introduced into older people's lives by the family life cycle. For the older person whose spouse is too frail to manage his or her role, or who has died, there are strong imperatives to take over the spouse's roles or, in turn, to perish or be institutionalized (Cameron, 1968; Neugarten, 1964). A permanent gender-linked division of labor is clearly dysfunctional for the aged. It would be my argument that the only gender role structure consistent with the idea of rapid shifts in marital household tasks is that of "role substitutability" or "role flexibility" (Litwak & Figueira, 1970).

I believe that pressures for such a concept of flexible role divisions are quite consistent with the moral imperatives of equity. The concept does not forego the idea that primary groups are important or that marital dyads are specifically important. It simply says that there is no reason in principle to argue that division of labor for men and women is permanently fixed. However, there is some reason to argue that in the recent past and to some extent in the present, men and women have been socialized so that women perform the bulk of household services.

For instance, Parsons (1944) was right in pointing out that a family with two major careers faces great pressures, because occupational demands often require spouses to locate in different cities (Mincer, 1978; Marwell et al., 1979). This systematic pressure is probably one reason why a considerable number of modern marriages tend to have one major career, even though both husband and wife may be in the labor force. However, Parsons was wrong in not noting the possible institutional changes that might moderate such pressures.[13]

Parsons was also correct in pointing out that there is invidious status competition between husbands and wives (Rapoport & Rapoport, 1976). However, there is good reason to believe that this invidious status competition is not intrinsic to the occupational system, but is based on attitudes derived from an earlier state of technology that is rapidly changing[14] (Litwak & Figueira, 1970).

There is yet one other pressure for a sex-linked division of labor: Having one person rather than two to manage most of the household tasks may be more effective. This may be the case because household activities are characterized by great nonuniformity, as well as by the fact that they occur within the same geographic boundaries and same time periods, which means that it is not efficient to divide them up. Thus, for example, shopping for food is often best done in conjunction with shopping for household cleaning supplies, since they are both located in the same stores. Furthermore, it is most likely that the cook and the cleaner will have the kinds of supplies they need when they need them if they also purchase the supplies. Since cooking and cleaning in turn take place in the same house, it is often functional for the same person to handle the two tasks. A division of labor is generally justified not because it is more efficient for household services, but because it is more efficient for husbands and wives to maintain occupational careers.

To argue that there are pressures for a division of labor within the family is not to argue that such divisions are permanently linked to gender roles. Rather, the evidence on changing male and female norms, the institutional changes that permit entry of women into the labor force on a more equal basis, the fact that primary groups other than the conjugal unit are viable—all these suggest that the current division of labor is a transitional one. As such, it is more consistent with the concept of "role substitutability" than with a permanent sex-linked division of labor. Currently society seems to be moving toward a stage where it is recognized that the family may be crucial for many nonuniform tasks, but that either men or women can manage them. However, the empirical and theoretical literature suggests that if one has to choose who is currently more likely to maintain kinship exchanges in industrial society, then it is likely to be women.

The data from the 1978 survey suggest that gender roles are changing, which is consistent with the principle of role substitutability for men and women. To clarify this issue, it is necessary once again to introduce the concept of race–ethnicity and to recall that two groups (the Latin Americans and the East Europeans) consisted mostly of first-generation immigrants from less industrialized societies.[15] The Latin American group contained 99% who were first-generation immigrants, and the East Europeans had 78%. By contrast, the West Europeans had 52%, the Jewish group had 44%, and the blacks had 8% who were first-generation. If modern society is moving toward a more flexible definition of gender role, then the assimilated Americans should be least likely to have differences in the provision of marital services between male and female helpers, while the Latin Americans and the East Europeans should be most likely. That is precisely what the 1978 data show. The female helpers among the Latin American group were 13% more likely to deliver services than the male helpers (30% vs. 43%). The East European female helpers were 10% more likely than males to deliver services (35% vs. 45%), while among the Jewish group, the West Europeans, and the assimilated Americans, the superiority of female helpers was 7%, 7%, and 4%, respectively. The American blacks were more likely to have services delivered by male helpers (25%), but given the small numbers of blacks involved[16] and the lack of a self-evident rationale, I offer no explanation for this result. It could be argued that these findings spuriously reflect income—that is, that ethnics are poorer, and poor people use women for kin ties. The path model (see Figure 6-3) suggests that this is not the case. It should also be pointed out that the American blacks, who were poorest of all, did not have more help from women helpers.

In short, there is good reason to conclude (1) that in the recent past there was a "traditional division of labor" between men and women; (2) that this is part of an ongoing shift in gender roles; and (3) that this shift is consistent with the view that "role flexibility" is a necessary feature of a modern industrial society. At the same time, it is necessary to acknowledge that because of "culture lag" there may be many who still adhere to that traditional view, as well as that some division of labor, if not the traditional one, may still be encouraged under the present state of technology.

Granted the empirical fact that studies do show that women provide most kinship services, what are the probabilities that such a division will lead to women's bearing the entire cost of the institutional conflict that arises when the kin provide marital household services? There are three reasonable speculations that seem to follow. First, if the woman is the chief provider, she may also feel the greatest burden. Second, this burden will be increased if she has to provide services that are inconsistent with the female role. Finally, the conflict will be most severe if the woman has to deliver marital household services rather than normal kin services.

One additional comment and one major modification should be made on the speculations given above. For women to help older persons who are disabled is no small feat, given the increasing life span of the chronically ill aged. Such help may involve far more work for longer periods of time than most helpers are aware of (Rix & Romashko, 1980). If this demand remains unnoticed socially, it could lead to self-blame and animosity as people assume personal responsibility for the stress produced by larger social forces. An illustration of this same process already exists in women's entrance into the job market. It has led to some reduction in their household responsibilities, but not enough to compensate for the time spent in the labor force. The resultant stress (i.e., working women's having two full-time obligations) often leads to personal feelings of inadequacy, rather than to a judgment that society has not provided institutional support (Giele, 1978).

The modification of the analysis above is the hypothesis that even though women are the direct providers, they must require the indirect help of their spouses if they are in turn to deliver marital household services. As I have noted, marital household services require close proximity in order to be delivered effectively. In the most extreme case, if a woman brings an older person into her home, she needs her spouse's acceptance and a willingness to alter or even lower his life style to accommodate the "extra" person who is disabled.[17] This is a very important elaboration of past findings that show that women are more likely to provide direct services.

Let us begin the empirical analysis of gender roles with this point in mind. In the 1978 survey, helpers who were married were asked:

Considering you and your spouse, who is the one who generally keeps in contact with (INSERT NAME OF PARENT)? Would that be (1) you mostly, (2) your spouse, or (3) both equally?

Female respondents were more likely than males to say that they themselves kept in contact [78% (306) vs. 46% (193)]. It is also the case that women helpers almost never asked their husbands to manage the contact with the older persons (4%), while the male helpers asked their wives over four times as often (17%). Similarly, the male helpers were much more likely than the female helpers to share with their spouses the management of contact with the older persons (38% vs. 18%).

This pattern of findings could be anticipated on the basis of past studies. However, what was not expected was that helpers who said that their spouses shared the management of contact of older people were also more likely to deliver services. Thus, for helpers who had spouses who shared the management of contact (128), 35% delivered marital household services to older people in the community. Among those who said they managed contact with older people on their own (325), 20% delivered services, while among those who said their spouses handled the contact with the older persons (44), 19% delivered such services. With one exception, the same pattern held for both male and female helpers (see Table 7-4).

The underlying dynamics of this finding are very much the same as those that explain the ability of single helpers to provide more help than married helpers. To deliver marital household services, the helpers must be proximate to the older persons. Where the helpers and their spouse share management of contact equally, they are more likely to be living in the same house as the older person or within a five-block radius. Thus 23% of the helpers whose spouses shared equally in the management of contact with the older person (128) lived in the same house as the older person. This contrasts with those helpers who managed the kin tie by themselves (325), of whom 6% lived in the same house. It also contrasts with those whose spouses handled the contact alone (44), of whom 2% lived in the same house. One of the major differences between this finding and a parallel one showing that single helpers lived closer than married helpers is that one must ask of married helpers how their spouses would react to an older person's moving into the household. It is hard to conceive that the spouses will not be affected by such a decision, and their cooperation must be given if helpers are to arrange such a move.

At the same time, there is also a gender factor, as suggested by Sweetser (1966, 1968) and the path model (see Figure 6-3). The 1978 data show that the married female helpers were twice as likely to live closer to the older persons they helped than the married male helpers [13% (305) vs. 26% (192)]. Even among the helpers who shared the management of the older persons

Table 7-4. Percentages of Noninstitutionalized Older Persons Receiving Household Services, According to Sex Type of Services, Who Kept in Contact with Older Persons, and Gender and Marital Status of Helpers

Type of Services Received	Percentage Receiving Services			
	Helpers Married			Helpers Not Married
	Helpers Alone	Helpers' Spouses	Helpers and Spouses Equally	
Mostly Female Tasks				
Doing light housekeeping				
Male	05	07	12	31
Female	18	18	57	41
Doing laundry, cleaning, storage				
Male	08	03	18	28
Female	22	18	57	35
Mixed Male and Female Task				
Checking bills, Social Security checks, etc.				
Male	13	24	15	28
Female	20	46	33	30
Mostly Male Task				
Doing small household repairs				
Male	27	31	48	53
Female	26	27	53	34

Note. Population bases for subgroups:

Male	(87)	(32)	(73)	(51)
Female	(238)	(12)	(55)	(138)

These numbers vary slightly, depending on the nonanswers for each item.

with their spouses, it was true that women helpers were more likely to live in the same household with the older persons than male helpers [i.e., 40% (55) vs. 11% (73)]. It is still the case that male helpers who shared management with their spouses lived closer to their parents than male helpers who did not share management with their spouses. Thus, 11% of male helpers who shared management (73) lived in the same household with the older persons, while 3% of those who managed on their own (87) and 0% of those who turned the management over to their wives (32) lived in the same household with the older persons they were helping. Among wives who shared the management of contact with their husbands, 40% (55) lived in the same household, while this was true of 7% (238) who managed the contact alone and 8% (12) who turned the contact over to their husbands.

Three points are being made. First, those who can get support from their spouses (be they men or women) are more likely to deliver marital household services. Second, women are more likely to provide direct services than men. Third, this superiority of women is based on the indirect support of the spouses in permitting them to move their older parents into the same household or nearby. It has long been known that women play the major role in dealing with kin. What is new and is therefore being stressed in this discussion is the extent to which women become dependent on their husbands if they are to help older people in the second and third stages of their disability (i.e., when they are sick and live alone). For those men who seek to deliver services directly to their parents, the same point is made—that is, they will become very dependent on their wives' cooperation as the elderly enter the second and third stages of disability. But this is a more obvious finding.

It is not only the case that the woman is the chief provider of aid; as others have shown, the wife is more likely to choose her own parents rather than her husband's parents as the ones to whom she will provide aid (Rix & Romashko, 1980). A possible reason is that the woman is likely to have had a long term reciprocal tie with her own parents (i.e., from childhood through adolescence and early adulthood). Her wishes will also dominate because she is the major provider of household services that are basically nonuniform and therefore cannot be easily observed. This means that the husband cannot easily control these activities.

One qualification of this analysis is that though women are more likely to manage the contact with older people, there are some areas where men are socially mandated to help. For instance, the four marital household tasks used in the 1978 study can be graded in terms of fitting traditional female sex roles as follows: Doing light housekeeping and doing laundry are the most feminine; keeping track of household bills and Social Security checks is "neutral"; and doing small household repairs (e.g., repairing furniture) is least feminine. Women helpers in the 1978 study were more likely to deliver light housekeeping and laundry services than men (i.e., 26% of the women helpers did this, while 14% of the men did it). They had about an equal chance of keeping track of bills and Social Security checks (i.e., 23% of the women helpers did this, and 21% of the male helpers did it). Men were slightly more likely than women to provide small household repairs (i.e., 34% of the male helpers did this, while 28% of the female helpers did it). This finding is also supported by evidence provided by Rix and Romashko (1980) and Lopata (1979), as well as the path model (see Figure 6-3), which also controls for most other factors.

However, sex role distinctions seem to break down when a great need for help arises (as in the case of disabled older persons). In such cases, women also take over tasks generally assigned to males. Thus among older persons who were healthy and married, 30% of those with male helpers (185) received home repair services, while 13% of those with female helpers (244) received such services. However, where the older persons were sick and single, the reverse occurred. Those with female helpers received more such home repair services [50% (152)] than those with male helpers [43% (90)]. This reversal may have been caused by the fact that the larger magnitude of help required both time flexibility and very strong role commitments. For males, kin help may be secondary to occupational concerns even in male areas of kin exchange. It can also be seen that female helpers did even more than male helpers in providing female-type household services when the older persons were sick and living alone. Thus the average difference between men and women helpers in providing female-type services was 20% (44% for women minus 24% for men) when the older persons were sick and lived alone. When the older persons were well and married, then the average difference between men and women was 9% (18% for women minus 9% for men).

Such role reversals on the part of the women helpers could involve extra social strains. The empirical data show a small trend in this direction. Females who took over the male role of small household repairs had a slightly higher percentage of those who said that help involves sacrifice (25%) than those handling traditional female roles, such as housekeeping or laundry (where 21% and 22%, respectively, said that sacrifice is related to help).[18] By contrast, male helpers showed a reverse pattern. Male helpers had the greatest sense of sacrifice when handling typical female tasks: that is, 25% of those handling light housekeeping and 34% handling laundry had a sense of sacrifice, while 21% who managed household repairs had a sense of sacrifice.

The separate contribution of sex roles and marital status to a helper's sense of sacrifice can be seen by looking at these same services according to marital status of helpers, as well as according to sex of the helpers. As noted earlier, helpers who are single have a less competitive household structure with the elderly than those who are married. This is one reason why single helpers presumably live with or near the older person and deliver more services. However, for married women, for whom the delivery of household services is part of the traditional role, the difference in helping pattern from that of single people should not be so great. In Table 7-4, it can be seen that single men in the 1978 survey were more likely to provide all household tasks than the married men whose spouses were cooperative. However, the differences were greater for female tasks such as housekeeping (the difference was 19%) and laundry (the difference was 10%) than for typical male tasks (the difference for small house repairs was 5%). By contrast, married women whose husbands helped them were more likely to provide household services than single women (i.e., 16% more likely to handle light housekeeping and 22% more likely to do laundry). In short, some effects seem to be attributable to differences in marital status, while others are attributable to gender roles.

A married woman with a cooperative spouse seems better able to utilize the resources of the marital dyad to deliver services than a married man.

The need for women to have cooperative spouses in order to deliver the maximum number of services to the aged who are ill and single, as well as the conflict this entails with traditional women's roles, is reflected in the different patterns of sacrifice expressed by husbands and wives. For instance, women who incorporated their spouses in the management of the contacts with the older persons had a greater sense of sacrifice [23% (53)] than those who handled the contacts themselves [15% (238)]. By contrast, male helpers felt less sacrifice [8% (73)] when their wives shared the management of contact with their "parents" or when they handed it over to their wives [9% (32)] than they did when managing it themselves [16% (88)]. To put it another way, a married woman is able to optimize her goals of helping the older person if she has her husband's cooperation. However, asking him to help in traditional female roles is a source of stress for her, which would not be the case for the male helper who asks his wife to help. This differential stress between men and women should be viewed as an indicator of a much larger stress, which arises when (1) women have to take care of older parents and (2) the magnitude of the care is not socially defined as a major activity, so that the woman (3) is put under great cross-pressure to fill her regular job as well as the socially defined "minor activity," with (4) a resultant sense of burden.

The importance of the helper's spouse's cooperation, as well as the possible conflict between the helper's marital household and the older person's, can be seen from yet another perspective. Married helpers in the 1978 survey were asked how happy the relationship was between their spouses and their parents. Where the spouses of the helpers were unhappy with the helpers' parents, the helpers were more likely to have a sense of sacrifice [24% (136)] than where the spouses were very happy [10% (209)] or just happy [17% (151)]. The dynamics of the situation are suggested by yet another relationship: The feelings of happiness of the helpers' spouses were in turn related to the older persons' state of disability. When the older persons were healthy and married, 52% of the spouses of helpers (180) were very happy. This dropped to 31% (80) when the older persons were sick and lived alone. A likely sequence of events is that as an older person becomes widowed and disabled, he or she must move closer to the helper if services are to be provided. This in turn involves the spouse, whose life becomes progressively disrupted, which makes him or her unhappy. This unhappiness in turn affects the helper, causing him or her to feel that help involves a sacrifice.

The role of the helper's spouse is further clarified by examining the helper's sense of burden at providing services under varying conditions of spousal unhappiness. First, it can be noted that the spouses' unhappiness increased the helpers' sense of sacrifice, no matter what the level of disability of the older persons who were being helped was. Thus when disability was held constant, 10% of the helpers whose spouses were happy (208) said they felt a burden, while 25% of those whose spouses were unhappy (135) felt this burden. However, the spouses' unhappiness affected the helpers' sense of sacrifice much more when the older persons were single and sick than when they were healthy. Thus when the older persons were healthy and married, 8% of their helpers with very happy spouses (92) had a sense of sacrifice, while this was true of 14% of those with unhappy spouses (35). This represents an increase of 6%. By contrast, when the older persons were sick and single, 8% of those with happy spouses (25) had a feeling of sacrifice, while this was true of 36% of those with unhappy spouses (25), representing a 28% increase.

The data also suggest that a spouse's feeling of happiness can reduce the effects of an older person's illness on the helper. When the spouse is very happy, then the disability of the older person is not related to the helper's having a sense of sacrifice. It is only when the spouse of the helper is unhappy that an older person's illness is associated with the helper's sense of sacrifice. Thus, when their spouses were very happy, 8% of the helpers of healthy and married older persons (92) had a sense of sacrifice; this was exactly the same as the percentage for helpers with sick and single older persons [8% (25)]. By contrast, among the helpers whose spouses were unhappy, 14% of the helpers of healthy married older persons (35) felt a sense of sacrifice, while 36% of those with sick and single ones (25) said this. Thus among helpers with happy spouses, there was no increase in the sense of sacrifice because of illness of the older persons, while among the helpers with unhappy spouses, there was a 22% increase.

Two trends have been noted: A happy spouse can reduce the impact of the older person's disability, while a healthy older person can reduce the impact of an unhappy spouse. The worst possible situation is to have an unhappy spouse and a sick and single older person, and unfortunately this seems to be the relationship that develops most often. It would be of some interest to know to what extent it is possible to reduce the unhappiness of the spouse that arises from illness of the older person, since it is unlikely that much more can be done to reduce illness among the aged. In any case, a central consideration of these findings is to highlight the role of the spouse of the helper. The fact that women delivered the bulk of services to older persons in the past might have caused people to overlook the role of spouses in either providing indirect help or making the provision of such services harder or easier. It also highlights the institutional conflict built into the modified extended family structure when one marital subunit breaks down.

Thus far, the discussion has proceeded with the assumption that the helper has the time to devote to such services. I should now like to consider work as a factor that may be very competitive with the delivery of services. It was expected that helpers who worked full-time would have a greater sense of sacrifice than those who did not work; these expectations turned out to be untrue. Furthermore, a review of the literature (R. H. Sherman, Horowitz, & Durmaskin, 1982) shows that others have come up with the same finding. Of the 207 male helpers who worked, 12% had a sense of sacrifice, while 17% of those who did not work (42) had such feelings. For females, those who worked and did not work had the same percentage who felt that help involves sacrifice—that is, 15% (186 worked, 270 did not). In order to highlight the extent of the reversal of original expectations, the population was divided into those who provided household services and those who did not. The expectation was that helpers who both worked and provided household services would have the highest percentage who felt that providing services involves sacrifice. Among those providing household services, 16% of the working men (96) and 28% of the nonworking men (18) had a sense of sacrifice, while 19% of the working women (85) and 22% of the nonworking women (130) had a sense of sacrifice. For those providing no household services, there was virtually no difference between working and nonworking helpers, be they men or women.

Single women were the only group for whom employment seemed to lead to greater sacrifice. Single women who were employed had a greater sense of sacrifice than those not employed [15% (62) and 9% (89), respectively]. For the single males, the differences were in the opposite direction— that is, the employed had less sense of sacrifice [11% (38) vs. 31% (18)]. Given the small number and the lack of an obvious explanation, I am inclined to dismiss these differences.

What is clear is that for the majority of respondents, work did not hamper the delivery of services or the sense of sacrifice. This result was not anticipated. Without being able to offer a definitive answer, I would like to offer four possible explanations for the finding that helpers who worked did not experience a greater sense of sacrifice. First, it is possible that household services to an older person can be delivered at times that are noncompetitive with the work situation, such as weekends and evenings (Rix & Romashko, 1980). It should be noted in this regard that almost the same percentage of working people and nonworkers delivered household services. Of the non-working women, 48% delivered marital household services, and 46% of the employed women did so; for the men, the respective percentages were 46% and 43%. Closely related to this hypothesis is one that the measures of amount of services and sacrifice used in the survey were relatively crude. It is possible that if more detailed measures of number of exchanges or degree of sacrifice were available, the original hypothesis would be documented. In this regard, those who provided two to four services were examined, and no basic differences were found in the pattern of findings reported.

A third hypothesis moves in a very different direction. It suggests that helpers who are not working are doing so because of the need to help the older persons. As such, not working involves two major sacrifices: It may mean a significant drop in income for the helpers' families, and it may lead to a significant loss of the autonomy that earning money provides the helpers, as well as to a loss of job satisfaction if they have been working at jobs they find pleasing. This last hypothesis can be elaborated to show that working may have positive functions for the helpers. It may provide them with meaningful psychological distraction from the painful spectacle of the decline of a beloved older person. It may also provide money that enables the helper to use paid help.

It is quite possible for all of the speculations above to be true. The reader should note that these data do not seem to indicate any relationship between the working status of the helpers and either the amount of household aid they provided or the sense of sacrifice they felt about providing aid.[19] This unexpected finding clearly requires some further inquiry. It seems unlikely that working does not have a significant impact on the amount of help and the sense of sacrifice.

There is yet another factor that can increase or decrease the burden of helping, and may in part explain the previous finding that work is not related to the number of services delivered by the helper. This is the income of the older persons. It is possible that those with higher incomes may be able to purchase some of their help from institutions and therefore may not require service in kind from their chief helpers. It will be recalled that earlier chapters have shown that those older persons and their helpers who are poorer tend to deliver more kin services, and the point has been made that such deliveries may be based on the fact that richer persons can purchase some forms of help for dealing with illnesses, in cases where the ill persons or spouses can provide supervision.

Also suggested earlier has been an alternative explanation—namely, that the poorer people (such as recent immigrants) hold to traditional family norms, according to which it is the duty of the helper to help the elderly. This question then arises: What about the poor who are not recent migrants? Do they also have more traditional norms that justify the delivery of services? If poor people are supplying services because they do not have money to purchase them, then it should be the case that they will have a greater sense of sacrifice than those who can purchase services. On the other hand, if people are providing services because of a sense of duty, then they should not have a sense of making a sacrifice.

What the 1978 data indicate is that the poor were more likely to associate service with burden or sacrifice than the rich. Thus, overall, 17% of the helpers of the very poor elderly (193) experienced a sense of sacrifice, while this was true of 8% of the helpers of the wealthiest elderly (229).[20] In other words, the delivery of kin aid by the poor may reflect the inability to purchase help, rather than the cultural norm that kin rather than formal organizations should provide help.

If these speculations are correct, it may also be assumed that the sicker the older person is, the less income will play a role in the helper's feelings of sacrifice. As can be seen in Table 7-5, when the older persons were sick and single, 25% of the helpers of the poor felt a great sacrifice in delivering services, while 20% of the helpers of the rich experienced a great sacrifice. This is only a 5% difference. By contrast, when the older persons were healthy and married, 24% of the helpers of the poor saw help as leading to a sacrifice, while this was true of only 5% of the helpers of the rich. The difference is 19%, or almost five times as great as when the older people were sick and single.

In short, the problems of conflict between the needs of the marital dyad for autonomy and the needs to exchange services with the kin are exacerbated for the poor much more than they are for the rich. However, when an older person becomes seriously ill, the conflict is almost as great for both. This is because severe illness requires extremely close proximity of primary-group members, be they rich or poor. It is this demand for close proximity at the same time that the larger society demands differential mobility and economies of small scale that leads to tensions.

In this discussion, attention has been focused on the dilemmas that arise in the kinship system when the marital household breaks down. Practitioners in the field of gerontology must deal with these problems in a very immediate sense. As a result, they have suggested a series of proposals for managing this breakdown. These include proposals to re-establish laws on filial responsibility; programs for subsidization of kin, neighbors, or friends to help out older people who are chronically ill; and the provision of such organizations as meals-on-wheels programs, homemaker services, foster parent programs, small communes of elderly with paid staff persons, and respite care, as well as nursing homes. What must be understood is that the principle of matching

Table 7-5. Percentages of Helpers Saying Help Involves Sacrifice, According to Older Persons'[a] Stage of Disability and Income

Older Persons' Income	Percentage Saying Help Involves Sacrifice		
	Older Persons Married and Healthy	Older Persons Married and Ill or Single and Healthy	Older Persons Single and Ill
$0–3999	24 (21)	11 (108)	25 (64)
$4000–6999	5 (79)	12 (108)	20 (40)
$7000 or more	5 (133)	7 (81)	20 (15)

Note. The populations for the subgroups appear in parentheses.
[a] Older persons lived in community.

groups and tasks permits the evaluation of the strengths and weaknesses of each of these proposals. In fact, such an evaluation is carried out in a later chapter on social policy (see Chapter 10). However, at this point, a few general implications of the principles of matching can be stated as follows: Any use of formal organizations and paid individuals to take over primary-group activities must deal with problems of routinization and the fact that staff members motivated primarily by economic incentives do not handle nonuniform activities very well. Any stress on use of primary groups must keep in mind that age peers usually do not have the physical resources necessary to manage marital household tasks, and that most primary-group members, unless they are children or spouses, do not have the necessary long-term commitments. Moreover, any rules that bind children and parents into a common household or make one the economic responsibility of the other are likely to lead to violations of geographic and occupational autonomy of the household, which in turn will in the long run undermine the conditions necessary for formal organizations to allocate labor rationally. With these criteria in mind, I use the principles of matching in Chapter 10 to show which populations each of these solutions will ideally fit.

Summary and Conclusion

In summary, it has been stressed that there is no way the marital dyad can supply the complete set of marital household tasks without inflicting considerable damage on the autonomy of the helper's marital dyad. What is important to keep in mind is that the problems are not a product of individual ill will or incompetence, but of a larger institutional conflict between the needs of formal organizations for differential mobility among kin members and the need for kin to provide marital household services. Thus it has been shown that the helper's sense of burden arises far more from the provision of marital household services than from the provision of normal kin services. Furthermore, the sense of burden develops from the violations of the helper's own household autonomy, not just from the physical burden of caring for an ill or disabled parent. In addition, where the helper's marital status (i.e., being single) permits a relationship with the older person that more closely resembles a regular marital household, the helper can deliver more services with no greater sense of burden. It has further been shown that a helper and an older person tend to form a joint household precisely when it is least likely to conflict with the autonomy of either marital household—that is, when they are both single.

Past studies have indicated that women provide the chief services to the elderly. As such, it is possible that the institutional dilemma described above might fall completely on a woman's shoulders. The data and theory suggest that such a formulation would be a partial truth. What it overlooks is that the woman can best provide marital household services by moving the older person into her house. Where the helper is married, such a move requires the cooperation of the spouse. The 1978 data show that married helpers who had help from their spouses delivered more services.

Of course, all of this analysis assumes that there is some intrinsic need to divide labor by gender roles. The argument made here is that nonuniform tasks may indeed require some division of labor within the marital dyad. However, the particular division of labor varies with stage of the life cycle and the state of science and technology. It is unlikely that these events will work in such a way that it is always best for husbands and wives to split household tasks equally. This is clearly impossible for older persons when one of them becomes disabled or ill. The key element in such a division is that spouses should be prepared to shift this division as circumstances change and that the woman's role should not be viewed as an inferior one. Thus, central to the marital dyad is the need for "role substitutability" or "role flexibility."

In this chapter, some of the key simplifying assumptions of the prior analysis have been dropped. No longer is it assumed that the helper's services are cost-free; no longer is it assumed that either the helper or the older person has the ideal marital household (combinations of each are examined); and no longer is it assumed that men and women provide the same amount of help. The more complex situations have been incorporated into the principles of matching group structures with services to show how one can elaborate and account for aspects of kinship exchange that other models of family structure cannot explain.

However, what must be kept in mind is that the analysis of marital structures and the larger kinship structure has taken place under the assumption that there are other primary groups, such as the neighborhood and friendship groups, which manage services that kinship cannot provide. It is to the analysis of this assumption that I now turn.

Notes

1. It is important to understand that this question referred to all forms of help, not just the nine exchanges measured in the survey. This variable was dichotomized by placing all those who said "no sacrifice" or "minor sacrifice" in one group and all the others in a second group.

2. In this chapter, I am dealing with a limited sample of older people whose helpers were interviewed by telephone. Such interviews were conducted for approximately 50% of our sample. The marital household services consisted of (1) doing light housekeeping, (2) doing laundry, cleaning, or storage, (3) keeping track of household bills, and (4) doing small household repairs. Normal kin services included (1) checking daily, (2) inviting respondents over to dinner, (3) buying small household gifts, (4) helping respondents keep in touch with relatives, and (5) cheering up respondents when low.

3. However, this interpretation must be tempered by the fact that included in the measure of burden were those who said they could not deliver services because the burden was too much.

4. However, it should be noted that where people were healthy and single or married and ill, living nearby but not in the same house seemed to lead to the same or a greater sense of sacrifice. I speculate that this group included single healthy people who lived in a common household and provided services to the older persons.

5. There are, of course, major sources of psychologically based conflict that are not covered in this analysis, though they are very important.

6. For those arguing for the isolated marital unit or the autonomous individual, the exchange between marital household units is unimportant, so consideration of the marital status of the helping units is unimportant. For those arguing for the traditional family formulation, there is no real distinction between the marital household unit and the larger kin system, and therefore the marital structure of the helping unit is not as important.

7. Table 7-1 has some peculiarities. For those helpers who delivered services, the fact of the older persons' being single or ill led to a greater sense of burden. However, for helpers who did not deliver services, the reverse was true: The helpers felt the most burden when dealing with married couples and healthy ones. One speculation is that where helpers do not deliver services, the chief friction comes from the threats to autonomy produced by two complete marital units interacting. By contrast, those delivering services have as their chief concern the amount of time and energy required, as indicated by the degree of disability of the older people.

8. For a description of this index, see Appendix B.

9. This study had a stratified random sample, so that 399 respondents were from nursing homes. This was 22% of the total respondent population. In a national sample, only about 5% should be in institutions. Therefore the probabilities in the tables presented are all on the high side. However, there is no reason why the different groups should not be ordered the same way, even if the probabilities are lower. It is the relative ordering of groups that is being stressed in the text. This ordering is consistent with those reported by others (Townsend, 1965; Palmore, 1976).

10. Since this study only examined people in institutions who could talk, this figure must be treated with caution. It would be a guess that if the most severely disabled had been included, the trend of convergence between married and single with severity of illness would have been even clearer. That is, roughly the same rate of married and single would have been institutionalized among people who were so crippled that they could no longer talk or hear and required 24-hour care.

11. Counterarguments to this theory could easily be made. Thus it would be easy enough to argue, following Freudian psychoanalytic theory, that sons and mothers have a special attachment, as do fathers and daughters.

12. The position of Parsons was vigorously attacked by many people as sexist or immoral. However, many did not challenge his sociological analysis; they simply said that his conclusion led to inequity. This also sidestepped his moral statement, since Parsons recognized the "inequity": He posed a dilemma in which he said that one accepts this form of inequity or another one—that is, a class-stratified society based on nepotism, or a society that advocates lower standards of living because it cannot maintain high levels of science and technology. I reject the dilemma posed by Parsons and accept the conclusions reached by those who have said that a permanent gender-linked division of labor is wrong. But I do not accept some of the solutions offered by Parsons's opponents, such as the uselessness of the marital dyad or the rejection of a need for a division of labor between spouses.

13. With awareness of the problem, there have been various suggestions raised as to how to insure equality of career aspirations. For instance, one suggestion is career rotation between husband and wife, with one spouse's career taking precedence at one point in time and another's taking precedence at a later period. Another concept is that of commuter marriages (Gerstel & Gross, 1982). In this case, the husband and wife do live in different cities, but commute to see each other very frequently. Gerstel and Gross thought this to be feasible for short periods of time, but not as a permanent or long-term arrangement. Yet another solution is for husbands

and wives to go into occupations where they can work together or where one of them can work in the home (Rapoport & Rapoport, 1976). Still another solution is to raise the status of the housekeeper to a much higher level, so that it would become a highly desirable position for both men and women. All of these are attempts to deal with the requirements of rational allocation of labor and the fact that this may lead members of the primary group who are in the labor force to different cities.

In addition, the pressures for differential mobility have two constraining influences. First, the development of large metropolitan areas and rapid modes of transportation means that most people can find jobs within daily commuting distance, if given several years to look around. Second, people who have reached career plateaus can make geographic moves to optimize spouses' jobs. Finally, in the case of retirements, there is no pressure for differential mobility at all.

14. In the immediate past, men were judged by their ability to be the major providers. Some would argue in addition that men, by controlling the economic sources, also controlled women (Engels, 1902), and that it is the idea of being dominant that is central (Dahrendorf, 1959). In either case, the fact of a wife's having an equal or better career would lead to invidious status comparison. The attitude on male–female status competition is changing (Giele, 1978). It is especially changing in a modern industrial society, because formal organizations have made housework as well as other occupations less demanding in terms of time. As a result, a woman in an occupation can bring in much more income, relative to the loss of household services, than in the immediate past. Given that the marital household is a common consumption unit, the man benefits as much as the woman from her employment. This common status unit is further reinforced by the occupational norms of merit, which say that women are as capable as men for most jobs.

15. The reader is reminded that the other groups were assimilated Americans, West Europeans, Jewish, and American blacks. For the definition of each category and of all the specific ethnic groups that fit under each category, see pages 106 and 141–142 (footnote 9).

16. The differences for Jewish people were 12% versus 19%; for West Europeans 18% versus 25%; for assimilated Americans 19% versus 23%; and for blacks 51% versus 39%. There were 22 black males and 35 females; 186 assimilated American males and 252 females; 87 West European males and 123 females; 54 East European males and 83 females; 37 Latin American males and 50 females; and 126 Jewish males and 236 females.

17. If a chronically ill older person lives in the same household as a married child and his or her spouse, it raises problems of inviting friends to the home (is the parent included in the gathering or not?) and of providing someone to watch the parent if the couple goes out. It also raises questions as to who watches the parent if the helpers go on vacation, have to leave on a business trip, or must go in an emergency to help the other spouse's parents. Finding daily food that is consistent with three persons' tastes is a further difficulty. Moreover, such an arrangement raises fundamental issues of privacy between husband and wife, since they may feel inhibited about discussing many issues with a parent present.

18. This interpretation cannot be disentangled from the earlier-mentioned one that women provided more when older persons were very ill. However, the fact that men felt a greater sacrifice when managing "female" services reinforces the idea of a separate stress from role reversal.

19. It bears some striking resemblances to the finding that women who enter the labor force still manage the bulk of household activities. What may not be the same is the finding that women do not feel a greater sense of burden.

20. The population was divided into thirds as follows: those whose family income before taxes was $0–3999, $4000–$6999, and $7000 and over.

8

Ideal and Nonideal Forms of Neighborhood Structure and Exchange: Another Elaboration of the Principle of Matching

This chapter focuses on the neighborhood and how it is shaped by modern institutions. It will be recalled from Chapters 2 and 3 that neighborhoods deal with the occupational demands for differential mobility of members by emphasizing only short-term residence. They maintain cohesion by evolving mechanisms of rapid integration and egress. Therefore, they have structural features that are very different from those of kinship units and marital households, both of which stress long-term members. In this chapter, the simplifying assumption that most neighborhoods have mechanisms for quick integration is dropped, and three alternatives are examined: (1) the mobile neighborhoods with rapid modes of integration; (2) the traditional neighborhoods, which instead rely on long-term members; and (3) the mass neighborhoods, which have short-term members but no rapid means of integration. The principle of matching group structures and dimensions of tasks is used to show which types of services each neighborhood can provide and which were indeed typical for the 1978 survey sample. Once this is established, the principles of matching are coupled to the dynamics of changing health stages to show that older people are under institutional pressures to make at least three major moves, which in turn radically alter the types of neighbors they must have and the mechanisms they must use to become integrated. Next, the simplifying assumption that there is one ideal-sized neighborhood is dropped, and neighborhoods of various sizes are considered. It is shown how the theory of matching group and service dimensions permits one to anticipate which tasks neighborhoods of different size can optimally manage. Finally, all elements are brought together to show how forms of integration, changes in health status, and size of the neighborhood affect the delivery of services.

Alternative Neighborhood Types and
the Consequences for Exchange

Mobile Neighborhoods

Let us begin the discussion with "mobile neighborhoods." These are neighborhoods that retain their cohesion despite rapid changes in membership.
The traditional theorists assumed that rapid turnover in membership was
antithetical to group cohesion. How could people who are only in a group a
short time or who intend to stay only a short time develop any meaningful
commitment to the group? To this question, there are two answers. First, it is
possible to speed up integration into a group. Though people may be part of
the neighborhood for a very short time, they spend more of it in an integrated
state because of the rapid modes of integration (Litwak, 1960b, 1961a; Fellin
& Litwak, 1963; Wilensky, 1961; W. H. Whyte, 1956; Gans, 1969; Festinger
et al., 1963). Second, there are many activities that do not require long-term
commitments, so that even though the mobile neighborhoods cannot deal
with all the things that the traditional neighborhood can deal with, it can still
handle a sufficiently important segment to make them meaningful groups.
This is especially the case if other primary groups (such as the kin) can pick
up those tasks that require long-term commitments.

The concept of mobile neighborhoods is especially important for the
aged population. There are substantial reasons, such as illness, disability,
and death, for neighborhood turnover. In addition, older people like all
others are subject to changes produced by the "rational" use of land, and to
neighbors' moves based on occupational demands and stages of the family
life cycle (Fellin & Litwak, 1963). In the 1978 sample, individuals were asked
how long they had lived within a 10-block radius of their present place. The
response was that 46% had lived in the same area 10 years or less, and that
72% had lived in the same area 20 years or less. Inasmuch as the respondents
were all over 65 and the median age was 74, these figures mean that almost
three-fourths of them spent the major part of their lives outside of the
"community neighborhood" (i.e., 10-block area) within which they were
living at the time of the survey. Clearly, traditional "community neighborhoods," in which families live for several generations within a 10-block area,
were not an important factor in this population.

It is also the case that this measure could underestimate the effects of
mobility for older persons, since, even though they stay, their neighbors may
die or move on. Such trends for mobility increase as the population grows
older and more disabled. Thus in many nursing homes, one may have a 30%
turnover of residents each year.

If it is agreed that many retirees are subject to problems of neighborhood
turnover, then it becomes clearer why mechanisms of quick integration are

so important. Without trying to provide a complete statement on mechanisms of quick integration (Litwak, 1960b; Fellin & Litwak, 1963), I should like to cite three of the mechanisms. One of the important mechanisms is the norm of ordered change (Litwak, 1960b; Wilensky, 1961; Fellin & Litwak, 1963). This notion of ordered change has two components to it: The first is the idea of order, and the second is the idea of progress. I have elsewhere referred to the combination (Litwak, 1960b) as a "stepping-stone" norm toward change. Each group is considered a prerequisite for joining a more desirable future group. The analogy made elsewhere is to the educational system, where in order to advance to a higher and more desirable grade, one must do well in the lower grades. I believe that the majority of the aged lack a concept of ordered change in retirement.

This lack is not accidental. It is due to the fact that the end product of this change—that is, death or disability—is undesirable. As such, it has the reverse implication of the stepping-stone notion. In nursing homes that cluster patients physically by their state of impairment, it is often the case that healthier residents will have nothing to do with those more impaired.

Under such circumstances, most older people do not dwell on future moves, because these often can only lead to lower status. In the 1978 sample, only 7% contemplated any move in the "near future." Yet, because of the high future rates of illness, it is very likely that older persons who are currently healthy will be subject to pressures to move. In the 1978 study, one item attempted to get an estimate of the neighborhood norm on ordered change by asking the respondents:

> How would most people on your block[1] treat newcomers? Would they make it their business to: (1) go over and welcome newcomers, (2) be friendly if newcomers came to them, (3) be cautious with newcomers, (4) ignore new-comers, (5) be unfriendly to newcomers, or (6) something else (please explain).

The responses were as follows: 28% said that their neighbors would employ the extreme mechanism of quick integration (i.e., go over and welcome the newcomers); 42% said that their neighbors would use a more passive mechanism of acceptance (i.e., be friendly to the stranger, but not initiate the contact); approximately 30% said that their neighbors employ the norm associated with traditional primary groups (i.e., treat strangers cautiously or display hostility to them); only 2% of this group said that their neighbors would be downright hostile. All told, a substantial part of the sample, 70%, lived in neighborhoods that have adopted a positive orientation to newcomers.

Another mechanism of quick integration stresses the need for strangers' first contacts to take place over mutually familiar and nonconflicting roles (Lazarsfeld & Merton, 1954). Such contacts are possible because in a modern industrial society, people have many overlapping groups. Thus rich and poor may share a common religion; people from different religions might share common ethnic origins or regions of the country. The political scientists say that American society is particularly dominated by overlapping group members and a lack of polarization (Dahl, 1966). What this means is that at any point in time, two people who are otherwise strangers might find some group that they share in common. One of the major mechanisms by which quick integration takes place is for groups to be structured to stress those roles and identities on which people are likely to overlap and least likely to conflict. Thus among the older population, the stress on common age, common problems of retirement, and common leisure-time activities tends to lead to rapid integration. In some retirement areas, like Florida, emphasis has been put on regional affiliation (e.g., the Detroit Club, the Cleveland Club, etc.). In the field of aging, substantial evidence has been gathered to show that where people live in age-homogeneous areas, they feel better (Beckman, 1969; Carp, 1976; Lawton & Cohen, 1974; Sheley, 1974; Siegel, 1982), as well as receive more services from their neighbors (Rosow, 1967; Beckman, 1969; Carp, 1976; S. R. Sherman, 1974; Siegel, 1982).

Another mechanism for rapid integration is that of local voluntary associations. In such associations, local issues are explicitly discussed, so newcomers learn local norms quickly. They are made up of local neighborhood people and are also run on a human relations model rather than a rationalistic one, so that they give maximum opportunity for newcomers to meet neighbors (Litwak, 1961a).

In addition, voluntary organizations can increase the speed by which individuals get integrated by assigning people to go out and greet newcomers. In some communities, there are "Welcome Wagons"; in some, members of the clergy systematically canvass all newcomers; in others, a member of the tenants' councils may greet recent arrivals. Voluntary organizations may not only assign people to actively seek out newcomers in order to integrate them; they may also arrange for social affairs designed to incorporate newcomers, such as a newcomers' welcoming dinner, a getting-acquainted dance, or bingo games for new arrivals.

In order to get some measures of this mechanism of quick integration, respondents in the 1978 survey were asked the following:

Now, here is a list of clubs and organizations. Please tell me how many of these organizations you or your spouse belong to or go to.

a. Senior citizen center, community center, or Y's, or organizations for senior citizens
b. Fraternal, veterans', political, cultural, charitable, or recreational
c. Unions or professional groups or their retirement associations
d. Church or synagogue or church-connected groups
e. Neighborhood block clubs, homeowners' clubs, block watchers' groups

Of the sample, 61% belonged to at least one organization. Furthermore, the greater the number of organizations the respondent belonged to, the higher the percentage of respondents who said that neighbors delivered services. The largest increase in the use of neighbors occurred in activities requiring immediate proximity but few physical resources or little long-term commitment, such as spotting break-ins, emergency borrowing of household items, and daily checking. In addition, it occurred for a service emphasizing common life style—that is, choice of free-time companions. The 1978 data show that among those belonging to three or more organizations, 16% to 21% more had neighbors who delivered these services than did those belonging to no organizations. For those services requiring long-term commitment, such as caring for respondents when bedridden, doing laundry, and keeping track of bills, the advantages of affiliating with formal organizations ranged from 1% to 11%. The average advantage was 19% for the first set of services and 9% for the second.[2,3]

These findings are consistent with the view that a substantial part of the sample (61%) lived in neighborhoods that had mechanisms of quick integration: That is, they belonged to voluntary associations, which were associated with neighbors' delivering services.[4]

However, it must be recognized that such integration means that neighbors cannot handle the same range of tasks as the traditional neighborhood or the traditional kin group. It is limited to tasks that involve short-term commitments. Such tasks are vital and provide more than enough bases for group cohesion, but it would be a mistake to assume that they cover the whole range of activities.

Thus, as indicated in Chapter 3, strong neighborhood groups can provide protection against thieves, can give emergency first aid, can call the doctor in cases of sudden illness, can hold spare keys, can provide information on local shopping, and can furnish the group support needed to deal with a common landlord or city agency. But neighbors cannot manage an older person's money or provide daily meals.

Traditional Neighborhood

By contrast to the mobile neighborhood, the traditional neighborhood assumes long-term members and stability. Movement in or out of the group is considered disruptive. Traditional neighborhoods are often associated with traditional extended families. They are also associated with the idea that strangers are bad and that "strangers" include members of formal organizations, unless they happen also to be members of the neighborhood. As a result, members of traditional neighborhoods, like members of traditional extended family groups, handle all matters on their own. Such neighborhoods have been described by Gans (1962) in a study of an Italian community in Boston, by R. L. Warren (1963) in a study of Hispanics in New Mexico, and by Young and Willmott (1957) in a study of Britons in central London. It is true not only that traditional neighborhoods might resist newcomers, but that members of traditional neighborhoods who are forced to move (because of illness, drop in income, sudden population shift, etc.) might find it difficult to integrate themselves into a new neighborhood (Merton & Kitt, 1957).

According to the theory of shared function, traditional neighbors should do extremely well when dealing with neighborhood exchanges that involve nonuniform problems, and when there are no pressures from the outer society to alter their membership. However, in a large, urban, modern industrial society, neighborhoods must confront the larger society's demands for rational land use, which might cause their land to be redeveloped right under them. To fight this situation requires some ability to deal with bureaucracies and to be represented by bureaucracies. The members of traditional neighborhoods find it difficult to use formal organizations, and as a consequence frequently lose such battles (Gans, 1962; Davies, 1966). In addition, they must confront problems of population movement when younger residents move to better housing elsewhere and when strangers seek the empty places in their community. The traditional neighborhoods generally cannot handle the problem of strangers; as a consequence, such moves lead to conflict and often to disorganization of the traditional neighborhoods. Where such traditional neighborhoods are able to defend themselves against the larger society, it generally is at the expense of individual mobility of its members (e.g., Young & Willmott, 1957). For the given neighborhood and the given members, the loss of individual mobility can be a solution as long as they do not particularly prefer upward mobility. However, if a significant part of the larger society were to adopt a similar stance, then it is questionable whether the society could maintain its high-technological base or its open-class society.

Older people are especially vulnerable when a traditional neighborhood is in a state of transition because of an invasion from a new group. The older people are often too poor to move and least able to defend themselves against the animosity of the newcomers. Insofar as traditional neighborhoods exist, they are probably most useful when the aged become ill and disabled and when cross-generational exchanges become vital. Crucial to this analysis is the fact that very few of the respondents in the 1978 survey lived in traditional neighborhoods. It will be recalled that 72% had lived in their current neighborhood less than 20 years, and, as suggested in Chapter 3, 53% had known their neighbors only 10 years or less.

Mass Neighborhoods

Yet another neighborhood type is what some have called a "mass neighborhood." This is a neighborhood in which there is mobility but no mechanism of integration. Whatever services a neighbor provides are not a result of a deliberate exchange, but occur inadvertently because all of the neighbors are exposed to the same stimulus. Thus, there may be a traffic jam in a given neighborhood because all of the people in the area go to work at the same time. People who live in mass neighborhoods will be at a systematic disadvantage in getting nonuniform requirements attended to. Neighbors may not report break-ins because they may not know each other well enough to know whether the burglar is indeed a criminal or some member of the family who has lost his or her keys. For older persons, nursing homes often are viewed as mass neighborhoods. Their immediate neighbors consist of paid attendants with instrumental orientations, and fellow residents who are strangers and often not able to interact or exchange except in the most limited ways.

Types of Exchanges Best Suited to
Different Neighborhood Types

With these thoughts in mind, I should like to present some data on the traditional and mobile neighborhoods and the types of exchanges they can best manage. In order to empirically examine the concept of neighborhoods organized to deal with mobility as opposed to those that are stable, the 1978 study attempted to isolate two elements: first, the effects of being in the neighborhood a long as opposed to a short time, and, second, the extent to which neighbors legitimated mobility by virtue of their acceptance of newcomers. In order to measure the stability of the individual, respondents were asked how long they had lived within a 10-block area of their present location. In general, there was little relation between length of time of residence and neighbors' providing services. The only time period that significantly diminished exchange was a residence period in the neighborhood of less than 1 year. For instance, among those respondents receiving services clearly classifiable as neighborhood services (i.e., reporting break-ins and emergency loans of household items), there was virtually no difference between the average percentages of those receiving such services from neighbors who had lived in the neighborhood 1 to 2 years [69% (104)] and those who had lived in the neighborhood 21 or more years [71% (370)]. The highest percentage of respondents using neighbors for such services was 74%, and this group consisted of those who had lived in the neighborhood for 3 to 10 years. The differences are very small. The only one that might be large enough to note is the difference between the other groups and those who had lived in the neighborhood for less than a year, of whom 62% said they received such services from their neighbors.

I speculate that the lack of association between length of residence in the neighborhood and the use of neighbors was due to the fact that the majority of the respondents were members of mobile neighborhoods, in which speedy mechanisms of integration permit neighbors to handle neighborhood tasks even when they have lived in the neighborhood for a short time.

To highlight this point, I should like now to consider the mechanism of integration inherent in neighbors' orientation to newcomers. The item measuring this mechanism and the item measuring the length of time in one's neighborhood can be used to classify all respondents as belonging to short-term neighborhoods with a positive orientation toward strangers, which is the classic mobile neighborhood situation; to traditional neighborhoods, consisting of people who have lived in their neighborhoods a long time and have negative or very negative orientations toward newcomers; or to mass neighborhoods, consisting of people who are mobile but have neutral or negative orientations toward newcomers. There is at least one logical type that I have not discussed up to this point, and that is those people who have lived a long time in their neighborhoods and have a positive attitude toward newcomers. This can occur for people who have reached a plateau in their occupational careers. To say that there are imperatives for large groups of people to be on the move does not mean that there are not also very substantial numbers who remain stable for long periods of time once they reach their occupational peak, or who retire. Older persons who move to a retirement community while vigorous and who remain very healthy, for example, may live in the same area for 15 years. The factors that distinguish their neighborhoods from traditional ones are these: (1) Residents welcome newcomers, and (2) there may be many who come and go.

In order to clarify this analysis further, I introduce one more question designed to measure length of residence. Respondents were asked how long they had known the neighbors they knew best. This item was included because it is very possible for a person to live in a neighborhood for a long time and yet for the neighborhood to be highly mobile. The reason for this is that an older population often gets left behind when neighborhoods change.

Length of residence was therefore measured by using two extreme groups. Those who had remained in their neighborhood above the median length of time and who knew neighbors who also had remained in their neighborhood above the median length of time were considered "long-term residents." Those who had lived in their neighborhoods fewer than the median number of years for the sample and who had known their best-known neighbors less than the median length of time were considered "short-term residents." However, the reader must remember that these are only relative definitions, since the median number of years a respondent had lived in a neighborhood was 12, and the median number of years people had known the neighbors they knew best was just over 10. With these measures of stability and mobility in mind, let us now examine Table 8-1. What is evident is that the chief factor affecting the delivery of services by neighbors was the norm legitimating the acceptance of newcomers. For instance, on the average, 79% and 81% of those who lived in mobile neighborhoods (i.e.,

Table 8-1. Percentages of Noninstitutionalized Older Persons Who Said That Neighbors Helped, According to Type of Service and Neighborhood Type

| | | Percentage Using Neighbors for Service | | |
| | | Neighbors' Orientation toward Newcomers | | |
Type of Services Neighbors Provided	Length of Community Neighborhood Residence[a]	Welcoming or Friendly: Positive	Cautious: Neutral	Ignoring or Unfriendly: Negative
	Neighborhood Services			
Reporting break-in when older person out	Long	82	59	41
	Short	80	64	42
Providing emergency loan of small household items	Long	75	54	44
	Short	81	52	45
Average for neighborhood services	Long	79	57	43
	Short	81	58	44
	Friendship Service			
Serving as companion for free-time activity	Long	34	22	9
	Short	37	13	19
	Kin Services			
Checking daily to see if respondents all right	Long	39	29	23
	Short	40	21	17
Talking to respondents when feeling low and cheer up	Long	30	19	20
	Short	34	17	11
Providing household services if bedridden for 2 to 3 weeks	Long	23	10	11
	Short	23	11	4
Average for kin services	Long	31	19	18
	Short	32	16	11
	Marital Household Services			
Keeping track of bills, Social Security checks, bank accounts	Long	0	0	2
	Short	1	0	2
Doing seasonal storage, laundry, or cleaning	Long	1	1	0
	Short	2	2	2
Average for marital household services	Long	1	1	1
	Short	2	1	2

Note. Population bases were as follows:

	Long	349	106	56
	Short	395	103	54

[a] Long-term residents were those who said they had lived in their neighborhoods longer than the median for the population (12 years) and who also said they had known the neighbors they knew best longer than the median (slightly over 10 years). Short-term residents were those who had lived in neighborhoods less than the median number of years and also had known their best-known neighbors less than the median number of years. The other groups are left out of this table.

positive orientations toward newcomers and either short-term or long-term residents) used neighbors for typical neighborhood services, such as watching the house to report break-ins while the respondents were out of the house on their daily chores. By contrast, 43% from the traditional neighborhoods (i.e., long-term residents with negative attitudes toward newcomers) and 44% from mass neighborhoods (i.e., short-term residents with negative views toward newcomers) used neighbors for such services. As the reader can see, the average difference between long-term and short-term residents was 2%, while the average difference for those who lived in neighborhoods with positive and negative orientations toward newcomers was 39%. These findings illustrate the argument that where a neighborhood can evolve mechanisms of quick integration, it can overcome many of the problems of short membership duration.

However, a glance at the rest of Table 8-1 also indicates the limits of this position. For if one looks at typical tasks performed by friends and marital dyads, it is obvious that neighbors were seldom used for kin or marital services, such as managing finances or doing laundry, cleaning, or storage. More generally, the point is being made that it is possible to use mechanisms of quick integration to overcome problems of short tenure for tasks that do not require long-term commitment. But this is less possible for services requiring long-term commitment.

In this presentation, I have sought to illustrate two mechanisms of quick integration. However, it must be understood that these are only two of a long list of possible mechanisms.[5]

How then are "mobile," traditional, and mass neighborhoods to be assessed? What the findings suggest is that the bulk of our sample (70%) lived in mobile neighborhoods that could deliver limited but vital services. I would further argue that traditional neighborhoods would be able to deliver a whole range of services (not considered here), but that the fact that so few respondents lived in such neighborhoods was no accident. Traditional neighborhoods are inconsistent with a modern industrial society.[6] The reader might well ask how it can be concluded that traditional neighborhoods can deliver the whole range of services; the answer is that because traditional neighborhoods are characterized by an overlap between neighbors and kin. Past studies suggest that the kin–neighbors do indeed help each other (Gans, 1962; Young & Willmott, 1957; R. L. Warren, 1963). What the 1978 data also show is that "mass neighborhoods" delivered the fewest services of all.

Three Basic Neighborhood Moves and
the Consequences for Exchange

Granted that the mobile neighborhood has outstanding virtues in a modern society, the question arises as to how it relates to older people who must inevitably confront the problems of illness and, for those married, the death of a spouse. In Chapter 5, it is pointed out that the principle of matching makes it possible to anticipate which primary groups can substitute for the marital household. In this chapter, this same principle suggests that older people will be under pressure to make at least three major moves from the time of their retirement to their death (Lee, 1980; Bowles, 1980; Yee & Van Arsdol, 1977).

In the first stage, when older people are healthy, the major goals are sociability goals and normal kin services that can be managed across distance. This is based on the assumption that, because of retirement, older people have unique daily time schedules and sociability interests that put a stress on common generation. As a result, there are strong incentives for them to move to retirement communities in warm climates, where age homogeneity and large numbers provide economies of large scale (e.g., specialized recreational organizations for the aged), as well as providing a base for primary groups by putting them in close contact with friends and neighbors sharing common life styles (Cribier, 1980; Flynn, 1980; Biggar, 1980; Fuguitt & Tordella, 1980; Longino, 1980).

A second stage begins when the older persons become disabled and their spouses die. As suggested in the preceding chapters, at this stage it is necessary to have household services delivered by kin on a regular basis. To do so requires living near kin. Age peers generally lack both physical resources and long-term commitments, especially among the advanced aged (Wiseman, 1980; Longino, 1979). To meet this condition, the older people have to move from their first-stage communities.

The third imperative to move occurs when individuals are so disabled that they require 24-hour care. As pointed out in Chapters 6 and 7, the helpers' marital households do not have resources to manage such care. It requires a move to institutions (Wiseman, 1980).

In short, to match the dimensions of groups with those of tasks at each stage of health optimally requires three different kinds of neighbors. Not all people live through all three stages. Even for those who do, many do not make these three moves (e.g., the poor). The principle of matching suggests that where people do not make these moves, they will lose key services as well as express specific complaints.

To clarify this point, the consequences for several groups who are least likely to follow this pattern are discussed here. The very poor might not be able to follow this pattern because they do not have the money in the first stage to move into retirement communities. For the poor who cannot move to age-homogeneous communities, one would anticipate complaints about being homebound during winter, a sense of cultural alienation, lack of age-appropriate companions, and inaccessibility of social programs for the aged. Another group that might not fit this pattern might be those who do not have children or who are alienated from their children. Often, these individuals form pseudofamily groups with close friends. It is my hypothesis that these groups serve them well until the second stage of aging, when friends are no longer able to help because of their own disabilities or because of high mortality rates. For this group, one would expect those at the second and third stages to complain about primary groups as either not having resources to help or not having long-term commitments—that is, to complain about being abandoned by friends. Many of this group would end up in institutions much earlier than those with children (Townsend, 1965). Still another group that might not fit into this idealized pattern may be people who are too fearful or unknowing of the virtues of retirement communities to make a move. They should suffer from many of the same problems as the poor.

There are some groups for whom predictions of loss of primary-group services will not hold. Those who hold a traditional family value are such a group. They will get maximum joy out of living near their children during all three phases of retirement (Cribier, 1980). They will also generally be poorer and suffer losses from their inability to use formal organizations, as noted in Chapter 6. Those people who never retire and who stress work or occupational values will also not benefit from such moves. I would submit that the pressures of the larger society are such as to minimize both of these orientations. That is, the traditional family orientation is held by very few people in our society, nor can it be held by many if the society is to stress science and technology. The effect of large-scale bureaucracy is to force retirement on the aged, where age is related to lower work productivity.

Another group that might not clearly fit the pattern consists of those who biologically do not go through all stages of aging. Thus people, after their robust initial period, might simply die and thus might not be affected by the subsequent stages. Modern medicine, however, seems to be increasing the number of chronically disabled who live for long periods of time.[7]

In the discussion that follows, I do not seek to provide all of the alternative sequences of moves and their consequences, but rather to deal with those for the three basic moves as made by the typical group defined above and by the group least likely to make the three moves, the poor. A more elaborate analysis of what happens to the poor highlights what happens to groups who choose various alternatives to the three proposed moves. As noted, the very poor have limited options to make the three moves.

In large urban areas, those who retire and have little money have at least two major options, aside from going immediately into the second stage (living with children). As suggested, they can remain in the neighborhood they are in. Another alternative for older people who are poor is to go into low-income public housing set aside for the aged. These are generally located in poor areas. As a consequence, the older persons are located among age peers and have some advantages of economies of large scale in their immediate neighborhood, but their larger neighborhood might be exceedingly rough. The nature of complaints should be different from the complaints made by those who remain in their old neighborhood (e.g., fewer complaints about alien age cultures and immediate economies of scale, but still complaints about general safety and inability to use wider community resources).

In either of these cases, the poor older persons are under great pressures to move if they become seriously incapacitated, because they need individuals with long-term commitments when they become ill. As suggested earlier, poor persons might experience this need more quickly than wealthier persons, because the rich can buy time through the purchase of aid from formal organizations.[8] In the case of the poor, in their need to move near relatives, they must confront the possibility that neither they nor their kin have the money for the move or a separate household for the older person. Therefore, the poor cannot move, or they must move into the same household as their children, if they are to receive kin aid during the second stage. In the latter case, there will be complaints from the older persons and their helpers that are basically derived from sharing a common household.

Finally, when the poor become so incapacitated that they must be institutionalized, they will be pressured to move again. This move confronts them with two opposing problems. Because they are poor, they may have more limited choices as to which institution they can enter. This limitation usually requires a move that takes them further from their kin. Second, because their kin are also poor, they should choose an institution that is relatively close to kin to avoid costs of transportation and time. Complaints may be expressed by the helpers because they cannot locate a home for their elderly parents, or by the elderly because they suffer a drop in services in the institution as a result of their children's not visiting often enough. In short, the stages of aging produce the same pressures for moves on the poor as wealthier groups. But because of their lack of resources, the poor cannot meet these pressures as well. Therefore, they are less likely to receive services and to have special forms of discontent.[9]

The central point of this discussion is to make clear to the reader that the process of matching groups with tasks, in conjunction with stages of health, forces older people to make at least three moves or alternatively to suffer loss of services.

Empirical Data on the Three Basic Moves

I should like to illustrate the dynamics of the three basic moves by treating the 1978 cross-sectional data as if they were longitudinal records consisting of four points in time.[10] The first point is when the respondents were healthy or had minor ailments and an intact marital unit. The second stage is when they either were widowed with minor ailments or were married with major ailments. A third stage is when they were single and had severe ailments, and a fourth stage is when they had an institutional living arrangement. For some purposes, this fourth stage is divided into groups—that is, those who had minor ailments and needed only minor help, and those who had severe ailments and needed 24-hour care. These stages are roughly related to the ages of older persons. Thus people from the 1978 study in the first stage had an average age of 71, those in the second stage 74, those in the third and fourth stages 78, and those in the fifth stage 79.

I have argued that among those living in the community, people in the first stage would be under social pressures to move to age-homogeneous retirement communities.[11] South Florida, consisting of the Miami and Miami Beach areas (Dade County) as well as the area just north (i.e., Broward County), was a prototypical retirement community at the time of this study, 1978. The contrast between those living in the New York metropolitan area (only the part in New York State) and those living in Florida should provide a rough test of this initial proposition. Basically, more people in the first stage of health should be found in Florida, and more people in the third stage should be found in New York.[12] Of the Florida sample, 42% were in the first stage of the disability cycle, while only 24% were in the first stage in the New York sample. The assumption is made that those in Florida who enter the second and third stages in the disability cycle tend to leave. It could, however, be argued that this pattern of data simply reflects Florida's being a newer community—one to which only vigorous younger people can move, but which older sick people do not leave. In 50 years, it may be like New York. Clearly, the present hypothesis partly overlaps with this reasoning, but is not the same. However, Longino (1979, 1980) has provided supportive evidence for the idea of older and sicker people leaving Florida. In a study of people who migrated to Florida and those who had returned to their home towns, he found that those who had returned to their home towns were older and in poorer states of health.

The hypothesis also suggests that during the first stage of the disability cycle people will live at greatest distance from helpers, closer to them in the second and third stages, and at an in-between distance in the fourth and fifth stages. Of the respondents in the first stage (340), 20% lived within five blocks of their helpers; of those in the second (446), 24% lived this close; and of those in the third stage (174), 37% lived this close. Furthermore, people in institutions (245) virtually never lived within five blocks of their helpers (1% lived this close). The distance at which institutionalized older people clearly predominated over others was the intermediate distance of over five blocks and up to 30 minutes: 40% of the institutionalized aged lived at this distance, as contrasted with a range of 22–26% of those in other stages of health. In short, the empirical findings follow the theoretically expected results.

The formulation further suggests that poor people will live next to each other, regardless of health status, while richer people are more likely to move next to each other only when parents are disabled. If living within a five-block area is an indicator of living close together, then among the poorest respondents 35% (34) lived this close when they were healthy, while 42% (89) lived that close when they were disabled and single. There was only a 7% difference between the healthy poor and the disabled poor. The difference for those in middle-income groups was 12% [i.e., 27% (44) minus 15% (90)]. It was largest for the highest-income group: 21% of the married and healthy wealthier group (175) lived near their helpers, while 45% of the ill and single wealthy group (18) lived near their helpers. This was a 24% difference, over three times as great as the difference for the poorest group.

I have argued that the reason for this difference between the poor and the wealthy is because the poor, having limited resources, are forced to move closer to their kin even when they are healthy. As suggested in Chapter 7, this implies that the wealthy have the same kin norms as the poor, but do not have to call on kin as much when they are healthy because they can pay for formal organizations to supplement kin assistance (e.g., housekeeper or shopping if sick for a day or so). At the stage of chronic illness requiring continual household help, even the wealthy need kin to handle services, because face-to-face contact is required for the supervision of household help if the older person is too ill to supervise personally.

It is further assumed that younger children do not live nearby when older people are healthy because the principles of matching suggest that most healthy older people will optimize their services if they live in an age-homogeneous neighborhood. Let us now examine this assumption and these principles in conjunction. To get some idea of the age homogeneity or heterogeneity of the older persons' neighborhoods, each respondent was asked:

> Now, considering all the people living on this block, what percent are 65 years or older? Would you say more than half are 65 and older, between 25% and 50% are 65 and older, fewer than 25% are 65 or older?

First, let us see to what extent the delivery of household services by the helpers was associated with age heterogeneity of the neighborhood. It will be recalled that the marital household services assessed were light housekeeping; cleaning, laundry, and storing of clothes or valuables; keeping track of household bills and bank accounts; and doing small home repairs. The data show that those living in age-homogeneous neighborhoods always had a lower percentage receiving two or more marital household services. This was true for respondents at each stage of health. Where people with similar health statuses are compared, 19% of those (333) in age-homogeneous areas received two or more household services, 30% of those (329) living in intermediate-type neighborhoods received household services, and 36% of those (299) living in age-heterogeneous areas received such services.[13] These data are consistent with the assumption that helpers find it easier to deliver marital household services to older persons in communities that are age-heterogeneous. The same pattern holds for those who receive normal kin services. However, the effects of neighborhood homogeneity were muted. This is consistent with the principle of matching, since such services can be delivered over distance.

I would like to contrast activities requiring a common life style with those requiring cross-generational help, such as the marital household tasks just considered.[14] Let us first examine the activity that most clearly involves a common life style. Respondents were asked:

> If you wanted someone to join you in your favorite free-time activities, tell me which of the following people, if any, would join you. (CHECK AS MANY AS APPLY.) Neighbor, close friends, children, husband/wife/companion, someone else (WHO?), or no one.

If choice of free-time companions by those who lived in age-homogeneous areas versus those who lived in age-heterogeneous areas is examined, it can be seen that older people living in age-homogeneous areas were less likely [10% (463)] to have "no one" than those living in the most age-heterogeneous areas [18% (410)]. In the intermediate age-homogeneous areas, an intermediate percentage had no one [12% (459)].

Respondents were also asked whether anyone checked on them daily to see if they were all right. In this case, checking can be a simple procedure of seeing whether the older person is up and around, whether the newspaper has been taken in, whether the window shades are up or down, and so on. However, checking on others can also be done by younger people and is therefore not as exclusively dependent on common age as choosing a companion for one's free-time activities. In this case, there was little advantage in living in an age-homogeneous neighborhood—that is, 16% in age-homogeneous neighborhoods said that no one helped, as opposed to 18% in the more age-heterogeneous neighborhoods.

Let us now contrast these activities with those of two household activities for which age homogeneity is thought to be even less helpful. The people in the survey were asked who would take care of them if they were sick in bed for 2 or 3 weeks and needed everyday help. They were also asked whether anyone in the last 6 months had helped them keep track of bills, Social Security checks, and bank accounts. Both of these activities are probably best handled by younger kin, such as children; the first because it requires time, physical energy, and economic resources, the second because it requires helpers with long-term future commitments. Neither of these activities requires immediate next-door living if an older person is healthy. However, the more chronic the ailment of the older person, the easier it is to handle these services if people live nearby.

In regard to these activities, there was a reversal of the previous pattern, though the differences were small. People who lived in age-homogeneous neighborhoods were more likely to have no one to take care of them when bedridden than those who lived in age-heterogeneous ones [13% (463) vs. 10% (410)]. The respondents who lived in moderately age-homogeneous areas (459) had 11% who did not receive this service. There was a similar reversal for the item on keeping track of bills and Social Security checks. Those living in the most age-homogeneous areas had a higher percentage who said that no one helps [62% (463)] than those in the extremely heterogeneous areas [55% (410)], while the middle group was intermediate [53% (459)]. In short, as one moves from exchanges emphasizing common life styles to those stressing physical resources, respondents who live in age-homogeneous areas are less likely to have help. Let us now connect this analysis to the states of health to see whether people who are ill are also least likely to receive services in age-homogeneous areas.

The survey respondents least likely to get help if bedridden for 2 or 3 weeks were those who were physically disabled and living in age-homo-geneous areas. Of those in that situation (233), 20% said that they got no help. By contrast, of those who were ill and living in age-heterogeneous neighborhoods (202), only 11% said that they would get no help. To remain in an age-homogeneous area means that one runs a risk of losing such services.[15]

If the theory of matching is correct, services that stress common life style, but not physical resources or long-term commitment, will not be similarly affected. In examining the service that most clearly emphasizes common life style—that is, serving as a free-time companion—it can be seen that even people who were ill were likely to be as well off, if not better off, in age-homogeneous areas. Thus 16% of those who were ill and lived in age-homogeneous areas (233) had no one to turn to for companionship during their free time, while this was true of 19% of those who were ill and lived in age-heterogeneous areas (202). Furthermore, older people clearly benefit by living in age-homogeneous areas if they want a companion during their free time when they are healthy. Among those living in homogeneous areas who were healthy (220), 5% said they had no one for a free-time companion, while among those living in age-heterogeneous areas (172), there were almost three times as many without help—that is, 14%.

To further highlight how the pressures to have consistency between dimension of groups and services combine with health status to encourage older people to change neighborhoods with major health changes, I now examine who is most likely to deliver household and sociability services in age-homogeneous and age-heterogeneous areas. In Figure 8-1, I have indi-cated the percentages of healthy and disabled respondents whose neighbors were their free-time companions and the percentages of those whose kin provided this service. The respondents who were most likely to receive such services were those who were not disabled, lived in age-homogeneous areas, and had neighbors who provided this service—40% for the healthy (220) and

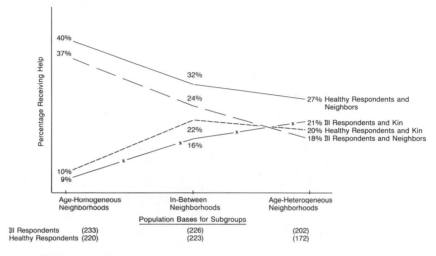

Fig. 8-1. The use of kin and neighbors as "free-time" companions, according to age homogeneity of neighborhood and health status of respondents. (Ill respondents were those who could not do at least one of the following without help: walk stairs, handle shopping, take pubic transportation, read, walk, or talk. Those missing a limb were also considered ill.)

37% for the ill (233). Those least likely to receive such services lived in age-heterogeneous areas, were ill, and relied on neighbors—18% (172). At no point did kin deliver much in the way of such services, but, unlike the neighbors, they were least likely to provide them in age-homogeneous areas —10% for the healthy (233) and 9% for the ill (220). Kin were 9% more likely to supply them in age-heterogeneous areas—20% for the healthy (202) and 21% for the ill (172). In short, for anyone who wants companion services, it is best to reside in age-homogeneous areas and have congenial neighbors. However, in Figure 8-2, where the graph on home care services for the bedridden is presented, the opposite picture emerges. People were most likely to get home care services if they had kin as providers and lived in an age-heterogeneous area—35% for the ill (202) and 30% for the healthy (172). They were least likely to have them delivered if they utilized kin and lived in age-homogeneous areas—15% for the healthy (220) and 19% for the ill (233). If neighbors were used for this service, it was always better to live in age-homogeneous areas (24% and 22%, vs. 19% and 15% for age-heterogeneous areas). However, that should not obscure the fact that those who lived in age-heterogeneous areas received optimal home care services from kin, while optimal companionship services were received from neighbors in age-homogeneous areas. It is not simply a question of receivng fewer services; as

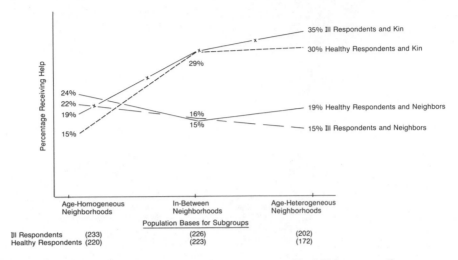

Fig. 8-2. The use of kin and neighbors for home care of bedridden, according to age homogeneity of neighborhood and health status of respondents. (Ill respondents were those who could not do at least one of the following without help: walk stairs, handle shopping, take public transportation, read, walk, or talk. Those missing a limb were also considered ill.)

the earlier findings suggest, it is a question of not getting services at all if one is in the wrong setting. This is the basic pressure behind the notion that older people must move as they go from states of health to illness.[16]

However, these figures go beyond my original statement and suggest a dilemma. If it is the case that "companionship" during one's free time is best provided by neighbors in age-homogeneous areas and that household services are best provided by kin in age-heterogeneous areas, which alternative should older persons take when they become ill and need someone else to provide household services? If they wish to maintain their sociability goals, they should remain in age-homogeneous areas, while if they desire to maintain their household functions, they should move to age-heterogeneous areas near their children. I would speculate that this dilemma is especially severe for those who are only mildly disabled or recently widowed and must leave their current residence. For the severely disabled, there may be little choice, since they probably do not really have the resources to maintain sociability relations with neighbors. The only time that such relations may be possible for them is in a nursing home environment, where resident–neighbors are thrown into such close contact that it virtually takes no effort to be together.

How does this analysis on stages of health relate to the prior one on types of neighborhoods? I should like to suggest two major implications. When older persons are in good health, to a very large extent they can play a major role in the mechanisms for quick integration. In addition, one of the mechanisms that speed up integration is common life style, and the older persons can take advantage of that mechanism (Litwak, 1960b; Fellin & Litwak, 1963). When people are sick and living alone, it is argued that they do best if they move nearer their helpers in an age-heterogeneous neighborhood. Insofar as that is the case, the persons who will play a much more important role in the integration of the older persons are their helpers. This is in part the case because the older persons might be too enfeebled and in part because the helpers are likely to be better acquainted with the neighborhood.[17] Where older people live in an age-homogeneous area and do not have children or access to children, they often do not have sufficient resources to maintain the mechanisms of integration. This produces the population of isolated "frail elderly" who have high mortality rates or survive only because they are located by agency personnel. When older persons are so ill that they require nursing home attention, the staff of the nursing home is most likely to be central to their integration. In this setting, they are again in a situation where other residents share the same life style, but in a condition where they have minimal ability to take advantage of it.

These are speculations to give the reader a sense of how to relate the need for mobile neighborhoods to the stages of health so as to generate the unique forms that mobile neighborhoods must take as older persons move from states of health to states of severe and chronic illness.

Defining Neighborhood Boundaries and
the Associated Exchanges

Before the discussion on neighborhoods is concluded, one further simplification is dropped—that is, the assumption that the optimal boundary of the neighborhood is known. In the past, one term—"neighborhood"—has been used to describe next-door neighbors, people on one block, people within a public-grade-school area (five blocks), and people within a high-school area, like Greenwich Village in New York (Davies, 1966). Much of the confusion in defining neighborhood boundaries can be eliminated if different-sized units are given different names and the principle of matching is applied to define tasks. Following Spiro (1968), I would like to suggest that the following terms be used for different-sized units.

The smallest neighborhood unit is that of next-door neighbors. I call this the "nuclear neighborhood"; it consists of all people who are immediately adjacent to the individual being considered. The characteristics of such neighbors are their immediate physical proximity and their small number. In terms of the principle of matching structure of group and structure of task, this means that this group can handle tasks that involve the most immediate time emergencies and immediate visual or hearing contact, but not great numbers. For instance, a next-door neighbor who is within immediate sight and hearing of the older person can spot someone trying to break into a house or hear cries for help from an older person who has broken a hip and cannot reach a phone.

The second smallest unit is called the "extended neighborhood"; it consists of those living on the same block or those living in a building with more than 15 units. The characteristics of this group are moderate closeness and moderate number. Therefore, it can handle tasks that require some dispatch, but not immediate visual or hearing presence. Thus an individual seeking to borrow some sugar or salt or a Band-Aid can go to a neighbor who lives on the same block and still achieve his or her time goal. Some problems, however, concern a total extended neighborhood group. A next-door neighbor can watch one's house while one is out, but who is to watch an older person when he or she is walking down the block or is entering a large apartment house? For that kind of protection, a block club or a building group that monitors the block or the building is necessary.

A third neighborhood unit consists of those within a five-block radius; I call this unit a "subcommunity." The qualities differentiating it from the other two neighborhood groups are that it is much larger in size, and its members take much longer to get in touch with each other. This group is not very good for watching one's house or responding to enfeebled cries for help. However, it can address itself to problems that are locally based but require large numbers. For instance, if there is a busy thoroughfare that runs through a residential area and the residents would like it diverted or traffic lights in, or if the neighborhood has many older people who have been victimized and the residents want more police patrols, these are locally based issues that involve members of a subcommunity. Furthermore, the more people who can be brought to bear on the city government, the more likely it is that the neighbors can achieve their goals.

The largest unit—that is, a 10-block area—is designated a "community neighborhood." Such community neighborhood units are often involved when the city decides it wants to put in a substantial urban renewal project (Davies, 1966; Gans, 1962). Such projects have consequences for very large areas (e.g., 10-block radius). Fighting or supporting this kind of development often requires substantial numbers of people.

For older persons, subcommunity neighborhoods and community neighborhoods become very important in considering concepts of retirement communities, or, as in the case of southern Florida, whole retirement regions. For instance, it often requires an area of this size to give a feeling of safety to older people.

Having provided the concepts of nuclear, extended, subcommunity, and community neighborhoods, I do not mean to insist that all functions will fit neatly into these particular categories. What the theory tells us is that a continuum of sizes and a continuum of tasks exist. However, it may be hard for the reader and the social planner to make use of such continua unless very precise measures and some mathematical formulae for relating the two are available. Therefore I have supplied names for points on the continua as a rough and ready indicator.[18] The dilemma of prior investigators and planners who did not know which unit to use for their studies can now be partially solved. There are, in fact, many different groups that have been identified with one concept—the "neighborhood." Using one term to describe different neighborhood structures produces a dilemma.[19]

In order to provide some empirical illustrations of this argument, the following question from the 1978 survey is used as a rough indicator of the respondents' orientation to a given neighborhood size. Respondents were asked:

> Where does the neighbor you know best live? Would you say, (1) next door or across the way, (2) in this building or on this block, (3) within five blocks, (4) within 10 blocks, (5) further than 10 blocks?

Under the present formulation, those who chose next-door neighbors would be oriented toward a nuclear neighborhood; those who chose neighbors on the same block or building in which 15 or more families live would be oriented toward an extended neighborhood; those who chose neighbors within five blocks would be oriented toward a subcommunity neighborhood; and those who chose neighbors within 10 blocks would be oriented toward a community neighborhood.[20]

It turned out that 50% of the respondents said that their best-known neighbors were nuclear neighbors (next door or across the way), and 38% of the respondents chose extended neighbors (on the same block or in the same building for apartment dwellers). Only 7% chose subcommunity neighbors (within 5 blocks), 2% chose community neighbors (within 10 blocks), and 3% chose as neighbors persons who lived beyond the community and were apparently using the city as their neighborhood base. The latter two groups are combined here because of the small number.

I now go on to examine the function of different types of neighborhoods for handling older people. Those who were healthy and married are examined first, with regard to exchanges that require immediate proximity. The survey item that asked respondents who would be able to spot an attempted break-in in their house while they were out on their daily activities provides a measure of a nuclear neighborhood activity. Such a service requires that people be within immediate visual contact—that is, next door or across the way. Others who live on the block but are several houses away may not be able to spot an intruder.

The results were as follows: 80% (264) of the respondents who said that their close neighbors lived next door or across the way said they would choose a neighbor to perform this kind of activity for them. This figure dropped to 68% for the respondents who said their best-known neighbors lived on the same block (134) and to 62% for those who said that their best-known neighbors lived beyond that (47). The figures show an uneven rate of decline, with the biggest drop coming between those choosing neighbors who lived next door and those choosing neighbors who lived on the block. It is the size of the drop that indicates which is the most significant group. To get a standardized estimate of this, the differences between respondents who had best-known neighbors at adjacent distances are divided throughout by the first distance. Using this measure of decline, the rate of decline between those who chose neighbors in the nuclear neighborhood and those who chose them in the extended neighborhood was 15%, while the decline between the extended neighborhood and the next larger group was 9%.

Four exchanges assessed in the 1978 survey seem to stress the extended neighborhood (i.e., people who live on the block). The first is the use of neighbors as companions for favorite free-time activities. Respondents whose best-known neighbor lived on the block were as likely to choose them [30% (134)] as those who said that their neighbors lived next door [31% (264)]. The real drop in choice of neighbors occurred for those who said their neighbors lived more than one block away [22% (47)]. Thus the percentage of decline between the extended and the next larger neighborhoods was 27%, while there was only a 3% difference between the nuclear and extended neighborhoods.[21]

The second exchange that seems to stress the extended neighborhood is respondents' choice of neighbors to provide daily household help if they were bedridden for 2 or 3 weeks. The rate of decline between nuclear and extended neighborhoods was 10%; that between the extended neighborhood and the next larger group was 28%. The services of checking daily and of talking to people and cheering them up also appeared to be optimally performed by neighbors who lived within the extended neighborhood area. The rate of decline for checking daily was 10% between nuclear and extended neighborhoods, and 28% between the extended and the next larger neighborhoods. For talking and cheering up, these rates were 16% and 42%. Providing emergency loans of small household items appeared to follow a pattern in between those exchanges stressing the nuclear neighborhood and those stressing the extended neighborhood: The decline rates were 11% and 9%, respectively.

From these data, one might argue that the nuclear and extended neighborhoods are central to neighborhood services. But the theory makes it clear that this finding is a consequence of the particular services assessed in the 1978 study.

To clarify this point and to illustrate the role of the region or city as the major geographical unit, I discuss a survey item not mentioned before. Respondents were asked:

How safe is it to walk around this block during the evening? Would you say it is: (1) very safe, (2) safe, (3) okay, (4) not too safe, or (5) very unsafe?

People who lived in Florida always said it was safer to walk around the block than people who lived in the New York area. This held true regardless of whether New York was divided up into suburbs and city, and despite income levels, which ordinarily relate to crime. For instance, among the poorest ($0–3999) older people, 22% of those living in New York City (148) said they felt very safe or safe, and 11% of those who lived in the New York suburbs (36) said this; by contrast, 59% of the poorest Floridians (182) said this. Among the more affluent ($7000 or more) of the older people, these figures were 28% (90), 45% (61), and 72% (209), respectively.[22] The differences between those living in New York City and Florida are substantial; that is, when respondents were matched for income, 36% more of the Floridians felt safe compared to those living in New York City (i.e., 61% vs. 25%), while 33% more felt safer than those living in the New York suburbs (61% vs. 28%).[23] By contrast, when respondents were standardized for region, the wealthier group had 17% more who felt safe than the poorest group.[24] The effects of region were twice as high (35%) as those of income (17%). These figures seem to suggest that fear of crime may be substantially defined by the larger community neighborhood.

But to assess the role of the larger unit versus the smaller one more closely, respondents were divided up into those who said they had a neighbor who was likely to spot a potential break-in in their homes and those who used other people or who had no one. All those who selected neighbors were presumed to have in mind someone living within a five-block area. The reader will recall that when individuals were asked where their best-known neighbors lived, a total of 88% said that they lived next door or on the block, and a total of 95% said that they lived within a five-block area. With this assumption in mind, the respondents in the New York and Florida regions who said that neighbors would watch their houses can be contrasted. New Yorkers and Floridians who did not use close neighbors can also be compared. Among the poorest New Yorkers (see Table 8-2), 24% of those with neighbors who watched their houses felt safe on their blocks at night. By contrast, 63% of the matching group in Florida felt safe. The average difference between New Yorkers and Floridians for all three income groups was 28%. Among those without neighbors they could count on to watch their houses, the difference between New York and Florida was 37%. If the use of neighbors were held constant, it would still be the case that 33% more Floridians felt safer than New Yorkers. There does seem to be a regional effect that is separate from income and having close neighbors available.

However, close neighbors played a role as well. Thus if those who used close neighbors versus those who did not are contrasted, and people are matched on income and regions, 18% more of those who used close neighbors felt safe than those who did not. In short, there seem to be both a local neighborhood effect and a large regional effect on the respondents' sense of safety, but the regional one is almost twice as large as the local one (33% vs. 18%).

Table 8-2. Percentages of Noninstitutionalized Older Persons Who Felt Very Safe or Safe Walking Around at Night, According to Reliance on Neighbors to Watch Home, Income, and State in Which They Lived

	Percentage Satisfied with Safety	
Older Persons' Income	New York	Florida
Neighbors Would Watch Home		
$0–3999	24 (107)	63 (141)
$4000–6999	42 (123)	51 (148)
$7000 or more	37 (107)	73 (156)
Missing income data	37 (70)	50 (55)
Other Primary-Group Members[a] but Not Neighbors Would Watch Home		
$0–3999	21 (33)	51 (8)
$4000–6999	23 (28)	63 (33)
$7000 or more	31 (25)	75 (37)
Missing income data	30 (22)	61 (11)
"No One" Would Watch Home		
$0–3999	10 (40)	47 (25)
$4000–6999	12 (25)	34 (16)
$7000 or more	24 (17)	50 (11)
Missing income data	28 (18)	29 (6)

Note. The populations for the subgroups appear in parentheses.
[a]Others could be spouses, children, relatives, or friends.

It would be my hypothesis that the local neighborhood effect had to do with the immediate aspects of crime detection and prevention, while the regional fears related to issues of crime arising from wider community sources, such as the number of new immigrants, the degree of unemployment, and the budget allocation for police.[25]

The central point to be illustrated by these data is that each type of neighborhood unit is able to manage different problems.

In this section I have dropped the simplifying assumption that all neighborhoods are the same size. How can this material be related to the earlier discussion on the mobile neighborhood and the hypothesis that older people are under pressure to make three basic moves? Without getting into all the complexities, I should like to suggest several central points. First, large-sized neighborhoods will probably need different mechanisms of coordination than smaller ones. They will need mechanisms associated with voluntary associations, such as block clubs, churches, and the like. By contrast, the nuclear neighborhood can coordinate through face-to-face contact, with only the shadow of organizational structure. Though the nature of these voluntary organizations does not require many resources, it is still true, as Piven and Cloward (1979) suggest and Rosow (1967) documents, that those who are very poor or physically disabled have a much harder time developing organizations based on large units than on small ones.

This in turn suggests a second basic point—that is, that individuals can have different-sized neighborhoods, some of which have optimal structures and some of which do not. Thus the poor might have nuclear and extended neighborhood groups that are organized on a mobility basis, while having a larger community organization that is set up on a mass basis. This is often the case for very poor older people who go into public housing specifically set up for the aged. The next-door neighbors and those in the building might indeed have mechanisms of quick integration. However, the building may be set in a larger neighborhood that is hostile and has little sense of community.

This leads to the third point: Individuals can systematically confront different types of organizations as a consequence of their stage in the health cycle. Thus people who are healthy and married have the best chance of moving into different-sized neighborhoods, each of which is optimally organized (i.e., mobile neighborhoods). Those who are sick and ill might find their immediate nuclear and extended neighbors dropping away. The kin as neighbors become vital, but may be drawn from the community neighborhood. When individuals enter nursing homes, it is generally the case that they face the equivalent of a mass neighborhood, in that the fellow residents are often too infirm to provide anything but the most minimal services.

These points are not even given the status of hypotheses. They are only meant to sensitize the reader to the true complexities of the neighborhood structure; one must take into account the form of organization, the size of the neighborhood unit, and the stage of the health cycle.

Summary and Conclusion

In this chapter, the assumption that all neighborhoods are of the idealized type called "mobile" neighborhoods has been dropped. Rather, three types have been conceptualized: the mobile neighborhoods, which have mechanisms of quick integration that permit them to deal with short-term members; the traditional neighborhood groups, which have mechanisms to prevent mobility; and the mass neighborhoods, which have short-term members but no mechanisms for quick integration. It has been pointed out that most of the people in the 1978 sample seemed to live in neighborhoods with mechanisms of quick integration. Two such mechanisms were assessed in the study: norms of welcoming newcomers, and locally oriented associations that integrated newcomers. The paradoxical fact that the delivery of services by neighbors was not related to length of stay in the neighborhood has been explained by the fact that most people have mechanisms of quick integration.

The 1978 data have been shown to be consistent with the principle of matching group structure with task structure by showing that survey respondents in mobile neighborhoods were more able than those in traditional or mass ones to use neighbors. This was especially true for services requiring short-term commitments.

The principle of matching group structure with task structure also suggests that most older people will have to make three basic moves (or suffer loss in services) as a consequence of changes in health status. When older people are healthy, they benefit most from age-homogeneous communities. When they are severely disabled but still in the community, they benefit most from living in age-heterogeneous communities near their children. When they are so disabled that they require 24-hour care, they benefit from a move to a nursing home. For those who do not make these moves, the principles of matching suggest the nature of their discontents, as well as the nature of services they will lose. I believe that many prior writers who have shown that older people in age-homogeneous communities have higher morale may have been reflecting the views of people who are in healthy stages.[26]

Next, the assumption that all neighborhoods are the same size has been dropped. The theory of matching the structures of groups and tasks has been employed to show that different-sized groups are best able to manage different tasks. Thus the nuclear neighborhood is best for managing tasks such as spotting and reporting break-ins, while the extended neighborhood is good for tasks such as emergency borrowing of small household items. It has been shown that the fear of crime is most related to the community neighborhood concept. Much confusion in defining boundaries of neighborhoods can be avoided if people assign different names to different geographically based groups and use the theory of matching to predict which group will best manage which task.

Finally, the type of neighborhood, the stage of health, and the size of groups have been considered simultaneously. Two points have been highlighted: First, different types of people may play key roles in the mechanisms of integration at different stages of health. Second, the same person may live in different-sized neighborhood units, each with a different mechanism of integration.

In conclusion, it has been shown that when one drops the simplifying assumptions about neighborhoods, the principle of matching task structures with group structures permits the analysis of very complex neighborhood structures. It brings to the fore some important concepts, such as mechanisms of quick integration, that deserve further inquiry. These formulations have some very important policy implications. They suggest that retirement villages that try to accommodate people in all three stages of health may be in error, since they generally do not permit children the kind of proximity they need when older persons are disabled and need household services; they assume that neighbors and paid staff can substitute for kin. The present formulations have similar implications for the development of large retirement regions. I explore some of these implications in the discussion of policy in Chapter 10.

Notes

1. For those living in apartments with more than 15 dwelling units, the term "building" was substituted for "block."

2. Among those not belonging to any organization (440), an average of 50% received services characterized by long-term commitments, and 12% received the other services. The respective average percentages for those belonging to one organization (410) were 57% and 16%; for those belonging to two organizations (285), they were 61% and 18%; and for those belonging to three or more (253), they were 67% and 21%.

3. In addition, if one examines the relationshp according to specific types of voluntary associations, there is a trend for those belonging to organizations designed for local neighborhoods (e.g., neighborhood block clubs and churches) to receive more neighborhood services from neighbors than those belonging to non-neighborhood ones (e.g., unions, fraternal clubs). The difference in percentages between the joiners and the nonjoiners in the first set was 13%, while in the second set it was 8%.

4. Elsewhere, we (Fellin & Litwak, 1963) suggest a series of other mechanisms that should clearly be explored. The particular finding in regard to voluntary organizations must be treated with caution, since it is also possible that people who are sociable both join clubs and seek out activities from neighbors without the two being causally related. It is also the case that in the 1978 study there was only a 60% response rate. This is typical for surveys of older people in large cities. Insofar as the nonrespondents lived in mass neighborhoods, the estimate on "mobile" neighborhoods may be optimistic.

5. The idea of mechanisms of quick integration has not as yet captured the imagination of students of modern neighborhoods, though one has only to go to any new retirement village to see that in fact the managers of such villages display a great awareness and use such mechanisms.

6. Planners often see the virtue of traditional neighborhoods for managing the whole range of services, and they argue for their return without seeing the larger consequences to society or the loss in educational and occupational opportunities to the individuals. Faced with such a dilemma, it is suggested that planners focus more on mechanisms of swift integration, as well as recognize that other primary groups pick up the "lost" neighborhood functions.

7. It is also possible that people might go from the first to the third stage. A person who goes from robust health to a stage of paralysis caused by a massive stroke would be a case in point. There are even more unusual cases of people who go from the first to the third stage and back to the second or first stage. For example, the stroke victim might spend a year in an institution, recover at the end of the year, and re-enter the community. In each of these cases, the present formulation would still indicate which type of community such persons would need and the kinds of pressures they would confront.

8. To some extent, our society has sought to equalize the use of organizations by providing institutional aid to the poor "free of charge," such as meals-on-wheels programs and homemaker services.

9. There is some evidence to suggest that society recognizes the dilemma of the very poor and does provide services free of charge. It is the lower-middle-income groups that are most likely to be caught in a cost bind. For the very wealthy, the problem of mobility becomes simplified: They have residences in several places and find the cost of moving back and forth trivial. The problem of migration becomes increasingly meaningless in that context. When the rich become seriously ill, they also require kin's presence, but insofar as the kin are also rich, they might provide supervision at greater geographic distances. In cases of chronic severe illness where others would be institutionalized, the very rich might hire 24-hour care, thereby converting their residences into institutions and requiring no moves. The very rich would have the same needs for age peers and kin as the others, and these would require some shifts in emphasis among their various residences, so that the general pattern would parallel those of the less wealthy. However, the problems would be obscured by their multiple residences and the ease with which they travel over large distances.

10. I am well aware of the danger of using cross-sectional data as though they were longitudinal data. That is why I deliberately use the phrase "to illustrate" (Palmore, 1981). I am presenting these data because longitudinal information is not available and I think the issues are sufficiently challenging to warrant speculations of this kind, if for no other reason than to encourage future investigators to collect such material. It is also the case that policy makers must make decisions before all the data are in. For them, I present these data as a "best bet." However, they should be cautioned that using cross-sectional data to estimate longitudinal data is very risky. As such, they should pay special attention to the nature of the explanation to make sure it makes sense to them.

11. The material on age-homogeneous and age-heterogeneous areas rests fully on the work of Siegel (1982), who tested out the principles of matching.

12. This hypothesis cannot be tested on the fourth and fifth stages, because the survey included a stratified sample of older people in institutions, with an equal number in New York and Florida.

13. Both stages of health and age homogeneity of the neighborhood contributed autonomously to the delivery of services. When the degree of community homogeneity was held constant, the percentage of healthy respondents receiving services (412) was 14%; for those with intermediate states of health (602), it was 27%; and for those who were sick and single (229), it was 43%. When both health and neighborhood homogeneity were considered together, the persons most likely to get two or more services were those who were sick and single and living in an age-heterogeneous area (56), 52%, while those least likely to get such services were those living in age-homogeneous areas and married and healthy (118), 8%.

14. This section is based on an analysis made by Siegel (1982), with some minor variations.

15. When in good health, most people do not need household services. The major exception is the poor single parent. In any case, for healthy respondents, the degree of neighborhood homogeneity played little role in determining loss of services [6% (200) vs. 7% (172)].

16. There are two assumptions involved in this notion—that older people will place a greater value on sociability when they are healthy, and that they will place a greater value on home care when they are ill. The principle of matching suggests why each service requires a different type of helper and neighborhood.

17. At this stage, the older persons are less likely to have neighbors with common life styles; rather, they have to locate people in the larger community with common interests. This probably means the need to depend more on local associations (e.g., churches, senior citizen centers, etc.) as the chief mechanisms for integration.

18. It is, of course, also true that I am using terms such as "five-block radius" and "10-block radius," when in fact there may be natural barriers, which mean that there may not be perfect concentric circles. For the situations I am talking about, this adds some complexity but does not basically change the point I am making: that tasks can be classified in terms of the amount of proximity they require and the number of people they require. The use of terms like

"five-block radius" and "10-block radius" is only a convenient way of describing most situations in large cities.

19. This means that planners and builders should not strive for some mythical unit that will optimize all neighborhood tasks; rather, they should determine which goals they want to give priority to and choose the neighborhood size accordingly.

20. This is admittedly a very rough indicator, since in principle people can and do use all neighborhood units, depending on the goals they are seeking.

21. The reader should be aware that the use of "percentage of decline" in this case inflates the absolute differences, which were 1% rather than the 3% indicated by the "percentage of decline," and 8% rather than 27%. What must be understood is that I am dealing with services that, as indicated in Chapter 3, are not best managed by neighborhood groups but by other primary groups. Therefore, the absolute percentages of neighbors managing these services are always low. Given these small absolute percentages, differences between them will always be low. The reader seeing these small differences may overlook the crucial theoretical properties they represent. The "percentage of decline" index takes into account these initial low percentages. Whether the reader sees this as a bit of puffery or as a realistic assessment depends on whether he or she sees the theoretical arguments as persuasive.

22. For those with a family income of $4000–6999, the respective figures were 26% (124), 27% (54), and 52% (199). For those who refused to give income, they were 39% (39), 28% (61), and 53% (72).

23. What is of some interest is that interviewers were also asked to rate the safety of the neighborhoods, and the Florida interviewers provided a higher percentage of safe ratings than the New York City interviewers. The average difference between Florida and New York City for the three income groups was 26%, and the difference between the New York suburbs and Florida was 19%. Since the interviewers were middle-aged or younger, one cannot ascribe the sense of safety (or the lack thereof) to older person's fears.

24. When standardized for region, the poorest group (366) had 31%, the next group (377) had 35%, and the richest group (360) had 48%. Those not giving income (188) had 48%.

25. The reader should be aware that these data were gathered before Cuba permitted the large emigration to America in 1980. Since that event, crime rates in the Miami area have gone up. Since these data were gathered, Miami has also been subjected to several race riots and seems to have become a center for importation of illegal drugs. All of these factors have probably altered the feelings of safety among older people living in the Miami area. If so, it would clearly show the extent to which community-wide and even nationwide factors can effectively alter individuals' feelings of safety.

26. It is also the case, as pointed out by Siegel (1982), that "morale" is a global measure that is affected by many different things. It does not really reflect changes in services, especially if the loss of one service is balanced by the gain of another. It may also be a relative measure, in which the respondent speaks about the situation relative to reasonable alternatives.

9

Ideal and Nonideal Forms of Friendship Groups, Networks, Subsocialization Groups, Volunteers, and Exchange

In Chapters 2 and 3, it has been pointed out that friendship groups put an emphasis on the structural properties of affection and common life style, but not necessarily on duty for the survival of the relationship per se. This combination gives friendship groups a flexible structure that is especially suited to deal with services that require precise matching of social statuses (e.g., ethnic, race, sex, age, economic, etc.). This is certainly consistent with the major findings described by many investigators studying friendships (Lazarsfeld & Merton, 1954; Z. S. Blau, 1961; Rosow, 1967; Lindzey & Byrne, 1968; Laumann, 1966; Jackson, 1977).

One of the simplifying assumptions made in the earlier analysis is that the length of time people must know each other to maintain close friendships is known. The implicit ideal was that close friends would be long-term or lifetime ones as well. In this chapter, this simplifying assumption is dropped. A major hypothesis is advanced that individuals can make use of three different types of friends: short-term, intermediate-term, and longer-term. However, for society in general and for the aged in particular, the intermediate- and short-term friends play far more important roles than they have in the recent past.

Another simplifying assumption that has been made is that friends match each other on all statuses simultaneously and continually over the life cycle. This assumption is now dropped. It is suggested that age, as a status indicator, becomes more important for older, retired people, while such factors as gender and occupation become less important (Riley *et al.*, 1972). The hypothesis is advanced that the pressures for friends to match on gender is especially damaging to older males.

Finally, the assumption has been made that friends constitute a closed group—that is, that most friends know one another. This assumption is also dropped, and two types of large open groups are discussed: those called "networks" (Bott, 1955; Mitchell, 1969; Horwitz, 1977; Granovetter, 1974), and those referred to as "subsocialization groups," such as ethnic (Zola,

1966) and class (Kohn, 1969) groups. In addition, volunteers are examined. The structural properties of each type of group are examined, and, utilizing the principle of matching, the various services each type can provide are discussed.

General Dimensions of Friendship Groups:
Freedom of Membership Choice and
Precise Status Matching

As indicated above, the chief structural characteristic of friendship is the continuing freedom of individuals to enter and leave the group; this reflects the fact that membership in such groups is based on mutual affection and choice, but not necessarily on the idea that the tie must survive as an end in itself. In this respect, friendship ties are often the opposite of kinship ties. Kinship ties are based on both a concept of duty to the survival of the total group and affection. However, compared to the friendship group, the stress is far more on duty than on affection. This emphasis on duty is reflected in laws that make parents responsible to children; laws that make children responsible for parents; laws on inheritance, which give priority to family members unless they are explicitly excluded; and divorce laws, which mean that marital ties cannot be severed without legal approval. By contrast, if affection ceases in friendship ties, there is virtually no concept of duty or law that would maintain the relationship. Having made this point, it should be added that in the past people often entered friendship ties with the hope and expectation that they would last a lifetime. However, these hopes must not be confused with the kinds of constraints society puts on marriages and kinship ties.

Friendship ties are also more flexible than neighborhood ones. To change neighborhood ties requires a major household move. To change friendship ties only requires that one party alter the tie for whatever reason he or she chooses.

The distinctive characteristics of friendship groups become obvious in societies where individuals are subject to differentiation and rapid role changes. Where individuals are not subject to these changes, then friends, neighbors, and kin may intermingle, and the expectation of a "lifelong friendship" can be met. As discussed in Chapter 2, there are two aspects of a modern society that make it difficult for kin or any group with long-term commitments to provide members with matching statuses. The first factor is the incredibly detailed division of labor that modern large-scale organizations encourage, and the second is the rapidity of change introduced by science and technology. These factors mean (1) that people in the same generation have different roles, and (2) that people in different generations have different definitions of common roles. It will be recalled that those in the same occupations share in common a set of family and community problems, as well as nontechnical work problems that make it necessary to have primary-group support if they are to be solved (LaRocco *et al.*, 1980; Cobb, 1976; W. H. Whyte, 1950; Clark, 1969). Only spouses or people in the same occupation have the necessary knowledge to deal with these unique problems.

The fact that kinship ties have been separated from work ties and that the latter are controlled by nonfamily members makes it decreasingly likely that kin members will be in the same occupation. Even if they are in the same occupation, the detailed forms of division of labor might cause them to have different specialties, which in turn produces very different pressures. The reader will recall the illustration of two siblings who become engineers but go into different branches of engineering, or go into firms with different degrees of success, or take different mobility paths within engineering. Any of these variations would lead to different problems requiring different people for friends.

Given the complexity and changing character of the occupational–industrial structure, it is hard to envision that any group that is relatively small and has a fixed membership commitment, such as the kinship group, can provide primary-group members who will have the same precise occupations. The exceptions are the poor, who generally have unskilled and semi-skilled occupations that are interchangeable.

It will also be recalled that in a society dominated by science and technology, people of one generation might confront very different life cycle problems from those faced by an earlier generation. The substantial increase of retired people, as well as the increase of chronically ill people, has led to unique problems not experienced by earlier generations (e.g., retirement communities, the need for large numbers of people to deal with nursing homes, and, among the very advanced aged, the fact that single women become the norm as well as being a substantial-sized group).

To point out that modern society puts special emphasis on changing roles raises at least two issues. The first is this question: Are there not some roles that remain relatively unchanging or that change more slowly than others? For instance, ethnic and religious roles can remain fairly constant over time (Jackson, 1977; Wolf, 1966). The second issue is that of what services, if any, shorter-term friends can provide if it is indeed true that the ideal in the past has been long-term commitment. The principle that group structures must match those of tasks would suggest that if short-term friends are to play a significant part, there must be tasks that call for matching statuses but only short-term time commitments. Furthermore, if it is the case that some roles change slowly and some quickly, then it is necessary to have friendship groups with different time bases—some long-term, some inter-mediate-term, and some short-term—that each provide different services.

Some investigators have implied that this may be the case (Wolf, 1966; Jackson, 1977).

Furthermore, it should be the case that these time-based friendships should have different structures. The short-term ones must have mechanisms of quick integration that resemble those of neighborhoods, while the long-term ones must have mechanisms for crossing geographic distances like those of the kinship units. However, these mechanisms would not be precisely the same as those for neighbors or kin. For instance, neighborhood mechanisms are based on close geographic proximity, while friendship mechanisms are not. Friendship mechanisms must also meet the demands for maintaining deep bonds of affection, while neighborhood mechanisms need only retain moderate noneconomic orientations. With regard to family mechanisms of exchange over distance, they are buttressed by the norm that the relationship has a value in its own right. This means that kin ties that have been dormant for many years can be activated by an appeal to this norm. By contrast, friendship ties are based on affection, and the question thus arises: If they are not reinforced by contact, will they not dissipate?

Variation in Time-Based Friendships and the Relevance for Older People

A major hypothesis to be examined here is that there are different types of time-based friendships, which can be roughly categorized as long-term, intermediate-term, and short-term (Jackson, 1977; Wolf, 1966). Older people are optimally served if they can have all three types of friendships. However, with advanced aging, the latter two take on special significance.[1]

How these differences might specifically affect the aged are now explored. Let us start by illustrating a service that requires the short time commitments and matching roles typical of friendship groups: the aid required by recent widows seeking to cope with the everyday immediate problems produced by their change in status. Only another woman who has recently undergone widowhood can provide advice on how to deal with shopping and cooking for one, how to cope with the fear of being alone at night, how to go to social gatherings by oneself, how to meet potential new spouses, and so forth. A new widow's long-term friends may not as yet have undergone such experiences. Even if they have, such long-term friends may not live nearby, since all long-term relationships (except marital ones) are subject to problems of differential geographical mobility. Therefore, long-term friends might not be able to provide services that require moderate degrees of proximity, such as playing cards together, going to movies together, or spending time in each other's houses to prevent fear and loneliness.[2] However, as indicated, long-term friends are often the only ones who can help a new widow with maintaining positive memories of the dead spouse, provide companionship during annual vacations, help plan moves to a new retirement community when widowed, and (if the friends are wealthy) even provide financial loans.

To point out that short-term and long-term friends can do different things is only one part of the problem. As indicated above, the long-term friendships require different structures to survive. A further examination of such structural requirements is useful because it may be difficult if not impossible for the aged to meet some of the requirements.

For instance, can older people use mechanisms of quick integration to maintain strong ties of affection as younger people might do? This is a question for which the answer may be "no" among the advanced aged. The reason is that among younger people shorter-term friendships may be terminated by changes in jobs or changes in status that are associated with success and happiness. By contrast, for the advanced aged, changes in friendship are usually associated with illness, death, and grief. Furthermore, among younger people, there is always the possibility that shorter-term friends can meet again or even develop into intermediate- or long-term friends if they can manage mechanisms of exchange over distance. However, for the advanced aged (those over 75), there are no such future prospects. Thus the very advanced aged (e.g., nursing home residents), faced with the decision to form a short-term friendship, might have to confront the probability of great trauma if the relationship becomes more affectionate. What seems to be implied is that very old people can maintain short-term friends only by limiting the amount of affection they expend. If so, there are clearly certain kinds of services that short-term friends cannot provide for the advanced aged but that younger persons may receive.

A graphic illustration of this point was made by some relatively intact people who resided in a nursing home. They made the argument that they could provide companionship and help as long as too much was not asked of them. As an illustration of "too much," they indicated that when fellow residents approached them weeping, they would avoid them. They would certainly not ask the weeping person what was wrong or whether they could help. This reaction was necessary for self-preservation. Residents of nursing homes have both very limited resources and severe problems. To attempt to provide succor to all the people who may request it can quickly overwhelm a "robust" person and can be an absolutely terrifying prospect to those who are barely holding on.

In addition, mechanisms of quick integration used by friends differ from those used by neighbors, in that friends cannot rely on immediate proximity. Thus a voluntary association that may be used to integrate neighbors quickly is generally located within a short walking distance, while those used to integrate friends may be city-wide and may require the use of a car or public transportation. As such, they require more physical vigor as well as greater economic resources. The advanced aged and the poor may not be as able to use mechanisms of integration for friends as they are to use those for neighbors. This would certainly explain those findings (Rosow, 1967) showing that with illness and poverty, older people draw their friends from those who live nearby. This suggests that, though both older and younger people must use mechanisms for quick integration as well as for spanning geographic distances, they may still differ in the specific mechanisms and the extent to which they can use them.

It is also important to keep in mind that though long-term friends, like kin, require mechanisms that involve maintaining exchanges over distance, these mechanisms may be used differently. As pointed out above, the friendship tie, unlike the kinship tie, is based only on personal affection and may require far more reinforcement than the kin tie to remain viable. This becomes a very important issue for the very old, since they are least likely to be able to use mechanisms for spanning geographic distance, such as cars, public transportation, and airplanes. As a result, long-term friends of chronically ill older people may have to live closer or suffer the danger of lapsed friendships.

So far, time has been used as a dichotomy to describe long- and short-term friends. However, for older people, unlike the very young, it is quite clear that there are groups in between the extremes of lifetime friends and very short-term friends. Thus a lifelong friend for someone who is 70 may be someone who has been known for from 40 to 60 years. A short-term friend may be someone known for less than 3 years. Where does that leave those who have been friends for from 3 to 40 years? Thus an individual can retire at 65, move to a retirement community, make a new friend, and have that friend for 3 to 20 years before one or the other dies. The designation of short-term and long-term friends ignores all such subtleties. Yet such intermediate-term groups do have a very special importance for older people. As suggested above, friendships of 5 to 10 years in duration may be sufficiently short-term to provide precise matching for changing statuses (e.g., retirement status, widowhood, illness, etc.), yet sufficiently long-term to build up reciprocities to handle most tasks requiring long-term commitments.

With these thoughts in mind, let us now turn to the empirical data from the 1978 survey to see whether some of these speculations can be documented.

Empirical Documentation of the Relationship between Variation in Time-Based Friendships and Exchanges

First, to what extent is it the case that older people who are disabled must rely increasingly on shorter-term friends? To get some estimate of the probability of this, the types of friends that older people in various health stages had were examined. The results were only partially confirming. Among those who were healthy and married (433), 60% said they had known most of their friends for 10 or more years. By contrast, among those who were sick and institutionalized (230), 41% said they had such long-term friends. What was unexpected was the result for those who lived in the community and were single and ill (263). Approximately as many of these had long-term friends (64%) as those who were healthy and married (60%). According to the theoretical speculations, fewer of the single and ill should have had long-term friends. The fact is that all those living in the community had about the same percentage of long-term friends, regardless of their state of health.

However, one aspect of the speculation was borne out. Those who were living in the community and were sick and single were much more likely to have younger friends [42% (219)] than those who were married and healthy [23% (400)], or those in an intermediate state of health [27% (579)]. This raises a paradox, since, as I indicate below, short-term friends were also younger. The answer to this paradox lies in the limited measure of long-term friends that was employed—that is, "those people who have been friends for 10 or more years." This definition incorporates within it people who have been friends from 10 to 20 years, who, in a population whose median age is 74, can be friends made in retirement, or intermediate-term friends. If the measure had allowed respondents to differentiate very long-term friends—those who had been friends for 45 years or more—I think the paradox would have been resolved.[3] What is emphasized by this discussion is the need to differentiate time-based friendships more precisely than has been done in the past.

A second feature of friendship bonds, suggested above, is that because of the rapidity of geographic movement, only short-term friends will be associated with close proximity. The 1978 data do indeed show that among those (49) who had short-term friends (3 years or less), 65% said that most of their friends lived within 10 blocks, whereas 26% of those (815) who said that most of their friends were of 10 years' duration or longer had friends who lived this close. What is equally important to note is that among those (304) with intermediate-term friends (i.e., of 4 to 10 years' duration), 55% had friends who lived that close. This suggests that intermediate-term friends share some of the advantages of short-term ones when proximity is central to the delivery of services.

A third feature of friendships in the speculations made above is that short-term friends may be drawn from younger and healthier age groups. However, it also means that they may be less likely to share a life style based on common generations, which is a major factor defining life style for older people. Of those respondents living in the community who had long-term friends (819), 71% said that they had friends who were the same age;[4] this figure was higher than the 55% of those who had short-term friends (49), but not significantly higher than the 68% of those who had intermediate-term friends (307). In other words, intermediate-term friends share with long-term ones a common life style based on age.

The central role of intermediate-term friends for delivery of services can be seen. They are like short-term friends in proximity and like long-term friends in age homogeneity. However, for them to compensate for the longer reciprocity of the long-term friends, the intermediate-term friends must have mechanisms of rapid integration.

There was no specific measure of such mechanisms for friends in the 1978 survey. However, there was a general indicator—the number of voluntary associations, which is frequently used for such purposes (Fellin & Litwak, 1963); it has been shown to operate in this manner for neighbors (see Chapter 8). What was found for friends was that those with short-term friends, intermediate-term friends, and long-term friends all had very high percentages (80%, 73%, and 70%, respectively) who belonged to one or more organizations.

This in turn permits the exploration of yet another underlying assumption, which is that people can retain affection even when they have only short-term friends, (i.e., friends of less than 3 years' duration). Respondents were asked:

> How about the friends you are close to: Do you have feelings of love and affection for [them] all the time, most of the time, half of the time, some of the time, or never?

Among those who said most of their friends were long-term ones, 88% said they had affection for them all or most of the time. This was true of 82% of those with intermediate-term friends and 77% of those with short-term friends. Though those with long-term friends did indeed have a higher percentage than those with short-term ones, the difference was not very large; the central point is that an overwhelming majority had affection for all three time-based categories of friends. There may be some inclination to dismiss this finding because the percentage of a single item is being used to measure a very complex feeling. However, there are some face validity data that suggest that bonds of affection do not require long periods of time to evolve. Premarital courtships that last 1 year, for example, are generally considered to involve an adequate time base for building affective ties. Courtships that last 3 years would be considered to involve a long time period. There is no reason to believe that building bonds of affection based on friendship where mechanisms of rapid integration are available should require a longer time period.

To summarize, what the empirical data do seem to suggest is that those who have long-term friends are more likely to have friends who match them in age or life style, but who do not live close by. Short-term friends are very likely to be younger and healthier and to live closer. Intermediate-term friends share with long-term ones the common life style defined by age homogeneity; with short-term friends, they share proximity and health. All of these types of friendships stress affection, and this is partly possible for the short-term and intermediate-term friendships because they stress mechanisms of quick integration.

Given the theory of matching group structure with task structure, it should be the case that these different types of friends will provide different types of services. Let us now see whether this can be empirically illustrated. Unfortunately, the 1978 study did not assess the full range of services. Of the services available for examination, the one that most clearly stressed short-term commitment and immediate proximity was the provision of emergency loans of small household items. In earlier chapters, this has been shown to be a service typically provided by neighbors. What is now being suggested is that it is the one service the short-term friend is also most likely to provide. This is a relative expectation, when comparing one type of friend with another, since the service is still most likely to be provided by neighbors.[5]

The task assessed in the survey that was least likely to call for proximity, but most likely to require an age-homogeneous life style, is the one that was originally viewed as ideal for friends—namely, serving as free-time companions to older persons. This should be a service that would more nearly match the long-term friend.[6]

The services that are most likely to be managed by intermediate-term friends are those requiring some physical resources and age homogeneity as well. Of the services examined in the survey, those best managed by kin come closest to fitting these demands. Providing emotional support to older persons who are feeling low and checking on them daily to see if they are all right are two such services. These would both involve much physical effort if they had to be managed by friends who lived at some distance, since friends are generally age peers who need such services as well.[7]

What these last-mentioned services highlight are the different functions of friends as one moves through the family life cycle (Fischer, 1982). When people are younger, their long-term friends, who are age peers, have more than sufficient physical resources to manage both of these tasks over distance. However, when they become older, they may have to turn to more intermediate-term friends who live closer and are younger to provide these services.

What the 1978 data indicate is that these four services are related to proximity, age homogeneity, affection, and mechanisms of quick integration in ways that are consistent with the speculations above. For instance, if one compares those whose friends lived within a 10-block area with those whose friends lived outside the 10-block area (see Table 9-1), 16% more of the former said that friends would check on them daily, 18% more said that friends could provide emergency loans of small household items, 8% more said that friends would cheer them up when they were feeling low, and 2%

Table 9-1. Percentages of Noninstitutionalized Older Persons Receiving Services from Friends, According to Proximity of Most of Their Friends

Type of Services Delivered by Friends	Percentage Receiving Services		
	Most Friends Lived within 10 Blocks ($n = 412$)	Friends Equally Mixed between Those Living within and outside 10-Block Area ($n = 485$)	Most Friends Lived outside 10-Block Area ($n = 259$)
Serving as companions for free-time activity	39	58	41
Talking to respondents when low and cheering them up	41	47	33
Checking daily to see if respondents were all right	34	34	18
Providing emergency loans of small household items	23	17	5

Note. Populations varied by 1 to 10, depending on the number of those who did not answer for each item. There were 196 people who had no close friends who were not included in this analysis.

less said that friends would serve as companions for their favorite free-time activities. Thus providing companions for free-time activities was least affected by proximity of friends, while providing emergency loans of small household items was most affected.

What were the effects of common life style, as measured by age, on friends' serving as companions for free-time activities? Among those with age-homogeneous friends (see Table 9-2), 13% more received such services from friends than those with friends who were younger, and 19% more received such services from friends than those with friends who were older. It was also the case that among those with age-homogeneous friends, 7% more had friends who cheered them up when they were feeling low than did those with younger friends, and 13% more had friends who provided this service than those with older friends. Practically the same percentage (0 to 3% difference) of those with age-homogeneous friends as those with younger or older friends had friends who checked daily to see if the respondents were all right. As far as providing small household items in an emergency was concerned, 3% fewer of those with age-homogeneous friends had friends who would do this than those with younger friends, and 4% more had friends who would do this than those with older friends. In short, homogeneity among friends had almost the reverse effect of proximity among friends in the delivery of services.

Table 9-2. Percentages of Noninstitutionalized Older Persons Choosing Friends for Various Services, According to Age Homogeneity of Friends

	Percentage Choosing Friends		
Type of Service Delivered by Friends	Friends Same Age ($n = 782$)	Friends Mostly Older ($n = 40$)	Friends Mostly Younger ($n = 313$)
Serving as companions for free-time activity	52	33	39
Talking to respondents when low and cheering them up	44	31	37
Checking daily to see if respondents were all right	30	30	27
Providing emergency loans of small household items	16	12	19

Note. This population consisted only of those with one or more friends.

Let us now see which, if any, services were influenced by affection. Of people who felt affectionate toward their friends all or most of the time, 12% more had friends who were their free-time companions, 10% more said that their friends checked on them daily, and 15% more said that their friends would talk to them and cheer them up. The only service for which affection did not lead to higher percentages of friends delivering services was emergency loans of small household items.[8]

Using the number of voluntary associations as an indicator of a mechanism of quick integration, it can be seen that those who belonged to voluntary associations were more likely to have friends deliver these services (see Table 9-3). However, in the case of emergency loans of small household items, the advantage was very small. People who belonged to two or more voluntary associations had 27% more than those who belonged to no voluntary association saying that they would use friends as companions for their favorite free-time activities. This was a little more than twice the advantage for the next highest service (i.e., cheering respondents up when they were feeling low). In that case, among the people who belonged to two or more voluntary associations, 12% more used friends than those who belonged to no organization. The advantage of belonging to organizations was 8% for those who used friends for checking on them daily, while it was 4% for those who received emergency loans of small household items from their friends.

If all of these factors (i.e., proximity, age homogeneity, affection, and mechanisms of quick integration) are considered, it seems that there is one service (that of serving as free-time companions) that is most likely to be congenially provided by long-term friends. The reason is that it does not require proximity and it does stress common age and affection, which are characteristics of the long-term friend. However, there is one qualification: This service is the one most affected by mechanisms of quick integration. Therefore, the intermediate-term friend, who has almost the same properties of age homogeneity as the long-term friend, can use such mechanisms to deliver these services almost as well.

By contrast, there is one service (the provision of emergency loans of household items) that does not seem particularly suited to long-term friends, in that it stresses proximity and does not especially require an age-homogeneous life style or great affection. It is more likely to be provided by short-term or even intermediate-term friends, since both of these friendship structures stress proximity.

There are two services that seem to be "in-between," in that they require some affection, some proximity, and some age homogeneity. These two services are checking daily and providing emotional support when the older person is feeling low. As such, they might be best managed by intermediate-term friends.

Table 9-4 shows which services were predominantly provided by friends of different duration. Thus, older people with intermediate-term or long-term friends were more likely to receive companionship for their favorite free-time activities from friends. Those with intermediate friends were most likely to be checked daily by friends, as well as to say that friends cheered

Table 9-3. Percentages of Noninstitutionalized Older Persons Choosing Friends for Services, According to Number of Voluntary Associations to Which Older Persons Belonged

| | Percentage Choosing Friends | | |
| | Number of Voluntary Organizations | | |
Type of Service Delivered by Friends	None ($n = 340$)	One ($n = 342$)	Two or More ($n = 480$)
Serving as companions for free-time activity	33	45	60
Talking to respondents when low and cheering them up	33	44	45
Checking daily to see if respondents were all right	25	29	33
Providing emergency loans of small household items	10	11	14

Note. Populations varied from 1 to 20, depending on the number of those who did not answer for each item.

Table 9-4. Percentages of Noninstitutionalized Older Persons Receiving Services from Friends, According to Length of Time They Had Known Most of Their Friends

	Percentage Receiving Services		
	Length of Time Most Friends Known		
Type of Service Delivered by Friends	1 to 3 Years ($n = 49$)	3 to 10 Years ($n = 305$)	More than 10 Years ($n = 816$)
Serving as companions for free-time activity	34	49	48
Talking to respondents when low and cheering them up	33	49	39
Checking daily to see if respondents were all right	30	37	27
Providing emergency loans of small household items	25	24	14

them up when they were feeling low. By contrast, older people with short-term and intermediate-term friends were more likely to receive emergency loans of small household items.

In other words, each type of time-based friend provides a different combination of services. Though the patterns are there, they do not seem to be defined as clearly as the theoretical statements would suggest. As indicated above, I believe that this is the case because the full range of friendship services was not included in the survey. But equally important, and also as suggested already, there was really no distinctive definition of "long-term friends." Given these handicaps, the persistence of the empirical patterns suggests that different types of time-based friends are important in the delivery of services.

Some further evidence for these speculations is the much greater dependence of intermediate-term friends than long-term ones on proximity and mechanisms of quick integration. It has been argued that intermediate-term friends can compensate for the relatively brief duration of their friendships by the fact of living closer and having mechanisms of quick integration. If one contrasts those with intermediate-term friends who lived within a 10-block area and those with intermediate-term friends who lived outside a 10-block area, the average difference between the groups in the delivery of the four services was 14%. By contrast, for those with long-term friends, this difference was 8%. Those with intermediate-term friends were almost twice as likely to be affected by proximity. Similarly, if one looks at mechanisms of quick integration that are associated with proximity (i.e., neighbors' norms toward welcoming newcomers), those with intermediate-term friends were more affected by such norms than those with long-term friends. For instance, 11% more of those with intermediate-term friends who lived in neighborhoods where neighbors were friendly to strangers used friends to deliver services than those with intermediate-term friends who lived in neighborhoods where neighbors ignored newcomers. By contrast, those with long-term friends had only a 2% difference. These findings are quite consistent with the idea that intermediate-term friends can compensate for their comparative lack of long-term commitment by mechanisms of quick integration and proximity.

From a theoretical point of view, it was not possible to demonstrate one of the major propositions—that individuals would do best if they had all three types of time-based friends. This was the case because people were asked how long they had known most of their friends, not how many of each type they had. However, there is one indirect measure that can be used to illustrate the value of different types of friends and to show why the intermediate-term friend is of particular value for older people and possibly for the general population as well. I should like to consider those who said that they had an equal number of friends living inside and outside the 10-block area as being most likely to have all three types of friends, those with friends living primarily outside the 10-block area as most likely to have long-term friends, and those with friends living primarily within the 10-block area as most likely to have short-term friends. If this assumption can be made, then those friends who lived equally close and far should have been able to manage those services requiring great proximity almost as well as those friends who lived only within the 10-block area, but they should have been able to manage these services better than those friends who lived outside the 10-block area. In addition, they should have been able to manage those services requiring age matching and common styles of life better than those friends who all lived in the 10-block area, and as well as those friends who lived outside of the 10-block area.

If one looks at the service least affected by proximity (that is, serving as free-time companions), an average of 58% of those whose friends were equally spread in and out of the 10-block area (485) received this service from their friends. By contrast, among those whose friends were all within the 10-block area (412), 39% received such services, while among those whose friends all lived outside the 10-block area (259), 41% received services. If one now looks at the service that required the most proximity (i.e., emergency loans of small household items), 14% of those whose friends were equally spread near and far (485) received the services from friends, while only 5% of those whose friends lived outside the 10-block area (259) received this service. But in this case, those with friends who lived within the 10-block area (412) had a higher percentage, 23%, who received this service than those with friends who were equally spread. Yet, the central point is that a person with different types of friends (as indicated by friends who are spread geographically) has an advantage in receiving a range of services over those who have only one type of friend. In three of the four comparisons, this was clearly the case.

Of course, this discussion on different types of time-based friends and mechanisms of quick integration only touches on a very complex issue, which cannot be fully developed here (Fellin & Litwak, 1963). However, one additional issue can be raised: What are the circumstances under which such mechanisms of quick integration are likely to be employed? It is hypothesized that those in retirement communities or communities that are old-age-homogeneous are likely to be very sensitive to the development of mechanisms of quick integration. Not only are these frequently new communities, but the density of older persons in such communities makes it easier to develop formal organizations that are specifically designed to incorporate the aged. They can hire staff members to greet newcomers and can set up formal organizations that seek to incorporate newcomers (e.g., hold dances and other gatherings for newcomers). If this explanation has merit, then those moving to retirement communities should have a higher percentage of short-term friends, because such communities are most likely to have mechanisms of quick integration as well as many people seeking friends.

Some insight can be gained on this issue by contrasting Florida and New York communities. Florida was prototypical of a retirement region when this study was done in 1978. In Florida, 35% of the community people in the sample (621) had short- to moderate-term friends, while in New York (682), 19% had such friends. In both communities, those with short-term friends were more likely to live within 10 blocks of their friends than those with long-term friends. Thus in New York, 81% of those (16) with very short-term friends (i.e., less than 3 years) said that most of their friends lived within 10 blocks; this percentage declined moderately to 76% for those (113) with friends of from 3 to 10 years' duration and dropped precipitously for those (465) with long-term friends (more than 10 years' duration) to 31%. In Florida, these same percentages were 58% (32), 43% (186), and 19% (336), respectively.[9] The underlying assumption that people who move to age-homogeneous neighborhoods will make short-term friends who live close by receives support from the data on those living in age-homogeneous neighborhoods in Florida and New York. In Florida, 48% of the respondents lived on a block in which the majority of neighbors were 65 or older. In New York, this was true of only 25% of respondents.[10] These findings are consistent with the view that retirement communities might be the spawning grounds for mechanisms for quick integration.

To get some further insight into this point, one can examine services delivered by very short-term friends in Florida and New York. Though the number of people with short-term friends was extremely small, the pattern of findings is of some theoretical interest. The group with short-term friends in Florida (33) had on the average 37% who received the four services discussed here from friends, while those in New York (16) had on the average 18% who received such services from friends. I suggest that this result is due to the facts that communities in Florida are much more likely to have mechanisms of quick integration, and that newcomers in Florida are likely to be younger and live in communities where people are similar to one another and seeking friends. By contrast, those living in New York with short-term friends are more likely to represent those who have been abandoned in their neighborhoods. I have suggested in Chapter 8 that mechanisms of quick integration may be radically different at different stages of health. The material presented above suggests another consideration—the density of the older population in a community.

Variations in Matching of Social Status and the Consequences for Exchange

At this point, I should like to direct attention to another central feature of friendship—the need for friends to have matching statuses. As indicated earlier, past researchers have stressed the fact that matching statuses seem central to friendship formation. Some current theorists go much further, arguing that communality of statuses is the key to most social ties (Fischer, 1982). Yet such an assertion must confront the fact that one of the key primary groups, the marital household, is based on differences in a major status position—that is, the gender role. Furthermore, it cannot ignore the multiplicity of relations between staff members of bureaucracies and clients, which invariably are defined in terms of different statuses (e.g., store clerk and customer, doctor and patient, etc.), as well as the division of labor within bureaucracies; all of these emphasize the need for people with different statuses and roles to exchange services.

In part, the resolution of this conflict between major investigators and face validity observations takes place from the recognition that services, like groups, differ in structure, with some requiring matching statuses and others not. The conflict may be partially resolved once it is understood that people in the United States have a multiplicity of roles (e.g., breadwinner; spouse; parent; man or woman; member of a social class, religious sect, and ethnic group; etc.), and that these roles may not be correlated. America is a society that political scientists refer to as a "depolarized" one (Dahl, 1966); this means that people might match on some of these roles but not others. When people speak about friends' sharing a common status, they implicitly have two things in mind. First, they are assuming that only some of the individuals' many statuses are relevant for a given service; thus they are saying that a large number of roles will be matched without necessarily saying that all must be matched. Second, they do not insist that all services be linked to each other, so that services delivered to the individuals may vary in the degree to which they require the same matching roles. Jackson (1977) points out that ethnicity, age, and occupation are bases for friendship, but they are not very highly correlated with one another. As a result, they lead to different types of friendships.

If the two considerations noted above are taken into account, some of the earlier ambiguities about friendship can be reduced. For instance, Winch's (1958) formulation on complementary needs really does not address the question as to whether the members of primary groups must in addition share a common language, common age, common sense of clothing style, common religious or ethnic interests, or common views on important social issues. There is clearly no reason why Winch's formulations on psychological complementarity should not coexist with a formulation on cultural similarities if it is recognized that individuals have multiple roles that are more or less independent of each other. What must be emphasized when one speaks about friendship groups having matching statuses is that one is referring to only a limited set of an individual's services and statuses (Jackson, 1977; Wolf, 1966).

If these speculations are correct, one of the critical problems that arises in the study of friendship ties is the definition of the central status around which groups will be organized (Laumann, 1966). The study of older people is fascinating because the aging process involves some major shifts in friendship criteria. One of the major shifts in emphasis is from occupation to age. Another shift that occurs among the advanced aged is from healthy states to states of chronic illness. Both of these shifts have been noted by students of gerontology. Perhaps not as well understood is the shift from distinctive gender roles to a situation where gender plays less of a role, or, alternatively a shift of both men and women to traditionally female-type roles (Palmore, 1981; Cameron, 1968; Neugarten, 1964). In this section, I should like to discuss the problem of friendship as it pertains to age and gender, and to show how the process of aging in conjunction with the principles of matching groups and services permits an assessment of which friends will provide which services.

Age Homogeneity

With these thoughts in mind, I now briefly review the impact of age on the delivery of services. So that age homogeneity of friends could be assessed, survey respondents were asked:

> Would you say that most of the friends you are close to are about the same age (within 3 or 4 years), or are mostly older, younger, or very much younger, or is there a pretty even mix of some older and some younger?

In what follows, I have treated those who said they had an equal mix of younger and older friends as though they had age-homogeneous friends.[11] It will be recalled that 69% of the community sample had friends who were the same age or an equal mixture of young, old, and those of the same age. Very few people had only older friends (4%), but a substantial minority had younger friends (27%) (cf. Palmore, 1981). In short, the aged have substantial age homogeneity with friends. This is, of course, what others have found (Z. S. Blau, 1961; Rosow, 1967). The analysis to this point has suggested that age homogeneity among primary-group members for the aged represents a potential structural strain. The virtues of homogeneity must be balanced against the fact that age peers among the advanced elderly suffer from high rates of disabilities and death. Therefore, they may not be available to provide help. Also, those who are disabled will need helpers who are more vigorous.

This becomes increasingly clear in looking at the aged at each stage of disability. As indicated earlier, among the people who were married and healthy (400), only 23% had friends who were younger. Those who were married and ill or single and healthy (579) had practically the same percentage—that is, 27%. But of those who were both ill and single (219), almost twice as many, 42%, had only younger friends.

The discussion on the value of age homogeneity makes one assumption that must now be explicitly investigated. The assumption that it is functional for older people to select people from the same generation as friends is true only where one is talking about exchanges that are related to the specialized interests of the aged. It will be recalled from the discussion to this point that among the services examined, the one that has been empirically shown to relate to age peers is the provision of companions for free-time activities. However, in the performance of tasks that require more physical resources, such as checking daily, and of tasks that require only proximity, such as providing emergency loans of small household articles, the importance of age homogeneity has been shown to be diminished. These data suggest a possible dilemma, as well as an elaboration of the rationale for older people's choosing friends. The dilemma for the aged arises if they have to choose between the need for more resources and the need for cultural compatibility. The elaboration consists of the understanding that age matching, which typifies friendships among the general population, has obscured the fact that this younger population has sufficient resources to handle most friendship tasks.[12]

Sex Role Homogeneity

Perhaps more dramatic in their implications for shifts in statuses that are central in forming friendships are gender roles. Earlier writers have shown that friendship generally takes place between people of the same sex (Merton, 1948; Z. S. Blau, 1961), and they have assumed this to be the case because of common interests. At first this seems reasonable, in that there is considerable evidence that gender roles in American society are very different (Giele, 1978). However, a second consideration may be that the very differences might also be a basis for friendship to cross sex role lines. Thus it has been pointed out that men and women in marital dyads have "complementary needs," which bind the couples together (Winch, 1958). Can this reasoning be applied to friendship? If a male wanted a friend to talk to about his ill spouse, would he find another male or a female more reassuring? It is very possible, given the traditional role divisions, that a woman might provide greater comfort in this situation. On the other hand, it is true that a male might find it easier to enjoy sporting events such as baseball with another male. At the same time, a man would enjoy social dancing with a female rather than with a male. In short, the past findings that people select their friends on the bases of sex role homogeneity is not on the face of it so obvious, if the full range of tasks for which friends might be used is considered.

It would seem that the ideal structure for friendship would be where there is a mix of friends, some female and some male. Such a mixture could handle the full range of friendship services. The question thus arises as to why there are not such mixtures. One major constraint on cross-gender ties is the extent to which they are viewed as either threatening to existing marital ties or as precursors to new ones (Lopata, 1979). People not prepared to enter a marriage or to break up an old one may therefore resist such ties, even when tasks can be better managed by cross-gender relations.

Such restraints would be less operative where joint friendships exist between married couples (Lopata, 1979). The question arises as to whether they are as operative among older people as well. The demographic fact of life for older persons is that a majority of them are single women who cannot marry (or remarry) because there are not enough eligible men. Given a group where the majority of the members are single women, is the norm that prohibits cross-gender ties enforced? It may be that there is a lesser sense of competition between single women and married ones, because it may be very apparent to the married ones that they may be in the same situation as the single ones in the near future. It may also be the case that elderly males are not so readily induced to leave a marriage of long standing, because it is apparent that long-term reciprocity is necessary for household help, which they may require in the immediate future. For those reasons, the advanced aged may have very different norms on cross-gender ties. However, these speculations must not obscure the powerful competition between marital units and cross-gender ties that force most single older women into one another's company.

In any case, the 1978 data show some very interesting trends with regard to sex homogeneity of friendship structures. Respondents were asked the gender of most of their close friends. They could say that most of them were male, that most were female, or that they were equally divided. The overall percentages are consistent with the idea that people will seek out others of the same gender. Thus 51% said that most of their friends were of the same gender as they, and only 3% said that most of their friends were of the opposite gender. What was surprising was the 46% who said they had friends who were equally divided between their gender and the opposite one.

This surprise was even greater when males' and females' responses were separated. The female respondents in our study provided the basis for the idea that friendship exists between people who are the same gender: Thus 69% of the female respondents (765) said most of their friends were female. Among the men (374), only 20% said their friends consisted mostly of other males. The largest group of men consisted of those who said that their friends were equally divided between men and women (72%).

Why is there this difference between men and women? One obvious explanation is that there are far more women than men at this age level, and if there is a pressure for sex homogeneity, the women have a much larger pool of people from which to select. However, in this case, the proportions were greater than would be expected by statistical chance. Another possible interpretation is that the bulk of tasks that friends have to perform for each other at this stage of life are women's tasks, so that both men and women select women more. A third possibility is that mixed-sex friendships require married persons. It is only in that context that people from the opposite sex can meet without seeming to engage in preliminary courtship behavior. Since men are more likely to be married in this age group, they may be more likely to have cross-gender friends.

Table 9-5 illuminates the finding that married persons were the respondents who were most likely to have both male and female friends. Thus among the married males, 79% said that their friends were equally male and female, while among the single males there were 54% who said this. Among the married females, 58% said they had an equal mixture of men and women friends, while among the single women only 21% said this. In short, being married seems to encourage having an equal mixture of male and female friends.

However, Table 9-5 also suggests that men are more likely to have such mixtures of friends than women. Thus both single and married men had a higher percentage of male and female friends than single and married women. If mixed-gender choices are ignored, it can be seen that both men and women were more likely to choose friends exclusively from their own gender group. Given that fact, it was still the case that men were more likely to choose women than women to choose men (5% vs. 1%). As to the possibility that this is a statistical artifact, because there are more women than men, it should be again noted that these findings go beyond chance levels.[13] This highlights a second reason as to why women *may* play a more important role in friendship among the aged: The traditional woman's roles may be more congenial for the kinds of activities needed by older people.

Table 9-5. Percentages of Noninstitutionalized Older Persons Having Same-Sex or Mixed-Sex Friends, According to Sex and Marital Status of Older Persons

Sex of Older Persons	Marital Status of Older Persons	Percentage Having Same-Sex or Mixed-Sex Friends			Total	Population
		Mostly Men	Mostly Women	Mostly Mixed		
Male	Single	31	15	54	100%	(111)
Male	Married	16	5	79	100%	(263)
Female	Single	1	78	21	100%	(505)
Female	Married	1	41	58	100%	(160)
						(1039)

Thus, as mentioned above, friends might be necessary for providing consolation and handling household tasks among the older population, and females may have better training for such roles than men. Also, many leisure-time activities that involve sex differences may become less important with retirement and advanced aging. As mentioned above, there are strong incentives for men and women to move toward a daily life pattern in which both do the same things (i.e., share household duties as well as leisure-time activities). The fact that husbands are older and may therefore have greater physical frailties may make wives ideal partners for sports that require physical resources, such as tennis and golf. At the same time, physical frailties may lead to activities that are suitable to both sexes, such as playing cards or going to movies or concerts.

The importance of marriage can be seen from yet another angle. In regard to marital status and illness, Table 9-6 makes it clear that illness leads to a decline in mixed friendships among the married and to a stress on friends of the same gender. For single people, this pattern has no consistent direction. Thus among the males in the married and healthy group (230), 14% had friends of the same gender, while for those who were married and ill (33), this figure increased to 27%. For those who were single, whether healthy or ill, there were approximately the same percentages—30% and 33%, respectively. The married women followed a similar pattern: 39% of the healthy ones (134) chose friends of the same gender, while those who were ill (26) had 54%. For the single, there was little difference between the healthy (79%) and the ill (74%). It seems that good health, in conjunction with marriage, produces a friendship set that consists of men and women. By contrast, being ill or single moves the friendship network toward a sex-homogeneous set, and this is a large factor for women.

I believe the reason for this pattern is that spouses pick up those aspects of the service that require cross-gender ties when people are ill. What is necessary in such cases are friends from the same gender to deal with the services that require gender homogeneity. Single people by contrast require both cross-gender as well as same-gender help if they become ill. These speculations receive some support if one looks at the four services for which the respondents were most likely to use friends.[14] First, single people were more likely to use friends for these four services than married people: 42% of the single people (611) received these services from friends, while 30% of the married ones (422) did so. But I believe that this is the case because 66% among the married people said that their spouses delivered these same services to them. Since it is possible for more than one person to deliver these services, it is of some interest to note that single people were in fact more likely to have no one to deliver such services than married people—that is, 13% (611) versus 8% (422). In this case, there was a distinctive sex difference: Single men were more likely to have no one delivering services, [23% (111)] than single women [11% (500)]. The married men and married women were in a virtual tie, with 7% (263) and 8% (159), respectively, having no one delivering services.

I think the fact that single males were least likely to get help is to some extent based on the services examined in the survey. All of the services require two persons, and with one exception, they are slanted toward the

Table 9-6. Percentages of Noninstitutionalized Older Persons Having Same-Sex or Mixed-Sex Friends, According to Older Persons' Sex, Marital Status, and Health Status

Marital Status	Health Status	Most Friends Same Sex	Most Friends Opposite Sex	Most Friends Mixed	Total	Population
		Percentage Having Same-Sex or Mixed-Sex Friends				
		Male Older Persons				
Married	Healthy	14	6	80	100%	(230)
Married	Sick	27	3	70	100%	(33)
Single	Healthy	30	16	54	100%	(87)
Single	Sick	33	13	54	100%	(13)
		Female Older Persons				
Married	Healthy	39	1	60	100%	(134)
Married	Sick	54	0	46	100%	(26)
Single	Healthy	79	1	20	100%	(345)
Single	Sick	74	1	25	100%	(152)

traditional socioemotional household role of women. However, these particular kinds of services may be crucial for older persons, and this may go a long way toward explaining why it is that single men have a much higher mortality rate than any other group. What seems to be suggested is that to have the optimal delivery of services, such as these, it is best to have friends from both sexes. The 1978 survey found this to be the case for men, regardless of marital status, and for single women.[15]

However, if one concentrates on friends delivering services, it can be seen that single men and women were equally likely to get services from friends, whether these were of the same gender or equally mixed (i.e., between 42% and 45%). The same was true for married women (33% and 36%), but married men did better if they had friends from both sexes (18% vs. 29%). What is very important in this analysis is that female respondents virtually never had friends from the opposite gender delivering services, which is perhaps another way of suggesting that single men do not play a central role in the delivery of services to women.

The central point is that for the 1978 sample of aged persons, earlier investigators' findings on gender and friendship must be modified. The prior finding that people form friendships with those of the same gender was very true of single women. For men and married women, respondents were more likely to stress friendships that consisted of both men and women in equal numbers. Furthermore, the argument is advanced that for the kinds of services that older people typically need, having friends from both genders may be helpful. This is especially the case for males, since the key services required among older people who are ill are the traditionally defined female type of services. I would speculate that gender difference may play a decreasing role for older people, especially for males who are chronically ill.[16]

Networks, Subsocialization Groups, and Volunteers:
Their Variation in Structure and Exchanges

In the discussion so far, the implicit assumption has been made that in discussing friendships, one is dealing with small closed groups—that is, that most friends of older persons know one another. However, the term "friends" has been used to encompass large networks (Bott, 1955; Mitchell, 1969; Fischer et al., 1977; Horwitz, 1977; Granovetter, 1974); in addition, the key features of friendship groups bear strong resemblances to informal ties among members of ethnic-racial and other subsocialization groups, and among volunteers. The features being referred to are (1) noneconomic motivation, (2) stress on common statuses, and (3) the capacity of either party to terminate the tie by simply saying they do not want to be associated any more. In this section, I drop the simplifying assumption that all friends know each other; I examine the unique structural features of each of these groups; and, by using the principles of matching group structures with task structures, I indicate the unique services these various groups can provide.

Networks

Let us begin our discussion with "networks" of friends, as defined by Bott (1955), Granovetter (1974), Horwitz (1977), and Mitchell (1969). These writers have pointed out that friendship groups can be closed groups, in which all friends know each other, or they can be open groups, with many members having no direct contacts. There are several distinctive attributes of these networks. First is their very large size. The networks have as their subunits traditional friendship groups, which often are as small as a dyad. Each of these traditional friendship groups is joined to another by at least one overlapping member. Thus older person A may have a close friend B, who in turn has a close friend C; however, A and C are not close friends. Person C may have a close friend D, who is unknown to either A or B, and this type of chain can continue so that the overall network includes many people. It is for this reason that large size is one of the features of these networks. A second feature is that all the members of this large network never meet together or have any centralized coordinator. Rather, coordination takes place through the overlapping members' communicating to one another. This is a very slow coordination process.[17]

A third feature of this network is that there are many people in it who have no deep bonds of affection to others, since most of the others are strangers. However, they still have a noneconomic orientation, since these strangers are always friends of friends. Granovetter (1973) has referred to such ties as "weak ties." From the present point of view, it is sufficient to say that there are motivations based on moderate forms of affection, not bonds of love at one extreme or impersonal economic incentives at the other. A final feature of such a network is the instability of the network as a whole (Mitchell, 1969), even though the subunits within may be very stable. Thus if any member of the network dies or terminates a relationship because of anger, then the entire chain below is cut off. By the same token, if someone forms a new friendship, then an entirely new chain may come with the new friend.

What the large network shares in common with the traditional friendship group are that people within it may share common statuses or interests, that members utilize noneconomic forms of motivation, and that the relationships can be terminated unilaterally by any member. With these structural features in mind, the principle of matching suggests the question of what kinds of services require large size, but not very quick coordination, and can be managed with moderate forms of internalized noneconomic motivation. Granovetter (1974) has suggested that such networks are extremely useful for helping people currently holding jobs to find better ones. Horwitz (1977) suggests that they are also useful for helping people locate mental health clinics.

In considering the underlying dimensions that tie these two services to each other, three central features emerge. First, associated with the formal organizations' tasks (i.e., hiring people and providing mental health services) are not only demands for technical knowledge, but nonuniform demands as well. For instance, Granovetter (1974) points out that if an organization must hire one engineer and 100 qualified engineers apply, then the organization will go to a secondary set of criteria. These secondary criteria are nonuniform. Thus it is important to know whether an applicant can get along with his or her colleagues, since breaks in communication caused by animosity or lack of understanding can hamper production. The assessment of such characteristics at this point is very difficult to make, since it involves not only assessments of the candidates' personality and socialization, but that of their colleagues as well. Often the best estimates can be made by primary-group members with good knowledge of a candidate's interpersonal quirks. Thus employers, once they can establish the technical qualifications of an applicant, can often proceed most quickly and efficiently by making use of primary-group sources to establish his or her ability to get along with the present work force. From the candidate's point of view, the same process works to tell him or her whether this will be a good working situation.

The underlying dimensions can be better highlighted by taking another illustration from a different field—that is, Horwitz's (1977) analysis of people seeking mental health care. First, one must have a technically competent therapist. In addition, one must have a therapist who can take account of a client's primary-group culture (Spiegel, 1959/1965; Bernstein, 1964/1970). Spiegel points out that Irish patients might have very different values from those of assimilated Americans and that the therapist will have to know this to be successful. Presumably, a therapist who comes from the same setting will be more able to do so.

What characterizes both the Granovetter (1974) and Horwitz (1977) studies is that the researchers have dealt with individual relationships to formal organizations that have much nonuniformity attached to them. Presumably, filling jobs on an assembly line would require less nonuniformity. The second feature of these studies is that the services are optimized by larger size because they involve somewhat esoteric activities. Thus for most people looking for most jobs, the larger the number of people looking on their behalf, the better their chances of finding a job. Similarly, finding a mental health clinic, unlike grocery shopping, involves a relatively esoteric service. Before clients are ready to commit themselves to a service that is very unfamiliar, they would like some assurances from someone who knows who they are that such a service would be appropriate for them.

A third feature of these studies is that the services assessed do not make such large demands on those providing the services that only those with very deep commitments can meet the demands. Thus providing the information that a job is available, and even making assessments of the kind of temperament needed for the job, involve no real energy on the part of those providing such information. To the recipient seeking employment and to the company seeking to hire, the decision is extremely important, but this must not be confused with the effort to provide nonuniform information.

Finally, in these studies, the services provided by the members of the network do not involve any time urgency. Granovetter (1974), for instance, is talking about people who already have jobs, so there is no great time urgency involved in their locating new ones. Horwitz (1977) does not supply information on the time urgency of those seeking mental health clinics. But I would suggest that the extent to which the need for such a clinic is an emergency determines the extent to which people would have to use professional advice rather than network members.

The question arises: Are there services with such characteristics required by older people? I think the following might be tasks where older people would find networks especially valuable: seeking housing in a retirement community; seeking a medical specialist for a newly discovered chronic ailment; seeking advice on how to deal with the staff of a Medicare or Medicaid bureaucracy, when some forms have been lost and one has run into a recalcitrant bureaucrat; tracking down organizations that provide discount tickets to various social activities; and so forth. More generally, most relations to formal organizations are likely to have these characteristics.

Subsocialization Groups: Ethnic–Racial, Class, and Religion

Closely related to social networks and often overlapping with them are large primary-like groups that I have labeled "subsocialization groups"; examples of these groups include the informal ties among ethnic–racial group members, church members, and members of the same social class or region. Like networks, members of such subsocialization groups often are motivated to provide services on a noneconomic basis. They are further distinguished by the requirement that ties are based on common status characteristics. It is also true (but less so) that these informal ties may be ruptured by any member's unilateral withdrawal from them.

What chiefly differentiates membership in these subsocialization groups from those in networks is the form of coordination. Members of these groups share a common subsocialization that sets them off from other groups and is the basis on which they coordinate. To understand what is meant by "subsocialization," one must first keep in mind that all major groups in the United States make use of the English language, but that each subgroup may vary in the extensiveness of its vocabulary (Bernstein, 1964/ 1970), the form of vocabulary it uses (Labov, 1972), and the values it stresses (McCready, 1974; Zola, 1966; Spiegel, 1959/1965; Hyman, 1953; Kohn, 1969).

It is the unique subsocialization that they share in common that permits people from the same subsocialization group to communicate and exchange quickly and effectively, even though they may otherwise be complete strangers. Thus if one again considers that staff members of formal organizations and their clientele must exchange not only technical information and services, but nonuniform ones as well, then those sharing a common subsocialization group often have a great advantage. Zola (1966), for example, points out that Italians stress different symptoms of the same medical problems than do the Irish. A doctor who is Italian can more readily understand what his Italian patients are describing. Bernstein (1964/1970) and Hollingshead and Redlich (1958) make this same point with regard to working-class clients and middle-class psychiatrists. Katan (1974) points out that the use of indigenous workers (those who share the same subsocialization as their clients) will lead to better social services.

What differentiates this form of coordination from that of the network is that it does not need to go through a long chain of overlapping members. Any two members from a common subsocialization group can communicate instantaneously, once they meet. The disadvantage of such a subgroup is that it is very unlikely that the resources of the entire group can be mobilized at any one time. To do so requires the use of a network or some voluntary association, or, in a rare case, all members of the subsocialization group reacting to a common stimulus that simultaneously confronts them (e.g., voting for a political candidate who shares the same subsocialization status).

It must be recognized that many nonuniform transactions between staff members of bureaucracies and their clients require instantaneous reactions between "strangers," but not the resources of the entire group. Thus, one of the advantages of a sectarian nursing home, in which staff and clients share the same ethnic or religious background, is that staff members can react instantaneously to the special language patterns, clothing patterns, and eating patterns that characterize the residents' subsocialization group. Residents, in addition, can interact with one another in a more "comfortable" way when they share the same subsocialization. To illustrate the differences between networks and subsocialization groups, it is the capacity to mobilize the total group that enables a network to locate a doctor or a nursing home that matches the nonuniform needs of a client as well as the technical ones. However, it is the common subsocialization between the doctor or the staff of the nursing home and the client that permits the instantaneous communication required for diagnosis or delivery of a service requiring immediate action.

Caution must be exercised when discussing such groups as networks and subsocialization groups and their relationship to formal organizations. It is very clear that the stress on common subsocialization groups and networks can also lead to discrimination. The idea that people should "match up with their own" can leave poor minority groups at considerable disadvantage. Granovetter (1974) recognizes this possibility with regard to networks. The traditional response to such considerations is to suggest the elimination of networks and subsocialization groups. Granovetter (1974) does not take this alternative, nor do I suggest it. The theoretical reason is that there is no way that formal organizations can eliminate the nonuniform aspects of their tasks without partially destroying their own goals. What Granovetter suggests is that one must equip minorities with powerful sub-networks of their own. Dono and I (Litwak & Dono, 1977) suggest a theoretical solution that is based on the need to balance both formal organizations and primary groups. We suggest that those groups that are weak politically and economically, as well as occupying lower-status positions in the bureaucracy, can benefit from attempts to build their primary groups; however, those groups that are powerful in the organization and are economically and politically powerful outside do indeed run a risk of introducing nepotism into the organization. Therefore they should not be encouraged so strongly to build powerful informal networks or subsocialization groups. Thus, the use of indigenous workers to provide the poor with better medical services (Strauss, 1974), better legal services (Weinstein, 1974), or better social services (Katan, 1974) is seen as legitimate, while the attempt to use this same principle of matching staff and clients on subsocialization may be viewed as evidence of racism, prejudice, or nepotism if used by the rich and powerful.

Volunteers

Yet another group that shares the features of large size, noneconomic orientation, matching statuses, and unilateral choices to withdraw consists of volunteers in voluntary organizations. However, volunteers differ from the first two large primary groups in that they have centralized coordinating procedures (i.e., hierarchies and rules), which permit the rapid mobilization of the total organizational resources. To maintain these central coordinating activities, voluntary organizations require a small paid staff or a small group of volunteers who have a commitment that is like that of a full-time paid worker. The factors that differentiate the voluntary organization from a formal organization are that the vast majority of its members are motivated not by economic incentives but by altruistic ones, and that they have extremely short time commitments, which are further characterized by their secondary nature. These commitments are, with the rare exceptions mentioned above, always secondary to their family and occupational commitments. That means that the average volunteers will provide several hours a week, but cannot guarantee their presence over a long stretch of time or even for any given week.

This highlights a unique structural feature of the voluntary association. The organization, because of its large numbers and centralized administration, can generally provide a long-term commitment, while the individual members cannot. Thus the organization can make a commitment to provide a chauffeur to an older person who needs to go to the doctor weekly, because its large size and centralized coordination permits it to say with some certainty how many volunteers will be available on a given day. However, what it cannot guarantee is that the same person will do the driving each time, because the individual volunteers can give no long-term commitment.

Given these structural features, the question can be asked: What services require long-term commitments but do not require that the same individuals provide the services? In general, this is the case where a given service delivered at one time is completely independent of its being delivered a second time. For instance, what one eats during one meal is in part related to what one ate in an earlier meal. It is not a good idea to have the same food or the same amount of food for all meals. Thus having a different person cook different meals each day would be considered disadvantageous, because different people are unlikely to take into account what has been served before. If there is, in addition, a series of activities such as shopping and cleaning, which are performed together and are interdependent over time, then chaos can reign if a different person does these tasks every day. By contrast, where a service does not involve any interdependencies over time and can be more or less isolated from other services, then it is ideal for volunteers. These are the characteristics of such services as chauffeuring people to doctors, putting together sandwiches at a low-cost food center, writing letters that are dictated by older people who can no longer write, bringing snacks and magazines to bedridden patients, and the like.

What is clear is that voluntary organizations, because of their structure (i.e., noneconomic motivation, large size, centralized coordination, and limited commitment of their members), are severely limited in what they can do. Some might object to such an appraisal and might mention cases where volunteers have taken in older people and treated them as their own parents, or they might point to those volunteers who treat their work as though it were a full-time job and give it priority over their families and occupations.

I think that such cases are atypical. The typical citizen cannot give up his or her own primary groups or occupation without suffering very significant losses in services. A few extraordinary individuals might manage to do this because of unusual energy, intelligence, or circumstances. Unfortunately, such atypical behavior often comes to the attention of the larger public and of policy makers. Having no theoretical understanding of the role of various primary groups in society, these policy makers operate on the assumption that these unusual groups should be prototypical for a larger social movement. When such enlargements are tried, they invariably end up in failure, with the policy makers bemoaning the lack of integrity and devotion of the larger public. This is an erroneous diagnosis. Any delivery of services that depends on volunteers to make full-time commitments must be based on the assumption of very limited personnel, because typical individuals cannot provide such full-time commitments without destroying their own primary groups or their careers. That is why, for those jobs in the voluntary organization that require full-time commitments (i.e., the jobs of central coordinators), voluntary organizations often have to pay individuals.

Let us now clarify what has been suggested in this section on large primary groups. The term "friendships" has been used to describe what I have called "networks," as well as informal ties among members of ethnic, racial, religious, and social class groups. I have used the principles of matching to show that these groups have slightly different structures, and then have illustrated the nature of the services that each group can optimally manage. I have done the same with volunteers. What should be clear to the reader by this time is that principles of matching can be applied to all forms of informal groups, and that a statement of the kinds of services each group can provide can be formulated as a result.

I do think that intrinsic to modern society is the need for some forms of large primary groups. This is a function of the fact that traditional primary groups, such as families, neighbors, and spouses, have been separated from large organizations that carry on such activities as business, medicine, and government. As a result, most individuals must interact with the staffs of these large bureaucracies in a context where traditional primary-group members are not likely to be found. Since this context always includes some nonuniform events, it becomes imperative to have some form of noneconomic ties based on large groups if one wants to optimize one's goals.[18]

Summary and Conclusion

In this chapter, the simplifying assumptions as to the length of time friends know each other have been dropped. It has been suggested that in a modern society there may be at least three different types of time-based friends—short-term, intermediate-term, and long-term—and that, following the principle of matching the structures of groups and services, the different types will deliver different types of services. It has been further suggested that older people and possibly the society in general may find a special significance in intermediate- and short-term friends. For older people, this is the case because long-term friends are a very small subgroup of one's age peers, and the older an individual is, the less likely long-term friends are to be alive or well. Intermediate-term friends are thought to be particularly crucial, because they have known each other for enough time to provide services requiring commitments of reasonable length, but have known each other for a short enough time that they can provide matches for major shifts in roles. Empirical evidence has been brought to bear to show that different types of time-based friends do indeed provide different types of services.

Crucial to the concept of friendship is the idea of matching statuses. Earlier investigators discussing this idea have tended to make the simplifying assumption that it is necessary to match friends on all statuses. In this chapter, a counterassumption is made that all statuses are not relevant for the delivery of any given service. Thus people can stress one set of matching statuses for one type of service and another type for another type of service. For instance, it has been pointed out that age-defined style of life is crucial for serving as companions for favorite free-time activities, so that those having friends with matching ages are more likely to get this service from them. By contrast, providing emergency loans of small household goods requires no age matching, but does require that friends share the same neighborhood. If one has two different sets of friends, some the same age (e.g., long-term) and some of different ages but in the same neighborhood (e.g., short-term), one can have both services delivered by friends, since the friends match on different characteristics.

The principle of matching statuses becomes very clear when gender roles are considered. Insofar as men and women are socialized along different lines, there are certain areas where gender similarities are crucial for the delivery of services by friends. If people want to have friends who provide the optimal range of services, they should have friends from both gender groups. It has been noted that men and married women in the 1978 survey chose their friends equally from both gender groups.

The basic proposition is still asserted that friendship groups are optimally structured to manage services that require close matching of roles. However, it is now suggested that not all roles are crucial to all services, and therefore that what is necessary to match for any given service may vary. Furthermore, it is suggested that what constitutes crucial roles may change within the life cycle.

Finally, the assumption that friends must be part of a small, close group has been dropped. It has been argued that the principle of matching group structures with services can be applied to large networks of friends and to informal ties in subsocialization groups, as well as to volunteers. The basic point has been to sketch out for the reader how the principle of matching group and task structures can be applied to many different "friendship" groups. A full exploration of the implications for each of these groups must await a separate work. However, I would hope that the reader is by now satisfied that the principle of matching can be applied to just about any type of primary group.

Notes

1. The more general hypothesis can be raised that intermediate-term friendships should receive far greater emphasis in modern industrial societies as contrasted with societies of the immediate past, because they are long enough to provide the reciprocity required for most services but short enough to provide the precise matching required for friends in a society that emphasizes change.

2. The stress on long-term and short-term friends may very well vary over the life cycle (Stueve & Gerson, 1977). One of the speculations that has been made in this book is that age peers or friends become decreasingly helpful as a person reaches very advanced stages of aging, because they die out or become too enfeebled to help. By implication, this suggests that when people are younger—that is, in their 20s through their 50s—friends are capable of performing many of the services that in later years only younger kin can perform. Clearly, persons in their 20s cannot have the same mix of long-term, intermediate-term, and short-term friendships as those in their 70s.

3. These findings might also be a function of selective loss; those who do not have long-term friends might enter institutions at an earlier stage (Townsend, 1965) or die earlier (Berkman & Syme, 1979). In regard to the former, it is instructive to note that among those institutionalized in our sample who were not severely disabled (163), 48% had long-term friends, as contrasted to those who were living in the community and severely disabled, of whom 64 % had long-term friends.

4. "The same age" means that respondents said their friends were within 3 or 4 years of their own age. It also refers to those respondents who said that their friends were more or less equally divided between those who were younger and those older.

5. What would have been preferable is a question that asked, "If you were widowed, who could give you advice on the everyday problems of living, such as preparing meals for a single person, arranging for escorts to parties, or dealing with household bills?"

6. However, it would have been better yet if there had been a question that asked, "Suppose you were nostalgic and wanted to talk to someone about your earlier years. Whom would you talk to?"

7. Ideally, there should have been a question that asked, "Suppose you wanted to go on a vacation for 2 weeks with someone with whom you could share your favorite free-time activities. Whom would you ask?"

8. Those who were most affectionate actually had 3% less of this service from friends.

9. But the data do reveal a seeming paradox. Florida, where there were more short-term friends, as expected, tended also to have a population in which friends lived further apart, which was not expected. I think the reasons for this may be that New York has more high-rise buildings and people tend to live closer together, and that people in Florida are younger and healthier, and so can maintain friends (short-term and long-term) over greater distances.

10. This occurred despite the effort to insure that New York and Florida would have the same percentages of sampling points, with at least 30% of the people being 65 or older. It is very possible that the differences reported might be even greater, because the sampling procedure did weigh the New York respondents to be more age-homogeneous than in fact they were. (See Appendix A, Table A-1.)

11. This is an assumption with which I am not completely comfortable, since it obscures a

prior hypothesis that people with different types of time-based friends are better able to manage a range of tasks. In this regard, I have pointed out that short-term friends are also generally younger.

12. In the general population, the question of resource limits may arise for poor people, for those suffering from chronic illness, and for those who are striving for occupational mobility by seeking out older, more prestigious people to help (Lin, Ensel, & Vaughn, 1981).

13. The chi-square is beyond the .01 level.

14. The four tasks (as indicated in Chapter 3, Table 3-3) are serving as free-time companions, cheering respondents up when feeling low, checking daily to see if respondents were all right, and providing household help if respondents were bedridden for 2 to 3 weeks.

15. Thus among single men who had friends from both genders (60), 17% had no one to help them, while those with friends from the same gender (34) had 23% and those with friends from the opposite gender (17) had 29%. For married men, these percentages were 6% (207), 12% (42), and 9% (14), respectively. For the single women who had friends from both genders (108), 9% said no one helped them, while 12% of those having friends from the same sex (392) said no one helped. By contrast, married women had 10% (93) who said no one helped when they had friends from both genders and 6% (66) when they had only female friends.

16. This very much depends on the assumption that certain tasks are crucial. It is easy enough to think of services that could be delivered only by those having the same gender, such as the provision of information to a new widow on managing the nitty-gritty of everyday life. This particular speculation requires more research.

17. For underground movements, such as the resistance movement in France during the Second World War, the difficulty of coordination was considered a very desirable feature. Thus if one member of the underground was caught by the Germans, it would take them a long time to unravel the network, and this would give the remaining members time to escape.

18. This is a simplified statement; the more precise statement is traced out in Chapters 1 and 2. For a complete statement of the role of large primary groups, see Litwak and Dono (1977).

10

Social Theory and Social Policy

This chapter on policy implications has several underlying assumptions. First, policy makers are frequently put in the position of having to act before complete information can be gathered. They therefore must ask their social science advisors to provide their "best bet" when the knowledge base is limited. In this chapter, the policy recommendations are my own "best bets," with the understanding that the knowledge base is limited.

Second, only some of the policy implications have been traced out, mostly those that deal with typical populations. Finally, what are being discussed are policy orientations and not detailed policy recommendations. A detailed policy statement would require estimates of costs as well as of political feasibility. Granted these limitations, the reader can still see how basic sociological theory and research have very direct and far-reaching implications for social policy.

This chapter is divided into four basic parts: first, policy considerations with regard to helping older persons who are chronically ill; second, policy implications as they affect the three major moves based on changes in health; third, policy considerations relating to those who are poor and ill; and finally, a general proposition about administering programs for the aged.

Some Alternative Policies for Helping the Chronically Disabled

There have been a series of proposals for helping the chronically disabled. At one extreme, some people have argued for the reinstitution of laws on filial responsibility; other proposals include subsidies to encourage kin to help older people, programs for paid homemaker services (or programs to pay kin to supervise homemakers), the use of foster parent programs, the use of communal living arrangements (or the payment of neighbors or friends to help the chronically ill), and the creation of relatives' advocacy groups for nursing home residents. The major theoretical propositions advanced in this volume provide criteria for assessing all of these proposals.

Laws on Filial Responsibility

There has been increasing pressure from some groups to reinstitute laws of filial responsibility, which would make children and close relatives financially responsible for their aged parents. Past evidence suggests that laws of filial responsibility have seldom been enforced in modern industrial societies (Schorr, 1960) and that, insofar as they were enforced in the earlier stages of industrialization, they actually led to the disruption of the kinship system among middle- to lower-income groups (Anderson, 1977).

From a theoretical point of view, what must be recognized is that such laws bind parents to adult children on the issue of basic shelter, clothing, and food, which in turn means that the parents and adult children must be tied together occupationally. Parents who know that in their old age they will be supported by the earnings from their children's occupations will make far greater efforts than now to insure that their offspring will have good jobs, which in turn is bound to lead to much greater violations of norms of merit. Children who have to provide for parents out of their income will have to give up the resources necessary to maintain their current standard of living, as well as those necessary for their or their children's mobility opportunities. As a result of all this, laws on filial responsibility will lead to a class-crystallized society (i.e., keeping the poor at a low income) and to lower levels of science and technology. Without a theoretical understanding of the role of kin, the obvious short-term advantages of the traditional family structure obscure the long-term negative consequences. What laws on filial responsibility should focus on are the nonuniform aspects of aid that children can provide to parents without disturbing the rational distribution of labor.

Subsidization of Kin to Help the Chronically Ill

Somewhat different in character are programs designed to provide government subsidies for kin who help chronically ill older persons. These subsidies might take the form of tax benefits given to those who take in elderly relatives who are sick, or outright payment for those who take in older people. Such subsidization does not tie the marital household of child and parent to the occupational income of the child, nor does it force the child to choose between his or her mobility and care for parents.

However, the principle that groups can optimally manage tasks that match their structure forewarns us that any time kin must provide marital household services to an older person, there will be problems. Putting the kin in charge of managing a chronically ill relative can strain the resources of the helper's unit and destroy the semiautonomous role of both units. For instance, in the present society, a goodly proportion of both husbands and wives work. For those involved in professional and managerial jobs, giving up their jobs to take care of the chronically ill might lead to a loss in status and in major life interests. It also raises an economic issue: Can society afford to meet the pay scale of the middle- and high-income groups?

An equally important consideration is this: What happens to the altruistic internalized motivation of kin ties if there is an overlap in which one kin member becomes the economic employer of the other? Historians of the family have pointed out that when family and occupation were intertwined, family members often treated each other in a very instrumental, "brutal," economic way (Ariès, 1962). On the other hand, we also know that when older persons have some income to pay for their services, this permits a degree of separation and leads to a strengthening of family ties (Anderson, 1977). What is suggested is some optimum point of subsidization—not enough to make the helper completely dependent on the older person, but enough to relieve the burden of care.

Such subsidization does not take into account yet another factor: The bringing of the elderly person into the home cannot help but alter the life style of the helper's family. The disruption will be more severe where there are strong generational and class differences between the two units. The conflicts will range from the choice of daily food, to the exclusion of the older person from social affairs carried on in the house, to the arrangement of "babysitters" when the helpers go out for an evening or an extended vacation.

It should also be noted that, though subsidization provides the family unit with considerably more resources to meet occupational demands for mobility, there is nevertheless still some strain. The individual who is offered a better job out of town must now not only consider the spouse, but must also consider how such a move might disrupt the life style of the chronically ill person who is living with them. It is true that, since that person is out of the labor force and mostly dependent on the helper, these restraints are less than would exist if a healthy individual moved into the household. The general point is that the healthier and more socially involved the chronically ill person housed at home is, the more he or she will resist any move from the community. This, in turn, acts to inhibit the helper's occupational mobility and the rational distribution of labor. On the other hand, if the parent is extremely sick, he or she may so overwhelm the marital household (Sussman, 1980) that it can no longer function. This situation will lead to states of depression and marital disruptions, which in turn may make it difficult to move and may decrease work productivity. Our theory suggests that between these extremes there is a small range of the chronically ill who can be ideally managed in the home by children or other kin helpers. This range is further limited if the helpers hold well-paying jobs. It is important for policy makers to understand the limits of this range when advocating direct-payment subsidy programs.

Use of Paid Help Such as Homemaker Services

One possible alternative solution, especially for cases where helpers hold well-paying and interesting jobs, is to have the government provide formal organizational services, such as homemaker programs, meals-on-wheels programs, or low-cost subsidized community meal programs. Our theoretical formulation indicates that this alternative is only possible if the organization routinizes the services. If it does not, there is a very serious risk that staff members (motivated basically by money) will exploit the older persons. This is precisely the problem that occurs when homemakers are sent into the homes of older people who are very ill, senile, or depressed, and consequently cannot provide close supervision. Such programs are continually plagued by problems of exploitation and abuse. The policy maker who keeps in mind that economic reward is not sufficient to motivate people whose work cannot be supervised or evaluated will understand the inevitability of such complaints. How does understanding this principle direct policy makers to ways for improving homemaker programs? One solution to which policy makers have turned is to try to get responsible agencies to become the major subcontractors of homemakers, rather than permit each individual older person to negotiate for such services himself or herself. The theory tells us that this is still not a good solution, the reason being that formal organizations are not in a very good position to supervise such homemaking services unless they can routinize them. A theoretically more satisfactory set of policy alternatives would be the recruitment of homemakers who would have internalized commitments, the restriction of such homemaking services to older persons who are still well enough to provide their own supervision, or the provision of such services only when there are vigorous kin immediately adjacent who can provide enough supervision to prevent exploitation. All of these solutions are ways by which people with internalized commitments provide or supervise the provision of household services.

Let us examine each of these alternatives briefly. What is the possibility of recruiting people with internalized commitments? Efficient ways to do this do not exist, and a knowledge of socialization processes suggests that such internalization requires long periods of time to develop. One of the best possibilities is to recruit people who come from the same subsocialization group—that is, the same religious, racial, or ethnic group. People from common subsocialization groups are much more likely to have the same standards of homemaking, to prepare the same style of food, to use language the same ways, and, as such, to be more congenial to older clients. The one major problem with this solution is that the job of homemaker is of such low status and is so poorly paid that such programs could not supply homemakers with matching statuses for those in the upper three-quarters of the income brackets. It does raise a policy issue as to whether one could train homemakers in the culture of higher-income groups as well as to form altruistic commitments to them. The first is very possible, while the second is improbable. Nevertheless, the idea should be explored.

However, if such a program is used in conjunction with a homemaker program restricted to people who are still sufficiently vigorous that they can supervise homemakers closely, it would work. This point recognizes that there is a very long tradition of middle-class people who have hired domestics from low-income groups to clean their homes. In general, such relationships have not been coupled with similar problems of exploitation by the home-makers, the reason being that the clients in this case are vigorous and can closely supervise the paid persons. It is worthwhile for the policy maker to explore those physical attributes that the chronically ill must have to super-vise homemakers, despite their illnesses. For such chronically ill persons, the homemaker program is good as it now stands.

The third solution suggests that supervision might be undertaken by kin who live nearby. While they cannot be in the home every minute, they can be there enough to prevent major forms of exploitation by homemakers. The conditions of success of such a program are that the kin must live close enough so that they can keep track of the homemakers, and that the elderly persons must still retain enough rationality and capabilities to observe, so that in combination with their kin they can supervise the helpers. Our theory tells us the policy makers would do better to try this and the other alternatives suggested here with the specified population, rather than asking formal organizations to supervise programs like homemakers.

Many of the problems of supervision can be eliminated if the formal organization can routinize the primary-group tasks. Meals-on-wheels programs, low-cost meals programs at senior citizen centers, and the serving of food in a nursing home provide illustrations of situations in which the formal organizations seek to manage primary-group tasks by eliminating contingencies. Basically, the same meal is offered to many. The problem of supervision of staff is solved, but at a cost of eliminating individual choice. Meals-on-wheels programs and low-cost meal centers are best for older people who are still vigorous enough to supplement the routine fare with more idiosyncratic choices. Alternatively, it is necessary to have relatives nearby who can provide such nonuniform services.

Foster Parent Solutions

Yet another solution suggested for managing the chronically ill is a foster parent service, which is meant to parallel programs for foster children. By this time, the reader is alert to the fact that the use of any paid person, unless he or she has internalized commitments to the older persons, can lead to exploitation when providing household services. This point is recognized in regard to foster children, and adults who take in such children are closely supervised by social workers with internalized commitments and are tightly screened for internalized commitments. Since there are no good ways to assess internalized motivation, this is a slow and very labor-intensive program, not suitable for the very large numbers of people represented in the growing population of the aged. In addition, it is much easier for adults to develop internalized commitments to children, because children typically are growing healthier and stronger, whereas older people with the passage of time become sicker and die. In fact, there is some very serious question as to how many older persons a "foster child" could take care of if he or she closely identified with them and they died.

In any case, where older persons are so severely ill that they require 24-hour continuous monitoring, such a solution is not adequate. Maintaining 24-hour shifts on an individual basis would be too costly (Sussman, 1980). It is true that "foster children" are on 24-hour duty, but the assumption is normally made that it is a rare event when their sleep will be disrupted. When all is said and done, the theory suggests that such programs are most likely to work if they are kept small, so that atypical people who can maintain internalized commitments to dying people can be found, or if they are restricted to cases of fairly intact older people, with the understanding that when their illness becomes severe they will move to an institution. The programs may also work for older people who are less intact but have spouses or children nearby who can maintain a close check on the caregiver.

Use of Alternative Primary Groups to Provide Care: Communes, Neighbors, and Friends

There have been a variety of other policy suggestions, such as setting up groups of older persons in large apartments, with paid help for housekeeping functions. Still another solution is to hire friends or neighbors. What the theory tells us is that neighbors do not have the necessary long-term commitment and therefore might be exploitative like paid employees, while friends with long-term commitments are likely to be disabled. Paying friends or neighbors is a workable solution only for older people who are sufficiently intact to supervise and can call on kin if problems arise.

How will a commune of older persons living in an apartment get along? Generally, they will do very well when all members are healthy. However, as time goes by and one or more of them becomes chronically ill, the others, as age peers, are in no position to help out. The one paid worker would be quickly overwhelmed also. Furthermore, if the group members' ties were initiated with the commune, they would not have the past or future possibilities of establishing long-term reciprocities. Therefore, they would have little incentive to take care of a chronically ill person. In addition, such communes may encounter special problems when one person is too ill to stay.

The original group members, often starting off as age peers, might find including replacements who are younger and more vigorous into such a small, intimate group to be culturally disconcerting. Alternatively, if the replacement is the same age and equally infirm, the person's tenure might be too short to develop commitment. In other words, such communes are no panacea for the chronically ill. Theoretical considerations suggest that they are a solution for single people who are a little frail, but not so chronically ill that they cannot manage most daily activities on their own.

Institutional Care and Advocacy Groups for the Elderly

In Chapter 4, I have highlighted the dilemmas of institutional care and some of the possible solutions to these dilemmas. In this section, I should like to suggest that for nursing home residents who are severely ill, it is important for their children or other relatives to supervise staff members, as well as to have an advocacy organization made up of children and relatives.

To understand this emphasis, let us look at alternatives. Some policy makers have suggested a residents' bill of rights and a council of fellow residents as the chief safeguards against staff exploitation. Why cannot fellow residents help? The reason is that fellow residents are usually so disabled and so much dependent on the staff that they would not, if rational, dare to criticize them. The criticisms of those who are not rational are simply ignored, or they are asked to leave. Why not use volunteers to act on the residents' behalf? Because there must be persons who maintain close contact with the individual patients over a very long period of time, so that they know which of their daily possessions are in fact missing, or which of their expressions of rage indicate realistic complaints and which stem from a generalized discontent. They must have sufficient commitment to undertake continual conflict with the staff, as well as to bear the responsibility that their actions might provoke the staff into punitive acts against the residents. As indicated in Chapter 9, the typical volunteer cannot make such a long-term commitment to a specific resident.

What about ombudsman programs? First, ombudsmen are too few in number to deal with the daily observation of all patients in a nursing home. Secondly, they are generally employees of the state, which in any conflict is very much subject to lobbying influences of nursing home associations and staff unions. Currently, residents have weak or no organizations that support systematic counterlobbying efforts. Ombudsmen seem to function best when someone comes to them with a problem that requires information rather than conflict resolution.

The mention of lobbying provides a partial answer to the question as to why children and relatives must form an organization. State and federal legislation can affect the reimbursement rates and the standards for nursing homes. To deal with state legislatures and nursing home regulatory agencies, paid lobbyists and threats of political action are needed. Organizations of children and relatives provide the kind of resources that most individuals simply cannot manage.

Another reason for the need for an organization is that children and relatives as individuals must be cautious in the criticism of staff, because the elderly patients are very vulnerable to staff punishment. In addition, they can be invited by the staff to take the patients and leave. This is a potent threat where beds in nursing homes are scarce. To avoid such danger, the children and relatives of residents need the power of an organized group, as well as the anonymity that such a group can give.

Why cannot state regulatory agencies provide such services? First, state regulatory agencies as formal organizations cannot provide the daily observations necessary to deal with the staff's nonroutine activities. Secondly, state regulatory agencies are, like ombudsmen, agents of government and thus liable to lobbying efforts. The administrators and staff of nursing homes are represented by associations and unions that have funds for lobbying on their behalf, while children and relatives of residents do not have such formal organizations. As a result, the governmental agencies are faced with continual organized pressure on one side, and sporadic, weakly financed efforts on the other side.

This raises a policy issue: To what extent, if any, should funds be provided to children and relatives of residents to develop their own organization? Nursing home administrators and staff are clearly using money that is derived from residents' fees to finance the associations that produce lobbying and legal activities on their own behalf. The theory tells us that if the primary-group needs of residents in nursing homes are to be protected, there must be provision of some kind of funding or encouragement for children and relatives of residents to develop an advocacy organization.

Summary

In policy makers' considerations of all of the alternatives described above, when the assumption has been stated that each primary group can manage only certain tasks, many typically respond by saying they have personal knowledge of exceptions (e.g., neighbors who have undertaken long-term daily household services for a chronically ill older person). The policy makers are faced with a dilemma: Are these exceptions prototypical models, or are they atypical events, impossible to develop on a larger scale without destroying the basic structure of the society? The use of the larger theoretical principle permits one to distinguish whether innovations are either consistent or not consistent with modern society. Thus, the fascination of some policy makers with traditional neighborhoods and kin structure is based on short-term, immediate considerations, without thought to long-term or larger implications. The call for neighbors, friends, or volunteers to take over typical kin functions rests on the analysis of very few atypically dedicated people whose personalities could not be easily duplicated, given the demands of the larger society. Policy makers who understand the larger needs of the society can take advantage of the atypical circumstances without pushing them so far as to create long-term problems for individuals or for the larger society.

Policies Relating to Major Moves
Required by Shifts in Health Status

Major policy implications also arise from the view that people must make at least three major moves after they retire because of changes in health status. The reader will recall that the first move is to age-homogeneous neighborhoods, the second is to be near children in age-heterogeneous neighborhoods, and the last is to a nursing home.

There are some housing developments that seek to take into account these three stages of aging within one retirement village. Thus a retirement village may have single dwellings for those who are healthy, a hotel-like arrangement with staff members to take care of people who must be in a protected environment but can still manage in the community, and a nursing home for those who need 24-hour care. The theory of matching group structure and task structure suggests that such housing arrangements will break down in the second and third stages. The reason is that such solutions assume that staff and possibly neighbors can manage to deliver household services at the second and third stages. As already indicated, the theory tells the policy makers that staff can only deliver primary-group services in a uniform way, or, alternatively, exploit the older residents, or both. It further tells them that neighbors who are age peers of older people will have a good chance of being too disabled themselves to help out, or will not have sufficiently long-term commitments to provide key household services on a continuing basis. For these reasons, it is argued that a housing policy that assumes it can manage all three stages of health in one retirement village is incorrect, unless the village is sufficiently small so that children can live nearby, or unless people do not have children or younger relatives who can help.

There are at least two major alternative policy directives suggested by this analysis. First, people who are about to retire should be informed of the need to consider all three stages before making a choice as to where they want to move. At present, many people choose their residence at retirement on the assumption that they will not have to move again. Second, the theory suggests three very different types of housing construction for the aged, rather than one solution for these different populations: first, the large age-homogeneous retirement communities that now seem in vogue; second, a series of very small housing developments scattered throughout the community, so that there is a good chance that any elderly parent would be able to find one within a child's extended or subcommunity neighborhood; third, a series of nursing homes that are sufficiently small so that they are within a community neighborhood of all children, yet large enough to take advantage of the economies of scale. Within this framework there may be room for alternatives—for instance, the notion of tax subsidies to permit people to add on to their homes or remodel their homes for parents would also be suitable for the second stage (Sussman, 1980). Furthermore, building smaller retirement communities within cities where children reside, rather than having whole retirement regions like southern Florida, might make the moves from one stage to the next easier for older people. Granted that many policy makers in housing see these alternatives, this theoretical formulation provides a rationale for selecting one alternative over others.

Policies Relating to Economic State and Health Status

The considerations above can be further elaborated if one takes into account the fact that older people have differential incomes. For instance, it is quite possible that older people with low incomes cannot afford three moves. Only the moderately well off and the wealthy can afford to move to retirement communities. Paradoxically, the extremely poor may be able to afford a version of a retirement community—that is, public housing that is devoted to the aged. However, such public housing is usually located in communities and subcommunities that are very hostile environments for the aged. The question thus arises: For those in modest circumstances, and for the poor who do not like the location of current public housing, what should government policy be? Should it provide cheap forms of transportation to those older persons financially unable to make these three moves? What about people who do not have children or whose relationship with their children has been completely ruptured? For such individuals, the ideal solution would be to have what the anthropologists refer to as "fictive kin"—that is, people with whom they develop a parent–child relationship over the years. Given that development, the same three moves would be in order. If the fictive kin are age peers, or if older people do not have fictive kin, then there will be no good solution in the second and third stages of health. In such cases, there will have to be some consideration to supplying professional workers (e.g., foster parent programs, communes of aged, nursing homes, etc.)—that is, people with much internalized commitment, even though paid—to provide social supports in the second and third stage of disability. Such provision will be very costly and will only be effective if efforts are kept small to take advantage of atypical people.

Modified Extended Family and Policy for the Poor and Ill

The modified extended family can supply two types of family help. There is the household help that spouses provide for each other and that directly rests on the occupational income of one or both spouses. There is also the help that one marital household normally provides to another marital household and that makes only the most modest demands on occupational income. Both types of services are necessary to optimize the life chances of older people. This is sometimes not understood by policy makers designing subsidy programs for the poor aged (e.g., typical laws on filial responsibility). Thus policy makers should not reduce the amount of subsidy when the kin supply normal kin help. To do so would be to force the very poor into an isolated marital household structure that is not suitable in a modern society, rather than to support the modified extended one that is suitable. This is something that policy makers are not always aware of; as a consequence, they sometimes institute needs tests, which force the poor to choose between receiving household services from government subsidies or normal kin services from relatives.

One of the key elements of the modified extended family is the ability to provide exchanges over geographical distance. This is especially crucial in the first stage of health, but is also important in the third stage. However, to do so requires resources to use the technologies for spanning distances—that is, telephones, airplanes, cars, trains, and buses. The poor and the disabled might find it more difficult to use these technologies. Policy makers should give serious attention to subsidies that permit the poor and infirm to exchange services over distance. Prototypes are already in place, with many cities offering public transportation discounts to older people. Should these not be extended to telephone bills and air fares, and made available to helpers as well as older people?

In addition, there must be an educational policy that sensitizes upwardly mobile children to the legitimate role of kin in helping older people. For instance, people must be educated to know that many services can be delivered despite class differences, as well as sensitized to the value of maintaining multiple-class cultures.

Immigrants from less industrial societies must be especially educated on the way in which the family shares tasks with formal organizations. This is especially crucial when older people must go into nursing homes. People who adhere to a traditional family structure, with the norm that the family must take care of its own, may keep the older person at home much too long and thereby damage the functioning of their own marital unit. When the older person is finally put into a nursing home they may feel enormously guilty, or may ask for special privileges that destroy the organization's merit principles and insure that some residents will receive poorer services. People who hold to an isolated marital household concept, in which kinship aid is considered nonessential, will not feel that it is important to provide any services to older persons once they are in nursing homes; this will lead to serious losses to older people. It is only persons who hold to the modified extended family concept who can put their parents in the nursing home without feeling either that they have no further responsibilities or that they have violated basic family norms.

Though the problems are particularly clear-cut in the nursing home setting, the same logic would hold true when older persons have to use any organizational service, such as homemaker services, meals-on-wheels programs, or inexpensive meal programs. Though the data in the 1978 study clearly show that substantial majorities of the sample in fact acted on the principles of the modified extended family, it is my own feeling that they often did so without an overall understanding of the model. As a result, helpers often suffered unnecessarily when having to make such decisions as putting older persons into nursing homes, moving the older persons closer to them, and so forth.

Neighborhood Structures and the Poor and Ill

Key to the structure of modern neighborhoods is the ability to maintain cohesion, despite the fact that people are constantly moving. However, there is good reason to believe that many of these mechanisms are learned as part of one's job and educational experience in middle- and higher-level jobs (Fellin & Litwak, 1963). Furthermore, there is good reason to believe that to use some of these mechanisms calls for financial resources and good states of health. Therefore the question arises as to what extent policy makers can devise mechanisms that can be used by the poor and ill, as well as to what extent, if any, these groups can be subsidized to utilize the mechanisms of the healthy and moderately well off.

For instance, one mechanism for quick integration is that of local neighborhood-based organizations. However, to form and maintain such clubs may require resources that are beyond the capabilities of the very poor (Piven & Cloward, 1979) and the disabled. The question arises for policy makers as to how these groups can be helped to develop these mechanisms or some alternatives.

Friendship Structure

Social policy with regard to friendship structure tends to overlap with that of neighborhood structure when people become very old. It has been shown that with advanced aging one can no longer count on long-term friends, because they are decimated by death and disability. It is suggested that of particular importance to older persons might be intermediate-term friends.

These are people with whom one has sufficient contact (perhaps 3 to 10 years) to establish some long-term reciprocity, while the time is short enough to insure a match in changing statuses. What policy makers have to do is to educate older people as to the necessity of forming these shorter-term friends, as well as to the unique mechanisms of integration required to form short- and intermediate-term friends.

The Poor's Use of Family versus Friends and Neighbors

There is yet one other empirical regularity concerning the relationship of neighbors, friends, and kin that suggests some policy implications. The poor in the 1978 study used friends and neighbors far less than others. I have hypothesized that this was the case because they did not have the money to purchase marginal services from formal organizations. As a result, they needed many more services for a longer period of time from primary-group members. It was also the case that helpers of the poor were likely to be poor as well. For them to give the same level of services as wealthier groups involved a greater sacrifice.

For both of these reasons, primary-group services to the poor demand long-term commitments. That is why the poor use kin so much more than neighbors and friends. However, the kin cannot really substitute for neighbors and friends without reducing their mobility opportunities (i.e., living in the same extended neighborhood). Therefore, one of the major policy questions that should be investigated is this: What are the marginal services formal organizations provide, and to what extent, if any, are policy makers prepared to supply the poor with enough resources to purchase such services so that they might use neighbors and friends as frequently as wealthier groups? Medicaid, low-cost meals, and shopping services are all prototypes. However, they are oriented to the sick poor, and the theory suggests that much can be gained by considering the well poor.

Overall Policy for Administration of Programs for the Aged

The theoretical perspective of this book argues that older people optimize their goal achievement if they have a network consisting of friends, neighbors, spouses, kin, and acquaintances. Furthermore, these groups cannot easily substitute for one another. One implication of this theoretical statement is that there is no single program of services that can provide all the answers for the aged. Neighborhood programs that seek to support older people by organizing block watcher clubs, escort services, and buddy systems cannot duplicate the services for the chronically ill that the kin can provide, nor can the latter duplicate the former. Furthermore, senior citizen centers, which are designed to provide places where those of a common generation can meet for recreational, political, and other social activities, cannot replace the neighborhood or kinship services. Too often policy has evolved on a "catch as catch can" basis. Each new innovation is greeted with great fanfare as the ultimate solution for the problem of the aged. The theoretical principles advanced in this volume, however, argue that all efforts to find one program to manage all services are futile. Such efforts are the policy makers' version of the primrose path.

What policy makers must understand is that, in principle, they must develop designs for a series of interrelated services. Furthermore, it is probably best that each of these services be developed as a semiautonomous unit. The reason for this is that, on the one hand, their goals are complementary, and success for one is helpful to the others; on the other hand, these services tend to be funded from the same budget source and must compete for money. Therefore, if they are in a single agency with strong centralized authority, it is very likely that the first time one of these subgroups gains control of the central authority, it will adjust priorities so that it gets the lion's share of the funds. Since all of the subgroups are all equally important at one time or another, this type of takeover should and can be minimized by giving each program semiautonomy.

I now conclude the discussion on social policy—not because the policy implications have been exhausted, but because there are too many to develop in a volume such as this. Rather, the purpose here has been to highlight some of the more obvious policy implications, as well as to illustrate how basic social theory can be translated into social policy directives. I hope that those interested in policy can apply the same logic to issues that specifically concern them and can develop the policies that are indicated. I do not mean to imply that this is an easy matter. In the physical sciences, it is well understood that there is a need to develop special occupations (such as engineering) to translate basic theory into practice. In the social sciences, we need similarly specialized professionals. However, what this volume seeks to stress is that an understanding of basic social theories may be a very important source of social policy, and one that has been too often overlooked. It provides a kind of long-term perspective that supplements immediate pragmatic considerations. In this volume, it has been shown that such long-term perspectives can have an enormous impact on our everyday lives.

11

Summary and Conclusions

At this point, a brief summary of some of the major conclusions of this book is in order. The initial observations point out a seeming paradox that has confronted modern social scientists. On the one hand, there are those who in one form or the other have proclaimed that modern society is tied to the emergence of large-scale formal organizations and the consequent decline of "family" and "community." On the other hand, contemporary researchers have continually "rediscovered" the importance of informal primary groups in all areas of life. It is not just that these groups exist, but, wonder of wonders, the large-scale formal organizations seem to do best when they work in close conjunction with them.

Who can deny that large-scale organizations have increased their role in modern society? Furthermore, who can deny that they operate on different and even contradictory principles than family and friends do? How, then, is one to explain the paradox of two kinds of groups with contradictory structures, achieving their goals by working closely with each other?

The answer to this seeming paradox is twofold. First, formal organizations and primary groups manage different and complementary aspects of the achievement of these same goals. Therefore, both types of groups are required for optimal goal achievement. Second, it is possible to mute the conflict sufficiently so they can work alongside each other, despite their differences.

There are two basic sociological questions that follow from this formulation. First, what are the mechanisms that permit groups to mute conflicting structures? Second, what aspects of group structure as well as task structure permit different groups to manage different tasks optimally? The answer to these larger sociological issues provides general guidelines to understanding how older people survive in modern society. With regard to the mechanisms that permit groups with conflicting structures to work alongside each other, several have been suggested, as follows:

1. Primary groups can modify their structures so that they minimize conflict.

2. Formal organizations can modify their structures so that they minimize conflict.
3. Linkage mechanisms between the two types of organizations can
   keep them at a midpoint of social distance—that is, close enough to
   coordinate their efforts, but not so close that their conflicting structures will lead to fatal warfare.

In this book I have explored the first solution and touched on the second
(Litwak & Spilerman, 1982; Spilerman & Litwak, 1982); the third has been
developed elsewhere (Litwak & Meyer, 1966, 1974; Litwak *et al.*, 1977;
Dobrof, 1976; Dobrof & Litwak, 1977; Litwak, 1978a).

   With regard to primary groups, I have pointed out that a variety of
structures have evolved, each stressing a different mechanism for meeting the
organizational demands for merit, differential mobility, and rapid change.
The marital household retains all of the features of the traditional primary
group except that it stresses the smallest possible size—that is, spouses and
young children. The kinship system gives up continual face-to-face contact
and common class culture, but retains long-term commitments. The neighborhood relinquishes long-term commitment and common culture but keeps
continual contact. The friendship group partially gives up long-term commitment and continual face-to-face contact, but keeps the communality of
culture and bonds of affection. By so doing, each of these groups manages to
handle the demands of formal organizations that people be moved differentially, geographically, and occupationally, depending on their ability; the
groups also manage to deal with continual change. Thus the marital household by its small size will have only one and possibly two people with major
career lines, and thus reduces the problems of differential mobility. The kinship system, which has many people in the labor force, permits differential
mobility because it does not insist on a common household or common class
position. Rather, it has mechanisms that permit it to exchange services over
geographical and social distance. The neighborhood, which does require
continual face-to-face contact, meets the demands for differential mobility
by giving up long-term commitment. It manages to survive by having
mechanisms for quick integration and egress. The friendship groups, because
of their stress on affection and common cultural interests but not on long-
term commitments, permit individuals to select others with matching interests
under conditions of rapid change.

   Those who are not social scientists, as well as those social scientists
wearied by the seemingly endless promulgation of theoretical propositions,
may well inquire as to the importance of these distinctions and the consequent principle that groups can ideally manage those tasks that match
them in structure. Some might see the theory as another piece of academic
esoterica, having as much usefulness as the debates on how many angels can
dance on the head of a pin. Yet the claim is made that this principle provides

researchers and policy makers with specific guidelines as to which tasks each group can optimally handle in caring for the aged. Is this an empty claim? This is precisely what is covered in Chapters 3 through 5 in this volume. In Chapter 3, the dimensions of primary groups have been used to classify both groups and their tasks, and it has been shown that in fact different primary groups manage different activities.

What Chapter 3 demonstrates is that the principle of matching group structure with task structure is not a form of futile scholasticism or an exercise in meaningless truisms. Quite the contrary: An understanding of this abstract sociological principle provides a set of criteria for classifying tasks and groups so that one can understand which primary groups can best handle which services required by the elderly.

In Chapter 4 of this volume, I have sought to link the analysis of organizational structure to primary-group structure through two procedures. First, I have pointed out that the dimensions used by organizational theorists to describe group structure are not that different from those used to describe primary groups, despite the substantial differences in terminology (Litwak, 1978b; Litwak & Kulis, 1982). The different characteristics of the two groups are generally opposite ends of the same dimensions (Litwak, 1978b). Second, I have shown that the principle of matching can be used in regard to the structure of formal organizations as well as that of primary groups. Again the question must be asked: Is this abstract statement very useful for explaining the world around us? In this regard, I have stated (Chapter 4) that the key job of one group of formal organizations is to take over services that the primary groups can no longer manage. This is true for such organizations as nursing homes, for homemaker services, or for meals-on-wheels programs. What the principle of matching immediately highlights is that there is an inherent dilemma when a formal organization takes over primary-group tasks, because primary groups manage tasks that are least consistent with the characteristics of formal organizations (i.e., tasks involving many contingencies, unpredictability, and frontier areas of knowledge). The question arises as to how formal organizations can manage primary-group tasks if they are structurally unsuited to do so. According to the principle of matching, the only way the formal organizations can manage is either to convert such a task to a routine one that eliminates contingencies and unpredictability, or, alternatively, to change their structure to resemble that of primary groups (Litwak & Spilerman, 1982). Formal organizations such as nursing homes do both. Thus a nursing home is able to hire one person to cook meals for 100 residents by simply removing the contingencies involved in the residents' choice of meals: the time they eat, the place they eat, and eating companions. Primary-group tasks that are handled through such routinization are generally experienced as inadequate and humiliating. The principle of matching explains why even the best nursing homes must follow this course.

Other difficulties arise if the nursing home uses the alternative option to routinization of tasks, which is to change the structure of the organization to resemble that of a primary group. First, it is difficult to find staff members who will work for money and at the same time have an altruistic motivation. Yet without such altruism, a staff dealing with nonuniform events cannot be properly motivated. Second, such a program is labor-intensive and therefore very costly. This means that nursing home administrators have a moral dilemma: Should they provide optimal services for a few, or less than optimal but still live-preserving services for many? In Chapter 4, an attempt is made to show how this dilemma can be moderated by matching tasks to administrative styles. Thus it is shown that the routinization of such tasks as eating, room furnishing, and emotional support can be partly compensated for if the children of nursing home residents provide special food treats, bring small gifts for their rooms, and maintain emotional support with weekly contacts. Other tasks are lost because they are too idiosyncratic for staff members and require too much continual contact for kin in the community; guarding everyday personal possessions is illustrative of such tasks.

In short, understanding the principle of matching group structure with task structure provides general principles for explaining why in nursing homes the formal organizations handle some tasks and primary groups handle the others, as well as why some administrative styles are optimal for one set of tasks while another style is best for different tasks. Again, the seemingly abstract principle has very specific applications.

In Chapter 5, the principle of matching groups to tasks for optimal delivery of services is applied to one of the critical questions in the field of aging: How can another primary group substitute for the marital household when it is weakened by death or disability? The answer offered by the theory of matching structures of groups and tasks is that one group can never fully substitute for another. However, some can substitute better than others. Three alternatives have been examined. First, primary groups can best substitute for those activities of the marital household that come closest to matching their structure. Second, formal organizations can substitute where no primary group exists, and the tasks can be routinized. Third, some services may be lost because there are no groups with matching structures.

In Chapter 5, I have attempted to illustrate this procedure with 13 services assessed in the 1978 study. More precisely, what I have done is to divide the 1978 population into three groups: those healthy and married, those single and sick, and those institutionalized and sick. Using the principle of matching group structure with task structure and treating the data as though they were longitudinal, five typical patterns of network help have been illustrated: (1) partial primary-group expansion, (2) complete primary-group expansion, (3) primary-group continuation, (4) primary-group decline, and (5) lost function or use of atypical primary groups.

The important point for the reader to keep in mind is that the application of the abstract principle of matching group structure to task structure enables the researcher and the policy maker to specify which tasks will be taken over by primary groups, which will be taken over by formal organizations, and which will be lost as the marital unit goes from a state of health to a state of illness to the state of institutionalization.

In Chapter 6, some of the key simplifying assumptions about the modified extended family have been dropped, and the principle of matching the dimensions of groups and services has been examined under more complex assumptions. The assumption that all people in the society have the same pressure to maintain autonomous marital households, as suggested in the original description of the modified extended family concept, has been dropped. Thus I have shown that in the 1978 sample, people predominantly held a modified extended family norm. However, when they did not, they still followed the principle of matching. Those with traditional family orientations were better able to manage tasks that required continual proximity, such as the marital household services. However, they were less able to manage tasks that required cooperation with formal organizations, and their members paid the predicted price of lower occupational and educational achievement.

I have also shown that the atypical kin patterns in the 1978 survey, such as joint parent–child households, came from the sources predicted. Thus, first-generation immigrants from less industrialized countries were more likely to live close to or with each other, because they were less likely to be socialized within the modern industrial society. Poor people (with no labor skills) were under less pressure from the occupational structure to move differentially, and had greater need for kin because they lacked resources to use formal organizations. The chronically ill were also under less pressure to move differentially, because they were also out of the labor market and in great need of household services.

The simplifying assumption that people could transmit services across class and generational differences has also been dropped, and an examination has been made as to which services can and cannot be transmitted across each of these barriers. I have pointed out that services associated with life style issues (e.g., taste in music, movies, furniture, etc.) are not transmitted across class and age lines. However, normal kin exchanges are, because they can be transmitted across distance and are continued throughout a life, permitting continual small adjustments. Marital household services are also more likely to be delivered across class lines, because for ill older people they require long-term reciprocity as well as physical and economic resources, rather than matching life styles.

The simplifying assumption that all services can be dichotomized into those that can be managed at a distance and those that require immediate proximity (i.e., within a common household) has likewise been dropped. I have shown that services vary in regard to the distances over which they can be managed. The degree of variation in turn depends on their relationship to modern technologies (i.e., the extent they can be managed through the use of the telephone, airplanes, cars, etc.). I have further argued that technology is in turn related to three basic factors: the frequency with which the service must be performed, the degree to which it requires a face-to-face presence, and the extent to which it demands resources (i.e., money or specialized knowledge) for its use. Using these formulations and data on frequency of face-to-face and telephone contacts, I have presented a set of curves that suggests for the 1978 sample how one could estimate for all services their relationship to proximity. From a conceptual point of view, this analysis permits one to speak of a modified extended family with a wide variety of proximity patterns, and to specify for each pattern the kinds of services that can optimally be delivered.

Simplifying assumptions on size of the group have also been dropped, and it has been shown that older people with more children receive more services because they have greater chances of living near a child. The assumption that all helpers have long-term commitments has likewise been dropped, and it has been shown that in the 1978 sample, long-term commitments were most likely to exist between parents and children, not between other relatives or friends. This in part accounted for the fact that children could manage tasks better than others. Finally, the assumption that older people are all affectionate toward their helpers has been dropped; it has been empirically shown that in the 1978 sample the overwhelming majority of older persons were affectionate, that such affection could be retained over class and geographic distance, and that affectionate ties were indeed associated with more services. All these factors have been put into a path model, which bears out my hypothesis as to how the factors relate to one another. The basic hypothesis is that ethnic status, illness, number of children, and social class tend to affect services indirectly by geographically moving people closer to each other. This is less true of normal kin services, as would be predicted by the principle of matching.

In Chapter 7, the simplifying assumption that older persons and helpers have complete marital households has been dropped, and it has been shown that helpers who are single are more likely to deliver services, but feel no greater burden because they are least likely to violate the norms on semi-autonomy of the kinship system. The 1978 data showed that when helpers and older persons were both single, they were best able to form a common household, while if they were both married they were least likely to do so. Having a common household was the single most powerful guarantee that marital household services would be delivered.

The simplifying assumption that male and female helpers provide equally is also dropped in Chaper 7. It is shown that female helpers provide more marital household services. However, this occurs because women helpers are more likely to take their parents into their homes. But there is no way that females can provide help by bringing their parents into their households or having them move nearby without significantly altering the life style of their spouses. The 1978 data showed that spouses had to supply help to the female helpers if they in turn were to deliver household services.

Nonetheless, the data did suggest that the sex-linked division of labor currently puts the most direct burden on women to manage ties of older people who are sick. It has also been suggested this role may be changing, in that the first-generation immigrant groups in the 1978 survey were the most likely to emphasize the woman's role. It has been argued that a "role substitutability" model is optimal in a modern society, especially for the aged. Older people whose spouses are ill or dead are severely hampered if they cannot take over their spouses' roles.

In Chapter 8, the simplifying assumption that all older persons live in "mobile neighborhoods" (i.e., have mechanisms of quick integration) has been dropped. Three major types of neighborhoods have been examined: (1) mobile neighborhoods, which have mechanisms of quick integration; (2) traditional neighborhoods, which can be cohesive only if members make long-term commitments; and (3) mass neighborhoods, where individual neighbors have little to do with one another. I have shown that the majority of the 1978 sample did live in neighborhoods where people had positive orientations toward newcomers and belonged to local associations. Furthermore, those having such mechanisms were most likely to get services delivered by neighbors, even if they had only lived in the neighborhood a short period of time.

The simplifying assumption that older people optimally remain in one neighborhood has also been dropped. It is argued that older persons are under institutional pressure to make at least three basic moves after their retirement. When they are healthy and vigorous, they benefit most from age-homogeneous communities. When they are sick and single, they optimize their life chances by living near or with children in age-heterogeneous areas. When they need 24-hour care, it is necessary for them to move to a nursing home within commuting distance. The 1978 data showed that older people were most likely to use neighbors and friends as companions for their free-time activities when they were healthy and lived in age-homogeneous communities. However, when the older persons became seriously ill and needed household services, they were more likely to get such services if they lived in age-heterogeneous areas near kin. Finally, it is suggested that if older people who need full-time 24-hour care do not move to a nursing home, they will either die more quickly or, if they depend on a helper, will severly damage the marital household unit of the helper.[1]

The simplifying assumption that optimal size of the neighborhood is known has also been dropped. One of the more enduring enigmas confronting neighborhood researchers is establishing the "proper boundaries" of a neighborhood. This enigma rests on the assumption that there is one ideal type of neighborhood that can provide all neighborhood services. However, the principle that dimensions of groups and tasks must match, and the knowledge that one of the key dimensions of group is size, immediately alerts the reader to the possibility that one term, "neighborhood," is being used to describe a variety of different groups.

To make this clear, four types of neighborhoods have been defined in terms of their size, and the 1978 data have been used to show that "nuclear neighbors" (those who lived next door) were best able to manage tasks requiring a direct line of vision, such as reporting an attempted break-in. The next largest group, the "extended neighbors" (those living on the same block or in the same building), could handle tasks that permitted a little more time such as emergency loans of small household items. Finally, it is shown that some services, such as soothing fear of crime, could best be managed at the city or regional level. Concurrently, such fears were always higher in New York than in Florida, even when respondents were matched on income, suburban status, and the degree to which they had active nuclear and extended neighbors.

In short, the understanding that groups can optimally manage those tasks that match them in structure, when applied to neighborhood groups, has led to the conclusions (1) that neighborhoods in modern society are almost uniquely defined by short-term membership and the need for mechanisms of quick integration; (2) that older persons are under institutional pressure to make at least three major moves; and (3) that there are a number of neighborhood types based on size, and each contributes different neighborhood services.

In Chapter 9, the simplifying assumption that it is known what time base is necessary to maintain friendship is dropped. Three different types of time-based friends are considered: long-term, intermediate-term, and short-term. It is argued that long-term friends will generally play a lesser role in modern society as contrasted with intermediate-term and short-term ones, because changes in a modern society are so rapid that even two people starting out in the same age group and same career can experience different shifts in status over their life span.

From this line of reasoning, two major themes emerge about contemporary friendship ties for older people. First, intermediate-term friendships (between 3 and 20 years) may have special importance to older persons in contemporary society, as contrasted with long-term friendships (40 or more years) or short-term friendships (up to 3 years). The rationale is that intermediate-term friends have been friends for a sufficient length of time to develop bonds of affection and commitment, but for a short enough time that they can take into account current changes in roles. The second theme is suggested by the theory of matching groups with tasks—namely, that each type of friendship can manage different services for elderly people. The two themes are joined together in a third proposition: that it is best to have all three types of friends, but that intermediate-term friends are likely to provide the most services.

There is empirical support for these themes, in that intermediate-term friends were more likely to be called upon than any other group to deal with the range of tasks examined in the 1978 study. However, long-term friends did as well on tasks that required precise matching in age roles but did not require geographical proximity (e.g., serving as companions for free-time activities). Short-term friends seemed to do best for tasks that required very close proximity, little age homogeneity, and little in the way of commitment (e.g., providing emergency loans of small household items).

Behind these hypotheses on time-based friends is the simplifying assumption that there are mechanisms of relatively rapid integration that permit people to form friendships quickly. This simplifying assumption has been dropped, and data have been presented to show that mechanisms of quick integration do indeed permit people to exchange services more freely with friends.

Another pair of simplifying assumptions—that friends must match on all major statuses, and that the chief statuses upon which matching takes place are constant—has likewise been dropped. It is suggested that age may replace occupation and gender (Cameron, 1968) as the key defining status among the aged (Riley *et al.*, 1972; Palmore, 1978, 1981). It is further hypothesized that different services require different statuses for matching. This is the basic rationale behind the idea of three types of time-based friends. This same point is made with regard to gender. It is argued that for some services, having friends of different genders is important (e.g., a man and woman in the same occupational field discussing the nonuniform aspects of their job); for other services, having people with the same gender is important (e.g., getting advice on widowhood from a friend). The 1978 data were consistent with these speculations, in that they showed that for all groups (except single women), respondents were more likely to say they had an equal number of friends from both genders than to say they had only friends from the same gender. In addition, respondents were most likely, with one exception (married women), to receive the most services from friends when they had an equal number of friends from both genders. It is suggested that the varying role of gender may be obscured among a younger population because of the competition between cross-gender friendships and the marital dyad.

The discussion of friendship also makes the simplifying assumption that friends are part of a small group in which members more or less know each other. This assumption has been dropped, and two types of large primary groups have been discussed: (1) networks that are coordinated through overlapping membership of small friendship groups, and (2) subsocialization groups based on race, ethnicity, class, or religion, which are coordinated because members share a unique subsocialization. The characteristics of both of these types of large primary groups are that members provide services to others in their group on a noneconomic basis; members share common interests; and individuals, with one possible exception, are able to leave if they choose.

The question arises as to why one has to consider such large friendship groups. The answer is that in a modern society, people must continually interact with staff members of formal organizations who are "strangers." Despite their being staff and strangers, many aspects of the exchange involve "nonuniform" matters that are best managed by primary groups. As a result, if some primary-group ties can be established within the rules of merit, the exchange can be materially improved.

There is another group that has some of the features of friendship groups—the volunteers. What differentiates volunteers from the other large primary groups is that they generally have a centralized decision-making apparatus, as well as rules governing all members. In that respect, they resemble formal organizations. However, unlike formal organizations, the majority of the members do not work for economic gain, nor can they give full-time or long-term commitments. This leads to a paradox: The volunteer organization can make long-term commitments, but individuals within it cannot. There are many tasks that do not always require the same person to provide the services, such as making sandwiches at a low-cost eating center. Volunteers are good for this. On the other hand, there are activities that do require that one person make a steady commitment, such as providing emotional support for the chronically disabled. Having a stream of different people do this could lead to chaos.

In conclusion, it has been argued that in a modern society it is necessary to have both large-scale formal organizations and small primary groups, despite the contradictions in their structures. Past commentators, seeing the contradictions, asserted that a choice had to be made between the goals of science and technology and those of love, family, and community. In this book, it has been argued that such a choice represents a false dilemma. What the past commentators overlooked was the basic sociological principle: Groups can optimally manage tasks that match them in structure. The fact that formal organizations and primary groups have such radically different structures means that they can manage different tasks. Furthermore, the types of tasks they can manage are both necessary to the achievement of most goals.

Past writers were correct in pointing out the radical differences in structure between formal organizations and primary groups, but they were incorrect in assuming that groups with radically different structures could not exist side by side in a society. The dilemma is not that of choosing between the community and science and technology, but rather of how to manage groups with radically different structures. In this volume, two solutions have been offered to this dilemma. One is the modification of the structure of primary groups, while the second is the modification of the formal organizations. I have argued that these modifications can mute the conflict sufficiently so that the groups can operate side by side, despite their differences. When this analysis is coupled with the principle that groups can optimally manage tasks that match their structure, it provides a very powerful set of guidelines for the nature of groups that can best "fit" a modern society, as well as the nature of tasks they can optimally manage. In this volume, it has been shown that when these abstract theoretical principles are applied to the field of aging, they provide very specific hypotheses as to which groups will provide which forms of services for older persons at each stage of health.

Although this has been a study of aging, a fundamental purpose of this volume has been to extend the boundaries of sociological knowledge by developing principles for understanding more deeply the dynamics of the interplay between large-scale organizations and primary groups.

Note

1. There are two obvious exceptions to these predictions, but they will always involve a small minority. For those who adhere to a traditional family orientation, association with kin is a major source of enjoyment. There will be no sense of discomfort involved in moving near kin in the first stage of health. However, the overall theory indicates that such groups cannot exist in large numbers in a modern industrial democratic society. Another exception comprises older people who do not retire. They will have occupational interests and time schedules that they share with younger people. Again, it is argued that this group will always be a minor exception. The reason is that formal organizations will always force the majority of older people to retire on the basis of merit.

Appendix A: Samples in the 1978 Study

There were three distinctive samples drawn in the 1978 study. The first consisted of community residents 65 and older living in New York City and surrounding suburbs, as well as in Broward and Dade Counties of Florida. The second consisted of residents of institutions for the aged—that is, health-related institutions such as nursing homes, and non-health-related institutions such as congregate living facilities —from the same two areas. The third sample consisted of children designated as helpers of the respondents from the first two samples. Respondents without children chose their helpers from people they knew best.

Sample I: Older Persons Living in the Community

The eligible community populations of persons 65 years of age or older resided in nine New York counties (New York, Kings, Queens, The Bronx, Staten Island, Westchester, Rockland, Nassau, and Suffolk) and two Florida counties (Dade, which includes Miami, and Broward, which includes Fort Lauderdale). The research design required stratification of the New York and Florida samples by old-age homogeneity of neighborhood (homogeneous vs. heterogeneous) and by socioeconomic status (SES) of neighborhood (predominantly working-class vs. predominantly middle-class). In order to achieve the desired goal of roughly equal proportions of the sample from each of the four strata formed by cross-classifying areas by homogeneity and SES in each state, multistage two-phase sampling procedures were applied. Major responsibility for the development of the sampling plan and its implementation lies with Audits and Surveys, Inc., the survey research company hired by Columbia University to conduct the field work.

Phase I began with the selection of census tracts with probabilities proportionate to their size in the 1970 census. In order to take into account changes in the geographic distribution of older persons between the 1970 census and the period of data collection (April–August 1978), more up-to-date estimates of age distribution (i.e., Social Security Administration data on the number of Social Security checks mailed to addresses in the appropriate zip code areas of New York and Florida in 1976) were utilized. The selected tracts were classified into three strata. Tracts in zip code areas that experienced large absolute increases in number of checks between 1970 and 1976 (increases of 1000 in Broward or of 2000 in New York and Dade) were included in Stratum I. The remainder of the tracts were ranked by percentage of older persons in the 1970 census. Stratum II was formed by tracts with the higher concentrations of older persons, and Stratum III by tracts with the lower concentrations.

The number of tracts was then reduced approximately 50% by selecting every other tract. "Locations," defined as blocks or groups of blocks having 60 or more households, were selected from the tracts. Random points were chosen around which boundaries were drawn encompassing at least 60 households. Three locations were chosen from tracts in Stratum I, two from tracts in Stratum II, and one from tracts in Stratum III. A preliminary field survey was then conducted in these locations. Interviewers were sent into locations with the Area Screening Questionnaire (see Figure A-1), and instructed to make observations and to speak to informants in the areas.

Phase II began with the stratification of the locations into the four strata in each state on the basis of the interviewer information. An "age-homogeneous area" was defined as a block or group of blocks having 60 or more households of which 30% or more had one or more persons 65 years or older. The status of an area on this dimension was determined by interviewer assessment on Question 5 of the Area Screening Questionnaire.

A "working-class area" was defined as one strictly or predominantly blue-collar or slum; a "middle-class area" was wealthy, white-collar, or predominantly white-collar. The status of an area on this dimension was determined by Question 7 categories; of these, 1–3 refer to middle-class areas, and 4–5 refer to working-class areas.

The joint distribution of 185 New York locations and 175 Florida locations is shown in Table A-1. The table clearly shows that the types of locations were not similarly distributed in New York and Florida. Age-homogeneous areas were more likely to be found in Florida, and working-class areas in New York; there was also an association between class and age homogeneity.

The stratified sample design called for 300 respondents to be interviewed from each cell in Table A-1. In fact, the study ended up with 219 more cases than the 1200 projected. This study did not reweight the sample so as to make population estimates. For those who may use the tapes and want to make population estimates, Audits and Surveys provided the following weights:

Neighborhood Age Homogeneity	Social Class	New York	Florida
Age-heterogeneous	Middle-class	1479	251
Age-homogeneous	Middle-class	426	596
Age-heterogeneous	Working-class	2158	366
Age-homogeneous	Working-class	434	239

Table A-1. Percentages of Population in Sample Locations[a] Living in Age-Heterogeneous and Age-Homogeneous Neighborhoods, and in Middle-Class and Working-Class Areas

Metropolitan Area	Middle-Class		Working-Class		Total
	Age-Heterogeneous	Age-Homogeneous	Age-Heterogeneous	Age-Homogeneous	
New York City and suburbs	30	5	56	9	100% (185)
Dade and Broward Counties, Florida	25	30	29	16	100% (175)

Note. The social class identification and the age homogeneity of each neighborhood was estimated by enumerators sent into the locations for that purpose. For definitions of "middle-class," "working-class," "age-heterogeneous," and "age-homogeneous" employed in this study, see Appendix A text.

[a] "Locations" were points taken at random from every other census tract in New York City and suburbs, as well as in Dade and Broward Counties in Florida. Each location consisted of approximately 60 households.

The average response rate for both New York and Florida was 60%. Responses were obtained with some difficulty, especially in the New York area. Only respondents who were healthy enough to be interviewed and could speak English were interviewed. Since this response rate includes people whom the interviewers were not able to contact, and since some of them may have been too ill to be interviewed or could not speak English, it may be slightly lower than it should be.

Sample II: Institutionalized Aged

The second sample consisted of those people 65 and older who were institutionalized. In both New York and Florida it was possible, through the state departments of health and welfare, to get a list of licensed nursing homes and congregate living facilities. In New York, it was necessary to eliminate homes that were predominantly for mentally ill persons released from state mental hospitals. The lists gave information on the number of beds, the skill level of care in the health-related institutions, and whether the home was proprietary, voluntary, or publicly owned.

A sample of 40 homes was drawn in new York and an equal number in Florida. The sample was drawn to represent the same proportions as in the entire list, of various size homes, skill levels, and forms of sponsorship. Of the homes approached, 80% agreed to cooperate with our study. A total of 199 respondents from New York and 200 from Florida were interviewed.

The nursing home staffs did not permit a random selection of their respondents, but insisted that staff members select those well enough to be interviewed. This led to few problems, since the number well enough to be interviewed was close to the quota for the nursing homes. However, in the congregate living facilities, far more residents were eligible than the sample called for. In these facilities, respondents volunteered and were interviewed on a first-come-first-served basis.

To summarize, there was a fairly good sample of institutions but not of residents within them. It is especially important to keep in mind that because of health considerations, the people we interviewed in nursing homes were far healthier than typical nursing home residents. In this sample it was not possible to calculate the respondents' refusal rate, since the nursing home staffs selected the people to be interviewed, and as far as we knew there were no refusals. However, it was possible that some residents had refused the staff's request; the research group would not have known of this. For the congregate living facilities, only volunteers were interviewed.

Sample III: The Children and Helpers of Older Persons

The third sample consisted of the children of the older persons who were designated by the older persons as their chief helpers. If an older person had only one child, that child was chosen as the person's chief helper. If respondents did not have any living children, they were asked who among the people they knew best would provide help if they needed it. There were 1746 interviews with older people. Of these, 87 (or 5%) either refused to give us the name and address of their helpers or said they did not have a helper. Of the remaining 1665, interviewers were never able to get in touch with the helpers of 30 (or 2%). Of those helpers who were contacted, 924 were able to complete a 20-minute telephone or mail questionnaire. This number represents 55% of those helpers whose names were made available to the interviewers. There appeared to be no obvious pattern to the refusal rates. The New York community sample had the highest refusal rate, 48%, but the New York institutional population had the lowest, 39%. The Florida community sample's refusal rate was 45%, and that for the Florida institutional sample was 43%. However, where the helpers lived closer to the respondents (e.g., in the same house), they were less likely to refuse. The results obtained by researchers doing studies like the present one, with one exception, were similar. The one exception was a study done in nursing homes before the emphasis on informed consent (Dobrof, 1976). The interview was done under the sponsorship of the nursing homes in question. Under such circumstances, the investigator got a response rate of 90% or higher.

Fig. A-1. Area Screening Questionnaire.

Audits and Surveys, Inc.   Project #4862
One Park Avenue   February 1978
New York, NY 10016

6-A

AREA SCREENING QUESTIONNAIRE
(SENIOR CITIZENS RETIREMENT STUDY)

Interviewer's Name: _____   Location #
                                           (map   12- 13- 14- 15- 16- 17- 18-
Interviewer's # | | | | | | attached)
                7- 8- 9- 10- 11-

Street Address: _____
                                           Date: _____
City/State: _____ 19
                               20-
County: _____ 21

Interviewer's Instructions:

The information in this questionnaire is to be completed for the location assigned (see number above and map) and returned to your supervisor as soon as possible.

In each location you are to verify the boundaries as identified on the map. And, based on your personal observations, and impressions and information obtained from local police, mail persons or postal officials, merchants and residents, etc., you are to determine the characteristics of the location, and answer the following questions:

22-

(continued)

Fig. A-1. (*continued*)

1. How would you describe this location?   a. Primarily residential   [ ]23-1
   (CHECK ONLY ONE.)   b. Primarily commercial   [ ] -2
                                              c. About half commercial–
                                                 residential   [ ] -3

2. How would you describe the structures/   a. Schools or other govern-
   buildings in this location? (CHECK AS   ment buildings   [ ]24-1
   MANY AS APPLY.)   b. Commercial or industrial
                                                 structures   [ ] -2
                                              c. Apartment buildings with
                                                 elevators   [ ] -3
                                              d. Garden apartments   [ ] -4
                                              e. Attached row (or town)
                                                 houses   [ ] -5
                                              f. Detached 3–4-family
                                                 structures   [ ] -6
                                              g. Two-family structures   [ ] -7
                                              h. One-family/detached
                                                 single family structures   [ ] -8
                                              i. Trailers/mobile homes   [ ] -9
                                              j. Other (SPECIFY)   [ ] -0

                                              _____

3. Does this location include a public   Yes   [ ]25-1
   housing project?   No   [ ] -2
                                               Don't know   [ ] -3

4. How many households are in this location? Please count the actual households within the boundaries described
   on the attached map.   #_____

5. Approximately what percent of these
   households are headed by a person   29-
   65 years old or over?   _____% 30-

6. Does this location include special   Yes   [ ]31-1
   housing (apartments, villages, etc.)   No   [ ] -2
   for the elderly?   Don't know   [ ] -3

7. Describe the type of neighborhood in this location. This should be done only in
   terms of how this entire location looks in the eyes of the people in the community.
   Those people you spoke to plus your own opinions, based on your awareness of
   the location's characteristics, must be considered. (CHECK AS MANY CATE-
   GORIES AS NECESSARY TO ACCURATELY DESCRIBE THIS LOCATION.)

   A wealthy or "society" type neighborhood—big business officials, very
   rich lawyers and doctors, and people with large, inherited incomes
   live here.   [ ]32-1

An excellent white-collar neighborhood—doctors, highly paid managers, strictly a professional and executive neighborhood.   [ ] -2

A better white-collar neighborhood—not many executives or doctors
live here, but there are probably no blue-collar people either.   [ ] -3

Predominantly a blue-collar neighborhood—not slummy, but a few
shacks and very poor housing mixed in; probably no white-collar
workers live here.   [ ] -4

A slum neighborhood; the people here are common laborers or people
on relief.   [ ] -5

8. Did you find the information you received from people in this neighbor-
   hood helped out in describing the   Yes [ ]33-1
   location?   No   [ ] -2

9. What kinds of people did you talk
   with?   Residents   [ ]34-1
                                             Merchants   [ ] -2
                                             Police   [ ] -3
                                             Post office personnel   [ ] -4
                                             Social workers   [ ] -5
                                             Other (SPECIFY)   [ ] -6

                                             _____

10. How would you describe the cultural
    or nationality make-up of most of the   _____35-
    people in this location?
                                             Mixed [ ]36-0

    OTHER COMMENTS ABOUT
    LOCATION:

    _____

    _____

    ┌──┐
    │   │
    │ I hereby certify that this information for the location is in accordance │
    │ with my instructions.   │
    │   │
    │   _____   _____   │
    │   Interviewer's signature   Date   │
    │   │
    └──┘

Appendix B: Health Indices

In this appendix, I discuss three different health indices that were used in the 1978 survey and are referred to throughout this book. The first was a respondent's individual health index. The second was a family health index, which included the respondent and the respondent's spouse or spouse-like companion (if there was such a person and if this person was still living). The third was a marital disability index, which consisted of the family index plus whether the respondent was married or single. On one extreme were those who were married and healthy; on the other extreme were those who were sick and single. In the middle were two groups that were often lumped together for statistical purposes—that is, those who were married and ill, and those who were single and healthy. With this introduction in mind, the specific construction of each index is discussed.

Respondent's Index

The respondent's index had eight components. The first three consisted of self-reports of functional disabilities. Community respondents were asked how much help they needed when (1) taking public transportation, (2) doing housekeeping chores (e.g., shopping, fixing small things, cooking, or housecleaning), and (3) climbing or descending stairs. For those who did not normally do these things, they were asked if they could do them if necessary (see Figure B-1, questions S2 a–c and S3 a–c). For each item a respondent could receive a score of 0 to 4, with 4 meaning that the person could not manage these activities and 0 meaning that he or she could manage them normally without any help. Institutional respondents were asked about the following activities: (1) dressing themselves; (2) buying extra food, tidying up their room, putting up pictures, or repairing small things; and (3) climbing and descending stairs.

The next three components referred to a respondent's seeing, hearing, and speaking problems. Respondents were asked to evaluate their vision and hearing capacities (see Figure B-1, questions S6– S10 and box D). The interviewer's estimate of hearing was also used, and if it differed from the respondent's self-estimate, it was used instead. Each interviewer was also asked to assess the respondent's ability to speak (see Figure B-1, box E). Each of the three items was scored from 0 to 4.

Interviewers were also asked to assess whether respondents had any missing limbs or were confined to wheelchairs or to bed (see Figure B-1, box A). This item was also scored from 0 to 4. Finally, the respondents were asked whether they had any

Fig. B-1. Items assessed for the respondent's individual health index.

S2. Now, I'd like to ask you a few questions about certain activities. As I read the list of activities, please tell me, would you require help from someone else to perform these activities, perform these activities yourself but with extra effort or the help of some device like a cane or a brace, or can you handle these activities normally? (REPEAT CATEGORIES AS NECESSARY.) (RECORD ANSWER BELOW IN GRID UNDER Q.S2.) IF RESPONDENT DOES NOT PERFORM A PARTICULAR ACTIVITY, CHECK BOX UNDER "DO NOT PERFORM" IN Q.S2 AND ASK Q.S3 FOR THAT ACTIVITY.

List of activities	Q.S2				Q.S3		
	(1) Help from others	(2) Extra effort	(3) Handle normally	(*) Do not perform	(1) Help from others	(2) Extra effort	(3) Handle normally
a. How about taking a bus or public transportation? (CHECK ONLY ONE ANSWER.)	SKIP 40 [ ]41-1	[ ]-2	[ ]-3	[ ]-4	SKIP 44 [ ]45-1	[ ]-2	[ ]-3
b. How about shopping, fixing small things around your place, cooking, or house-cleaning? (CHECK ONLY ONE ANSWER.)	[ ]42-1	[ ]-2	[ ]-3	[ ]-4	[ ]46-1	[ ]-2	[ ]-3
c. What about going up and down a flight of stairs? (CHECK ONLY ONE ANSWER.)	[ ]43-1	[ ]-2	[ ]-3	[ ]-4	[ ]47-1	[ ]-2	[ ]-3

(Do not perform column) SKIP TO INTERVIEWER INSTRUCTION "A" IN BOX — ASK Q.S3

IF "DO NOT PERFORM" TO Q.S2a, b, OR c, ASK HYPOTHETICALLY FOR THAT PARTICULAR ACTIVITY:

S3. If you had to [INSERT ACTIVITY] would you require help from someone else, do it yourself with extra effort, or could you handle this normally? (REPEAT CATEGORIES AS NECESSARY.) (RECORD ABOVE IN THE ANSWER GRID UNDER Q.S3.)

A. INTERVIEWER: DOES RESPONDENT HAVE OBVIOUSLY MISSING LIMBS (LEGS OR ARMS), OR IS RESPONDENT CONFINED TO A BED OR WHEELCHAIR?   Yes [ ]48-1   No [ ]-2

(continued)

273

Fig. B-1. (continued)

S4. Do you have any illnesses or disabilities at the present time?

Yes [ ]50-1 ASK Q.S5
No [ ] -2 SKIP TO Q.S7

SKIP 49

IF "YES" IN Q.S4, ASK:
S5. Can you tell me what they are? (ASK RESPONDENT TO SPECIFY NAMES OR ILLNESSES.)

51-
52-
53-
54-
55-
56-
57-
58-

S6. Do you have to be very careful as a result of this/these illnesses to perform everyday activities?

Yes [ ]59-1 GO TO INTERVIEWER INSTRUCTION "B" IN BOX
No [ ] -2 BELOW

B. INTERVIEWER: RECORD AGAIN RESPONDENT'S ANSWER TO Q.S6.

Yes [ ]60-1 No [ ]-2

S7. How about your eyesight? Can you see normally (with glasses) or do you have problems seeing?

See normally
Have problems
Blind

[ ]61-1 CHECK "NO" IN BOX C BELOW
[ ] -2 ASK Q.S8
[ ] -3 CHECK "YES" IN BOX C BELOW

IF RESPONDENT HAS PROBLEMS SEEING, IN Q.S7, ASK:

S8. Can you see the print in a regular newspaper?

Yes [ ]62-1
No [ ] -2 } GO TO INTERVIEWER INSTRUCTION "C" IN BOX BELOW

S9. Can you recognize people's faces across a normal-size room?

Yes [ ]63-1
No [ ] -2

C. INTERVIEWER: DOES RESPONDENT HAVE A PROBLEM READING THE NEWSPAPER OR RECOGNIZING FACES OR IS RESPONDENT BLIND?

Yes [ ]64-1   No [ ]-2

S10. How good is your hearing? Would you say you hear normally (with hearing aid), do you have minor hearing problems, or do you have a hearing problem that severely interferes with your activities?

Normal
Minor
Interferes with activities

[ ]65-1
[ ] -2 } GO TO INTERVIEWER INSTRUCTION "D" IN BOX BELOW
[ ] -3

D. INTERVIEWER: DOES RESPONDENT HAVE HEARING PROBLEMS WHICH SEVERELY INTERFERE WITH ACTIVITY? DOES RESPONDENT IN YOUR JUDGMENT HAVE DIFFICULTY IN HEARING?

Yes [ ]66-1   No [ ]-2

E. INTERVIEWER: DOES RESPONDENT HAVE A PROBLEM SPEAKING OR IS IT DIFFICULT FOR RESPONDENT TO CARRY ON A CONVERSATION?

Yes [ ]67-1   No [ ]-2

275

serious illnesses and how serious they were. This item was also scored from 0 to 4 (see Figure B-1, questions S4–S6).

The respondent could have a total disability score on these eight components that could range from 0 to 32 points. This score comprised the respondent's health index.

Family Health Index

Each respondent who was married or had a companion with whom he or she lived like a spouse was asked to evaluate the health of the spouse or companion on five of the eight items included in the respondent's individual index. The respondent was asked whether the spouse (1) could manage housekeeping activities (e.g., shopping, fixing small things, cooking, or housecleaning, and (2) was able to go up and down stairs (see Figure B-2, questions S15–S16). The respondent was also asked to evaluate the spouse's eyesight (see Figure B-2, question S17) and hearing (see Figure B-2, question S19). Finally, the respondent was asked if the spouse was confined to a wheelchair or bedridden or physically disabled in any way (see Figure B-2, question S19). Each of these five items was scored from 0 to 4. The family health score consisted of the joint scores of the spouse and the respondent. Since married respondents had five more items than single respondents, the scores of married respondents were multiplied by 8/13 so that their range would be the same as that of the single respondents.

For most of the findings in this study, respondents' families were described as healthy or not healthy. For the purpose of this classification, all those who had family health scores from 0 to 7 were considered as healthy or having minor ailments. All those who had scores from 8 to 32 were considered to be seriously disabled or ill. This particular cutoff point was based on two factors. First, it was the point that empirically differentiated the institutionalized aged from those in the community: For example, 43% of those with a score of 8 or more were institutionalized, as contrasted with 25% for those with scores of 4–7, 11% for those with scores of 1–3, and 8% for those with a score of 0. Second, this cutoff point still left enough people in the "ill" category for analysis purposes (i.e., 36%).

Marital Disability Index

Those who were married and had a family health score from 0 to 7 were considered to be healthy and married—that is, in the first stage of health. Those who were married and had a family health score of 8–32, and those who were single and had a score of 0–7, were considered to be in the second stage of health. Those who were single and had a score of 8–32 were considered to be in the third stage of health. Those who were institutionalized and had a family health score of 0–7 were considered to be in the fourth stage of health, while those who were institutionalized and had a family health score of 8 to 32 were considered to be in the fifth stage of health.

Fig. B-2. The spouse items for the family health index.

Now, I'd like to ask you some questions about your [INSERT RELATIONSHIP FROM Q.S12 OR Q.S14].

S15. As I read the list of activities again, please tell me, would your [INSERT RELATIONSHIP FROM Q.S12 OR Q.S14] require help from others, perform these activities herself/himself with extra effort or the help of some device like a cane or a brace, or can he/she handle them normally? (REPEAT CATEGORIES AS NECESSARY.) (RECORD ANSWER BELOW IN GRID UNDER Q.S15.) IF HE/SHE DOES NOT PERFORM A PARTICULAR ACTIVITY, CHECK BOX UNDER "DO NOT PERFORM" IN Q.S15 AND ASK Q.S16 FOR THAT ACTIVITY.

List of activities	Q.S15					Q.S16		
	(1) Help from others	(2) Extra effort	(3) Handle normally	(*) Do not perform		(1) Help from others	(2) Extra effort	(3) Handle normally
a. How about shopping, fixing small things around your place, cooking, or house-cleaning? (CHECK ONLY ONE ANSWER.)	[ ]71-1	[ ]-2	[ ]-3	[ ]-4	SKIP TO INTERVIEWER INSTRUCTION "F" IN BOX BELOW	[ ]73-1	[ ]-2	[ ]-3
b. What about going up and down a flight of stairs? (CHECK ONLY ONE ANSWER.)	[ ]72-1	[ ]-2	[ ]-3	[ ]-4	ASK Q.S16	[ ]74-1	[ ]-2	[ ]-3

IF "DO NOT PERFORM" TO Q.S15a, b, OR c, ASK HYPOTHETICALLY FOR THAT PARTICULAR ACTIVITY:

(continued)

Fig. B-2. (continued)

S16. If he/she had to (INSERT ACTIVITY) would he/she require help from someone else, do it himself/herself with extra effort, or could he/she handle this normally? (REPEAT CATEGORIES AS NECESSARY.) (RECORD ABOVE IN THE ANSWER GRID UNDER Q.S16)

S17. Now, how about your [INSERT RELATIONSHIP FROM Q.S12 OR Q.S14] eyesight? Can he/she see normally (with glasses), or does he/she have minor or major problems seeing, or is he/she considered blind?

Normal [ ]75-1
Minor [ ] -2   GO TO INTERVIEWER INSTRUCTION "F"
Major [ ] -3   IN BOX BELOW
Blind [ ] -4

F. INTERVIEWER: IS PERSON DESCRIBED IN Q.S17 BLIND OR DOES HE/SHE HAVE MAJOR PROBLEMS SEEING?
Yes [ ]76-1 No [ ]-2

S18. Is your [INSERT RELATIONSHIP FROM Q.S12 OR Q.S14] confined to a wheelchair or bedridden, or does he/she not have full use of his/her arms or legs?

1) Confined/bedridden   [ ]77-1
2) Not confined, but does not have full use of arms or legs [ ] -2
3) Not confined, has full use of arms and legs   [ ] -3

S19. How about your [INSERT RELATIONSHIP FROM Q.S12 OR Q.S14] hearing? Would you say he/she. . . ? (READ CATEGORIES.)

1) Is deaf   [ ]78-1
2) Has major hearing problems   [ ] -2
3) Has minor hearing problems   [ ] -3
4) Has no hearing problems   [ ] -4

Appendix C: Statistical Tables

Table C-1. Percentages of Respondents Receiving Services from Helpers at All Stages of Disability (the Complete Population)

Exchanges Provided by Helpers	Stages of Disability				
	Stage 1: Married and Healthy or Minor Disability (n = 371)	Stage 2: Married and Major Disability or Single and Minor Disability (n = 590)	Stage 3: Single and Major Disability (n = 227)	Stage 4: Institutionalized and Healthy or Minor Disability (n = 154)	Stage 5: Institutionalized and Major Disability (n = 219)
Partial Primary-Group Expansion (Kin)					
Doing small household repairs	20	33	41	7	9
Doing light housekeeping	13	21	31	5	6
Complete Primary-Group Expansion (Kin)					
Keeping track of bills, checks	14	24	43	36	51
Doing laundry, cleaning, storage	16	21	33	32	47
Primary-Group Decline (Kin)					
Checking daily on respondents	47	52	57	34	23
Taking care of respondents when bedridden	33	53	48	14	9

	Primary-Group Continuation (Kin)				
Taking out for meal or bringing food	42	56	57	47	51
Bringing small household gifts	40	46	47	47	44
Helping keep in touch with relatives	45	46	51	47	58
Cheering respondents up when low	68	72	79	80	71
	Primary-Group Decline (Neighbors)				
Reporting attempted break-in	80	72	67	35	30
Providing loans of small household items	74	69	61	39	29
	Primary-Group Continuation (Friends)				
Serving as free-time companions	41	47	32	33	49

Note. The population bases vary slightly for each item, depending on the number of "no answers."

Table C-2. Regression Constants and Coefficients (Unstandardized) for Income, Ethnicity–Race, and Distance Respondents Lived from Helpers

Type of Exchange	a	b_1	b_2	b_3	b_4	b_5	b_6	b_7	b_8	b_9	b_{10}	b_{11}	b_{12}	b_{13}	b_{14}	R^2***
Partial Primary-Group Expansion (Kin)																
Doing small household repairs	.20	.29*	-.08*													.11
	.14	.19*	-.03	-.04	.08*	-.01	.06	-.09*	-.15	-.06*	-.06*	-.04	.60*	.24*	.10*	.32
Doing light house-keeping	.15	.20*	-.08*													.07
	.01	.14*	.03	-.03	.15*	.07*	.07**	-.02*	.25*	.002	-.03	.04	.66*	.16*	.04*	.38
Complete Primary-Group Expansion (Kin)																
Keeping track of bills and checks	.08	.39*	.49*													.23
	.08	.32*	.45*	-.07*	.13*	.05	.01	.05*	-.17	-.11	.06**	-.10*	.31*	.04	.09*	.30
Doing laundry, cleaning, and storage	.14	.23*	.32*													.10
	.04	.15*	.37*	-.02	.16*	.07**	.01	-.01	.11	-.06*	-.08*	-.02	.62*	.09*	.11*	.30
Primary-Group Decline (Kin)																
Checking daily on respondents	.48	.16*	-.23*													.07
	.15	.07*	-.12*	-.06**	.10*	.16*	.13*	.08*	-.11	.07*	-.01	.01	.75*	.61*	.39*	.40
Taking care of respondents when bedridden	.35	.18*	-.25*													.10
	.22	.14*	-.17*	.01	.10*	.23*	.09**	.01	.03	.04	-.04	.01	.36*	.19*	.07*	.19
Primary-Group Continuation (Kin)																
Taking respondents out for dinner	.44	.19*	.12*													.03
	.32	.15*	.19*	-.05	.18*	.10**	-.04	-.04	.11	.03	-.11*	-.01	.39*	.22*	.20*	.13

	a	b1	b2	b3	b4	b5	b6	b7	b8	b9	b10	b11	b12	b13	b14	R²
Providing small household gifts	.41	.11*	.07*	−.004	.17*	.23**	−.03	−.09*	−.12	−.01	−.10*	−.03	.36*	.12*	.09*	.01
	.35	.06**	.13*	−.11*	.16*	.11*	.03	−.04	.15	.03	−.05	−.05	.25*	−.07	.03	.11
Helping respondents keep in touch with relatives	.46	.07**	.17*													.02
	.45	.03	.19*	−.11*												.08
Cheering up respondents when low	.73	.12*	.06		.10*		−.09*		.09*	.02	−.13*		.21*	.12*		.02
	.65	.09*	.07*	−.09*	.01	.05	.29*		.09*	.02	−.13*	−.02	.21*	.12*	.15*	.09

Primary-Group Decline (Neighbors)

	a	b1	b2	b3	b4	b5	b6	b7	b8	b9	b10	b11	b12	b13	b14	R²
Reporting attempted break-in	.80	−.13*	−.50*	.003	−.02	−.07	−.09*	−.001	.13*	−.03	.11*	−.05	.11*	−.05	−.06	.18
	.77	−.08*	−.42*		.02		−.001						.16*		−.04	.20
Loaning small household items in emergency	.75	−.14*	−.44*	.06**	−.10*	−.09*	−.08	−.10*	.058	.11*	−.02	.16*	−.13*	−.03	.13	.13
	.71	−.07*	−.36*	−.09*		−.08	−.10*		.11*	−.02		−.13*	−.03			.17

Primary-Group Continuation (Friends)

	a	b1	b2	b3	b4	b5	b6	b7	b8	b9	b10	b11	b12	b13	b14	R²
Serving as free-time companions	.42	−.07	.20*	−.04	−.06	−.10*	.02	−.03	.04	−.04	.16*	−.14*	−.15*	−.05	.04	.04
	.40	−.01	.24*				−.03			−.04						.08

*Figures significant at .01 level or less.

**Figures significant at .05 level or less.

Note. Population base for all regressions was 841.

Note. Key to table heads: a, constant: married and heads; low income; assimilated Americans; helpers lived over 30 minutes away; b_1, single and sick; b_2, institutionalized and sick; b_3, West Europeans; b_4, East Europeans; b_5, Latin Americans; b_6, American blacks; b_7, Jews; b_8, other ethnic groups; b_9, middle income; b_{10}, missing income; b_{11}, high income; b_{12}, helpers lived in same house; b_{13}, helpers lived one to five blocks away; b_{14}, helpers lived six blocks to 30 minutes away.

*Figures significant at .01 level.

**Figures significant at .05 level.

***R^2 values have all been adjusted for the number of independent variables.

Table C-3. Unstandardized Coefficients for Factors Affecting Services

| | Marital Household Services | | | | | Normal Kin Services | | | | |
Factors Affecting Services	A Doing Light House-keeping	B Doing Laundry, Storage, Cleaning	C Doing Small Household Repairs	D Managing Household Bills	E Checking on Respondents Daily	F Taking Respondents to Dinner	G Providing Small Household Gifts	H Helping Respondents Keep in Touch with Relatives	I Cheering Respondents when low	J Taking Care of Respondents when Bedridden
Helpers lived in same house	.68*	.60*	.64*	.33*	.72*	.38*	.34*	.24*	.14*	.10*
Helpers lived one to five blocks away	.18*	.14*	.28*	.10*	.62*	.29*	.10*	.002	.11*	.19*
Helpers lived six blocks to 30 minutes away	.02	.13	.15*	.05*	.38*	.17*	.06*	-.04**	.04*	.03
Married and ill	.13*	.19*	.11*	-.02	.09*	.04	.09*	.14*	.09*	-.03
Single and well	.03	.03*	.08*	.06*	.02	.06**	.05	.003	.02**	.11*
Single and ill	.11*	.13*	.14*	.24*	.01	.10*	.02	-.01	.06**	.07*
Norm—ill parents should live close by	.004	.02*	.002	.03**	-.006	.03*	.01**	.04*	-.01**	-.01
Traditional kin norm	-.05	.08*	.07	.09**	.26*	.01	.007	.09*	.12*	.08
Modified extended family norm	.01	.02	.05*	.02	.07*	.08*	.05*	.08*	.10*	.04
Illogical kin norm	-.10	.004	.07	.08	.15	.09	.008	-.11	-.08	.12

West Europeans	.04*	.03	-.07*	-.04**	.001	.02	-.08*	.06*	.05*	.02
East Europeans	.16*	.16*	.02	.10*	.05	.11*	.13*	.07**	.04	.08*
Latin Americans	.06*	.04	-.04	.06	.04	.04	.16*	.06	.11*	.07
American blacks	12*	.01	.05	.02	.15*	-.01	.03	.02	.00	.05
Jews	.006	-.01	-.11*	.03	.06*	-.10*	-.11	-.02	.05*	.02
Other ethnic groups	24*	.04	-.02	-.10*	-.11	.06	.05	-.08	.16**	.06
Number of respondents' children	.02*	.01**	.03*	.02*	.02*	.01**	.03*	.04*	.004	-.04*
Gender of helpers	.09*	.09*	-.11*	.02	.08*	.10*	.08*	.07*	.06*	.004
Respondents' affection for helpers	-.04*	-.04*	-.05*	-.04*	-.09*	-.10*	-.10	-.14*	-.14*	-.02
Marital status of helpers	.03*	-.05*	-.03	.03	.03	-.01	.009	-.07*	.04*	.07*
Age of respondents	-.02	-.03	.00	.004*	.00	.00	.001	.00	.00	.005*
Gender of respondents	.03	.05*	.10*	.10*	.02	.005	.04	.02	.02	.01
Education of respondents	.00	.0002	.00	-.007*	.002	.006*	-.002	.005**	-.009*	.01
Constant[a]	.59	.13	.62	-.18	.11	.31	.46	.57	.94	.47
Adjusted R^2	.43	.33	.29	.22	.15	.15	.15	.15	.11	.06
R^2	.44	.34	.31*	.24*	.44	.17	.16	.17	.13	.08

Note. Population base for all regressions was 1081.

[a] Comparison groups: Helpers lived more than 30 minutes away; married and well; isolated nuclear family norm; and assimilated Americans.

*Indicates the coefficient is significant at .01 or beyond.

**Indicates the coefficient is significant at .05.

Table C-4. Unstandardized Regression Coefficients for Variables Most Likely to Affect Telephone and Face-to-Face Contacts

Variables Affecting Services	Means	Telephone				Face-to-Face			
		Daily	Weekly	Monthly	Yearly	Daily	Weekly	Monthly	Yearly
Helpers lived in same house	.134	.686*	.301*	.003	−.052*	.937*	.904*	.837*	.235*
Helpers lived in same block	.101	.728*	.393*	.082*	.028	.849*	.947*	.855*	.242*
Helpers lived two to five blocks away	.0546	.781*	.492*	.217*	.163*	.440*	.939*	.851*	.243*
Helpers lived 6 to 10 blocks away	.060	.583*	.452*	.162*	.109*	.257*	.840*	.854*	.243*
Helpers lived 11 blocks to 30 minutes away	.187	.516*	.460*	.181*	.129*	.082	.743*	.809*	.212*
Helpers lived 31 minutes to 1 hour away	.139	.331*	.429*	.201*	.149*	.019	.516*	.781*	.226*
Helpers lived over 1 hour to 2 hours away	.071	.152*	.266*	.127*	.101*	.006	.175*	.534*	.193*
Helpers lived over 2 hours to 4 hours away	.143	−.019	−.036	.099	.071*	.009	.018	.005	.130*
Married and ill	.115	−.011	.024	−.009	−.029	−.001	−.018	−.038**	−.031**
Single and well	.652	.001	.015	.004	−.009	−.022	−.024	−.035*	−.014
Single and ill	.1885	.007	.026	.024	.016	−.042*	−.042	−.011	−.037*
Norm—ill parents should live close by	2.806	−.011	−.008	−.021*	−.016*	−.010*	−.004	−.005	−.006
Respondents' education	10.362	.002	.004	.005*	.004*	−.001	−.001	.0004	.001
Respondents' age	73.633	.001	−.001	−.002*	−.002	−.0001	−.001	−.0003	−.0005
Traditional kin norm	.049	.158*	.119*	.071*	.084	.037	.026	.070*	.060*
Modified extended family norm	.751	.075*	.104*	.061*	.061	−.005	−.015	.047	.067*

Illogical kin norm	.007	.134	.232*	.089	.070	.036	-.151**	.117	.138*
West Europeans	.168	.082*	.059*	-.008	-.011	.001	-.014	.019	.046*
East Europeans	.098	.048	.054	-.010	-.007	.031	-.013	-.037	-.003
Latin Americans	.068	.015	-.031	-.037	-.044	.050	.002	-.001	-.059*
American blacks	.047	.074	.050	-.004	.006	-.010	-.022	.001	.051*
Jews	.265	.088*	.118*	.050*	.046	-.006	.029	.001	.019
Other ethnic groups	.010	.081	.290*	.078	.052	-.006	-.030	-.055	-.068
Number of respondents' children	1.680	.032*	.022*	.018*	.013	.020*	.022*	.009*	.008
Helpers' gender (female high)	.597	.102*	.031	.007	.013	.024*	.040*	.001	.001
Respondents' affection for helpers	1.232	-.096*	.102*	-.076*	-.076	-.046*	-.060*	-.041*	-.034*
Marital status of helpers (married)	.327	.011	.007	.006	-.006	-.009	.022	.009	.013
Gender of respondents (female)	.652	.031	.045*	.013	.0131	.008	.001	.006	.006
Constant[a]	.030	.418	.979	1.016	.772	.181	.189	.768	
R^2	.41	.25	.14	.13	.70	.62	.65	.14	
Adjusted R^2	.39	.23	.12	.11	.69	.61	.64	.12	

Note. Population base for all regressions was 1098.

[a] Included in the constant were helpers who live more than 4 hours away, healthy and married respondents, those holding an isolated conjugal family norm, assimilated Americans, single helpers, and male respondents and helpers.

*Indicates the coefficient is significant at .01 or beyond.

**Indicates the coefficient is significant at .05.

References

Adams, B. N. Occupational status and husband–wife social participation. *Social Forces*, 1967, *45*, 501–507.

Adams, B. N. Isolation, function, and beyond: American kinship in the 1960's. In C. B. Broderick (Ed.), *A decade of family research in action*. Minneapolis: National Council on Family Relations, 1971, pp. 163–186.

Anderson, M. The impact on the family relationships of the elderly of changes since Victorian times in governmental income-maintenance provision. In E. Shanas & M. B. Sussman (Eds.), *Family, bureaucracy, and the elderly*. Durham, NC: Duke University Press, 1977, pp. 36–59.

Angell, R. *The family encounters depression*. Gloucester, MA: Smith, 1965. (Originally published, 1936.)

Arensberg, C., & Kimball, S. T. *Family and community in Ireland*. Cambridge, England: Cambridge University Press, 1940.

Ariès, P. *Centuries of childhood*. New York: Vintage Books, 1962.

Babchuk, N. Primary friends and kin: A study of the associations of middle class couples. *Social Forces*, 1965, *43*, 483–493.

Beckman, R. C. Acceptance of congregate life in a retirement village. *Gerontologist*, 1969, *9*, 281–285.

Bennis, W. G. *Changing organizations*. New York: McGraw-Hill, 1966.

Berkman, L. F., & Syme, L. S. Social networks, host resistance, and mortality: A nine-year follow-up study of Alameda County residents. *American Journal of Epidemiology*, 1979, *190*(4), 186–204.

Bernstein, B. Social class speech systems, and psycho-therapy. In E. O. Laumann, P. M. Siegel, & R. W. Hodge (Eds.), *The logic of social hierarchies*. Chicago: Markham, 1970, pp. 617–625. (Originally published, 1964.)

Biggar, J. C. Reassessing elderly sunbelt migration. *Research on Aging*, 1980, *2*(2), 177–190.

Blau, P. *The dynamics of bureaucracy*. Chicago: University of Chicago Press, 1955.

Blau, Z. S. Structured constraints on friendships in old age. *American Sociological Review*, 1961, *26*, 429–438.

Blau, Z. S. *Black children/white children: Competence, socialization, and social structure*. New York: Free Press, 1981.

Blood, R. O., Jr., & Wolfe, D. M. *Husbands and wives*. New York: Free Press, 1960.

Bonacich, E. A theory of ethnic antagonism: The split labor market. *American Sociological Review*, 1972, *37*, 547–559.

Bott, E. *Family and social network*. London: Tavistock Institute, 1955.

Bowles, G. K. Age migration in the United States: A brief review. *Research on Aging*, 1980, *2*(2), 137–140.

Burgess, E. W., Wallin, P., & Schultz, G. D. *Courtship, engagement and marriage*. Philadelphia: J. B. Lippincott, 1953.

Butler, R. N. *Why survive?: Being old in America*. New York: Harper & Row, 1974.

Cameron, P. Masculinity–femininity in the aged. *Journal of Gerontology*, 1968, *10*, 63–65.

Cantor, M. H. Neighbors and friends: An overlooked resource in the informal support system. *Research on Aging*, 1979, *1*, 434–463.

Carp, F. M. Housing and living environments of older people. In R. H. Binstock & E. Shanas (Eds.), *Handbook of aging and the social sciences*. New York: Van Nostrand Reinhold, 1976, pp. 244–263.

Clark, J. P. Isolation of the police: A comparison of the British and American situations. In R. Quinney (Ed.), *Crime and justice in society*. Boston: Little, Brown, 1969, pp. 126–146.

Cloward, R., & Piven, F. Hidden protests: The channeling of female innovation and resistance. *Signs: Journal of Women in Culture and Society*, 1979, *4*(4), 651–669.

Cloward, R. A., & Elman, R. M. The storefront on Stanton Street: Advocacy in the ghetto. In G. A. Brager & F. P. Purcell (Eds.), *Community action against poverty*. New Haven: College and University Press, 1967, pp. 253–282.

Cobb, S. Social support as a moderator of life stress. *Psychosomatic Medicine*, 1976, *38*, 300–314.

Coleman, J., Katz, E., & Menzel, H. The diffusion of an innovation among physicians. *Sociometry*, 1957, *21*, 253–269.

Cooley, C. H. *Social organization*. New York: Scribner's, 1909.

Cribier, F. A European assessment of aged migration. *Research on Aging*, 1980, *2*(2), 255–270.

Dahl, R. A. Patterns of opposition: Some explanations. Epilogue. In R. A. Dahl (Ed.), *Political oppositions in Western democracies*. New Haven: Yale University Press, 1966, pp. 332–402.

Dahrendorf, R. *Class and class conflict in industrial society*. Stanford, CA: Stanford University Press, 1959.

Davies, J. C., III. *Neighborhood groups and urban renewal*. New York: Columbia University Press, 1966.

Dobrof, R. *The case of the aged: A shared function*. Unpublished doctoral dissertation, Columbia University, 1976.

Dobrof, R., & Litwak, E. *Maintenance of family ties of long-term care patients* (Department of Health, Education and Welfare Publication No. (ADM) 77-400). Washington, DC: U.S. Government Printing Office, 1977.

Dono, J. E., Falbe, C. M., Kail, B. L., Litwak, E., Sherman, R. H., & Siegel, D. Primary groups in old age: Structure and function. *Research on Aging*, 1979, *1*(4), 403–433.

Emery, F. E., & Trist, E. L. The causal texture of organizational environments. *Human Relations*, 1965, *18*, 21–32.

Engels, F. *The origin of the family, private property and the state*. Chicago: Charles H. Kerr & Company Co-operative, 1902.

Etzioni, A. *Modern organizations*. Englewood Cliffs, NJ: Prentice-Hall, 1969.

Fellin, P., & Litwak, E. Neighborhood cohesion under conditions of mobility. *American Sociological Review*, 1963, *28*, 364–376.

Festinger, L., Schacter, S., & Back, K. *Social pressures in informal groups*. Stanford, CA: Stanford University Press, 1963.

Firestone, S. *The dialectic of sex*. New York: Morrow, 1971.

Fischer, C. S. *To dwell among friends: Personal networks in town and city*. Chicago: University of Chicago Press, 1982.

Fischer, C. S., Jackson, R. M., Stueve, C. A., Gerson, K., & Jones, L. M., with Baldassare, M. (Eds.). *Networks and places: Social relations in the urban setting*. New York: Free Press, 1977.

Flynn, C. B. General versus aged interstate migration, 1965–1970. *Research on Aging*, 1980, *2*(2), 165–176.

Foote, N., & Cottrell, L. S. *Identity and interpersonal competence*. Chicago: University of Chicago Press, 1955.

Fuguitt, G., & Tordella, S. J. Elderly net migration: The new trend of nonmetropolitan population change. *Research on Aging*, 1980, *2*(2), 191–204.

Furstenberg, F. F. Industrialization and the American family: A look backwards. *American Sociological Review*, 1966, *31*, 326–337.

Galbraith, J. R. *Designing complex organizations*. Reading, MA: Addison-Wesley, 1973.

Gans, H. J. *The urban villager*. New York: Free Press, 1962.

Gans, H. J. *The Levittowners*. New York: Vintage Books, 1969.

Gerstel, N., & Gross, H. E. Commuter marriages: A review. In H. Gross & M. Sussman (Eds.), *Alternatives to traditional family living*. New York: Haworth Press, 1982, pp. 71–93.

Giele, J. Z. *Women and the future*. New York: Free Press, 1978.

Goode, W. J. Theory of role strain. *American Sociological Review*, 1960, *25*, 483–496.

Goode, W. J. *World revolution and family patterns*. Glencoe, IL: Free Press, 1963.

Gordon, M. Primary-group differentiation in urban Ireland. *Social Forces*, 1977, *55*, 743–752.

Gottesman, L. E. *Nursing home performance as related to resident traits, ownership, size, and source of payment*. Paper presented at 100th Annual Meeting of the American Public Health Association, Atlantic City, NJ, November 15, 1972.

Granovetter, M. The strength of weak ties. *American Journal of Sociology*, 1973, *78*, 1360–1380.

Granovetter, M. *Getting a job: A study of contacts and careers*. Cambridge, MA: Harvard University Press, 1974.

Hill, R. *Family development in three generations*. Cambridge, MA: Schenkman, 1970.

Hollingshead, A. B., & Redlich, F. C. *Social class and mental illness*. New York: Wiley, 1958.

Homans, G. C. *The human group*. New York: Harcourt, Brace & World, 1950.

Horwitz, A. Social networks and pathways into psychiatric treatment. *Social Forces*, 1977, *56*, 86–103.

Houriet, R. *Getting back together*. New York: Avon Books, 1971.

Hyman, H. H. The values systems of different classes: A social psychological contribution to the analysis of stratification. In R. Bendix & S. M. Lipset (Eds.), *Class, status and power: A reader in social stratification*. Glencoe, IL: Free Press, 1953, pp. 426–441.

Hyman, H. H., & Sheatsley, P. Some reasons why information campaigns fail. *Public Opinion Quarterly*, 1947, *11*, 412–423.

Jackson, R. M. Social structure and friendship choice. In C. S. Fischer, R. M. Jackson, C. A. Stueve, K. Gerson, & L. M. Jones, with M. Baldassare (Eds.), *Networks and places: Social relations in the urban setting*. New York: Free Press, 1977, pp. 59–78.

Kahn, A. J., Grossman, L., Bandler, J., Clark, F., Galkin, F., & Greeawait, K. *Neighborhood information centers*. New York: Columbia University School of Social Work, 1966.

Kahn, R., & Antonucci, T. C. Convoys over the life course: Attachment, roles and social support. In P. B. Baltes & O. R. Brim (Eds.), *Life span development and behavior*. New York: Academic Press, 1980, pp. 253–286.

Katan, Y. The utilization of indigenous workers in human service organizations. In Y. Hasenfeld & R. A. English (Eds.), *Human service organizations: A book of readings*. Ann Arbor: University of Michigan Press, 1974, pp. 448–467.

Katz, E., & Lazarsfeld, P. F. *Personal influence*. Glencoe, IL: Free Press, 1955.

Kelly, E. Consistency of the adult personality. *American Psychologist*, 1955, *10*, 659–681.

Kohn, M. L. *Class and conformity: A study in values*. Homewood, IL: Dorsey Press, 1969.

Kohn, M. L. Bureaucratic man: A portrait and an interpretation. *American Sociological Review*, 1971, *36*, 461–474.

Komarovsky, M. *The unemployed man and his family*. New York: Dryden Press, 1940.

Komarovsky, M. *Women in the modern world, their education and their dilemmas*. Boston: Little, Brown, 1953.

Ktsanes, T., & Ktsanes, V. The theory of complementary needs in mate-selection. In R. F. Winch, R. McGinnis, & H. R. Barringer (Eds.), *Selected studies in marriage and the family* (Rev. ed.). New York: Holt, Rinehart & Winston, 1962, pp. 517–531.

Labov, W. *Language in the inner city: Studies in Black English vernacular.* Philadelphia: University of Pennsylvania Press, 1972.

Lansing, J. B., & Mueller, E. *The geographic mobility of labor.* Ann Arbor, MI: Institute for Social Research, 1967.

LaRocco, J., House, J. S., & French, J. R., Jr. Social support, occupational stress, and health. *Journal of Health and Social Behavior,* 1980, *21,* 202–218.

Laumann, E. O. *Bonds of pluralism.* New York: Wiley, 1966.

Lawton, M. P., & Cohen, J. The generality of housing impact on the well being of older people. *Journal of Gerontology,* 1974, *29,* 194–204.

Lazarsfeld, P., & Merton R. K. Friendship as a social process. In M. Berger, T. Abel, & C. H. Page (Eds.), *Freedom and control in modern society.* New York: Van Nostrand Reinhold, 1954, pp. 18–66.

Lee, E. S. Migration of the aged. *Research on Aging,* 1980, *2*(2), 131–136.

Lieberson, S. *A piece of the pie: Blacks and white immigrants since 1980.* Berkeley: University of California Press, 1980.

Lin, N., Ensel, W. M., & Vaughn, J. C. Social resources and the strength of ties: Structural factors in occupational status attainment. *American Sociological Review,* 1981, *46,* 393–405.

Lindzey, G., & Byrne, D. Measurement of social choice and interpersonal attraction. In G. Lindzey, & E. Aronson (Eds.), *Handbook of social psychology* (Vol. 2). Reading, MA: Addison-Wesley, 1968, pp. 452–525.

Litwak, E. Occupational mobility and extended family cohesion. *American Sociological Review,* 1960, *25,* 9–21. (a)

Litwak, E. Reference group theory, bureaucratic career, and neighborhood primary group cohesion. *Sociometry,* 1960, *23,* 72–84. (b)

Litwak, E. Geographic mobility and extended family cohesion. *American Sociological Review,* 1960, *25,* 385–394. (c)

Litwak, E. Voluntary associations and neighborhood cohesion. *American Sociological Review,* 1961, *26,* 258–271. (a)

Litwak, E. Models of bureaucracy which permit conflict. *American Journal of Sociology,* 1961, *67,* 177–184. (b)

Litwak, E. Extended kin relations in an industrial society. In E. Shanas & G. Streib (Eds.), *Social structure and the family generational relations.* Englewood Cliffs, NJ: Prentice-Hall, 1965, pp. 290–323.

Litwak, E. Towards a balance theory of grassroots community organization. In G. W. Magner & T. L. Briggs (Eds.), *Leadership training in mental health.* New York: National Association of Social Workers, 1970, pp. 22–60.

Litwak, E. Agency and family linkages in providing neighborhood services. In D. Thursz & J. L. Vigilante (Eds.), *Reaching people: The structure of neighborhood services.* Beverly Hills, CA: Sage, 1978, pp. 59–94. (a)

Litwak, E. Organizational constructs and mega bureaucracy. In R. C. Sarri & Y. Hasenfeld (Eds.), *The management of human services.* New York: Columbia University Press, 1978, pp. 123–162. (b)

Litwak, E., Count, G., & Hayden, T. Group structure and interpersonal creativity as factors which reduce errors in prediction of marital adjustment. *Social Forces,* 1960, *38,* 308–315.

Litwak, E., & Dono, J. *The organizational bases for ethnic relations in industrial societies.* Unpublished manuscript, 1977.

Litwak, E., & Figueira, J. Technological innovations and theoretical functions of primary groups and bureaucratic structures. *American Journal of Sociology,* 1968, *73,* 468–481.

Litwak, E., & Figueira, J. Technological innovation and ideal forms of family structure in an industrial society. In R. Hill & R. Konig (Eds.), *Families in East and West: Socialization process and kinship ties.* Paris: Mouton, 1970, pp. 348–396.

Litwak, E., & Kulis, S. *Networks, primary groups, and formal organizations: Alternative principles for matching group structures with tasks among the aged.* New York: Columbia University, Center for the Social Sciences (Preprint Series No. 88), 1982.

Litwak, E., & Meyer, H. A balance theory of coordination between bureaucratic organizations and community primary groups. *Administrative Science Quarterly*, 1966, *11*, 31–58.

Litwak, E., & Meyer, H. *School, family, and community: The theory and practice of school-community relations.* New York: Columbia University Press, 1974.

Litwak, E., Meyer, H., & Hollister, C. D. The role of linkage mechanisms between bureaucracies and families: Education and health as empirical cases in point. In R. J. Liebert & A. W. Imershine (Eds.), *Power paradigms and community research*. Beverly Hills. CA: Sage, 1977, pp. 121–152.

Litwak, E., & Spilerman, S. Nursing home administration, organizational theory, and social policy. In A. Kolker & P. I. Ahmed (Eds.), *Aging*. New York: Elsevier Biomedical, 1982, pp. 207–230.

Litwak, E., & Szelenyi, I. Primary group structures and their functions: Kin, neighbors, and friends. *American Sociological Review*, 1969, *34*, 465–481.

Longino, C. F., Jr. Going home: Aged return migration in the United States, 1965–1970. *Journal of Gerontology*, 1979, *34*, 736–745.

Longino, C. F., Jr. Residential relocation of older people: Metropolitan and non-metropolitan. *Research on Aging*, 1980, *2*(2), 205–216.

Lopata, H. Z. *Women as widows*. New York: Elsevier, 1979.

Malowsky, C. Personal communication, 1976.

Marris, P. African families and the process of change. In R. Hill & R. Konig (Eds.), *Families in East and West: Socialization process and kinship ties*. Paris: Mouton, 1970, pp. 397–409.

Marwell, G., Rosenfeld, R., & Spilerman, S. Geographic constraints on women's careers in academia. *Science*, 1979, *205*, 1225–1231.

Mayhew, L. Ascription in modern societies. In E. O. Laumann, P. M. Siegel, & R. W. Hodge (Eds.), *Logic of social hierarchies*. Chicago: Markham, 1970, pp. 308–323.

McCready, W. C. The persistence of ethnic variation in American families. In A. M. Greeley (Ed.), *Ethnicity in the United States*. New York: Wiley, 1974, pp. 156–176.

Merton, R. K. The social psychology of housing. In W. Dennis (Ed.), *Current trends in social psychology*. Pittsburgh: University of Pittsburgh Press, 1948, pp. 163–217.

Merton, R. K. The role-set: Problems in sociological theory. *British Journal of Sociology*, 1957, *94*, 106–120.

Merton, R. K., & Kitt, A. S. Contributions to the theory of reference group behavior. In R. K. Merton & P. F. Lazarsfeld (Eds.), *Continuities in social research: Studies in the scope and method of the "American Soldier."* Glencoe, IL: Free Press, 1957, pp. 87–89.

Mills, C. W. *The power elite*. New York: Oxford University Press, 1956.

Mincer, J. Family migration decisions. *Journal of Political Economy*, 1978, *86*, 749–775.

Mintzberg, H. *The structuring of organizations*. Englewood Cliffs, NJ: Prentice-Hall, 1979.

Mitchell, J. C. Concepts and use of social networks in urban situations. In J. C. Mitchell (Ed.), *Social networks in urban situations*. Manchester, England: University of Manchester Press, 1969, pp. 1–50.

Muir, D. E., & Weinstein, E. A. The formal debt: An investigation of lower class and middle class norms of formal obligations. *American Sociological Review*, 1962, *27*, 532–539.

Neugarten, B. *Personality in middle and later life*. New York: Atherton Press, 1964.

Nisbet, R. *Community and power* (2nd ed.). New York: Oxford University Press, 1969.

Ogburn, W. F. The changing family. In R. Winch & R. McGinnis (Eds.), *Selected readings in marriage and the family*. New York: Henry Holt & Co., 1953, pp. 75–77.

Palmore, E. Total chance of institutionalization among the aged. *Gerontologist*, 1976, *16*, 504–507.

Palmore, E. Facts on aging: A short quiz. *Gerontologist*, 1977, *17*, 315–320.

Palmore, E. Are the aged a minority group? *Journal of the American Geriatric Society,* 1978, *26,* 214–217.

Palmore, E. *Social patterns in normal aging: Findings from the Duke Longitudinal Study.* Durham, NC: Duke University Press, 1981.

Papajohn, J., & Spiegel, J. P. *Transactions in families: A modern approach for resolving cultural and generational conflicts.* San Francisco: Jossey-Bass, 1975.

Parsons, T. The social structure of the family. In R. Anshen (Ed.), *The family: Its function and destiny.* New York: Harper & Row, 1944, pp. 173–201.

Parsons, T. Pattern variables revisited: A response to Robert Dubin. *American Sociological Review,* 1960, *25,* 467–482.

Pennings, J. The relevance of the structural-contingency model for organizational effectiveness. *Administrative Science Quarterly,* 1975, *20,* 393–410.

Perrow, C. A framework for the comparative analysis of complex organizations. *American Sociological Review,* 1967, *32,* 194–208.

Piven, F. F., & Cloward, R. A. *Poor people's movements: Why they succeed, how they fail.* New York: Vintage Books, 1979.

Polsky, H., & Duberman, L. The changing American family: From traditional to companionship to existential. In H. Polsky (Ed.), *Social system, culture and role theory: Applications in the helping professions.* Lexington, MA: Ginn Custom Publishing, 1979, pp. 158–170.

Rapoport, R., & Rapoport, R. N. *Dual-career families re-examined.* New York: Harper Colophon Books, 1976.

Redfield, R. Folk society. *American Journal of Sociology,* 1947, *52,* 293–308.

Riegel, K., Riegel, R., & Meyer, G. Socio-psychological factors of aging. *Human Development,* 1967, *10,* 27–56.

Riley, M., Johnson, M., & Foner, A. *Aging and society* (Vol. 3). New York: Russell Sage Foundation, 1972.

Rix, S. E., & Romashko, T. *With a little help from my friends* (Final report to Administration on Aging, U.S. Department of Health, Education and Welfare, AOA Grant No. 90-A-1320). Washington, DC: U.S. Department of Health, Education and Welfare, 1980.

Rosow, I. *The social integration of the aged.* New York: Free Press, 1967.

Safilios-Rothschild, C. The study of family power structure: A review 1960–1969. In C. B. Broderick (Ed.), *A decade of family research and action.* Minneapolis: National Council on Family Relations, 1971, pp. 79–90.

Schnaiberg, A., & Goldenberg, S. Closing the circle: The impact of children on parental status. *Journal of Marriage and the Family,* 1975, *37,* 937–953.

Schorr, A. *Filial responsibility in the modern American family* (Social Security Administration). Washington, DC: U.S. Government Printing Office, 1960.

Shanas, E., Townsend, P., Nedderburn, D., Friis, H., Milhoj, P., & Stehouwer, J. *Old people in three industrial societies.* New York: Atherton Press, 1968.

Sheley, J.F. Mutuality and retirement community success: An interactionist perspective in gerontological research. *International Journal of Aging and Human Development,* 1974, *5*(1), 71–80.

Sherman, R. H., Horowitz, A., & Durmaskin, S. C. *Role overload or management?: The relationship between work and caregiving among daughters of aged parents.* Paper presented at 34th Annual Meeting of the Gerontological Society of America, Boston, 1982.

Sherman, S. R. Leisure activities in retirement housing. *Journal of Gerontology,* 1974, *29,* 325–335.

Shils, E. A. The study of the primary group. In D. Lerner, & H. D. Lasswell (Eds.), *The policy sciences: Recent developments in scope and method.* Stanford, CA: Stanford University Press, 1951, pp. 44–69.

Shils, E. A., & Janowitz, M. Cohesion and disintegration in the Wehrmacht in World War II. *Public Opinion Quarterly*, 1948, *12*, 280–315.

Siegel, D. *Differential structure and function of primary groups in age homogeneous versus age heterogeneous areas for the elderly.* Unpublished doctoral dissertation, Columbia University, 1982.

Simmel, G. The stranger. In K. H. Wolff (Ed. & trans.), *The sociology of Georg Simmel.* Glencoe, IL: Free Press, 1950, pp. 402–408. (Originally published, 1903.)

Smelser, N. J. *Social change in the Industrial Revolution.* Chicago: University of Chicago Press, 1959.

Spiegel, J. P. Some cultural aspects of transference and countertransference. In M. N. Zald (Ed.), *Social welfare institutions.* New York: John Wiley & Sons, 1965, pp. 575–593. (Originally published, 1959.)

Spilerman, S., & Litwak, E. Reward structures and organizational design: An analysis of institutions for the elderly. *Research on Aging*, 1982, *4*, 43–70.

Spiro, S. E. *Effects of neighborhood characteristics on participation in involuntary organizations.* Unpublished doctoral dissertation, University of Michigan, 1968,

Stein, M. *Eclipse of community.* New York: Harper & Row, 1960.

Steinberg, S. *The ethnic myth: Race, ethnicity, and class in America.* New York: Atheneum, 1981.

Strauss, A. L. Medical ghettos. In S. Huber & H. T. Chalfant (Eds.), *The sociology of American poverty.* Cambridge, MA: Schenkman, 1974, pp. 234–246.

Streib, G. F. Family patterns in retirement. *Journal of Social Issues*, 1958, *14*, 46–60.

Strodtbeck, F. L. Husband–wife interaction over revealed differences. *American Sociological Review*, 1951, *16*, 468–473.

Stuckert, R. P. Occupational mobility and family relationships. *Social Forces*, 1963, *41*, 301–307.

Stueve, C. A., & Gerson, K. Personal relations across the life-cycle. In C. Fischer, R. M. Jackson, C. A. Stueve, K. Gerson, & L. M. Jones, with M. Baldassare (Eds.), *Networks and places: Social relations in the urban setting.* New York: Free Press, 1977, pp. 79–98.

Sussman, M. B. Relationship of adult children with their parents in the United States. In E. Shanas & G. Strieb (Eds.), *Social structure and the family: Generational relations.* Englewood Cliffs, NJ: Prentice-Hall, 1965, pp. 62–93.

Sussman, M. B. Family, bureraucracy, and the elderly individual: An organizational linkage perspective. In E. Shanas & M. B. Sussman (Eds.), *Family, bureaucracy and the elderly.* Durham, NC: Duke University Press, 1977, pp. 2–20.

Sussman, M. B. *Social and economic supports and family environments* (Final report to Administration on Aging, U.S. Department of Health, Education and Welfare, AOA Grant No. 90-A-316). Washington, DC: U.S. Department of Health, Education and Welfare, 1980.

Sussman, M. B., & Burchinal, L. Parental aid to married children: Implications for family functioning. *Marriage and Family Living*, 1962, *25*, 320–332.

Sweetser, D. A. The effect of industrialization on intergenerational solidarity. *Rural Sociology*, 1966, *31*, 156–170.

Sweetser, D. A. Intergenerational ties in Finnish urban families. *American Sociological Review*, 1968, *33*, 236–246.

Talmon-Garber, Y. Social change and kinship ties. In R. Hill & R. Konig (Eds.), *Families in East and West: Socialization process and kinship ties.* Paris: Mouton, 1970, pp. 504–524.

Terryberry, S. The evolution of organizational environments. *Administrative Science Quarterly*, 1968, *12*, 590–613.

Thompson, J. D. *Organizations in action.* New York: McGraw-Hill, 1967.

Toennies, F. *Fundamental concepts of sociology* (C. P. Loomis, trans.). New York: American Book Company, 1940.

Townsend, P. The effects of family structure on the likelihood of admission to an institution in old age: The application of a general theory. In E. Shanas & G. Streib (Eds.), *Social structure and the family: Generational relations*. Englewood Cliffs, NJ: Prentice-Hall, 1965, pp. 163–187.

Warner, W. L., & Lunt, P. S. *The social life of a modern community*. New Haven: Yale University Press, 1941.

Warren, D. I. Power, visibility, and conformity in formal organizations. *American Sociological Review*, 1968, *33*, 951–970.

Warren, D. I. *Black neighborhoods: An assessment of community power*. Ann Arbor: University of Michigan Press, 1975.

Warren, R. L. *The community in America*. Chicago: Rand McNally, 1963, pp. 95–104.

Weber, M. *The theory of social economic organization* (A. M. Henderson & T. Parsons, Eds. and trans.). New York: Oxford University Press, 1947.

Weinstein, J. B. Delivery of legal services reviewed. *New York Law Journal*, 1974, *171* (85), 1–4.

Whyte, W. F. Human relations: A progress report. *Harvard Business Review*, 1956, *34*, 125–132.

Whyte, W. H. *Is anyone listening?* New York: Simon & Schuster, 1950.

Whyte, W. H. *The organization man*. New York: Simon & Schuster, 1956.

Wilensky, H. L. Orderly careers and social participation. *American Sociological Review*, 1961, *26*, 521–539.

Winch, R. F. *Mate selection: A study of complementary needs*. New York: Harper & Row, 1958.

Wirth, L. Urbanism as a way of life. *American Journal of Sociology*, 1938, *64*, 8–20.

Wiseman, R. F. Why older people move. *Research on Aging*, 1980, *2*, 141–154.

Wolf, E. R. Kinship, friendship, and patron–client relations. In M. Banton (Ed.), *Social anthropology of complex societies* (ASA Monograph No. 4). London: Tavistock, 1966.

Woodward, J. *Industrial organization: Theory and practice*. London: Oxford University Press, 1965.

Yee, W., & VanArsdol, N. D., Jr. Residential mobility, age, and the life cycle. *Journal of Gerontology*, 1977, *32*, 211–221.

Young, M., & Willmott, P. *Family and kinship in East London*. London: Routledge & Kegan Paul, 1957.

Zola, I. K. Culture and symptoms: An analysis of patients' presenting complaints. *American Sociological Review*, 1966, *35*, 615–630.

Author Index

Subject Index

Abandonment, fallacy of, 66, 67
Administrative style (*see* Formal organization)
Advocacy groups, institutional care and, 245, 246
Affection
  measure of, 132–134
  and social class, 134
  time-based friendship and, 213, 216
Affectional ties, 101
  variations in, 132–134
Age
  distribution, services and, 190–195
  effect on exchange, 126–128
  of friends, 212, 213, 261
  and friendship, 210
  homogeneity (*see* Age homogeneity)
Age homogeneity, 126
  and friendship, 222, 223
  and friendship services, 215, 216
  and household services, 191, 192
  life styles and, 192
Aged (*see* Older Persons)
Ageism, 123
Aging, Weber's formulations and, 9
Argicultural society, 158
Association, 123

Balance theory of coordination, between formal
    organizations and primary groups, 16, 26,
    27
Barriers, 27, 257
Burden, 146, 147 (*see also* Sacrifice, of helper)
  illness degree and, 151, 152

Career aspirations, equality of, 160, 174*n.*, 175*n.*
Children, number of, 131–133
Chronically disabled
  filial responsibility and, 240
  and subsidization of kin, 5, 240, 241
Class (*see* Social class)
Clubs, and neighborhood integration, 179, 180
Combination, in networks, 229, 238*n.*
Commitment
  length variations in, 128–130
  long-term, 100
  marital status and, 149

term of, 33
Commune
  Harrad West, 146
  of older persons, 5, 244, 245
  urban, 145, 146
Community neighborhood, 177, 196
Commuter marriages, 174*n.*
Companions, 216, 217
  health status and, 192–194
  and life styles, 191
  proximity of, 219, 220
Compartmentalized organizations, 25
Complementary needs
  in friendship, 222
  in marital dyad, 224
Conflict, between formal organization and
      primary groups
  altering organizational structure to minimize, 23
  altering primary group structure, 16
  coordination under, 26, 27
Contact
  face-to-face (*see* Face-to-face contact)
  by telephone, 115, 117–119
  type and frequency of, 121
Contingencies, 10, 29*n.*, 30*n.*
Continuum, organizational, 24, 25
Cooperation, spousal, 167
Coordination
  balance theory of, 16, 26, 27
  conflict and, 26, 27
  rules for, 8
  task simplification and, 13
  volunteers and, 235, 236
Culture lag, 162

Daughters, 158
Deference, 123
Depolarized society, 221
Disability
  chronic (*see* Chronically disabled)
  cycle of (*see* Disability cycle)
  effect on services, 50, 53*n.*
  and income, 189, 190
  and institutionalization, 152, 153
  and neighborhood moves, 186

Please remember that this is a library book,
and that it belongs only temporarily to each
person who uses it. Be considerate. Do
not write in this, or any, library book.

WITHDRAWN

DATE DUE